"This is a story that had to be tol[...] the skill and care of a historian and the warmth and concern of a pastor. Dr. Lucas is thorough, honest, fair, and accurate in unfolding the history of a complex movement that includes mixed motives, different hopes, complicated relationships, and inner controversies. In spite of the failures of the Presbyterian Church in America ('the purest churches under heaven are subject both to mixture and error'), its history is a good story, indeed a wonderful story, of God's grace and blessing on a group of southern Presbyterians who were committed, despite the cost, to establishing and maintaining 'a continuing church,' true to the Bible, faithful to Reformed theology, and obedient to the Great Commission. If you want to understand the Presbyterian Church in America, you must read this book."

—**David B. Calhoun**, Professor Emeritus of Church History, Covenant Theological Seminary

"This important work by my friend Sean Lucas is much needed, well researched, forthright, and comprehensive. It will be a tremendous resource for present and future leaders in the PCA in general and Covenant Seminary students in particular. Lucas gets the story straight so that we can see more clearly both the strengths and the blind spots of our past. He does this with a hope-filled desire for faithfulness in today's church as another new generation takes its place of leadership and joins God's mission in and through the PCA and beyond."

—**Mark L. Dalbey**, President and Associate Professor of Applied Theology, Covenant Theological Seminary

"Don't let the title fool you. This is about far more than the PCA. This book is nothing less than a history of Presbyterianism in the twentieth century—with all its theological wrangling, all its political maneuvering, all its failings, and all its faithfulness. This is certainly a story worth telling, and Sean tells it very well."

—**Kevin DeYoung**, Senior Pastor, University Reformed Church, East Lansing, Michigan

"Sean Lucas has given us an account of events leading up to founding of the Presbyterian Church in America that not only is informative from a historical perspective but could be valuable in helping to assess events taking place today. Some of the issues and concerns facing the church today are similar to, if not the same as, those that fed into the forming of the PCA. I believe this book not only will have an appeal to those involved in this history, but could be a resource for those who have come along at a later time to better understand where and why we are today."

—**Charles H. Dunahoo**, Chairman of the Board, Westminster Theological Seminary; Coordinator of Christian Education & Publications, PCA (retired)

"Take it from this Baptist. I don't care if you're not a conservative Presbyterian; you still need to read *For a Continuing Church*. It tells an important, yet often-neglected story in the history of American evangelicalism, combining original research and outstanding engagement with current scholarship. Writing with the empathy of an insider, but the historical honesty of a critical scholar, Sean Lucas has also told this story in a masterfully crafted narrative. The book makes a lasting contribution to our understanding of the American evangelical landscape, highlighting the complexity of denominational movements and institutions. It should be read widely, not only by historians, but by anyone else who wants to think carefully about the intersection of faith and culture."

—**Matthew J. Hall**, Vice President of Academic Services, The Southern Baptist Theological Seminary

"With *For a Continuing Church*, Sean Michael Lucas has remedied the neglect that southern Presbyterians have generally suffered at the hands of church historians. His story of conservatives in the Presbyterian Church in the United States follows carefully the Old School tradition as it developed and adapted to twentieth-century life, and then informed the founding of the Presbyterian Church in America. If history teaches lessons, Lucas's book has at least a semester's worth for both those who belong to the PCA and others who desire to promote and maintain the witness of Reformed Protestantism."

—**D. G. Hart**, author of *Calvinism: A History*

"I've always thought of my friend and former colleague Sean Lucas as a walking encyclopedia. Every page of this volume proves me right. Meticulously researched, this history of the founding of the Presbyterian Church in America will instantly become the definitive account of a significant movement in the history of American Presbyterianism. The detail is comprehensive, the writing is wonderfully engaging (as though the drama were being played out before our very eyes), and the sins of the past are neither downplayed nor exaggerated. As a church historian and pastor in the Presbyterian Church in America, I've waited a long time for this history. I was not disappointed. There were surprises, there were aspects of the story that filled in gaps in my own understanding, and there was a sense of encouragement as I turned the last page. It does seem that we can count ourselves as one example of an evangelical Presbyterian church that God has enabled to remain true to the Scriptures, the Westminster Standards, and the robust Reformed faith. Praise God from whom all blessings flow!"

—**Michael W. Honeycutt**, Senior Pastor, Westminster Presbyterian Church, Rock Hill, South Carolina

"This book offers the first comprehensive story of southern conservative Presbyterianism—a most important and too-often-neglected part of the larger story of American Christianity. It is full of both inspiring moments and cautionary tales. It is as church history should be: a faithful and engaging retelling of the church's past in the service of her present and future calling."

—**Stephen J. Nichols**, President, Reformation Bible College; Chief Academic Officer, Ligonier Ministries

"As God did a glorious work in the lives of his imperfect but beloved covenant people, he would at times tell them to 'pile up some stones' in order to remember what he had done and to teach the 'coming generations.' Sean Lucas has 'piled up some stones' to prod our remembrance of the gracious work of God's providence in establishing the Presbyterian Church in America. And the 'coming generations' are therefore sure to be both encouraged and equipped for a future that by God's grace will be marked with an imperfect yet loving obedience."

—**Harry L. Reeder III**, Senior Pastor, Briarwood Presbyterian Church, Birmingham, Alabama

"With first-rate scholarship, engaging style, and a pastor's insights, Sean Lucas provides the most perceptive history of the Presbyterian Church in America thus far. His proof that our forefathers intended for the PCA to be a new mainline denomination confirms that the growth pains so far have been worth it and inspires us to renew their vision to be a servant-leader denomination. According to Lucas's research, our mandate as a denomination is to make sure that our service to the gospel is not 'done in a corner.' My friend has once again been used of the Lord to refresh my commitment to the Scriptures, the Reformed faith, and the Great Commission!"

—**George Robertson**, Senior Pastor, The First Presbyterian Church, Augusta, Georgia

FOR A CONTINUING CHURCH

FOR A
CONTINUING
CHURCH

THE ROOTS OF THE
PRESBYTERIAN CHURCH
IN AMERICA

SEAN MICHAEL
LUCAS

P&R
PUBLISHING
P.O. BOX 817 • PHILLIPSBURG • NEW JERSEY 08865-0817

ISBN 978-1-62995-106-5 (pbk)
ISBN 978-1-62995-107-2 (ePub)
ISBN 978-1-62995-108-9 (Mobi)

Printed in the United States of America

Library of Congress Cataloging-in-Publication Data

Lucas, Sean Michael, 1970-
  For a continuing church : the roots of the Presbyterian Church in America / Sean Michael Lucas.
      pages cm
  Includes bibliographical references and index.
  ISBN 978-1-62995-106-5 (pbk.) -- ISBN 978-1-62995-107-2 (epub) -- ISBN 978-1-62995-108-9 (mobi)
  1. Presbyterian Church in America--History. I. Title.
  BX8968.52.L825 2015
  285'.13--dc23
                                                              2015025949

For
Sam, Liz, Drew, and Ben

Contents

Foreword

In just over forty years, the Presbyterian Church in America (PCA) has grown to be the largest conservative Presbyterian denomination in the English-speaking world. From a small evangelical splinter group that left the declining Presbyterian Church in the United States, the PCA has survived and continued and expanded and matured despite the early predictions of both enemies and friends. And while it is still relatively small in comparison to a body such as the Southern Baptist Convention, the PCA exercises a theological influence in the evangelical world, and a cultural influence in the United States, disproportionate to its size.

From the beginning, the PCA was committed to the inerrancy of Scripture, the Reformed theology of the Westminster Standards, and the fulfillment of the Great Commission. The founders of the PCA envisioned a conservative mainline Presbyterian denomination characterized by biblical authority, doctrinal orthodoxy, experiential piety, and missionary zeal. Unwittingly, they forged a body that has played a significant role in the resurgence of Calvinism at the end of the twentieth century and in the beginning of the twenty-first.

Yet from the outset of its history, the PCA has struggled with its identity. Early on, factions self-identified as "thoroughly Reformed" or "broadly evangelical," with one group claiming that the PCA had been started as a revival of Old School Presbyterianism (and was thus opposed to evangelistic and missionary cooperation with non-Calvinist evangelicals) and the other viewing the PCA as a Calvinistic denominational entry in the late-twentieth-century neoevangelical network (and was thus favorable toward missionary cooperation with non-Calvinist evangelicals). These perspectives were not entirely mutually exclusive, nor did these groups represent the only constituencies in the PCA, but their juxtaposition characterized many of the early debates in the young PCA.

This is, of course, not the only taxonomy that has been used to describe the PCA. The PCA has, for instance, also been depicted as tripartite, with doctrinalists, pietists, and transformationalists making up its ministry, along with competing visions of what it is and should be. And there have been specific issues that animated discussion at the General Assembly and highlighted very different ways in which people conceived of the PCA (and indeed of the mission of the church): the role of spiritual gifts (continuationism and cessationism); Christian reconstructionism (theonomy); marriage, divorce, and remarriage (especially the matter of biblical grounds for divorce and remarriage); Freemasonry; creation and the days of Genesis; paedocommunion; the validity of Roman Catholic baptism; confessional subscription; women in the military; the Federal Vision controversy; the "Insider Movement" (dealing with contextualization issues, especially in relation to Muslim mission work and Bible translation); and more. The joining and receiving of the Reformed Presbyterian Church, Evangelical Synod, into the PCA in 1982 added another layer of complexity to the PCA identity issue, and another historical experience.

Meanwhile, the PCA in its young history has lived through a cultural megashift. Today's judicial rulings about the definition of marriage were inconceivable in the world in which the PCA was born. During the early years of the PCA, which coincided with an era of unprecedented evangelical political influence, the "Moral Majority" aspired to cultural dominance. Bible-believing Christians today hold no such illusions, and frankly wonder how long they will even be allowed a place at the table.

There have been happy societal changes as well, though. Perhaps the most significant is in race relations. Though 2014 saw new disappointments and tensions in America, we are a world away from the era in which the conservative movement began in the old southern Presbyterian church. In those days, Jim Crow and segregation still haunted us; then came the civil-rights movement. The PCA's founders explicitly and officially stated their desires for a denomination that would include all races, but the PCA began overwhelmingly white. The children and grandchildren of the PCA founders, however, are part of a denomination that has witnessed and participated in a Reformed awakening in the African-American community, and that is planting multiethnic congregations, establishing campus ministries at historically black colleges and universities (which have a very substantial Asian membership), is deliberately reaching out into the Hispanic communities, and is intentionally and happily committed to a PCA that is increasingly multiethnic.

These cultural and societal changes have had a massive effect on the PCA, and are especially reflected in very different generational perspectives on how the church ought (or ought not) to address social issues. Those differing viewpoints and approaches have brought their own challenges to the formation of a coherent, compelling denominational identity.

Representing one's own denominational history, at point-blank range, with all these factors and perspectives, is a challenge, to say the least. Add to that the fact that Presbyterian history in general, and the history of conservative Presbyterianism in the twentieth century in particular, is not a well-known subject, even by Presbyterian ministers, and you have a real interpretive conundrum.

This is but one reason that I am so grateful for and excited about Sean Michael Lucas's new history of the PCA, *For a Continuing Church*. Dr. Lucas is a recognized church historian, an expert in American Presbyterianism, a respected pastor, a widely regarded churchman, a veteran theological administrator, and a master teacher. He brings a rich experience and profound historical insight to the task. This book itself, well researched, evenhanded, generous-spirited, offers a pathway to denominational self-understanding and on into the future of a Presbyterianism that is true to the Bible, in accordance with the Reformed faith, and obedient to the Great Commission.

Ligon Duncan, Ph.D.
Chancellor, Reformed Theological Seminary
John E. Richards Professor of Systematic and Historical Theology
Past Moderator, General Assembly, Presbyterian Church in America

Acknowledgments

This book would not be possible at all without the assistance of many folks through many years. First, I would like to acknowledge the session of First Presbyterian Church, Jackson, Mississippi, who graciously opened their session records to me during a visit in 2002. J. Ligon Duncan III, then senior minister at the church, and his staff, especially Mary Ball, made me feel welcomed. Later, the session asked me to write the church's 175th anniversary history that was eventually published in 2013 as *Blessed Zion: First Presbyterian Church, Jackson, Mississippi, 1837–2012*. The opportunity to think through the developments that led to the beginning of the PCA from the perspective of a historic, flagship congregation was extremely valuable.

Also, Wayne Sparkman, director of the PCA Historical Center, assisted me throughout my research, hosting me on several occasions as I did initial research in St. Louis and opening his doors to me after I arrived at Covenant Seminary to work and teach. Since I left St. Louis, Wayne has continued to be on the lookout for documents that would help; he has been a partner in this project. I am especially grateful to Jim Pakala and the staff at the J. Oliver Buswell Library at Covenant Seminary, who ran down scores and scores of books and articles for me through interlibrary loan. Several other repositories opened their collections to me: the James P. Boyce Library at the Southern Baptist Theological Seminary, Louisville, Kentucky; the Billy Graham Center Archives at Wheaton College; the Presbyterian Historical Society, at both the Montreat, North Carolina, and Philadelphia offices (after the Montreat office closed, all references to *PHS* in the notes are to the Philadelphia office); the Archives at Columbia Theological Seminary, Decatur, Georgia; the Morton Library at Union Presbyterian Seminary, Richmond, Virginia; and the library at Reformed Theological Seminary,

Jackson, Mississippi. I am thankful as well to David Peterson, who shared his research on Judge Samuel Wilson with me, and to Bill Smith, John Muether, and Brister Ware, who all supplied hard-to-find documents.

Projects such as this cannot happen without money, time, and feedback. I am pleased to acknowledge the 2004–5 research fellowship I received from the Presbyterian Historical Society to do research in Montreat. While at Covenant Theological Seminary, I enjoyed the support and confidence of many friends, particularly Bryan Chapell, Donald Guthrie, Mark Dalbey, David Calhoun, and Jimmy Agan. I am grateful to my faculty colleagues to whom I presented a section of chapter 5 at a colloquium for their interest and dialogue. In addition, I thank the seminary's president, Bryan Chapell, and the board of trustees for granting me a sabbatical for the spring 2009 term and for funding research trips to Richmond, Virginia, and Philadelphia. Since I have served in Hattiesburg, Mississippi, the session and staff at First Presbyterian Church have consistently supported my calling to write; the writing sabbatical that I enjoyed in 2013, as well as the regular writing days that I had, were a gift not only to me but to the church at large and significantly aided the completion of this manuscript.

Finally, I am grateful to all those with whom I have discussed this project, in churches and classes across my denomination and friends in southern studies across the country. In this regard, I would particularly like to mention Richard Bailey, David Chappell, Bobby Griffith, Keith Harper, Bo Morgan, Steve Nichols, Otis Pickett, and Nick Willborn. Portions of this book were presented as conference papers and lectures at the Conference on Faith and History, the University of Arkansas–Little Rock, Reformed Theological Seminary, Westminster Seminary California, the American Society of Church History, the Evangelical Theological Society, the University of Southern Mississippi, and the PCA General Assembly. Portions of chapter 3 appeared as " 'Our Church Will Be On Trial': W. M. McPheeters and the Beginnings of Conservative Dissent in the Presbyterian Church, U.S.," *Journal of Presbyterian History* 84 (2006): 52–66.

My family's support has been invaluable. My wife, Sara, came along with me on this journey into Presbyterianism. Steve and Susan

Lucas, my parents, encouraged me by reminding me often about the importance of this book. Ron and Phyllis Young, my parents-in-law, continue to maintain a close relationship with us and remind us that connectedness is important, whether within a church or a family. I hope they enjoy this story of a different kind of fundamentalism. This book began right after my third child was born; our oldest was not yet five. It has grown up with my four children; there has never been a day that they did not know about "the big book." It is fitting that this volume be dedicated to them. My prayer is that they will always love Jesus and this wonderful, flawed, beautiful Presbyterian church.

Abbreviations

BGC	Billy Graham Center, Wheaton College, Wheaton, Illinois
CLC	Covenant Life Curriculum
CO	*Christian Observer*
COCU	Consultation on Church Union
ECOE	Executive Commission on Overseas Evangelism
MGAPCUS	*Minutes, General Assembly of the Presbyterian Church in the United States*
NAACP	National Association for the Advancement of Colored People
NPRF	National Presbyterian and Reformed Fellowship
OPC	Orthodox Presbyterian Church
PCA	Presbyterian Church in America
PCAHC	Presbyterian Church in America Historical Center, St. Louis, Missouri
PCU	Presbyterian Churchmen United
PCUS	Presbyterian Church in the United States
PCUSA	Presbyterian Church in the United States of America
PC(USA)	Presbyterian Church (U.S.A.)
PEF	Presbyterian Evangelistic Fellowship
PHS	Presbyterian Historical Society, Philadelphia
PJ	*Presbyterian Journal*
PO	*Presbyterian Outlook*
RPCES	Reformed Presbyterian Church, Evangelical Synod

SPJ	*Southern Presbyterian Journal*
UPCUSA	United Presbyterian Church in the USA
UPS	William Morton Library, Union Presbyterian Seminary, Richmond, Virginia
WCF	Westminster Confession of Faith

1

Introduction: The Roots of the Presbyterian Church in America

The creation of the Presbyterian Church in America (PCA) on 4 December 1973 was an attempt to preserve a "continuing" Presbyterian church. Concerned by the apparent leftward drift of the Presbyterian Church in the United States (PCUS), colloquially known as the "southern Presbyterian Church," those who led in forming the PCA were concerned with doctrinal and ecclesiastical issues; they believed that the agencies and boards of the denomination, along with many of its ministers, had become apostate and that the only way in which the mission and tradition of the PCUS could be preserved was through a separation. When the separation happened, it brought to an end over forty years of conflict with the PCUS.

In forming this continuing Presbyterian church, the founding generation believed that it was preserving what was best from the PCUS. In particular, the leaders were trying to form a conservative "mainline" Presbyterian body, one that was committed to biblical inspiration and inerrancy, warm and winsome Calvinism, and aggressive local and global evangelization. The desire was that the new church would marry these emphases with a sense of cultural responsibility for American civilization. Like liberal mainstream Protestants, the southern Presbyterian conservatives who formed the PCA believed that the church had a responsibility to culture. These conservatives differed in how to relate to culture: while liberal Protestants issued prophetic statements or utilized educational processes to impact culture, conservatives tended to emphasize evangelism as the means of bringing cultural change. And yet these conservatives who formed the PCA were profoundly interested in preserving American civilization through their efforts.[1]

And so the PCA was formed to be a conservative mainline Presbyterian body. This claim undoubtedly surprises because the PCA could be read in the light of a number of other ecclesiastical divisions that littered the twentieth century. When the PCUS conflicts began in earnest in the late 1920s, the northern Baptist and Presbyterian churches were already convulsed by the fundamentalist-modernist controversy, which led to the creation of new Baptist and Presbyterian connections, the General Association of Regular Baptist Churches (1932), the Orthodox Presbyterian Church (1936), the Bible Presbyterian Synod (1937), and the Conservative Baptist Association (1947). As the strife in the PCUS came to a head in the 1960s and 1970s, there were similar troubles in denominations as diverse as the Southern Baptist Convention, the Lutheran Church–Missouri Synod, and the Episcopal Church. Hence, it is fair to say that the southern Presbyterian conservatives who formed the PCA bore some similarities with other fundamentalists: emphasis on key doctrinal issues, such as biblical inerrancy and the exclusive nature of salvation in Jesus Christ, a demand for evangelism as the primary mission of the church, and a willingness to separate from those deemed apostate. By separating from the PCUS to form a new denomination, southern Presbyterian conservatives followed a well-worn path.[2]

Yet while they followed a path that others traveled, it is notable that these church leaders actually formed a new denomination rather than joining with either the Orthodox Presbyterian Church (OPC) or the Reformed Presbyterian Church, Evangelical Synod (RPCES),

1. W. Jack Williamson, "To the Glory of God," *PJ* (26 December 1973): 19.

2. All issues raised in "A Message," *PJ* (26 December 1973): 7–8; Bryan V. Hillis, *Can Two Walk Together unless They Be Agreed? American Religious Schisms in the 1970s* (Brooklyn, NY: Carlson, 1991). For the history of that first generation of northern Presbyterian and Baptist fundamentalists, see George M. Marsden, *Fundamentalism and American Culture: The Shaping of Twentieth Century Evangelicalism, 1875–1925* (New York: Oxford University Press, 1980); D. G. Hart and John Muether, *Fighting the Good Fight: A Brief History of the Orthodox Presbyterian Church* (Philadelphia: Orthodox Presbyterian Church, 1995).

a successor denomination to the Bible Presbyterian Church. Such a determination reflects the different aims and goals that southern Presbyterian conservatives had for their new body—aims and goals that were distinctly mainline in orientation. To be sure, there were connections between followers of northern Presbyterian fundamentalist J. Gresham Machen and their southern counterparts that contributed to the development of conservative dissent within the PCUS. And Machen's Westminster Theological Seminary did play a role in supplying conservative ministerial leadership to the PCUS. Several leaders of the "Conservative Coalition" trained at Westminster—either graduating from the theological school or transferring to a PCUS seminary for the last year of school to ease placement. Some conservatives actually pastored churches in the OPC before coming south to serve conservative PCUS congregations. Even more, many of the issues over which southern conservatives agitated were issues that caused northern Presbyterians to bolt from that denomination, specifically the inerrancy of Scripture and confessional subscription.[3]

Yet there were important differences. For example, while many in the Machen cohort that led the OPC in its early days sought to maintain a confessional Presbyterianism for its own sake, the majority of those who helped to develop the PCA were less interested in arguing over secondary theological issues that would distract from the larger goal of evangelizing and renewing American culture. In fact, it appeared that conservatives within the PCUS were influenced more strongly by the rising "New Evangelicalism" and its luminaries, particularly Billy Graham, than by leaders or emphases from the OPC. For example, one important link between the New Evangelicals and southern Presbyterians was L. Nelson Bell, Graham's father-in-law and founder of both *Presbyterian Journal*, the magazine of southern

3. Rick L. Nutt, "The Tie That No Longer Binds: The Origins of the Presbyterian Church in America," in *The Confessional Mosaic: Presbyterians and Twentieth-Century Theology*, ed. Milton J. Coalter, John M. Mulder, and Louis B. Weeks (Louisville, KY: Westminster John Knox, 1990), 236–56; R. Milton Winter, "Division and Reunion in the Presbyterian Church, U.S.: A Mississippi Retrospective," *Journal of Presbyterian History* 78, 1 (2000): 76; William R. Glass, *Strangers in Zion: Fundamentalists in the South, 1900–1950* (Macon, GA: Mercer University Press, 2001); Vernon S. Broyles III, "Is the PCUS Problem 'Confessional Fundamentalism'?," *PO* (11 September 1972): 5.

Presbyterian conservatives, and *Christianity Today*, the magazine for New Evangelicals.[4]

Thus, rather than link arms with smaller, separatist northern Presbyterian bodies, the founders of the PCA forged a body that would emphasize conservative doctrine for the purpose of renewing American culture. But the PCA would be more than this. From the beginning, southern Presbyterian conservatives articulated right-wing social and political views that would shape the founding of the denomination and continue to characterize the vast majority of ministers and laypeople. In the post–World War II era, these conservatives articulated a religiously inspired version of conservative political ideology: anticommunism, anti-integration, and anticentralization. While the focus of much of their ideology was dedicated to critiquing leftward theological and social trends in the PCUS, many of the conservatives who would form the PCA would articulate a more positive vision of political, cultural, and religious conservatism, which would place the new body solidly on the right wing of American denominations and give it a larger-than-expected influence in the new Religious Right.[5]

In tracing out this argument, it is important to recognize that the creation of the PCA offered yet another example of the growing cultural divide between conservatives and liberals within American society as a whole and particularly in the South. Recent historians of the post–World War II period have noted the developing rift between progressives and conservatives throughout southern society. Before World

4. Kennedy Smartt, *I Am Reminded: An Autobiographical, Anecdotal History of the Presbyterian Church in America* (Chestnut Mountain, GA: n.p., 1998), 22, 56, 105, 115. Compare with Joel A. Carpenter, *Revive Us Again: The Reawakening of American Fundamentalism* (New York: Oxford University Press, 1997). For the contested relationship between the OPC and other evangelicals, see Sean Michael Lucas, "J. Gresham Machen, Ned B. Stonehouse, and the Quandary of Reformed Ecumenicity," *Westminster Theological Journal* 62 (2000): 197–222.

5. Rick L. Nutt, *Toward Peacemaking: Presbyterians in the South and National Security, 1945–1983* (Tuscaloosa, AL: University of Alabama Press, 1994); Joel L. Alvis Jr., *Religion and Race: Southern Presbyterians, 1946–1983* (Tuscaloosa, AL: University of Alabama Press, 1994); Jonathan M. Schoenwald, *A Time for Choosing: The Rise of Modern American Conservatism* (New York: Oxford University Press, 2001), 12; Sara Diamond, *Roads to Dominion: Right-Wing Movements and Political Power in the United States* (New York: Guilford, 1995); D. G. Hart, *From Billy Graham to Sarah Palin: Evangelicals and the Betrayal of American Conservatism* (Grand Rapids: Eerdmans, 2011).

War II, while the South may have been "solid" in a one-party way, it was far from monolithic. Deep divisions over industrialization, unionization, and desegregation wracked the Democratic party in the South, and created rival ideologies within the single partisan umbrella. While progressives articulated a worldview that exalted individual rights over societal norms, conservatives sought to buttress older social byways that maintained white supremacy, male hierarchy, and social-bond individualism. As the twentieth century progressed, southern Presbyterians would experience a "conflict of visions," a culture war that southern and American society at large was and would be experiencing. Ultimately, southern Presbyterians resolved the internal conflict through the departure of conservatives who formed the "continuing church." Still, the conflict within the PCUS provides yet another barometer of the changing cultural and social relations that the South and the nation endured in the final decades of the twentieth century.[6]

Although it was unrecognized at the time, the conflict that resulted in the formation of the PCA began early in the twentieth century. By the end of the nineteenth century, prominent PCUS ministers had moved away from the church's historic commitments to confessional Calvinism and the spiritual nature of the church by espousing progressive theological sentiments and urging the social gospel as an appropriate response to the social ills experienced in the New South. By the mid-1920s, not only had conservatives noted these trends, but they began to articulate a position of conservative dissent that stressed fidelity to the older ways. Conservative professors such as W. M. McPheeters, the longtime professor of Old Testament at Columbia Theological Seminary, partnered with pastors such as J. B. Hutton, the rock-ribbed leader of First Presbyterian Church, Jackson, Mississippi, to work through the challenges raised by this

6. Robert Wuthnow, *The Restructuring of American Religion* (Princeton, NJ: Princeton University Press, 1988); Numan V. Bartley, *The New South, 1945–1980* (Baton Rouge, LA: Louisiana State University Press, 1995); Pete Daniel, *Lost Revolutions: The South in the 1950s* (Chapel Hill, NC: University of North Carolina Press, 2000); Joseph Crespino, *In Search of Another Country: Mississippi and the Conservative Counterrevolution* (Princeton, NJ: Princeton University Press, 2007); Thomas Sowell, *A Conflict of Visions: Ideological Origins of Political Struggles* (New York: Basic Books, 2002); James Davison Hunter, *Culture Wars: The Struggle to Define America* (New York: Basic Books, 1991).

"liberal group" in the church. Conservative ruling elders and ministers began to write to the Presbyterian papers, warning of the effects
of the progressive agenda of confessional revision, social liberalism,
and ecumenical activity. These conservatives stressed the importance
of the "fundamentals" of the Christian faith as vital for the life of
the church. They even sought to convince the church that ministers should commit themselves to certain fundamental doctrines by
virtue of their ordination vows. By 1939, conservatives had come
to believe that the situation in the church was dire, and they determined to make a stand. Led by a ruling elder from Charlotte, North
Carolina, Tom Glasgow, conservatives attempted to charge the most
prominent and popular progressive minister in the church, E. T.
Thompson, with violating his ordination vows by teaching contrary
to the Westminster Standards. When the church not only failed
to discipline Thompson but exonerated him in 1941, conservatives
became convinced that the progressives had captured the machinery
of the church. In response, they determined to organize in order to
battle for their church's future.

While conservatives objected to the theological waywardness of
their liberal counterparts, always in the background were objections
to the progressives' political and social agendas. In seeking to over-
turn the church's long-standing commitment to the spiritual nature
of the church, PCUS progressives intended to speak "prophetically"
to their day and to work for the corporate reformation of American
society. Generally, that meant involvement in a variety of social issues
in the South, particularly racial integration. By pursuing social justice,
progressives within the church were convinced that they could maintain Presbyterianism's long-standing cultural hegemony. Maintaining
this leadership position was vitally important for those who had long
thought of themselves as the cultural custodians of American civilization. While southern Baptists and Methodists claimed overwhelming
numbers—out of every ten churchgoers in the South, approximately
five were Baptist, three Methodist, and one Presbyterian—southern
Presbyterians were still the intellectual leaders. In order to maintain
this position of leadership and to purify America from the dross
of social ills, progressive southern Presbyterians saw themselves as

"prophets in the Old Testament tradition, prophets who dare to speak out boldly and are prepared to meet the fate generally meted out to prophets, and which some have met in our own day."[7]

PCUS conservatives shared a similar goal with the progressives—to save Western civilization as represented in the United States of America. And they shared a similar identity as the progressives; both sides cherished the fact that they belonged to a mainline Protestant denomination. But the two sides differed profoundly over the method for achieving that goal. While progressives embraced a prophetic stance that sought social justice, conservatives stood as evangelists in the old-time sense, seeking for lost souls. Committed to mass evangelism as practiced by a long train of itinerants from Charles Finney to their new champion Billy Graham, PCUS conservatives worried that the denomination's movement away from the fundamental doctrines of the faith would hamstring evangelism. If individuals were not being transformed by the power of the gospel, then American society would begin to disintegrate.

By the 1960s, conservatives were convinced that the church's failure to maintain their historic evangelistic approach, which had been traded in for "evangelism as social justice," had led to the gross moral and social failures of the rising generation. As Presbyterian (and other) children rioted in the streets, used drugs and exalted free love, marched on Selma, or burned their draft cards—encouraged to do so by youth leaders trained in the progressive theology of the PCUS seminaries—conservatives wondered whether the apocalypse was truly coming in their times. If so, it was the fault of the progressives and their transformation of the mission of the church. Increasingly convinced that they were "unequally yoked together" with denominational progressives, and fearful of the effect that this was having on American culture, conservatives believed that it was necessary to separate in order to continue a "Presbyterian church loyal to Scripture, [true to] the Reformed faith, and committed to the spiritual mission of the Church as Christ commanded in the Great Commission." Only a

7. Ernest Trice Thompson, *The Spirituality of the Church: A Distinctive Doctrine of the Presbyterian Church in the United States* (Richmond, VA: John Knox, 1961), 45.

church thus committed would have the political and cultural clout necessary to save America in the midst of its profound moral malaise.[8]

In order to accomplish this separation, early in the 1960s, southern Presbyterian conservatives began to forge their own shadow organizations within the church. Already *Presbyterian Journal*, which had been in operation since 1942, had rallied conservatives to their causes. The *Journal* had proved its worth in the defeat of reunion with the northern Presbyterians in 1954; key to the strategy was not only information provided to the church's masses, but also inspiration through an annual rally each August in Weaverville, North Carolina. Eventually called "Journal Day," the event served as a major meeting place for conservatives to network. In 1958, Bill Hill, pastor of West End Presbyterian Church, Hopewell, Virginia, left his pastorate in order to go into full-time evangelism, preaching revival and leading evangelistic meetings in the Billy Graham style. Hill preached in over a hundred meetings in his first five years of full-time evangelism, but he soon concluded that in order to make a real change in southern society and morals, he required assistance. In 1964, Hill formed the Presbyterian Evangelistic Fellowship (PEF), which was soon stocked with fiery "soul-winning" evangelists. PEF became a rallying point for conservatives, and their annual summer conference at the Presbyterian Assembly Grounds in Montreat, North Carolina, was one of the best-attended conferences each year. Eventually, PEF would branch into international evangelism, forming the Executive Commission on Overseas Evangelism that would serve as a mission sending agency.

A third organization, Concerned Presbyterians, was led by Kenneth S. Keyes, a ruling elder and real estate developer from Miami. Keyes had long been involved in conservative causes within the church, working to defeat reunion with the northern Presbyterians in 1954. As the lay leaders involved with the *Journal* saw the leftward turn in the church, they became convinced that they needed to organize ruling elders as a mass movement to save the church. Keyes was willing to lead this organization funded with seed money from the *Journal*; in late 1964, Concerned Presbyterians had become a reality and a thorn

8. Williamson, "To the Glory of God," 11.

in the side of the liberal leadership. The initial success of the Keyes group in raising consciousness convinced several ministers to gather informally to pray for revival within the denomination. As they prayed, they began to wonder whether they, too, needed more formal organization in order to make a final stand for the reform and renewal of the PCUS. As a result, in late 1968, Donald Patterson led these ministers toward creating Presbyterian Churchmen United, which would ultimately take the lead in forging a continuing Presbyterian church.

These four organizations—*Presbyterian Journal*, PEF, Concerned Presbyterians, and Presbyterian Churchmen United—formed the basis for the new denomination that would emerge in 1973. Two years before, leaders from each of these groups met in order to discuss the possibility of separating from the mainline church. Those discussions revealed the deep fissures among those who participated in the conservative dissent. Some, most prominently Nelson Bell, could not envision abandoning the PCUS; Bell repudiated the continuing-church movement and died a few months after completing his term as moderator of the 1972 PCUS General Assembly. Others, who had banded together as the Covenant Fellowship of Presbyterians, were uncertain that separation was the proper procedure at that time. These ministers feared the growing polarization within the church and desired to bridge the differences between its conservative and liberal wings. When the PCA was formed in 1973, none of the Covenant Fellowship ministers joined, awaiting some future time when apostasy would be plain and would demand separation. Still others, such as Robert Strong, pastor of Trinity Presbyterian Church, Montgomery, Alabama, had gone through prior church separations and could not bear to go through another. In the end, Strong resigned his pastorate, after which his church immediately voted to leave the PCUS and to join with the new continuing church.[9]

The ambivalence that some felt for the new denomination was epitomized within the one other vitally important institution for the continuing-church movement, Reformed Theological Seminary in Jackson, Mississippi. Started with seed money from one of the leading

9. Robert Strong, "Why I'm Not Leaving My Church," *Eternity* (September 1973): 44–48; "Applause," *PO* (17 December 1973): 4.

conservative PCUS churches, the independent Reformed Seminary maintained an awkward relationship with the continuing-church movement. Founded to supply conservative ministers for the PCUS, the school produced a number of younger ministers who would support division in the church when the time came. In addition, Morton Smith, professor of systematic theology at the seminary, was one of the leaders promoting the separation, served as an adviser to the independent Vanguard Presbytery, and later acted as the PCA's first stated clerk. At the same time, Sam Patterson, president of the seminary, consistently repudiated separation as a strategy, going on record in late 1972 that he "was opposed, on the basis of Scripture as I understand it, to a division from or withdrawal from our denominational branch of the Church of Christ." Patterson was supported by recently hired Robert Strong, who had left his church to teach homiletics at the seminary, and by church history professor Al Freundt, who would never separate, maintaining his ministerial credentials in the Presbyterian Church (U.S.A.) until his death in 2001.[10]

These realities provide an important reminder: not everyone who was involved in conservative dissent necessarily viewed the issues the same way or believed that separation was the answer. One of the ironies is that Nelson Bell, who did more than anyone else to lead others toward the creation of the PCA, failed to support it when the time came. Likewise, other conservatives who worked within the Covenant Fellowship of Presbyterians felt that those who led in the formation of the PCA were power-hungry, divisive, and too theologically rigid to make a successful denomination. This perspective came through in *Eternity* magazine, which claimed that the group forming the PCA "does not represent the mainstream of Southern Presbyterian conservatism, symbolized by *Christianity Today*'s L. Nelson Bell, current moderator of PCUS." A couple of years before the PCUS merged with its northern counterparts in 1983 to form the PC(USA), many of those associated with the Covenant Fellowship withdrew and opted to start their own denomination, the Evangelical Presbyterian Church,

---

10. "Limited Appeal Is Made by Dissenters," *PO* (4 December 1972): 3; Patterson news item in *PO* (20 November 1972): 4.

rather than join with the PCA. A few conservatives associated with the Covenant Fellowship decided to lead their churches into the Associate Reformed Presbyterian Church, because they believed that the PCA was too fussy theologically. Clearly, the conservative-progressive division within the PCUS was far from neat and tidy.[11]

And yet even though the division was challenging for some and disappointing for others, the PCA has existed for over forty years and represented a conservative mainline Presbyterian tradition. To put it differently, the PCA has sought to be evangelical Presbyterians and Presbyterian evangelicals, which has given the church a voice to the broader culture. Holding the church together has not been easy. For some, frustrations have arisen from the church's tendency to opt for an identity that is more comprehensive than pure. Others are disappointed that the church often spends a great deal of time on relatively fine points of Reformed doctrine instead of focusing on mission, cultural engagement, or evangelism. As the church gropes toward what Presbyterian identity means in the twenty-first century, however, it does so with the clear sense of itself as a church that preaches an inerrant Bible, offers a robust and winsome Calvinism, and motivates believers to share their faith with others. In offering this kind of Christianity to American culture, the PCA stands in the broad Presbyterian tradition that goes back to the founding of American Presbyterianism and runs through three hundred years of debates over what it means to be a Presbyterian church in America. And that debate continues today.

11. "Fireman, Fireman!," *PO* (11 October 1971): 8; "Opponents of Withdrawal Speak Out," *PO* (11 June 1973): 8; "Conservatives Split Southern Presbyterians," *Eternity* 24 (July 1973): 33; David B. Calhoun, *The Glory of the Lord Risen Upon It: First Presbyterian Church, Columbia, South Carolina, 1795–1995* (Columbia, SC: R. L. Bryan, 1994), 297–321; "No Comment Department," *PO* (7 January 1974): 4; "Unwelcome Prospect," *PO* (7 January 1974): 8.

2

"The Odor of 'New Theology'": The Rise of Southern Presbyterian Progressive Thought

The rise of progressive theological and social thought in the PCUS came to notice simply enough. In 1898, James I. Vance, popular minister of the First Presbyterian Church, Nashville, Tennessee, preached a stirring sermon on the difficult Presbyterian doctrine called *predestination*. Later published with the imprimatur of the Presbyterian Committee on Publication, Vance modified the classic Calvinism of the Westminster Standards in an attempt to make predestination palatable to late-Victorian sensibilities. Unlike the theologians, whom he condemned for divorcing "God's decrees from God's heart," Vance rooted predestination firmly in God's love. "The tap-root of predestination," he observed, "grows out of the soil of divine love. God's decrees are not the manifestation primarily of power, wisdom, expediency, or foreknowledge, but OF ETERNAL AND UNCHANGEABLE LOVE." Far from being independent of his creation, "God is under obligation—the obligation of his love, of his mercy, of his nature." God was bound to save all his creation, to remake all the marred clay into vessels "for the Master's use . . . invested with imperishable beauty and worth." In the end, Vance's doctrine of predestination veered toward universalism. "God is not glorified by the damnation of his creatures. . . . God's glory is his goodness, his grace; and if he can be glorified by the redemption of one soul, much more by all," he claimed. Not only did Vance's understanding of predestination save God from Calvin's *decretum terrible*, it was the means for establishing human freedom and for saving all humankind.[1]

Conservatives were quick to discern the basis for Vance's sentimental revision of predestination. George A. Blackburn, son-in-law of famed southern Presbyterian theologian John L. Girardeau, attacked the pamphlet by claiming that "it has throughout the unpleasant odor of 'New Theology,' and the nauseous taste of 'Advanced Thought.' " By holding on to traditional language while forging a new universalistic meaning for the doctrine, Vance satisfied only those who "do not understand the doctrine, do not profess to understand it, do not propose to try to understand it, but [who] believe it, and [who] mean to keep on believing it." As evidence of Vance's vast misunderstanding, Blackburn pointed to the manner in which he read justice completely out of the doctrine's scope. Instead, "It is love, love, love, nothing but love; no justice, no righteousness, no holiness, except as they emanate from love." The effect of the pamphlet was so bad, Blackburn argued, that "the only proper disposition to make of it would be to recommit the whole case, with instructions to review and correct."[2]

Such an action was unlikely to happen, not only because Vance was extremely popular, but also because progressive thought was beginning to make serious inroads into the PCUS. This progressive thought not only redefined doctrines, but also reshaped historic southern Presbyterian commitments to the spiritual nature of the church. In the same year that Vance published his sermon, Alexander McKelway became editor of the *Presbyterian Standard*, the North Carolina Presbyterian newspaper. Until McKelway's editorship (and after he left), the *Presbyterian Standard* was an archconservative newspaper, standing firmly for the spiritual nature of the church and conservative Presbyterian doctrine. But during the seven years that McKelway edited the

1. James I. Vance, *Predestination: A Sermon* (Richmond, VA: Presbyterian Committee of Publication, 1898), 14, 17, 19, 26, 29 (emphasis his). For an account of predestination in America's religious history, see Peter J. Thuesen, *Predestination: The American Career of a Contentious Doctrine* (New York: Oxford University Press, 2009).

2. George A. Blackburn, "Vance's Predestination," *Presbyterian Quarterly* 12 (1898): 653–56.

paper, readers were exposed to a wide range of social reforms, most particularly to child-labor reform and prohibition. By using the newspaper as a vehicle for social-gospel progressivism, McKelway stood as an early voice for broadening the church's mission from individual salvation to social transformation. Though not as influential for the social gospel as others would later be, McKelway in his ascension to the editor's post signaled a new day for southern Presbyterians.[3]

Conservatives were lulled into believing that these progressive moves were only aberrations. Throughout the early decades of the twentieth century, they failed to recognize the importance of men such as Vance and McKelway in leading acceptance of new theological positions and the social gospel. These early leaders encouraged men such as Walter L. Lingle, professor at Union Seminary in Virginia, to consider Walter Rauschenbusch and other northern social-gospel crusaders. Lingle, in turn, significantly influenced a generation of students who would come together at Union Seminary and in Richmond pulpits in the 1930s. By the time conservatives noticed what was happening—shocked awake by the forthrightness of popular Arkansas minister Hay Watson Smith—progressive leadership was already in place in the important institutions and pulpits throughout the PCUS.[4]

JAMES I. VANCE AND SENTIMENTAL PRESBYTERIANISM

Of special importance to the growth of progressive thought in the PCUS was the influence of urban pulpiteers. As these men preached to their genteel audiences in New South cities at the beginning of the twentieth century, they eschewed doctrinal preaching for a more popular approach. These ministers recognized that they were participating

3. Glenda Lynelle Bridges, " 'Rescue the Perishing': Alexander Jeffrey McKelway, Social Gospeler and Social Reformer" (M.A. thesis, Western Carolina University, 1997); William A. Link, *The Paradox of Southern Progressivism, 1880–1930* (Chapel Hill, NC: University of North Carolina Press, 1992): 161–81. When McKelway became editor of the *Presbyterian Standard*, it was still called the *North Carolina Presbyterian*, a name that it did not change until 1899. In order to avoid confusion, I use the later name in reference to his editorship.

4. J. Wayne Flynt, " 'Feeding the Hungry and Ministering to the Broken Hearted': The Presbyterian Church in the United States and the Social Gospel, 1900–1920," in *Religion in the South*, ed. Charles Reagan Wilson (Jackson, MS: University Press of Mississippi, 1985), 83–137; Peter H. Hobbie, "Walter L. Lingle, Presbyterians, and the Enigma of the Social Gospel in the South," *American Presbyterians* 69 (1991): 191–202.

in a revolution of sorts. Samuel Hall Chester, secretary of the PCUS Foreign Missions Committee, observed that "the revolution in style of preaching from the elaborate theological discourse to the more practical style of the present day is doubtless due, in part at least, to the fact that all our Seminaries are now in cities where students come in contact with all sorts and conditions of men and have the opportunity of subjecting to clinical experiment the theories learned in the classroom." Not only was the seminary experience important for this transition, but the example of ministers who successfully downplayed doctrine for experience was vital as well. And no minister represented this trend better than James I. Vance, longtime minister at First Presbyterian Church, Nashville, Tennessee. As historian E. T. Thompson observed, "As a pulpit orator Dr. Vance was unexcelled, but in other respects typical of a new generation of preachers—little concerned with the niceties of Calvinistic dogmatics, greatly concerned with God's redemptive love, freely offered to all mankind through Jesus Christ."[5]

Born in Arcadia, Tennessee, on 25 September 1862, Vance received a fairly typical education for a postwar Presbyterian minister. After training at King College, the Tennessee Presbyterian school in Bristol where Vance received both bachelor and master of arts degrees, he attended Union Theological Seminary in Hampden-Sydney, Virginia. Vance arrived on Union's campus at a time of institutional transition. Robert Lewis Dabney, the longtime professor of theology and overshadowing force at the seminary, had just left for the University of Texas. Though both Thomas E. Peck and Benjamin M. Smith remained, new faculty members with greater attainments were also there. Thomas R. English joined the faculty to teach English Bible and pastoral theology in 1883, and James Fair Latimer, professor of ecclesiastical history with a Ph.D. from Leipzig University in Germany, joined the faculty in 1884. But most importantly, Walter W. Moore joined the faculty as an adjunct professor of Hebrew in 1883. Moore would influence generations of students at Union Seminary with his

5. Samuel Hall Chester, *Memories of Four-Score Years* (Richmond, VA: Presbyterian Committee of Publication, 1934), 82; E. T. Thompson, *Presbyterians in the South*, 3 vols. (Richmond, VA: John Knox, 1963–1973), 3:223.

"progressive conservatism," both as professor of Old Testament and later as the seminary's first president. Moore was personally conservative and held to "the plenary theory of inspiration," but hesitated to place certain views on the inspiration of Scripture out of bounds as long as the ministerial candidate held to the fundamentals of the system of doctrine contained in the Westminster Standards. Moore confided to A. J. McKelway, editor of the *Presbyterian Standard*, "We must have more liberty in our Church or there is going to be an explosion. . . . In my judgment there is nothing more certain as to the future of our Church than that we must allow a subscription to the 'system of doctrine,' without trying to tie men down to every statement of detail." Vance would embrace this broadening view of doctrine and apply it throughout his ministry.[6]

After leaving Union Seminary, Vance had a brief pastorate in Wytheville, Virginia. His preaching abilities, however, soon destined him for larger and more prominent pulpits: Second Church, Alexandria; First Church, Norfolk; and ultimately First Church, Nashville. Almost immediately at Nashville, Vance made an impression. He published his first book of sermons in 1895, entitled *The Young Man Four-Square*. Tapping into the same religious currents that produced D. L. Moody, the Young Men's Christian Association, and "muscular Christianity," Vance appealed directly to "every young man who has an ambition to make the most of himself and his opportunities."[7] His four sermons urged young men to display integrity in business, activism in society, and morality in politics. But Vance was particularly concerned about young men and their religion. In an age that viewed religion as

6. Basic information on Vance is from E. C. Scott, ed., *Ministerial Directory of the Presbyterian Church, U.S., 1861–1941* (Austin, TX: Von Boeckmann-Jones, 1942), 729; Walter W. Moore et al., eds., *General Catalogue of the Trustees, Officers, Professors, and Alumni of Union Theological Seminary in Virginia, 1807–1924* (Richmond, VA: Whittet and Shepperson, 1924); Moore's characterization can be found in J. Gray McAllister, *The Life and Letters of Walter W. Moore* (Richmond, VA: Union Theological Seminary, 1939), 206, 210; W. W. Moore to A. J. McKelway, n.d., in ibid., 208.

7. For example, see Gail Bederman, *Manliness and Civilization: A Cultural History of Gender and Race in the United States, 1880–1917* (Chicago: University of Chicago Press, 1995); Clifford Putney, "Character Building in the YMCA, 1880–1930," *Mid-America* 73, 1 (1991): 49–70; Clifford Putney, *Muscular Christianity: Manhood and Sports in Protestant America, 1880–1920* (Cambridge, MA: Harvard University Press, 2001).

feminine and sentimental, Vance told his young men: "Let yours be a manly religion. Don't let it degenerate into cant. Don't let it melt down into mushy sentimentalism. Don't let it die away into a starveling rite, the naked bones of formalism and ritual. Don't let it lapse into a moss-grown, mildewed theology. Let it be sincere and straightforward. Let it be clear-cut and stalwart. Let it be sympathetic and tender. Let it be fine-grained and broad-brained. Let it be rich, full, free, divine." Yet for all his emphasis on masculinity in religion, Vance's conception of religion was decidedly anti-intellectual and sentimental. Religious doctrine meant little, Vance claimed; what was required was for religious associations to "fill you, flood you, saturate you." In a similar fashion, Vance agreed with James Stalker in the claim that religion was "not a creed, but an experience; not a restraint, but an inspiration." As a result, religion meant that one had to "keep your mind free to every wind that blows, while your faith abides unwavering in Jesus Christ." Doctrines were a distraction to the type of voluntaristic religion that Vance meant to promote. While meant to be "manly," such a conception of religion was unmistakably sentimental.[8]

Vance tapped into this same sentimental religiosity in *Royal Manhood*, published in 1899. Opening the book with the bold statement, "True manhood is imperial. It does not need the rite of coronation, for it is crowned already. Its majesty is supreme in all lands, all ages, all worlds," he exalted the powers and abilities of human beings. So high were human beings in his estimation that Vance downplayed the traditional Calvinist doctrine of total depravity: "Over against total depravity let there be placed limitless possibility; over against original sin, original divinity." Human beings in their natural state could fulfill God's demands to "do justly, love mercy, [and] walk humbly with thy God" and approximate the ideal, the Divine Man. These basic human character qualities were to be coupled together with strength, manhood's greatest attribute, which stood opposed to weakness, "the damnation of manhood." To be a "strong man," he claimed, one had to care for the weak and be gentle to all, self-controlled and self-reliant.

8. James I. Vance, *The Young Man Four-Square* (New York: Revell, 1894), 92–94. The classic treatment of sentimentality in Victorian religion is Ann Douglas, *The Feminization of American Culture* (New York: Farrar, Straus and Giroux, 1998).

One also had to care for his body because "character has a physical as well as a spiritual basis." Thus, human beings had to keep their bodies in check in order to develop their full powers and abilities. Only with a body and soul rightly achieving their potentialities would Christianity come into its rights. Creeds and dogmas would not make men Christian unless they translated truth into experience: "A creed is worth nothing by itself. It must be incarnated. . . . We must do vastly more than hold our creeds. We must experience them." Yet when he attempted to describe what an experiential Christianity looked like, Vance slipped into the sentimental jargon of the age: "True religion is an experience. It is God in the life. It is not so much copying after Christ as it is having Christ formed within you, the hope of glory. . . . [It is] a religion that is not only a creed but an experience, a religion that incarnates its convictions, until its truths pulsate with the heart-throb of its own being."[9]

Not surprisingly, Vance's activistic, sentimental religion could not remain content in the relatively safe environment of a New South pulpit. In 1900, Vance accepted a call to North Reformed Church, a congregation of the Reformed Church in America, in Newark, New Jersey. While in New Jersey, Vance continued to promote a manly version of sentimental Christianity. In 1904, he published *A Young Man's Make-Up*. Once again stressing the character qualities that made up manly character and religion, he pointed to honesty, honor, courtesy, aspiration, and perseverance as vital characteristics of successful men, but chief of all stood "faith." Indeed, "the young man's crowning life-principle is the expression of his religious nature. The supreme conviction is a religious experience." This religion that young men were to embrace was no morbid experience; rather, God "wants you to be happy and stay as long as you can." In fact, according to Vance, "the church has harped too much on the duty of repressing nature. There is no such duty in sane religion. Nature is all right. It is the abuse of nature that is wrong. Be natural. Let nature lead to nature's God,

9. James I. Vance, *Royal Manhood* (New York: Revell, 1899), 11, 14, 16, 18, 27, 29, 75, 230–32. During his first pastorate in Nashville, Vance also published *Church Portals* (Richmond, VA: Presbyterian Committee on Publications, 1895) and *The Rise of a Soul* (New York: Revell, 1902).

where grace suffuses nature with faith, and love, the high-priest of the soul offers worship." But Vance wanted to be clear: Christianity was a masculine religion. He complained of those "who feel it is not quite manly to be religious. They characterize the religious young man as 'a perfect lady.' He is soft and juiceless." People could claim this only by misunderstanding what religion was. Religion was not "creed or ritual or dogma" or the "very small questions that get into the religious realm and about which the saints zealously differ." Rather, religion put young men into a right relation with "a God." This God should be one that could be respected and trusted, but ultimately had to be a being that was beyond humankind and that could provide an inspiring ideal. "Man needs God for his ideal, his faultless example, his inspiring standard, his holy, ineffable and ineffaceable light," Vance held. "God is an eternal light; a shining, deathless, everlasting sun." When men submitted their lives to God, they were fitted for service: "The people who serve society best are those through whom God expresses himself. The finest service is that which flows out of the fountain of infinite love. . . . The most glorious deeds are done when God and man strike hands to do."[10]

Perhaps Vance's most sentimental statement of religion was his 1907 book entitled *The Eternal in Man*. Within every human being, he averred, is eternity and immortality. While men and women wander away and abuse the eternal within, it still remains. What is necessary is for humans to embrace the gospel, for "the gospel is a plea for the recognition of the eternal in man. It is God coming to occupy the place He made for himself in the soul, when man was created. It is a summons to the temporal to obey the eternal." The way for men to obey the eternal is to believe in Christ, but Christ did not come to die for sinners as in traditional theology. Rather, "Christ came to recover the lost eternal accent in human life." He came to enable human beings to fulfill their eternal destinies. And so grace is not unmerited favor to wretches; instead, "grace wakes the eternal within us into living power and expression, until we hold eternal convictions."

10. James I. Vance, *A Young Man's Make-Up* (New York: Revell, 1904), 34–39, 138–39, 141–46.

Redemption is not being set free from trespasses and sins; instead, "man is redeemed when the eternal rules him." To be sure, Vance is forced to admit that humans do not obey the eternal; here was evidence of the traditional doctrine of total depravity. But the human will still had power to change its course and obey the eternal within: "[The will] is the element in whose might one may set himself against the tide. . . . Next to the Almighty it is the greatest force in the universe." When the will sought God, the eternal in man would come into its rights and rules.[11]

Vance's version of Christianity pointed men and women to religious sentiment and experience as the way to access the divine and to religious activism as the way to live out the faith. In this regard, his Christianity was far more progressive than most conservative Presbyterians recognized. Part of what made his liberalism difficult to discern was his ability to use traditional doctrines to speak new thoughts: predestination, original sin, regeneration, the incarnation of Jesus all found new content in Vance's preaching. But that was to be expected, for the minister's task was to proclaim the message of the gospel, which was not defined by "something Jesus said or taught or did or had." Rather, the gospel "is Christ himself," which was received by experience and life. And once people embraced this new life, they entered into service for a Christian civilization, which was nothing less than the kingdom of God.[12]

By 1910, Vance had decided that life in the northern United States was not all that he thought it would be; he accepted a call to return to his pulpit at First Presbyterian Church, Nashville, Tennessee, where he would serve until his retirement in 1936. As a sign of his influence in the PCUS, he was elected moderator of the General Assembly in 1918, was heavily involved in the Federal Council of Churches as a PCUS representative, and served as chairman of the Foreign Missions Committee. He would continue to expand his influence through his preaching ministry, eventually starting a radio evangelistic ministry in 1925 on WSM radio, the first fifty-thousand-watt

11. James I. Vance, *The Eternal in Man* (New York: Revell, 1907), 15–16, 21–22, 27.
12. James I. Vance, *Being a Preacher: A Study of the Claims of the Christian Ministry* (New York: Revell, 1923), 53–54, 61–62.

clear-channel station in the South. And most significantly, he was one of the early leaders for reunion with the northern Presbyterian church. As he would observe in 1918, if union with the northern church were considered simply as a question of "what will be for the best interests of the Redeemer's kingdom in the earth," Vance declared, "I unhesitatingly place myself on the side of the organic union of the two great Presbyterian bodies in this country." In so many ways, Vance would represent the major themes of theological liberalism that characterized mainstream Protestantism, whether north or south, above all in his sentimental, activistic approach to religion and his determination to adapt Christianity to the spirit of the age.[13]

A. J. MCKELWAY AND PROGRESSIVE SOCIAL REFORM

One who epitomized James Vance's sentimental, activistic religion was Alexander Jeffrey McKelway. McKelway was born into a Presbyterian minister's family: his father, John Ryan McKelway, was a northerner who was sympathetic to the southern cause in the Civil War. He did not, however, enlist in the Confederate Army because his own father was fighting on the Union side. Once the war was over, John McKelway, his wife, Catherine Scott Comfort McKelway, and their newborn son went to Albemarle County, Virginia, to serve a Presbyterian church there. John died in 1870, and Catherine, Alexander, and a younger brother relocated to Charlotte County, Virginia, where they found care and support in the home of Catherine's parents. Catherine was responsible for her sons' early education and prepared them for entrance into college.[14]

Like many Virginia Presbyterians, McKelway received his collegiate education from Hampden-Sydney College, from which he

13. Scott, *Ministerial Directory*, 729; Markku Rutosila, *The Origins of Christian Anti-Internationalism: Conservative Evangelicals and the League of Nations* (Washington, DC: Georgetown University Press, 2008), 74; James I. Vance, "Presbyterian Church Union," *Union Seminary Review* 29 (1918): 117.

14. Basic information on McKelway comes from Scott, *Ministerial Directory*, 472; William S. Powell, "Alexander Jeffrey McKelway, 1866–1918," in *Dictionary of North Carolina Biography*, ed. William S. Powell (Chapel Hill, NC: University of North Carolina Press, 1996), 4:157–58; Betty Jane Brandon, "Alexander Jeffrey McKelway: Statesman of the New Order" (Ph.D. diss., University of North Carolina, 1968); Bridges, "'Rescue the Perishing.'"

graduated in 1886. After graduation, he taught school in Virginia and Georgia as he sorted out his sense of calling. After deciding that he could do the most good as a Presbyterian minister, he returned to Farmville, Virginia, to attend Union Theological Seminary. During his seminary education, he won the heart of Lavinia Rutherford Smith, the daughter of seminary professor Benjamin M. Smith. They would marry in 1891 after he graduated from the school. Also during this time, he developed a close relationship with the young Old Testament professor Walter W. Moore. During those years, Moore was viewed as "a new Gamaliel" who was extremely loyal to Smith and so by extension to McKelway. Undoubtedly there was significant impact as Moore's "progressive conservatism" gave room for McKelway to consider new theological positions and new approaches to social righteousness. In later years, as McKelway challenged the southern Presbyterian church with social-gospel emphases, Moore would repeatedly extend his support; as McKelway's wife later remembered, "I make no claim that they always agreed, but as a friend [Moore] was one of our jewels."[15]

McKelway was licensed to preach by Roanoke Presbytery in 1890 and, like other student preachers of the period, served as an itinerant evangelist of sorts through small towns in central Virginia. In 1891, he was ordained by Albemarle Presbytery and served as an evangelist in Johnston County, North Carolina. Part of his responsibility was to preach at the Presbyterian church in Smithfield, but after a year of this, he accepted a call to the Presbyterian church in Fayetteville, North Carolina. Founded in 1800, the Fayetteville church was already a historic congregation by the time McKelway arrived in 1892. Many of the town's leaders were members of this congregation, and the church exuded respectability. While the congregation's pastors had not stayed for notably long tenures throughout the nineteenth century—with the exception of H. G. Hill, who served from 1868 to 1886—this was a plum pulpit for a minister a couple of years removed from seminary. McKelway threw himself into his work, engaging in the regular duties of ministry, leading the congregation through a building program for

15. McAllister, *Life and Letters*, 168–69.

a new Sunday school facility, urging them to pay attention to their responsibility to their community.[16]

Especially important to McKelway during his Fayetteville ministry was the temperance cause. He regularly preached sermons against the use of alcohol and especially the life-destroying work of the saloons. He viewed the Fayetteville saloons as "Satan's chosen instruments" and begged his congregation to stand against the saloon owners. If this generation did not do so, it may be "when your children will turn from your graves, drunkards' graves, with fierce resolve to root out the evil that destroyed you." McKelway favored replacing local bars with a state-regulated dispensary. In 1897, he led the town's religious leaders in circulating a petition that asked the state legislature to enact such a reform; legislators approved the dispensary system over the objection of the Liquor Dealers' Association.[17]

While he was at Fayetteville, McKelway received other opportunities to extend his service. One notable call came in 1896 from First Presbyterian Church, Jackson, Mississippi. McKelway took that call seriously, going so far as to come to preach at the church and visit the town. In the end, he declined the call and decided to stay in Fayetteville. The following year, he agreed to become superintendent of the Synod of North Carolina's department for home missions. It was during the three years that he served as the synod's representative that he saw the effects of child labor on the structures of southern families. As he became more concerned that the failure of educating the next generation would have disastrous effects down the road—alcoholism, health issues, and poverty—McKelway increasingly urged churches to take on these issues as part of a general approach to social Christianity.[18]

In 1898, McKelway would gain a larger platform from which to advocate his views. When *The North Carolina Presbyterian* was

16. Walter H. Conser Jr. and Robert J. Cain, *Presbyterians in North Carolina: Race, Politics, and Religious Identity in Historical Perspective* (Knoxville, TN: University of Tennessee Press, 2012), 164; "The First Presbyterian Church, Fayetteville, North Carolina: A Brief Historical Introduction," http://www.firstprez.com/wp-content/uploads/2014/06/HistoricalBrochure2011.pdf.

17. Bridges, "Rescue the Perishing," 94–95.

18. Sean Michael Lucas, Blessed Zion: First Presbyterian Church, Jackson, Mississippi, 1837–2012 (Jackson, MS: First Presbyterian Church, 2013), 63–64.

founded, it held a great deal of influence, reflecting the prestige of the original editor, George McNeill. But with his death in 1861 and the onset of the Civil War, the newspaper struggled. It continued to advocate a relatively conservative theological and social position, aligning with most conservative Presbyterians on issues as wide-ranging as the status of the freed African Americans after the war to whether James Woodrow should be allowed to teach evolution at Columbia Theological Seminary. By 1898, however, the newspaper required a new start—a new editor, a new name, even a new publishing location. In response, the synod elected McKelway to be editor; and shortly after his election, the stockholders of the Presbyterian Publishing Company decided to change the name of the newspaper to the *Presbyterian Standard* and to move it to Charlotte.[19]

McKelway embraced his new position as a "call from God" in which he would be "guided solely by the love of truth." That meant that the *Presbyterian Standard* had to be "the enemy of every abuse and the advocate of every reform" as well as "the earnest and effective promoter of all the great causes of the church, looking to the extension of the Kingdom of Christ."[20] Early on, McKelway distanced himself from many reform movements that would increasingly become part of progressive politics in the early twentieth century. For example, as editor of the *Presbyterian Standard*, he was not in favor of women's suffrage, suggesting that "women do not care to vote because they recognize that voting involves a fitness and willingness to fight, and because they recognize that fighting is not included in the duties that fall to them." Likewise, McKelway was a racial traditionalist, observing that "the Negro is not merely a sun-burnt white man. . . . In other words, a Negro is a Negro." He used his position as editor of the *Standard* to support North Carolina's White Supremacy Campaign at the end of the 1890s and defended *de jure* segregation. Like many other southerners, he believed that racial equality would lead to racial amalgamation, which was "abhorrent to the instincts of nature." That did not mean,

19. Thompson, *Presbyterians in the South*, 1:452.
20. A. J. McKelway, *Presbyterian Standard* (5 October 1904); A. J. McKelway, *Presbyterian Standard* (5 January 1899); A. J. McKelway, *North Carolina Presbyterian* (6 January 1898), all quoted in Bridges, "Rescue the Perishing," 38.

however, that white southerners could simply ignore African Americans in their midst; after all, "our brother in black is still our brother." Rather, McKelway urged educational development for black men and women so that they might fulfill their respective roles in southern society, under the oversight of "the stronger race." This was required by the white paternalism that shaped McKelway's worldview.[21]

One moral reform that was easy for McKelway to support was temperance. After all, he had been fighting against the alcohol interests since his early days in Fayetteville. In 1902, he became one of the charter members of the North Carolina Anti-Saloon League; he also served on the association's executive committee. In supporting this organization, McKelway observed that "we are not expecting the millennium immediately in North Carolina. But neither are we in favor of enlarging hell." The League achieved a notable victory in the state legislature's 1903 decision to provide for local option with the possibility of saloon, dispensary, or prohibition. Throughout 1904, McKelway utilized the pages of the *Standard* to urge Presbyterians to vote to close the doors of the saloons permanently; when they voted to do so, effective 1 January 1905, he praised their decision.[22]

Yet the same paternalism that caused McKelway to reject reforms connected to the rights of women and blacks also motivated his activity for child-labor laws. From the very beginning of editorship, McKelway had an eye to "the comfort of the sorrowing and the tender care of the little ones." While he initially hoped that factory owners, "earnest Christian men," might be able to come to a place of excluding children from their factories without the coercion of legislative action, it soon became clear that this would not be the case. He began a series of editorials that opposed the long days and unhealthy conditions

21. A. J. McKelway, *Presbyterian Standard* (14 October 1903), quoted in Bridges, "Rescue the Perishing," 74; Link, *Paradox of Southern Progressivism*, 68–69; A. J. McKelway, *Presbyterian Standard* (6 November 1901); A. J. McKelway, *Presbyterian Standard* (25 November 1903), both quoted in Bridges, "Rescue the Perishing," 80–81; A. J. McKelway, *Presbyterian Standard* (25 November 1903), quoted in Bridges, "Rescue the Perishing," 89.

22. A. J. McKelway, "The North Carolina Anti-Saloon Movement," *The Progressive Farmer* (11 March 1902): 7; A. J. McKelway, *Presbyterian Standard* (13 January 1904); A. J. McKelway, *Presbyterian Standard* (3 February 1904); A. J. McKelway, *Presbyterian Standard* (13 July 1904), all quoted in Bridges, "Rescue the Perishing," 95–96.

experienced by children in the textile mills. He declared that mill children "are slaves, made to work when they should be at play, made to work when they should be sleeping the deep sleep of childhood, hired into slavery under masters that are not always the kindest, for the sake of the pittance that they can earn upon which they have no claim." He also supported those in North Carolina and elsewhere who favored child-labor laws that set minimum ages and standard workweeks for children in the mills. As a result of his efforts, Davidson College awarded McKelway an honorary doctor of divinity degree in 1900.[23]

While McKelway was motivated by a general commitment to social Christianity, he also championed early Christian progressivism's defense of the white race. Hence, one of the key reasons to advocate for child-labor reform was to protect "the purest American stock[,] . . . the dominant race, the race of victorious achievement in war and peace, . . . a race whose integrity must be preserved as the only safeguard of the national greatness." This view was more similar to that of national liberal leaders Josiah Strong and Washington Gladden than to that of social-gospel theologian Walter Rauschenbusch. As historian William Link rightly observed, "McKelway was deeply suspicious of an independent, and potentially dangerous, southern proletariat," in which "Anglo-Saxon vigor" was weakened and replaced with "a debased, degenerate 'cotton mill type.'" Such degeneration would create social instability and eventually political instability. Fearful of the type of unrest that increasingly characterized Europe, southern progressives such as McKelway sought to remove children from the mills, place them in classrooms where they might be educated in American citizenship and basic skills, and so "purify this stream of life at its source."[24]

Eventually, McKelway saw that he needed to do more on behalf of the children. In 1904, when the National Child Labor Committee

---

23. A. J. McKelway, *North Carolina Presbyterian* (6 January 1898), quoted in Bridges, "Rescue the Perishing," 92; A. J. McKelway, *Presbyterian Standard* (3 September 1902), quoted in Thompson, *Presbyterians in the South*, 3:243; A. J. McKelway, *North Carolina Presbyterian* (15 December 1898), quoted in Bridges, "Rescue the Perishing," 110.

24. A. J. McKelway, "The Child Labor Problem: A Study in Degeneracy," *Annals of the American Academy of Political and Social Science* 27 (1906): 55; Link, *Paradox of Southern Progressivism*, 166–67.

organized in New York City, it chose McKelway to serve as assistant secretary for the southern states. While at first he tried to hold this position along with his editorship of the *Presbyterian Standard*, he decided that he could do more good working for the National Child Labor Committee. He would eventually move to Atlanta in 1907 and then Washington, D.C., in 1911 and would spend the rest of his days advocating for a federal child-labor law. Several hard-hitting attacks on child labor would come from McKelway's pen, comparing it to a feudalism that sucked children into the labor system through high wages while they were young but then gradually cut their wages as they got older and were stuck in the system. He would also become so identified with Woodrow Wilson's progressive politics that he would work on the Democratic Party's platform in 1916. He would later claim that nearly fifty different positions upon which the Democrats ran in 1916 had come from his pen, including the demand for a federal child-labor law. The first federal restriction on child labor was passed that same year, only to be struck down as unconstitutional two years later; the following year, the same Congress that would ratify the Volstead Act would pass it again. But McKelway would not be alive to see either of his two pet reforms succeed; he died on 16 April 1918.[25]

WALTER L. LINGLE, THE BIBLE, AND SOCIAL ISSUES

While McKelway's progressivism was significant for modeling the social gospel for southern Presbyterians, it was Walter Lingle who influenced a generation of reform-minded ministers through his teaching at Union Seminary and the Assembly's Training School and then as president of Davidson College and as a longtime columnist for the *Christian Observer*. Born in Rowan County, North Carolina, in 1868, Lingle followed a fairly typical educational route for North Carolina Presbyterians, graduating from Davidson College with undergraduate and graduate degrees before heading to Union Seminary in Virginia for his seminary training. While at Union, he became one of seminary president Walter Moore's favorites; upon graduation, Moore ensured

25. A. J. McKelway, "Child Wages in the Cotton Mills: Our Modern Feudalism," available at http://docsouth.unc.edu/nc/mckelway/mckelway.html; Betty J. Brandon, "A Wilsonian Progressive—Alexander J. McKelway," *Journal of Presbyterian History* 48 (1970): 2–17.

that Lingle was elected librarian and tutor in Hebrew and Greek so that he might remain at the seminary for a few years. A further mark of the trust that Moore had for Lingle was that he entrusted the younger man with the arrangements for moving most of the contents of the seminary—and especially the library's twenty thousand volumes—to its new location in Richmond, Virginia, in 1898.[26]

Lingle left the seminary that year for his first of three pastorates that would take him to Dalton, Georgia; Rock Hill, South Carolina; and Atlanta, Georgia. And yet even though he was not at the seminary, he continued to serve Union as financial agent while serving the Dalton church, raising funds for the school in northern Georgia, eastern Tennessee, and western North Carolina. But it was particularly when he was minister at First Presbyterian Church, Atlanta, that Lingle experienced a serendipitous moment that would shape his future direction. Around 1909, he was at the Carnegie Library, thumbing through periodicals, when he ran across an article by Ray Stannard Baker that dealt with the social teachings of the Bible. Baker's article enthusiastically recommended Walter Rauschenbusch's *Christianity and the Social Crisis*, which had been published two years before. Lingle "made haste to get the book, and read it with avidity." Not only did it push him to read other books on social Christianity, but it would prove to be a landmark in his thinking: "No other book," he later reflected, "has so stirred my soul as that first one." To be sure, Lingle dissented a bit from Rauschenbusch's theological position: when he reviewed the book for *Union Seminary Review* in 1912, he would emphatically distance himself from some of the northern Baptist's views. Still, the fact that he was still mulling over the book three years later and that he desired to share it with the review's readership was a mark of the book's significance to and influence on him.[27]

Two years after first reading Rauschenbusch, Lingle was invited to come back to Union Seminary to take over the McCormick chair

26. Basic information on Lingle comes from Scott, *Ministerial Directory*, 408; McAllister, *Life and Letters*, 281–82, 312.

27. McAllister, *Life and Letters*, 335; Walter L. Lingle, *The Bible and Social Problems* (New York: Revell, 1929), 7; Flynt, "Feeding the Hungry," 83; Lingle, "Review of *Christianity and the Social Crisis* by Walter Rauschenbusch," *Union Seminary Review* 23 (1912): 356.

of Hebrew Language and Literature from his mentor Moore. As part of his portfolio of classes, though, he would also teach a class on "sociology," which began to be offered as a result of a 1911 General Assembly's directive to its theological schools. Whatever the General Assembly meant by such a course, Lingle saw it as an opportunity to teach his seminarians the social Christianity that he had learned from Rauschenbusch; as one of his students noted, Lingle's course "The Social Teachings of the Bible" helped to "shape the mind of a new generation of theological students."[28]

In 1916, Lingle shared the flavor of this course in an essay for the *Union Seminary Review*. Originally an address to the North Carolina Conference for Social Service, Lingle's essay unpacked the "teachings of Jesus and modern social problems" along lines that would be recognizable to those paying attention to the developing social-gospel movement in the northern churches. Lingle began by recognizing that the spirit of the age was for "a change in the social order." And while socialism and other streams of thought recommended changes, all the proposals failed to recognize "that man is by nature a sinful, selfish, greedy creature" and that one could not simply transform humans into "an ideal, unselfish society simply by changing the external social order." The problem was deeper than that: "human solutions have failed and they are doomed to failure because they make no provision for changing the sinful and selfish nature of man, and because they have no power to make such a change." The problem was radical, and so the solution must be radical as well.[29]

Such a radical solution could be found in the teachings of Jesus, Lingle held. Taking Jesus' petition from the Lord's Prayer, "Thy kingdom come. Thy will be done on earth as it is in heaven," Lingle began to set forward his understanding of social Christianity. First, Jesus had come to bring about the kingdom of God. Defining this

28. McAllister, *Life and Letters*, 433; Flynt, "Feeding the Hungry," 83–84; Thompson, *Presbyterians in the South*, 3:504–5. For Lingle's influence on E. T. Thompson, see Peter H. Hobbie, "Ernest Trice Thompson: Prophet for a Changing South" (Ph.D. diss., Union Theological Seminary in Virginia, 1987), 107–8. Lingle would be transferred to the professorship of church history and missions in 1914.

29. Walter L. Lingle, "The Teachings of Jesus and Modern Social Problems," *Union Seminary Review* 27 (1916): 192.

term, "the kingdom of God," was key: "The kingdom of God includes the reign of God in heaven, in the human heart, in the Church, on the earth, and will include the final kingdom which Jesus establishes when he comes again." When Jesus prayed that God's kingdom would come, he asked that God's reign would come "in man, over man, through man, in all the relationships in man, and in all the earth." In other words, Jesus was expressing his ideal for the social order, "the perfect reign of God in all the earth." And the church, "God's greatest agent for advancing and establishing the kingdom," had the responsibility to bring about God's perfect reign into existence in the present age.[30]

The church advanced God's kingdom by actively bringing God's will to bear on human institutions and activities. After all, Lingle noted, Christians pray that God's will would be done on earth as it is in heaven; "in this petition, we are praying that the law of the kingdom may be as perfectly observed and obeyed in the earthly province of the kingdom as in the heavenly province." This touches "all of our duties as members of the social order." God's will, his law, had to be followed in every area of human endeavor so that God's perfect reign on earth would be advanced. What did that look like? It first required that men and women be "born again." The only way that the social order would be made new was for human beings to be made new: "This new creature, the redeemed individual, is the greatest contribution which the religion of Jesus Christ makes to the solution of our social problems." And yet personal regeneration was not enough to change the social order; changed individuals needed to learn and observe the laws of the kingdom, such as self-sacrifice, service, stewardship, the Sermon on the Mount, and the Golden Rule. Do away with selfishness and greed, do to others in commercial and industrial practices as one would have them do in return, live to serve God and humanity in business, and what would be the result? Become stewards of one's money so that "our money would not go into any business which our Lord could not approve and bless," follow the teachings of the Sermon on the Mount in their application to "every day life and every

30. Ibid., 193, 195–97.

day social problems," and what would happen? "Social problems will vanish and earth will be touched with heaven."[31]

To be sure, Lingle's version of social Christianity at this point was relatively moderate. After all, he maintained a stress on personal sin and regeneration that set his vision apart from that of Walter Rauschenbusch, who was revisioning Christian theology along corporate and systemic lines. Lingle would never be comfortable with the more radical approach of Rauschenbusch, questioning his understanding of biblical inspiration, biblical criticism, and the deity of Christ as well as his apparent embrace of socialism. Still, he continued to find things to appreciate in Rauschenbusch's vision, and he found ways to communicate the core ideas of social Christianity in a more acceptable form for southern Presbyterians: kingdom of God, laws of the kingdom, and the application to business and social relations.[32]

Even as Lingle gave this address, he was involved in other responsibilities that would extend the reach of social Christianity. Starting in 1910, he participated in conferences for rural pastors who needed to combine gospel preaching with social care; the third PCUS Rural Church Conference would take place under his leadership at Montreat in 1916. In these conferences, Lingle was able to share his lectures on "the social teachings of the Bible" with rural ministers, who would then implement the ideas in their local contexts. Another endeavor was the editorship of the *Union Seminary Review*, which he received when he returned to campus in 1911. Under his leadership, the review began to engage modern thought, taking up most of the key books of social Christianity and reviewing them in a generally positive way. In this way, the journal became "a forum on the Social Gospel" and heightened its visibility in the PCUS. In 1918, Lingle became acting president of the Assembly's Training School. Founded in 1911 through the leadership of A. L. Phillips and Walter Moore, the school was created to train women for missionary service as well as for leadership in

31. Ibid., 197–98, 202–3.
32. See, for example, Lingle's reviews of Rauschenbusch's books: *Christianity and the Social Crisis* in *Union Seminary Review* 23 (1912): 356; *Christianizing the Social Order* in *Union Seminary Review* 25 (1913): 63; *The Social Principles of Jesus* in *Union Seminary Review* 28 (1917): 182; and *A Theology of the Social Gospel* in *Union Seminary Review* 29 (1918): 274.

Christian education in the local church. Many of these women would find leadership opportunities in rural areas where social Christianity was required for any type of gospel witness. Lingle had taught at the school from its inception and then served as dean; but because of its precarious financial condition, he agreed to become acting president. Through his leadership, the school continued to grow. In recognition of his contribution to the church, Lingle was elected moderator of the 1920 General Assembly.[33]

Lingle's departure from Union Seminary in 1924 to become the full-time president of the Assembly's Training School did not stop his continued promotion of social Christianity.[34] He had invested too much to turn back, not only within his own denomination, but also in his involvement with the Federal Council of Churches and with the Interchurch World Movement, both ecumenical organizations that sought to promote the social gospel. When the opportunity came to summarize his views on the relationship between the Bible and social problems, he seized it: in 1929, just after he had assumed the presidency of Davidson College, he came back to Union Seminary to deliver the prestigious James Sprunt Lectures, which were published in the same year. As it would happen, *The Bible and Social Problems* would prove to be a landmark for the social gospel in the southern Presbyterian church.[35]

Lingle opened his lectures by recalling the pioneer work that he had done when he first began to teach the "Christian Sociology" course at Union Seminary. The most difficult work initially was simply helping people to understand what *sociology* entailed: most were convinced that the seminaries were teaching *socialism*. Actually, sociology was simply the study of society; and Christian sociology was the

33. McAllister, *Life and Letters*, 462–64; Flynt, "Feeding the Hungry," 100–101, 103, 105.

34. Hobbie, "Ernest Trice Thompson," 140–41; McAllister, *Life and Letters*, 512. Hobbie draws on E. T. Thompson's 1974 oral history interview with Edgar Mayse to suggest that Lingle was forced to resign from the seminary because of his advocacy of reunion with the northern church and his social-gospel advocacy; he suggests that "Lingle's fall from grace was but one example of the seminary's determination to keep out progressive and advanced thought." If so, it was simply a momentary blip, especially in the light of Thompson's own election to the Stuart Robinson chair of English Bible at the same board meeting.

35. Flynt, "Feeding the Hungry," 134.

application of biblical principles to the problems of human society. As such, it might or might not require someone to engage with socialism, to develop a social consciousness and a social message, or to engage in social service, all issues that were confused with sociology. Each of those responses was a reaction to the application of biblical principles to the problems of society, not the thing itself.[36]

Of course, Christian sociology presumed that society had problems, and significant ones at that. As a result, Lingle believed that the main question that every Christian needed to ask was "whether Christianity offers any solution for our social problems, and whether God has any ideal for His world." There were some who denigrated the historic theological answer, but Lingle was not one of them. He still believed that "the cross, the atoning death of Christ, is the great central theme of the Bible. [We] believe, with the Apostle Peter, that Christ bore our sins in His own body upon the tree, and that by His stripes we are healed." But the theological answer was not to be the only answer; rather, there was a sociological answer as well: "Centered about the cross is a great body of social and ethical teachings, which define our duties to others in all the relationships of life." Thus, the solution for our social problems was both theological and sociological, both individual and collective: the cross dealt with individual and corporate sin and sinning. "God's ideal for the individual is that he should become perfectly like Jesus Christ," Lingle taught. "God's ideal for the world is that it should become perfectly like heaven."[37]

The theological concept that brought together these twin ideals for the individual and the world was the kingdom of God. At this point, Lingle reiterated many of the themes from his earlier 1916 article. The Bible's teaching about the kingdom of God meant "the reign of God in the hearts and lives of men. It means the enthronement of God at the very center of our beings, and the doing of His will in all the relationships of life." One entered God's kingdom only through regeneration; thus, the first social implication was that Christians must continue to preach the gospel and see men and women become new

36. Lingle, *The Bible and Social Problems*, 11–29.
37. Ibid., 30–32.

creatures in Christ. Yet to believe that regeneration alone would solve the social crisis was mistaken. Born-again believers needed to embrace lives of self-renunciation and sacrificial love, serving those around them in large and small ways and stewarding their money and gifts for God's purposes. If Christians lived this way, God's kingdom would come to earth and his will would be done here as it is in heaven.[38]

A significant section of biblical teaching on the kingdom of God and social ethics was the Sermon on the Mount. Jesus showed "what manner of world this would be if the kingdom had fully come, and if the will of God were being as fully done on earth as it is in heaven." For one thing, when God's kingdom comes, righteousness would be done from the heart; it would be a regular feature of daily life and would affect every relationship. Certainly it was important to be engaged in corporate worship on Sunday, but God "expects to see our worship followed up by lives which are noted for their personal holiness and social righteousness. That kind of righteousness would solve most of the world's social problems, and cure most of its social ills." Christians' transformed lives would lead to transformed social relationships.[39]

Specifically, if Christians lived out the righteousness of the Sermon on the Mount, they would embrace Christ's cure for hatred. No longer would Christians engage in racial hatred, class division, national rivalry, or family fights. Rather, they would work to eradicate all traces of hate from the heart: "At their very first appearance, contempt and anger should be plucked up by the roots and cast out of our hearts." The pathway for doing this was forgiveness and reconciliation as quickly as possible; of course, this was easier on a personal level than on a class or national level, and yet it must be pursued at every level of life. Not only would Christians not hate, they would also be pure in heart—that was the solution to the various "sex problems" that plagued humans, from lust and adultery to divorce and remarriage. Especially in the social problem of divorce, if people simply rooted out "unchaste thinking," then the sole biblical ground for divorce— unchastity itself—would be avoided and marriages preserved. Further,

38. Ibid., 32–57.
39. Ibid., 58–64.

Christians would work toward reconciliation and purity to such a degree that this would be "a world in which it will not be necessary for boys and men and nations to use force" and to defend themselves. Until then, Christians might fight in self-defense, but they avoided revenge and retaliation exemplified by the old *code duello*; they lived lives of "non-resistance" as far as possible, seeking to love one's neighbor even when that person was unlovable.[40]

The central principle of the Sermon on the Mount was the Golden Rule. For Lingle, this represented the "one comprehensive" summary of "all the social teachings of the sermon and all the social teachings of the Bible." What made the Golden Rule such a powerful social teaching was that it was "positive and comprehensive." Not only did it summarize Jesus' teachings, but it was applicable to every relationship: "Jesus expects us to live by it in the home, in the school, in the community, in the social circle, in the church, in business, in industrial life, and in national and international affairs. He expects us to practice it toward all men of all classes, all races, all creeds, and all colors." Simply living by the Golden Rule would solve the majority of social problems in the world. And yet how little Christians practiced it and how infrequently preachers spoke on it and its application to life's relationships![41]

In the rest of the lectures, Lingle worked to demonstrate how the principles of the kingdom of God and the Sermon on the Mount applied to various areas, such as money, poverty, family, and war. He finished by urging the church, and especially its pastors, to deal with the wide range of social problems facing the world. While the church must work for the redemption of individuals, it also needed to educate the redeemed individual about the social problems in the world around him. The Christian should engage in personal Bible study and the study of social ills, but even this was not enough: the church needed to challenge the Christian "to put the social teachings of the Bible into practice in his own personal life in all of its relationships," whether the home, community, business, or city hall. To be sure, the individual Christian would go only as far in this endeavor as his pastor went.

40. Ibid., 64–75.
41. Ibid., 75–85.

Thus, ministers needed to study the social problems of the community as well as the teaching of the Bible on these matters; they should put into practice what the Bible taught in every relationship. But ministers needed to go further—they needed to preach the "comprehensive social and ethical principles" found in the Bible that "would help to guide the citizen in the proper exercise of his Christian citizenship." And sometimes they needed to lead the fight on some social issue in their role as citizens, though such action required wisdom and discretion.[42]

Still, people would not act if their pastors failed to do so. That was especially the case when the pastors and elders gathered in the church's courts. The organized church may rightly petition the state on various matters that could, in the judgment of the church, "affect the moral and spiritual life of the people." Of course, the church's main business was spiritual in nature: it was found in the Great Commission. And yet making disciples involved, as Jesus said, "teaching them to observe all things whatsoever I have commanded you" (Matt. 28:20 KJV). Hence, it was part of the spiritual mission of the church to teach Christians what the Bible demanded of them in their social relationships: "If the Church is going to teach men to live in all the relationships of life according to the teachings of Jesus, she must let me know what those teachings are, and she must make it clear that it is the duty of Christians to apply these teachings to business and to all kinds of social problems." The church must teach through the pulpit, but also "through the deliverance of church courts," on "the great ethical and social teachings of the Bible, which apply to the larger social problems of today." Surely the church could do this without "intermeddling with affairs which belong exclusively to the commonwealth." Anything less would be forsaking the very teaching of Jesus himself.[43]

On the one hand, Lingle's Sprunt Lectures seemed incredibly moderate. More times than not, his illustrations of how these social principles applied to life were personal and limited. Rather than demonstrating how Jesus' teaching on nonretaliation applied to international affairs such as World War I, he told a story about a duel that

42. Ibid., 170–82.
43. Ibid., 182–91.

had broken out over an unwillingness to drink alcohol. Instead of applying his principles on reconciliation to the crying need for racial justice, he illustrated from a conflict that he had had with an older man who was upset with him for no apparent reason. And yet it was this personal and limited approach that masked the revolutionary aspect of his argument: Lingle was trying to demonstrate that the historic southern Presbyterian commitment to the "spiritual mission of the church" had unnecessarily and unbiblically limited that mission simply to matters of individual salvation. In his final chapter, as he invoked both B. M. Palmer and James Henley Thornwell's "Address to all the churches of Jesus Christ"—key text and figures for those in the PCUS who affirmed the church's spirituality—he subtly drew them onto his own side. Those men and that text represented all that he was trying to say, namely, that the church's spiritual mission included teaching what the Bible had to say on social problems.[44]

In doing this, Lingle assisted the younger progressives in the church greatly. As E. T. Thompson noted, Lingle's lectures on social ethics "had great influence on successive generations of students." In fact, "most of the younger ministers who led in the social awakening of the church had been students of Dr. Lingle." Over the next several years, these younger ministers would have the courage to preach and teach the social gospel from their cosmopolitan pulpits, write about the social application of biblical principles in the *Union Seminary Review*, and work toward a denominational-level committee that would address the social and moral problems of the day. And they did so with Lingle's strong arguments that they actually agreed with the spirituality of the church, more so than the conservative reactionaries, who were agreeable toward preaching for abstinence from alcohol, but who were opposed to racial reconciliation and labor unions.[45]

For their part, Presbyterian conservatives as a whole failed to take seriously the progressive currents represented by Vance, McKelway, and Lingle. Every once in a while, someone would sound the alarm. The *Christian Observer* noted in 1909, "We have not drifted so rapidly or

44. Reference to Palmer, ibid., 180–82; reference to Thornwell's "Address," ibid., 185–87.
45. Thompson, *Presbyterians in the South*, 3:265.

so far as other bodies. But it is stated again and again that in some of our prominent pulpits the truth is either suppressed or perverted, and that pastors are sustained by their congregations and tolerated by their presbyteries, when they are known to be decidedly out of harmony with our confessional position." Such insight, however, was relatively rare. Most conservatives simply assured themselves that the southern Presbyterian church remained sound, standing in essentially the same place where Thornwell, Dabney, and Palmer had left it in the middle of the nineteenth century. Such was the claim, for example, by the *North Carolina Presbyterian* that "there was not a Presbyterian Church on the face of the earth so completely united as the Southern Church." Any theological or social questions that were raised "are more surface questions—they concern matters of administration chiefly—they do not go down to the roots of doctrinal belief, or touch the fundamentals of faith."[46]

The thoughtful, though, could clearly see the beginning of two parties in the church. Reflecting on the 1906 General Assembly, the *Central Presbyterian* observed, "It was clearly evident that there were two distinct parties in the Assembly that appeared again and again as particular subjects presented themselves for consideration. They were lined up with but slight variations on a number of issues. . . . Our church may as well recognize that she has a 'liberal' element of a milder type within her own fold, whether for her advancement or her embarrassment, and adjust herself to the new conditions." As the 1920s progressed, it would become clear that the progressive element was much larger than the conservatives believed, and that they were ready to modernize the PCUS and bring it into line with other mainstream Protestant denominations.[47]

46. "Our Doctrinal Drift," *CO* (7 July 1909): 2; *North Carolina Presbyterian* (19 January 1893), quoted in Thompson, *Presbyterians in the South*, 3:217.
47. "Our Assembly's Letter," *Central Presbyterian* (30 May 1906): 344, quoted in Thompson, *Presbyterians in the South*, 3:224.

3

"Reasons for a Separate Existence": Conservatives' Defense of the Spiritual Mission and Confessional Integrity of the Church

As progressive ministers came to prominent pulpits and professorships, conservatives generally remained uneasy and inactive, resting on the traditional reputation of the church in areas of doctrine and social action. Beginning in the late 1920s, progressive ministers—especially those serving in East Hanover Presbytery, which had Union Theological Seminary in Richmond, Virginia, within its boundaries—determined to bring change to their church. With an eye on the larger goal, reunion with the northern Presbyterian church, these ministers brought several overtures to the General Assembly that attacked two key conservative commitments: the "spiritual mission of the church" and full subscription to the Westminster Standards as the doctrinal statement of the church.

The commitment to the spiritual mission (or *spirituality*) of the church had a long history within southern Presbyterianism. Even before the division of the Presbyterian Church (Old School) in 1861, church leaders such as James Henley Thornwell and Robert Lewis Dabney had defended the idea that the church should not address social or political matters that were purely secular; rather, the church must focus on its spiritual mission of evangelism and worship, preaching the gospel and seeking individual conversions. If possible, the commitment to confessional integrity was of even longer standing: southern Presbyterian heritage was traceable back to the early-nineteenth-century debates in the Presbyterian Church between the Old and New Schools that centered on commitments to the Westminster Standards as originally adopted by the American church in 1729. To move away from the confessional standard was to jeopardize the church's commitment to rigorous Calvinism and set it adrift doctrinally.[1]

Even more, these identity markers served as major arguments for the PCUS's continued separation from the northern Presbyterian church. From the southern church's beginning in 1861, it had stood for the church's spiritual mission and its doctrinal integrity; when the northern church sought reunion after the Civil War, these were the reasons the southern church cited for not agreeing even to fraternal relations with its former churchmen. And conservatives held that these twin commitments continued to prevent reunion with the northern church in the 1930s. They believed that "almost alone among the churches of the world our church has stood as a stalwart champion of the spiritual mission of the church, and in its loyalty to, and emphasis upon, this great principle, which we believe to be fundamental to the attainment of the great purpose for which Our Lord gave His life, and for which He sent His church into the world." To forsake this position would be to forsake "the chief reason for her separate existence."[2]

Likewise, conservatives recognized that a major barrier to reunion with the northern church was differing confessional standards. One conservative theological professor had observed that "the Southern Presbyterian Church regards the preservation and propagation of this body of truth in its purity and entirety (referring to our church

---

1. Sean Michael Lucas, *Robert Lewis Dabney: A Southern Presbyterian Life* (Phillipsburg, NJ: P&R Publishing, 2005), 93–94; D. G. Hart and John Muether, *Seeking a Better Country: 300 Years of American Presbyterianism* (Phillipsburg, NJ: P&R Publishing, 2007). E. Brooks Holifield, *The Gentleman Theologians: American Theology in Southern Culture, 1795–1860* (Durham, NC: Duke University Press, 1978), 154, typifies scholarly opinion about the *spirituality* doctrine, namely, that it was an attempt to shut off debate on issues of slavery and segregation. While southern Presbyterians did utilize the argument in creative ways on issues of education and science, it was used most frequently to silence those who challenged the prevailing "racial orthodoxy."

2. *MGAPCUS* (1937): 59–60.

Standards) as constituting the sole justification for its existence." After all, northern Presbyterians had revised their version of the Westminster Standards in 1903 by adopting two new chapters—"On the Holy Spirit" and "On the Love of God and Missions." But now in the 1930s, buttressed by a younger generation of scholars trained on social-gospel emphases and openness to European critical scholarship, PCUS progressives desired to reshape the essentials of the church's doctrinal system. One pleaded, "Let us take down the picture of God which Calvinism has hung in them (the Standards)"; others saw such a redefinition as necessary "if there is not to be stagnation—and death." Conservatives looked at the movement for confessional revision as a step toward reunion with the northern church. Willis Everett feared, for example, that these changes were motivated by a "small group [within the PCUS] in cooperation with a like group in the Northern Church, who has visions of national bigness."[3]

And yet conservatives utterly failed in their attempt to defend the church's spiritual nature or its confessional integrity. In the decade between 1932 and 1942, progressive church leaders would successfully establish a denominational-level committee that sought to revise the church's understanding of its spiritual mission through its proclamations *and* would complete a revision of the Westminster Standards that would establish the principle of confessional revision and lead to further doctrinal changes in the years to come. Even more, conservative failures on these two issues—along with conservative inability to bring discipline to prominent progressive ministers, as will be seen in the next chapter—would serve to coalesce them as a minority group that would dissent from the denomination's direction and establish rival organizations to battle for the future of the southern Presbyterian church.

3. George Bitzer, "Changeless Gospel in a Changing World," *Union Seminary Review* 42 (1930–31): 413; E. T. Thompson, *Presbyterians in the South*, 3 vols. (Richmond, VA: John Knox, 1963–73), 3:326–28, 493; Walter L. Lingle, "The Five Points Examined," *CO* (1 September 1943): 3; Willis M. Everett, "A Questionable Procedure," *CO* (15 December 1937): 10. For a brief, general overview of confessional revision in American Presbyterianism, see John Leith, "The Westminster Confession in American Presbyterianism," in *The Westminster Confession in the Church Today*, ed. Alasdair I. C. Heron (Edinburgh: Saint Andrew, 1982), 95–100.

DEFENDING THE SPIRITUALITY OF THE CHURCH

Though conservatives did not realize it, the church's transformed understanding of its mission had begun in a musty theological journal. When Walter Lingle was a professor at Union Theological Seminary in Richmond, Virginia, in the 1910s and early 1920s, he held control of the editorship of the faculty's theological journal, the *Union Seminary Review*. He used the journal to expose southern Presbyterian ministers to the same social-gospel emphases that he was teaching seminarians in his classroom. As articles and book reviews shared the emphases of Walter Rauschenbusch and other key social-gospel thought leaders, younger ministers took note. When Lingle was forced to leave Union Seminary in 1924, the editorship went to E. C. Caldwell, described by his colleague E. T. Thompson as someone who "was little concerned with upholding the Calvinistic system; he was profoundly concerned with enabling students to discover the true meaning of Scripture. . . . He widened the horizons of a generation of students and was responsible for some of the new currents of thought that soon made themselves felt in the church." Thompson himself became the book-review editor. And through Caldwell and Thompson's leadership, the journal ran articles defending and promoting the church's involvement in economic, social, and political causes.[4]

Notably, most of these articles came from a cadre of young Richmond ministers who were determined to bring change to their church. One of the most influential came from W. Lapsley Carson, minister at First Presbyterian Church, Richmond. He held that "it is quite obvious that Jesus expected His spirit and teaching to transform human society, and that He expected His ideals and principles to influence all social relationships and to become enshrined in all social institutions." In fact, "to speak of saving the individual without attempting to reform society is a contradiction in terms." To be thoroughly Christian, individuals must apply the teachings of Jesus "in all of the relationships of life, in the home, in society, in business, in racial contacts, in international affairs, and in our treatment of our weaker or less fortunate fellow-men." Even more, ministers and church

---

4. Thompson, *Presbyterians in the South*, 3:224.

courts must take up the task of instructing Christians in their social responsibilities. "If the spiritual leaders of the Church do not discover for themselves the social implications of the teachings of Christ, and if they do not instruct the members of the Church concerning their social duties and responsibilities," Carson asked, "how can the Christian mind be informed?" And yet the church's failure on this very point accounted for "much of the modern indifference and hostility towards the Church." What the church required was a thorough engagement with its social tasks and responsibilities.[5]

Within the East Hanover Presbytery, the local judicatory for most of Union Seminary's professors, ministers were ready to take up Carson's challenge. In 1932, the presbytery replaced one of its standing committees with a new Committee on Moral and Spiritual Welfare that would focus on alerting presbytery to information concerning "moral and spiritual issues, that may be of interest or concern to the Presbytery, and to suggest any action that it may deem wise for the Presbytery to take." Leaders within the presbytery decided to overture the Synod of Virginia to establish a synodical Committee on Moral and Social Welfare in order to continue advancing the new social emphasis within the church. As it so happened, E. T. Thompson not only made the overture from presbytery to the synod; as the retiring moderator of the synod, he also served as the chairman of the Bills and Overtures Committee, which received his overture and recommended it to the body. The synod members agreed with their committee and its chairman and established a Committee on Moral and Social Welfare in 1933.[6]

---

5. W. L. Carson, "The Social Tasks of the Church," *Union Seminary Review* 43 (1931–32): 407, 411, 415, 418. Carson's sermon was delivered at the spring 1932 meeting of East Hanover Presbytery; see Peter H. Hobbie, "Ernest Trice Thompson: Prophet for a Changing South" (Ph.D. diss., Union Theological Seminary in Virginia, 1987), 229–30.

In 1932, James Gray McAllister would succeed E. C. Caldwell as editor of the *Union Seminary Review*, but E. T. Thompson would continue as book-review editor and a member of the Editorial Committee. He would exert significant influence over its direction: see Hobbie, "Ernest Trice Thompson," 223–24. The review also ran an article from noted modernist William Adams Brown on "Needed Emphases in the Church of Today," which highlighted ecumenism and the social gospel. *Union Seminary Review* 43 (1931–32): 387–406.

6. *Minutes of the Presbytery of East Hanover, PCUS* (April 1932): 47; Hobbie, "Ernest Trice Thompson," 230–31.

That same year, progressives decided to attempt establishing such a committee on the General Assembly level. At the 1933 General Assembly, Stuart Oglesby, minister at Central Church in Atlanta, offered a resolution on the moral conditions of the country and the disregard of American law. The subtext for the resolution was the ongoing ratification of the twenty-first amendment to the U.S. Constitution, which repealed prohibition and was completed in December 1933. The assembly responded well to Oglesby's resolution; J. E. Thacker moved that the resolution be read to every PCUS congregation. But then Oglesby followed his resolution with another motion: "that the moderator appoint a Permanent Committee of nine members on Social and Moral questions." This, too, was adopted by a standing vote of 139 to 34. Progressives had apparently won a smashing victory, establishing a committee to investigate a range of social issues.[7]

Conservatives quickly regrouped. The following day, they forced the Assembly to reconsider what had happened; the vote to reconsider was nearly identical on the opposite side of the issue, 134 to 49. Judge Samuel Wilson, a ruling elder from Lexington, Kentucky, led the argument against the committee, describing the proposal as "an unwarranted departure from our historic practices." In fact, as such a departure, the entire establishment of the committee should be expunged from the Assembly's minutes, Wilson argued. Debate on Wilson's motion to expunge was fast and furious; one observer noted that "this occasioned more debate than any other single matter to come before the Assembly." In the end, the Assembly reversed course and voted to expunge the entire matter from the minutes by a vote of 137 to 99. For the moment, the church clung to its commitment to the spiritual nature of the church.[8]

---

7. "The General Assembly Proceedings," *CO* (31 May 1933): 22; Thompson, *Presbyterians in the South*, 3:507. Somewhat disingenuously, Stuart Oglesby later claimed that "it was never his or anybody's purpose that such a committee should make deliverances on social and moral questions. It was the thought of those who were in favor of such a committee that the committee should study such questions and call the attention of the Assembly to anything along those lines which seemed to fall within the province of the Church and which seemed to call for the attention of the committee." Walter L. Lingle, "An Unusual Meeting," *CO* (1 November 1933): 3.

8. "The Montreat Assembly," *CO* (7 June 1933): 2, 14.

Yet progressives would not be so easily denied. It was clear that the momentum for establishing such a committee would continue to grow and that progressives would make the case for it in a variety of ways. The Synod of Virginia, where progressives maintained a significant stronghold, provided a model for how such a committee might work. Walter Lingle praised the synod's 1933 report, claiming that it was "the ablest and most comprehensive report along the line of Christianity and Social and Moral Questions that has ever been prepared by anybody in our Church, so far as I can recall." Progressives also hosted a ministers' forum at Montreat at the end of the summer, focused on these questions. The ministers invited Lingle to present addresses on how Christianity related to the Depression, war, and race. They also appointed a Findings Committee, led by the ablest progressive ministers in the denomination, whose committee report affirmed that "we hold that the Gospel of Jesus Christ has profound implications for the whole social, economic, and political order in which we live, and that this order cannot permanently ignore that Gospel without exposing itself to disastrous consequences."[9]

While making the case for the church's taking on a more prophetic role in speaking to social issues, progressive leaders tried to marry this to traditional emphases on evangelism. "Is the Church's primary business evangelism, the winning of individuals to faith in Jesus Christ?" Henry Wade Du Bose asked rhetorically. "Certainly; but in the Great Commission the risen Christ coupled with that supreme mission another, which yet is not another, but the inevitable supplement of evangelism . . . . A discipleship that does not bring the Sermon on the Mount to bear upon all the personal and social relations of life has read the Great Commission with one eye shut." Likewise, Stuart Oglesby argued that a focus on matters of social and moral concern would not cause the church to "lessen its spiritual power and its enthusiasm in evangelical work, but on the other hand the neglect of them may be fatal to any spiritual progress at

9. Walter L. Lingle, "Another Presbyterian Manifesto," *CO* (11 October 1933): 2; "Presbyterian Ministers' Forum," *CO* (11 October 1933): 15. The Findings Committee report was prepared by J. McDowell Richards, president of Columbia Seminary. Stuart R. Oglesby, "The Church and Social and Moral Problems," *CO* (14 February 1934): 6.

all." In fact, appointing a committee on social and moral problems could actually foster and sustain the cause of revival for which Presbyterians prayed.[10]

Conservative leaders tried to push back against the momentum that the progressives were building toward the establishment of such a committee. William Crowe, longtime minister at Westminster Church in St. Louis, argued that the church's mission was one of benevolence and evangelism; only such a view was "in accord with the doctrine of the spirituality of the church." In a similar way, Judge Samuel Wilson believed that "the creation of such a committee would be a grave mistake, injudicious, inexpedient and unwarranted." In particular, Wilson noted that though Jesus dealt with certain moral issues, he always "approached and acted upon specific, concrete, practical instances." Even more, nothing in the current Presbyterian order prevented social issues from being addressed by the General Assembly; to create a super-committee that would "throw out a mammoth and unlimited dragnet" and deal with any conceivable social or moral issue would ultimately lead to spiritual tyranny. Finally, Wilson represented other conservatives well when he pointed out that the main issue was simple: "Nothing should be done by the Presbyterian branch of [the Christian] church to obscure or subordinate the spiritual nature of Christ's Kingdom, the preeminently spiritual nature of his life and work and teachings. The Christian church received no commission from its divine Founder to occupy itself with social, moral, economic or political questions as such."[11]

At the 1934 General Assembly, the church moved decisively to establish a Permanent Committee on Social and Moral Welfare. Several presbyteries and two synods sent overtures to the Assembly to do just this. In response, the members of the Bills and Overtures Committee not only recommended that the Assembly establish such a

10. Henry Wade Du Bose, "Social Ethics at Montreat," *CO* (18 October 1933): 9; Oglesby, "The Church and Social and Moral Problems," 6.

11. William Crowe, "Some Reflections on the Business of the Church," *CO* (14 March 1934): 5–6; Samuel M. Wilson, "The Proposed Assembly's Committee on Social and Moral Questions Is Inexpedient, Unwise and Unconstitutional," *Union Seminary Review* 45 (1934): 189, 190, 191–92.

morals committee; they believed that it was necessary because "there is among us a grievous lack of systematic endeavor for better understanding of current evils and hardships and of proposed remedies." Such a Committee on Social and Moral Welfare would provide "concerted effort toward effective militancy" in the application of Christianity to the great social issues of the day. The Assembly voted to establish the committee with a limited purview: it was charged to produce a report that would suggest "a program of scope and attitude for our Church" and offer it to the 1935 Assembly for a vote and the establishment of the committee on a permanent basis. After debate, the proposal to set up the new committee was approved by a 163–103 vote. When the moderator appointed the initial committee, not only were progressive ministers Stuart Oglesby and E. T. Thompson on the committee, but Oglesby was the first chairman. As historian Peter Hobbie noted, "The progressives gained a precarious victory."[12]

It was a victory, however, that would be solidified over the following year. Once again, progressives would push their case in the Presbyterian newspapers. William Crowe Jr., minister at First Church, Talladega, Alabama, disagreed with his conservative father and urged a social application of the gospel as part of the "business of the church": "The social application of the Gospel is nothing new under the sun. It is written into the very heart of the Bible. Preaching a vision of an ideal and universal brotherhood simply means taking God at His Word regarding human relationships." One such relationship was the one between whites and blacks: "Let us be specific. We have a Negro problem—or is it a white problem? How far has the Church gone in trying to create a definite respect for the Negro on the basis of genuine, unqualified neighborly love?" In a similar fashion, Walter Lingle made the case again that because the Bible spoke to social concerns, the church must as well. In fact, "applied Christianity has a large contribution to make towards the solution of these social problems which afflict and vex the world today."[13]

12. *MGAPCUS* (1924): 33–34, 39; Thompson, *Presbyterians in the South*, 3:509; Hobbie, "Ernest Trice Thompson," 236.

13. William Crowe Jr., "Some Reflections on the Business of the Church," *CO* (1 August 1934): 9; Walter L. Lingle, "Christianity and Social Problems," *CO* (29 May 1935): 3.

Progressives also continued to host conferences that advanced their perspectives on social Christianity. The Synod of Virginia hosted one at its conference grounds in Massanetta Springs. Chaired by John MacLean, minister at Ginter Park Presbyterian Church in Richmond, and staffed with Richmond-area ministers as speakers, the Massanetta Springs Conference's Findings Committee declared, "We believe profoundly that the Church of Jesus Christ has a definite responsibility in Christianizing the social order." In order to do this, "the Church should clearly and definitely through her courts and from her pulpits denounce all un-Christian standards in industrial, political, interracial, and international relationships and that she should proclaim the Christian ideal of life, preaching and teaching definite principles of Christian conduct in human relations." Other conferences were held at Montreat and Kerrville, and presbyteries and synods continued to discuss the issues.[14]

Conservative ministers tried to make their case against the new committee, but found the going difficult. S. K. Dodson, minister of the Citronelle, Alabama, church, argued that "the Church should not through her courts endorse any specific social program, and that if any declaration is made by these higher courts as to the Church's social duty, it should be done very carefully in the broadest terms possible." William Childs Robinson, professor at Columbia Seminary, did not even want the church to do that. Concerned that the church was under the influence of leftist politics, he worried that "it may be that the economic and political 'center' and 'right' groups in our Church are asleep as to what the 'left' wing is doing." Even more, the church would be better off if it did not allow political, social, or moral questions into its courts: "In the interest of peace in our Church would it not be wiser to stop now ere these questions become acrimonious? . . . Is it quite right to turn a Church away from the very principle that gave it life and independent being? The non-secular character of the Southern Presbyterian Church is her 'raison

14. "Conference on Social and Moral Problems," *CO* (8 August 1934): 10; Samuel L. Joekel, "Massanetta Springs Conference on Moral and Social Problems," *CO* (12 September 1934): 10; Thompson, *Presbyterians in the South*, 3:509.

d'etre.'" The church should focus on evangelism and worship, not political concerns.[15]

While Robinson, Dodson, and other conservatives tried to argue against the new committee, a fundamental conflict was embedded in their case. Most conservatives actually believed that Christianity would have an effect on society—individual regeneration would lead to social transformation. Hence, their defense of evangelism was not isolationist, merely saving souls for a separated existence apart from civil society. Rather, they believed that the gospel would produce better citizens, parents, workers, and church members. Even more, over the past decades, conservatives had participated in and tried to involve their churches in social and political causes, most notably for prohibition and against teaching evolution in public schools. And so most conservatives would not disagree with Walter Lingle's claim that "the greatest contribution that Christianity can make towards the solution of our social problems is the regeneration and redemption of the individual." But they might quibble with his further claim that "in addition to the message of individual redemption, the minister will find in the Bible great teachings which define our duties and relationships to others. It is his duty to preach these also and to apply them to the hearts of the men and women before him and to the social problems that are all around them." And yet few conservatives truly doubted that individual redemption would produce social transformation.[16]

Perhaps that was why the permanent committee's report to the 1935 General Assembly was a nonevent. Upon closer inspection, however, the report truly was a change in direction that was, in E. T. Thompson's words, "a reinterpretation or reversal of the church's traditional view of the spirituality (or non-secular mission)

15. S. K. Dodson, "The Church and Social Service," *CO* (22 August 1934): 10; William C. Robinson, "Questions Which Divide Us as Citizens," *CO* (26 December 1934): 15.

16. Lingle, "Christianity and Social Problems," 3. For conservative Presbyterian involvement in prohibition and anti-evolution causes, see Gaines Foster, *Moral Reconstruction: Christian Lobbyists and the Federal Legislation of Morality, 1865–1920* (Chapel Hill, NC: University of North Carolina Press, 2002); Willard B. Gatewood Jr., *Preachers, Pedagogues, and Politicians: The Evolution Controversy in North Carolina, 1920–1927* (Chapel Hill, NC: University of North Carolina Press, 1966).

of the church." While the committee's report was careful to affirm southern Presbyterians' traditional emphasis on evangelism and worship as "the chief functions of the Church" and the traditional focus on the individual as "the primary mission of the Church," it noted that evangelism to individuals was only "the beginning of the Church's task." Beyond this, "the Church must also teach men to love their neighbors as themselves, and to do so in every area of life, in the social sphere, as well as in the individual sphere, in the home, in the school, and in the Church, in industry and in politics, in racial contacts, and in international affairs." In order to do this, the church must pay attention to social and moral issues and "interpret and apply the teachings of the Bible and the principles of Christianity to the solution of these problems and to the amelioration of distressing conditions of life." Nothing less must be envisioned than the time when "Jesus is Lord of all men, and until He is also Lord of all life." This report, which added social Christianity to the church's understanding of its own mission, was adopted without debate; in addition, four new members were added to the committee as it continued its work.[17]

Though conservatives did not realize it at the time, this permanent committee was firmly established and would serve as the most important progressive clearinghouse for the social gospel. The conservatives would challenge the committee's existence three times and fail to dismantle it each time. The first attempt came in 1936, when Central Mississippi Presbytery sent an overture to the General Assembly, requesting that the Social and Moral Welfare Committee be abolished; this was defeated. This failed overture would indicate conservatives' growing frustration with a permanent committee committed to the social application of the gospel and would set the stage for their second attempt to challenge it. The following year, a second attempt: the committee's report drew a protest, signed by twenty-three ministers and elders. The protest focused not only on the report, but also on the underlying rationale for the committee's work. In particular, these commissioners observed that the committee's work

17. Thompson, *Presbyterians in the South*, 3:509; *MGAPCUS* (1935): 93–94.

stood at variance with the procedure of Jesus himself: "Surely he was not lacking in interest or concern in such matters, but His plan was to approach them from another direction and to deal with them as essentially problems of individual sin or personal repentance and faith, rather than as a social or moral reformer." In addition, the committee's work moved the church away from its historic position as a "champion of the spiritual mission of the church." In doing so, the church was moving away from "the one and only remedy which can effect a real and permanent cure for the ills of the individual, and ultimately of human society." To respond to the protest, the Assembly appointed a three-man committee, headed by E. T. Thompson. The committee essentially sniffed at the protest, noting that "it is simply a blanket contradiction of the conclusion of the General Assembly" on whether a Social and Welfare Committee was legitimate. The Assembly adopted this response, and the conservatives were beaten back.[18]

The final conservative attempt to undo the committee came in 1939. In order to better mirror the means of reporting within the rest of the Assembly's operations, the church had set up a standing committee, drawn from commissioners attending that year's Assembly, to receive the report from the permanent committee and make recommendations. As it so happened, the chairman of the standing committee that year was Tom Glasgow, elder from Charlotte, North Carolina, and the author of the permanent committee's report was E. T. Thompson. Glasgow had begun his public question of Thompson's orthodoxy in this year, and undoubtedly this exchange

18. *MGAPCUS* (1936): 36; *MGAPCUS* (1937): 59–60, 74–75. Through an examination of the *PCUS Ministerial Directory, 1861–1941*, it appears that of the twenty-three signers of the protest, nine were ministers and the rest were elders. None of the ministers were especially prominent except for G. T. Gillespie, president of Belhaven College in Jackson, Mississippi; the rest hailed from churches in Knoxville and Bloutsville, Tennessee; Holston Presbytery; Bay Springs and Liberty, Missouri; Kanawha Salines, West Virginia; and Norfolk, Virginia. The one important name among the elders was Leon Hendrick from First Presbyterian Church, Jackson, Mississippi; he would be a major figure in the conservative movement and would serve as the third moderator of the PCA General Assembly in 1975. Hobbie, "Ernest Trice Thompson," 246, claims that Thompson chaired the committee that responded to the protest, but the minutes do not indicate this. D. C. MacGuire, minister in Montgomery, Alabama, presented the report on the committee's behalf.

fed his concern. The standing committee's majority recommended the adoption of the permanent committee's report, but Glasgow and five others had crafted a minority report. At the heart of Glasgow's report were recommendations that both thanked the committee for its work and then moved "that the Permanent Committee on Social and Moral Welfare be dissolved and desist from further active service." The minority report was debated for over an hour, with J. B. Hutton, pastor of First Presbyterian Church, Jackson, Mississippi, carrying the argument for the minority, suggesting that the committee's findings "were contrary to our Church's ideal of non-interference in political matters." But the minority lost, 104 to 132, and the Social and Moral Welfare Committee survived.[19]

In the end, conservatives would move on to other battles, especially focused on confessional revision. Still, this dustup over the Permanent Committee on Social and Moral Welfare would set the terms of debate between the progressive and conservative wings of the church for the next forty years. On the one side were those who wanted the church to speak from its highest court to the issues of social consequence; on the other were those who believed that social reform could come only through individual conversions and spiritual renewal. A young conservative leader, back from the mission field, recognized this: L. Nelson Bell, writing in the *Christian Observer*, suggested that these committees on social and moral welfare attempted to substitute moral reform for spiritual redemption. This was all wrong: "What America needs today is not reform . . . . We need a Spirit-sent revival, one prayed down by those who know and love God and who have a burden for the lost souls of men." Through his writing and family, Bell, along with other conservatives, would pray and work for such a spiritual renewal.[20]

TRYING TO PREVENT CONFESSIONAL REVISION

In 1934, the General Assembly received two overtures that would shape the face of the confessional-revision debate. The first, from the

19. *MGAPCUS* (1939): 61; "The General Assembly Proceedings," *CO* (7 June 1939): 17.
20. L. Nelson Bell, "Redemption vs. Reform," *CO* (29 April 1936): 22.

Presbytery of Meridian, asked the Assembly to "define the System of Doctrine as required of all officers, also to affirm the statement, 'the fundamentals of this System of Doctrine,' as found in the same obligation." In response, the General Assembly observed that "System of Doctrine" stood for "the exhibition of the essential doctrines of Scripture arranged in logical and systematic order as the Scripture is interpreted by the Presbyterian and Reformed Churches." The committee noted, however, that this did not mean that officers affirmed "that each doctrine of the Confession is an integral part of that system or an essential doctrine of Scripture." Further, the General Assembly could not set forth what the "fundamentals of the system of doctrine" were as required by one's ordination vows. Such fundamentals could be determined only through "regular judicial process." Anything else "would be in effect to amend the Constitution by extra constitutional methods." The second overture came from Enoree Presbytery, requesting that the Assembly "take steps to amend the Confession of Faith by adding a Chapter entitled 'Of the Holy Spirit.'" The Assembly answered this request in the negative, reasoning that "the 'brief statement' of faith adopted by the Assembly of 1912 and bound in the same volume with the recent copies of the Confession covers this matter sufficiently."[21]

The following year, spurred on by conversations within East Hanover Presbytery, several presbyteries petitioned the General Assembly on the matter of confessional revision. While the presbyteries of Abingdon, West Hanover, and Montgomery asked the Assembly not to pursue confessional revision, the presbyteries of Memphis and Western Texas as well as the Synod of South Carolina urged the Assembly to make appropriate changes. Even though there were only three church courts requesting the church to move forward, the Assembly answered the overtures with "the appointment of an Ad Interim Committee of the General Assembly to whom the whole matter shall be referred." The committee would consist of the current moderator of the Assembly, Henry H. Sweets, and the professors of systematic theology at the four

21. *MGAPCUS* (1934): 20–21, 32–33.

PCUS seminaries, J. B. Green (Columbia), George Summey (Austin), John Vander Meulen (Louisville), and J. Porter Smith (Union).[22]

While the committee had a fairly traditionalist tone—Summey, a former moderator of the General Assembly, and Green, professor at Columbia Seminary since 1921, were reputed to be traditional Reformed theologians—some PCUS progressives hoped that they would do more than simply tweak the doctrinal standards. Walter Lingle, for one, desired that the committee would heed the church's request that the confession's doctrines "be stated in a way that will be more effective for the century in which we live." Ultimately, Lingle believed, the committee should produce a "brief authoritative statement of the faith of our church in present-day language and in terms that laymen and young people can understand. Such a statement should face and meet present-day religious problems." At the end of the day, progressives expected that the committee would produce recommendations that would bring the church theologically into the modern age.[23]

Unable to pull its report together in 1936, the Ad Interim Committee reported at the next year's General Assembly. Of the recommended changes, some simply modernized the language of the confession: for example, in Westminster Confession of Faith (WCF) 1.8, the committee suggested reworking the statement that the Bible should "be translated into the *vulgar* language of every nation," so that it would now claim that the Bible should "be translated into *the language of every people.*" There were other suggestions that softened the confession's animus toward Roman Catholicism, reworking or deleting language in several places.[24]

Other recommendations were much more substantive. Perhaps the most important focused on WCF chapter 3, "On God's Decree." In that chapter, the committee recommended that the church excise two

---

22. Thompson, *Presbyterians in the South*, 3:490; Hobbie, "Ernest Trice Thompson," 263–64; W. P. Nickell, "Revising the Confession," *CO* (9 March 1938): 10; *MGAPCUS* (1935): 19–20, 43–44.

23. Walter L. Lingle, "Revision or Restatement," *CO* (30 October 1935): 3–4. Lingle observed that "the committee was composed of some of our most conservative men in our Church." "Predestination," *CO* (6 July 1938): 3.

24. *MGAPCUS* (1936): 36, 117; *MGAPCUS* (1937): 129–30, 133–34. Specifically, there were proposed revisions in WCF 25.5, 25.6, and 29.2.

paragraphs: paragraph 3, which noted that "by the decree of God, for the manifestation of his glory, some men and angels are predestinated unto everlasting life, and others foreordained to everlasting death"; and paragraph 4, which claimed that this predestination meant that those angels and men "are particularly and unchangeably designed and their number is so certain and definite that it cannot be either increased or diminished." In addition, the committee suggested that paragraph 7 be edited to read that God's passing by "the rest of mankind" would occur by leaving "them to the consequences of their sin."[25]

As significant as these recommended changes were, equally so was what the committee decided not to recommend. The committee decided not to offer new confessional chapters on the Holy Spirit, the love of God, and missions and social service. The bulk of its report provided a compendium of quotations from the Westminster Standards, suggesting that each of these topics were treated "adequately" in the confessional documents. To be sure, one had to collate the references from different portions of the Standards; still, this "adequate" treatment argued for focusing the confessional revision on the current chapters of the Standards instead of adding new ones.[26]

When the report came to the floor of the General Assembly, Columbia Seminary professor J. B. Green was selected to make the report. After a period of prayer and a recess for lunch, Green offered the committee's report, with the closing recommendation that the Assembly submit the report to the presbyteries for their advice and consent to incorporate the changes into the church's Standards. Almost immediately, E. T. Thompson, noted progressive church history professor

25. *MGAPCUS* (1937): 130–31. The original reading of WCF 3.7 is as follows: "The rest of mankind, God was pleased, according to the unsearchable counsel of his own will, *whereby he extendeth or withholdeth mercy as he pleaseth, for the glory of his sovereign power over his creatures, to pass by, and to ordain them to dishonor and wrath for their sin,* to the praise of his glorious justice." The italicized portion was changed.

The committee made other changes that appeared to soften the strict Calvinism of the documents. For example, the committee changed WCF 5.6 so that it no longer tied human wickedness to God's judicial hardening and blinding; deleted the word *wholly* in both WCF 6.2 and 6.4 so that the Standards would no longer claim that human beings were "wholly defiled" or "wholly inclined to all evil"; and reshaped WCF 10.3 so that the challenging language of "elect infants dying in infancy" was no longer there.

26. *MGAPCUS* (1937): 134–40.

from Union Seminary, offered a substitute resolution: that the report be submitted to the presbyteries "with the request that they consider the same at their fall meetings, and advise the Ad Interim Committee regarding any desirable changes or additions; the Ad Interim Committee, in the light of these recommendations, to resubmit its report to the next General Assembly." Over the protests of committee members, who noted that they had approved their recommendations unanimously after two years of labor, the substitute resolution was adopted and the report was referred to the presbyteries.[27]

This referral led to an all-out debate in the church's newspapers. The progressives generally cheered the proposed revisions, while often noting that they did not go far enough. T. J. Ray, pastor from Sharpsburg, Kentucky, applauded the proposed revisions as an "admirable restatement of our Confession, softening statements which in the light of the change in our language are unnecessarily harsh in their original form." He only wished that the committee had pursued a more thorough revision of WCF 10.3 on the status of children dying in infancy. Similarly, the minister at the Presbyterian Church in Hilton Village, Virginia, Willis Thompson, observed that the committee's work met "with the approval of those who are primarily interested in keeping themselves true to the Bible and at the same time intelligible." He, too, desired for the committee to offer more changes, especially in reference to the church itself as a means of grace.[28]

27. Ibid., 38; "The General Assembly Proceedings," *CO* (2 June 1937): 13. It is unclear what Thompson hoped to do with his substitute—whether to buy more time, convince the committee to do a more substantial revision with additional chapters, or prevent the defeat of the committee's report. One writer later observed that the move was "strange and adroit[,] . . . confusing the Presbyteries as to actually what was in the mind of the 1937 Assembly." A. A. Little, "What Is the Use?," *CO* (17 August 1938): 11.

Likewise, it is unclear what the Assembly meant: one observer claimed that this action was taken "because of the fact that previous reports presented to the Assembly had provoked an unexpected amount of debate and the commissioners were desirous of avoiding more debate on the floor of the Assembly." T. J. Ray Jr., "Revising the Confession of Faith," *CO* (30 June 1937): 11. Another wondered whether "the Assembly last spring may have been in too great a hurry to enter into serious and prolonged debate. Hence the happy thought to let the committee have another go at it; and to let the Presbyteries be heard from." Nickell, "Revising the Confession," 10.

28. Ray, "Revising the Confession of Faith," 11–12; Willis Thompson, "The Proposed Changes in the Catechisms," *CO* (8 September 1937): 10.

Opponents of the proposed confessional revisions found their arguments concentrating on several major issues. First, there was profound concern that the revisions were weakening the Calvinism of the Standards, which represented "the very heart of the system and not . . . some of its details." Some, such as home missionary H. F. Beaty, wondered whether the changes on the nature of original sin would lead the church to "deny the Bible and preach Arminianism." Others, such as W. P. Nickell, pastor from Tazewell, Virginia, suggested that "this new principle of creed-making by which we eliminate the so-called harsh, offensive, irritating, repulsive, alienating, undesirable statements, deserves careful scrutiny."[29]

Some simply wanted to leave the Standards alone because neither the church nor the age was ready for revision. Wick Broomall held that "we are living in a time when theology is at low ebb. There are powerful influences at work in the world and Church today. The tendency of our age is toward apostasy. Let us not succumb to the popular trend of the times in revising our doctrinal standards!" In a similar vein, W. P. Nickell noted that "speaking of the Christian Church as a whole, we venture to declare that no especial creed-forming genius has showed itself. On the other hand, no one will be found today who will care to deny that the Westminster Assembly did have unusual talents along this line. That we have such abilities is not plain." Another minister, W. A. Gamble from Raymond, Mississippi, proclaimed that "our Church's need is not revision of its beliefs, or revision of the expression of them, but the exposition and declaration and illustration of them." Still others worried that, rather than being led by the Holy Spirit, the church was instead being directed by ministerial "pressure groups" that were organizing laymen to support these changes.[30]

As a result of the responses gained from the eighty-seven presbyteries, the committee released its report two weeks before the 1938 General Assembly, recommending all its previous changes as well as

29. Nickell, "Revising the Confession," 10; H. F. Beaty, "Why Change the Constitution and Catechisms?," *CO* (1 December 1937): 10.

30. Wick Broomall Jr., "The Proposed Changes in Our Confessional Standards," *CO* (23 June 1937): 15; Nickell, "Revising the Confession," 10; W. A. Gamble, "Far-Reaching Assembly Proposals," *CO* (12 January 1938): 10–11; Everett, "A Questionable Procedure," 10.

new changes and the addition of two new chapters entitled "Of the Holy Spirit" and "Of the Gospel."[31] The debate at the Assembly was intense, lasting the better part of two days, as the commissioners considered the changes one by one. The initial, lengthy debate focused on the excision of the two paragraphs from the confession's chapter on God's decrees of predestination and foreordination; after a couple of hours, the recommendation to omit the paragraphs passed by a standing vote of 151 to 130. That debate set the stage for the rest of the two-day consideration of the report: one after another, the committee's proposed changes were adopted. The two new chapters on the Holy Spirit and the gospel were referred back to the committee for proof texts and to the presbyteries for their advice; these were to be brought back to the Assembly for a vote the following year.[32]

Throughout the year, Green defended other aspects of the committee's work. He tried to make a case that God did not use a "positive influence . . . upon the wicked" as WCF 3.5 suggested in its language of "blinding and hardening." He also suggested that other comments in the paragraph "come perilously near accusing God of tempting men to sin." In WCF 3.7, where the committee changed the language from "the glory of his sovereign power over his creatures" to "in the exercise of his sovereign right," he explained that the change referred "this mysterious act to infinite wisdom and refrain[ed] from assigning a reason for it." On the issue of human depravity as discussed in WCF 6.2, Green saw the committee as correcting what "appear to be overstatements of one of the historic Five Points of Calvinism." Softening "wholly defiled"

31. "Proposed Changes in the Confession of Faith and Catechisms," CO (4 May 1938): 2; "General Assembly Reports: Proposed Changes in the Confession of Faith and the Catechisms," CO (4 May 1938): 5–7. Between the release of the report and the 1938 Assembly, there was no discussion why the committee had changed its mind. One factor could be the changing composition of the committee: D. Clay Lilly, former moderator of the Assembly, was added to the committee to replace Vander Meulen, who had passed away in 1936. In addition, H. T. Kerr Jr., then professor of systematic theology at Louisville Seminary, met with the committee, and perhaps had some influence; Kerr would go on to have a long and distinguished career as a voice of liberal Protestantism at Princeton Theological Seminary.

32. "The General Assembly Proceedings," CO (1 June 1938): 11–13; MGAPCUS (1938): 39–40, 128–38. It is important to notice that opponents of the revision included several who would become leaders of the conservative movement in the church: J. E. Cousar Jr., W. Calvin Wells, and Tom Glasgow all spoke against revision.

through the deletion of "wholly" was "not un-Calvinistic and heretical," Green claimed. Rather, it brought the church's teaching and Standards into harmony with each other. In defense of the new chapters on the Holy Spirit and the gospel, Green suggested that while this teaching was scattered throughout the Standards, "it is a gain to have these scattered and implicit parts of the great body of truth brought together and laid open to the mind of the average reader."[33]

Green's advocacy of his committee's work would draw support and criticism from his colleagues at Columbia Seminary. New Testament professor Samuel A. Cartledge supported Green, warning that "we must be careful, however, that we do not think too highly of [the Westminster Standards] and give to them an authority that should be reserved for the Bible alone." Because the Standards were not "inerrant," and because the Westminster divines "were children of their time and suffered from the limitations of their age," it was only right to expect that the modern generation would need to revise them. In fact, such changes were necessary so that the church did not become "so opposed to change of every kind that we shall become fossilized and drive out and keep out many who are real conservatives and should be our friends."[34]

Cartledge and Green received a strong pushback from their colleague William Childs Robinson, professor of church history, polity, and apologetics. Robinson observed that "the movement for modification is the outcome of anti-confessional 'liberalism,' which has reached our Church at a time when the tide of Christian thought has turned and is running in the opposite direction." Even more, these changes were "based too much on rationalistic and not sufficiently on exclusively scriptural grounds, and that at the moment when there is less confidence in fallen human reason than at any time since the Reformation." Several of the changes simply accommodated contemporary sensibilities not used to thinking

33. J. B. Green, "A Second Statement for the Committee on the Revision of the Standards," *CO* (20 July 1938): 10–11; J. B. Green, "A Third Statement on Behalf of the Committee on Revision of the Standards," *CO* (27 July 1938): 11; J. B. Green, "The Revision of Our Standards: Fourth and Final Statement on Behalf of the Committee," *CO* (14 September 1938): 10–11.

34. S. A. Cartledge, "Shall We Change Our Standards?," *CO* (3 August 1938): 10.

about God as the sovereign, transcendent, almighty God. In the end, the confessional changes before the church "definitely move away from the doctrine of the sovereignty of God as taught by consistent Calvinism in an Arminian direction."[35]

By the time southern Presbyterians gathered for their 1939 General Assembly meeting at Montreat, North Carolina, the initial results of the presbytery voting were known: the presbyteries had defeated the excision of the two paragraphs on predestination from the chapter on God's decree as well as the attempt to remove the language of "elect infants" from the confession. The presbyteries also defeated all the proposed changes to the Shorter Catechism and approved only the change to the Larger Catechism that would bring it in line with the approved version of WCF 1.8. On the floor of the Assembly, Robinson led the charge against the most controversial remaining changes. For the change that would have deleted language from WCF 3.7 that God "extendeth and withholdeth mercy as he pleaseth," Robinson successfully moved the original confessional language as a substitute; the revision was defeated. He also argued against the change in WCF 5.6, which would have taken out language of God's active "blinding and hardening." The Assembly agreed and defeated that change, along with changes to the confessional chapter on original sin.[36]

Robinson's most controversial action of the Assembly occurred toward the end of the voting on the confessional revisions. A ruling elder, Judge Richard V. Evans, had offered a personal resolution from the floor of the General Assembly; it would have tightened up the ordination vows of ministers and elders, requiring that they affirm

35. William C. Robinson, "The Proposed Changes in the Standards," *CO* (31 August 1938): 11–12; John S. Foster, "A Calvinistic Church Should Have a Creed Completely Calvinistic," *CO* (22 February 1939): 9–10. Green eventually responded point by point to Robinson in "Further Statement on Behalf of the Committee on Revision of the Standards," *CO* (15 March 1939): 10, 15. The proposed language for WCF 10.4 was: "Others, not elected, although they may be called by the ministry of the Word, and may have some common operations of the Spirit, yet they never truly come to Christ, and therefore cannot be saved; much less can men, not professing the Christian religion, be saved in any other way whatsoever than by Christ, be they never so diligent to frame their lives according to the light of nature, and the law of that religion they do profess; and to assert and maintain that they may is without warrant of the Word of God."

36. *MGAPCUS* (1939): 36, 66–71; "The 1939 General Assembly," *CO* (7 June 1939): 2–3; "The General Assembly Proceedings," *CO* (7 June 1939): 12, 14, 18.

"five essential doctrines" as part of those vows. Perhaps recognizing that the proposal was not passable and yet also believing that the church needed to go on record for the central doctrines of the Christian faith, Robinson moved a substitute, which was subsequently adopted: "The General Assembly hereby declares that it regards the acceptance of the infallible truth and divine authority of the Scriptures and that Christ is very and eternal God who became man by being born of a Virgin, offered up himself a sacrifice to satisfy divine justice and reconcile us to God, who rose from the dead with the same body with which he suffered, and that he will return again to judge the world as being involved in the ordination vows to which we subscribe." While traditionalists hailed such a move as the church's highest court authoritatively interpreting the ordination vows, others demurred. Walter Lingle, for one, sniffed that "such deliverances are to be 'considered as only didactic, advisory and monitory.' "[37]

The rest of the Confessional Revision Committee's report was unable to be heard. Because the Assembly's time was taken up with other matters, most notably the issue of union negotiations with the northern Presbyterians, the report was "docketed for consideration by a later Assembly." Importantly, the committee was not dismissed or disbanded; it continued on. In addition, eleven changes were approved to the Westminster Confession and the Larger Catechism. If nothing else, the principle of the acceptable nature of confessional revision was well established.[38] Progressives viewed the entire scene as a speed bump for their hopes to broaden the church theologically and pave the way for reunion with the northern church. As liberal leader E. T. Thompson looked back on these events, he took comfort in the fact

37. *MGAPCUS* (1939): 71; "The General Assembly's Proceedings," *CO* (7 June 1939): 14; Walter L. Lingle, "Minutes of the General Assembly," *CO* (24 July 1940): 3; William C. Robinson, "The Doctrinal Deliverance of the 1939 Assembly," *CO* (28 August 1940): 10. Interestingly, the minutes recorded the resolution as coming from Evans, while the *CO* claimed that it was H. J. Spencer, a ruling elder from Charlotte. I followed the Assembly minutes.

38. *MGAPCUS* (1939): 75, 139. By this time, only three members had signed the committee's report: Sweet, Green, and Summey. Lilly died on 28 May 1939; there is no record of what happened to Porter Smith or Hugh Kerr. Hobbie mistakenly views this as a defeat "by the conservative power of the 1939 General Assembly." Hobbie, "Ernest Trice Thompson," 264.

that though "the harsher statements of a polemic Calvinism remained," the tide was running toward the progressives: "Since responsible professors in the four theological seminaries, two General Assemblies, and two-thirds or more of the presbyteries had voted for the elimination of these more difficult portions of the Confession, [these statements] could hardly claim to reflect the mind of the church."[39]

Thompson was right—the tide was running toward the progressive element in the church. Historians sometimes view the 1939 General Assembly as the first high-water mark of conservative resistance to the progressive ecclesiastical agenda, and yet that General Assembly began a process of church union with the northern Presbyterians, discussed tightening control over local church properties, and established confessional revision as an acceptable principle in southern Presbyterian life. What looked like conservative victory on one issue—defining the "essential doctrines" in the system of doctrine and defeating a few of the proposed revisions—was actually closer to a Pyrrhic triumph in the light of the whole. In addition, the new chapters on the Holy Spirit and the gospel were still on the table, waiting for the proper time for the church's consideration and incorporation into its doctrinal standards.

Although the committee apparently did not meet in 1940, the General Assembly, meeting in Chattanooga, Tennessee, took up the tabled 1939 report during its May meeting. Motivated to finish its work, in part, because of the continuing unrest in the church on the issue, the Assembly gave "intensive consideration" to the rest of the committee's 1939 report. D. J. Woods, minister at Clinton, South Carolina, moved that the Ad Interim Committee's recommendation that the two new confessional chapters on the Holy Spirit and the gospel be sent to the presbyteries for their advice and consent. J. B. Green spoke in favor of this, noting that "a large majority of favorable votes on these changes have come from the presbyteries." The Assembly voted overwhelmingly (196–75) to adopt Woods's motion and refer the two new chapters to the presbyteries for their consideration.[40]

39. Thompson, *Presbyterians in the South*, 3:492; Walter L. Lingle, "Notes on the General Assembly," *CO* (28 June 1939): 3–4.
40. "Important Matters before the 1940 General Assembly," *CO* (8 May 1940): 2; "The General Assembly in Chattanooga," *CO* (22 May 1940): 2; "The 1940 General Assembly,"

In a last-ditch effort to prevent this from happening, Tom Glasgow—an elder from Charlotte, North Carolina, who was also in the midst of alerting the church to E. T. Thompson's progressive theological positions—moved that the Assembly reconsider its action, refer the proposed changes back to the committee, and enlarge the committee. Somewhat surprisingly in light of its previous vote, the Assembly agreed to this; eventually, the committee would have only one continuing member—J. B. Green—with four new additions: B. R. Lacy Jr. (president of Union Seminary), Frank Caldwell (president of Louisville Seminary), E. W. McLaurin (new professor of systematic theology at Austin Seminary), and Judge Samuel Sibley. Unlike the previous version of the committee, which had a traditionalist flavor, the new committee was made up of several progressive leaders.[41]

Not surprisingly, when the committee members brought their report the following year, they presented their recommendations, having "unanimously" approved the new chapter on the Holy Spirit and "without dissenting vote" the chapter on the gospel. Immediately, William Childs Robinson was on his feet to protest. He presented objections to the phraseology of the new chapters, suggesting that they might even teach universalism. "Why should we strive to stream-line our standards?" he asked. "Let us be done with this matter of revision." Nevertheless, the momentum was on revision's side; the church adopted the committee's recommendation to send these chapters to the presbyteries for their advice and consent.[42]

CO (29 May 1940): 4; "The General Assembly Proceedings," CO (29 May 1940): 13, 15.

41. "The General Assembly Proceedings" (1940), 13, 15.

42. "General Assembly Reports: Changes in the Confession of Faith and Catechisms," CO (30 April 1941): 5; "The General Assembly Proceedings," CO (4 June 1941): 11; MGAP-CUS (1941): 38, 111–13.

Robinson's fear that there was some form of universalism in the proposed chapter was not unfounded; Thomas Hooper, long-serving clerk of Potomac Presbytery, wanted to revise the proposed chapter on the gospel to broaden it in exactly this way: "To say that there is no other way of salvation than that revealed in the Gospel is a very different thing from saying that we know of no other way of salvation. The language sent to the presbyteries by the Assembly states categorically that there is no other way of salvation. . . . That means that God cannot save a man, woman, or child, who is or has been respectively a believer in any other religion, even though that man, woman, or child never had an opportunity to hear about the glorious Gospel of Jesus Christ. That seems to some of us to put a definite and distressing limit on the mercy of God, with regard to a large majority of the human

Though Robinson kept on fighting against the new chapters, his was a losing battle. He continued to argue that these chapters were unnecessary and sometimes even biblically and theologically erroneous; he also hinted at the larger issues in play. He noted that "these two chapters have been taken over from the close of the [Presbyterian Church] U.S.A. Confession for insertion into the center of our Confession." These chapters marked "a further step in the direction of broad-churchism" in the northern church and would be used in a similar way in the southern church: " 'Stream-lining' the Confession may make our Church more inclusive; it will not make it more harmonious or happy or united in loyalty to the whole counsel of God."[43]

By the time the commissioners arrived in Knoxville, Tennessee, for the 1942 General Assembly, the conclusion was rather a formality. Both chapters had been approved by three-fourths of the southern church's presbyteries; there was apparently little debate on the Assembly's floor. The chapters were adopted with the requisite majority. There was little public comment in the aftermath. Walter Lingle took the opportunity of an error in the *Christian Observer*'s reporting of these actions to notice how difficult it actually was to amend the church's doctrinal standards. But by the time conservatives had organized their own paper, the *Southern Presbyterian Journal*, right before the 1942 General Assembly, more pressing matters had come before the church: doctrinal error, church union, and social, cultural, and political liberalism. It was over those issues that the conservatives would raise their banners.[44]

Among the chief arguments that conservatives would raise against reunion with the northern Presbyterian church in the days ahead were the northerners' laxity on doctrine and their social activism. And yet what they missed was that the 1930s had brought the southern church into greater conformity with the northern church and paved the way for future reunion. By sharing the same essential doctrinal standard,

---

race." Thomas W. Hooper, "The Addition of Chapter X to the Confession of Faith," *CO* (31 December 1941): 10.

43. William C. Robinson, "Plea for Careful Consideration before Adopting the Proposed Revision of the Westminster Confession," *CO* (23 July 1941): 9; Walter L. Lingle, "The Two New Chapters," *CO* (27 August 1941): 3.

44. "The General Assembly's Proceedings," *CO* (10 June 1942): 16.

with the new chapters on the gospel and the Holy Spirit, there was little need to be concerned about harmonizing two differing sets of confessional statements. Even more significant was the shared conception of the church's role in social reform. While far behind the social activism of the northern church's highest court, the PCUS establishment of the Permanent Committee on Social and Moral Welfare signaled a new willingness by southerners to engage in social activism. By producing reports on a range of social issues—poverty and economics, alcohol and gambling, war and racial justice—this committee not only offered a response to the crises of the day in the name of the church, but also made the possibility of future reunion with the more politically active northern Presbyterians palatable.

Southern Presbyterian conservatives knew this to be the case. When they started the *Southern Presbyterian Journal* in 1942 and provided rationale for the new conservative organ, they noted how the actions of recent days affected the church's future. While the fundamental issue at stake was "the integrity of the Scriptures," the church also displayed "misapprehension as to the mission of the Church" and "desire for reunion" with the northern church, which was itself the result of "misunderstanding of the mission of the Church." These three issues—doctrine, mission, and reunion—threatened the existence of the PCUS, whether by absorption from the larger northern body or by decay from within. The only thing to do was to raise the banners and rally the troops in order "to keep our Church true to, not only her historical position, but also to the path God wants us to walk today."[45]

45. L. Nelson Bell, "Why?," *SPJ* (May 1942): 2–3.

4

"How Far Will the Progressives Go?" The Coalescing of Conservative Dissent

"How far the 'progressives' in our Church want to go no one knows," Columbia Seminary professor William Childs Robinson complained in the midst of the debate over the proposed revisions of the Westminster Standards. Referring to the PCUS and its failure to discipline Hay Watson Smith for his deviant theological views, Robinson continued, "Many of them supported a minister who was received on the basis of a statement that liberty of conscience was the essence of Calvinism. . . . Another minister asserts that love to God and man is the essence of religion and that all the rest is theological tarnish which the heretic should remove that religion may shine more resplendent."[1]

Starting in the late 1920s, it came clear that the progressive "wing" of the church was on the move and that conservatives were poorly organized. Throughout the 1930s, as confessional revision progressed and the Committee on Social and Moral Welfare was established, conservatives saw their church moving away from the general conservative evangelicalism of its past. What brought them to high alert, however, was the apparent doctrinal deviancy of Hay Watson Smith and E. T. Thompson and the failure of the church to discipline them. Such a situation would galvanize those who felt that something was drastically wrong with the

1. William C. Robinson, "The Proposed Changes in the Confession and Catechisms," *CO* (29 September 1937): 10–11.

PCUS. J. E. Cousar, a Virginia Presbyterian minister, wrote to Columbia Seminary professor W. M. McPheeters in 1934, expressing his conviction that conservatives needed to organize or else the PCUS would be lost to "modernism," as had happened to the northern Presbyterian church. "What I am doing is motivated by the profound conviction that unless we are willing to draw a line NOW and fight there to the finish, there will be but little left to us in years to come but to come out and pursue our way alone," Cousar wrote. "The church would appear to be well on the way to being completely dominated by the Modernist element in the pulpit, and, though more slowly, in the pew and we can expect to be in the position of Dr. Machen and his fellow-helpers in five or ten years' time if we are content to remain asleep for just a while more." Still, Presbyterian conservatives would not truly unite together to "preserve southern Presbyterianism" until McPheeters's nephew, Tom Glasgow, would engage in his own failed crusade to force Thompson's resignation from Union Theological Seminary. By 1941, conservatives had become convinced that progressives had full control of both the church structures and the Presbyterian papers. In response to the church's failure to discipline, along with the failures on the spirituality of the church and confessional revision, these conservative leaders banded together the following year to form the *Southern Presbyterian Journal*, which would serve as the rallying point for conservative dissent in the years to come.[2]

MCPHEETERS, SMITH, AND THE FAILURE OF PRESBYTERIAN PROCEDURES

By all accounts, W. M. McPheeters should have been enjoying the end of a long and fruitful ministry. Son of a Presbyterian minister,

2. J. E. Cousar to W. M. McPheeters, 26 April 1934, J. McDowell Richards Papers, box 78, PHS (emphasis his). Glasgow and McPheeters engaged in a number of letters about the Smith case: see Tom Glasgow to W. M. McPheeters, 5 May 1930; Tom Glasgow to W. M. McPheeters, 26 May 1931; Tom Glasgow to W. M. McPheeters, 27 May 1931; Tom Glasgow to W. M. McPheeters, 5 June 1931 (all in J. McDowell Richards Papers, box 78, PHS). Also, McPheeters often stopped in Charlotte during this period, and Glasgow would host his uncle; it is not too much to imagine a number of conversations about these things. The fact that Glasgow's method of attacking—focusing on Thompson's Sunday school articles and highlighting his departure from biblical inerrancy—paralleled his uncle's is also suggestive for seeing a link.

he was born in St. Louis in 1854. After the Civil War, his father took a church in Shelbyville, Kentucky, where the family relocated. McPheeters soon enrolled at Washington and Lee College, graduating with his undergraduate degree in 1874. He matriculated the following year at Union Theological Seminary in Virginia, where he was deeply influenced by longtime professor of polemic and didactic theology Robert Lewis Dabney. Graduating in 1878, McPheeters served a number of smaller churches in Virginia until he received a call to teach at Columbia Theological Seminary in 1888. Befitting his new status as professor of Old Testament, Presbyterian College in Clinton, South Carolina, conferred on him the doctor of divinity degree the following year. By 1929, he had served the church long and well, editing a number of religious periodicals and journals, writing tracts and articles, and training ministers through the sometimes tenuous days when the seminary struggled in South Carolina and finally at its new campus in Decatur, Georgia.[3]

Yet McPheeters could not rest easy. He had long feared and struggled against the rising historical-critical views in the world of biblical studies and now saw those views being promoted in his church's seminaries. He likewise observed with increasing apprehension the church's departure from its stance on the nonsecular character of the church and protested its continued dalliance with the Federal Council of Churches.[4] But the evolution controversy that developed in the South, in particular, grabbed his attention. It was not so much the issues debated or even the fact that some of his dear friends, such as Albert Sidney Johnson, pastor of First Presbyterian Church, Charlotte, North Carolina, were in the lead. Rather, the evolution controversy

3. E. C. Scott, ed., *Ministerial Directory of the Presbyterian Church, U.S., 1861–1941* (Austin, TX: Von Boeckmann-Jones, 1942), 488; W. M. McPheeters to Robert Lewis Dabney, 7 February 1896, Robert Lewis Dabney Papers, UPS.

4. W. M. McPheeters, "Dr. Briggs' 'Higher Criticism of the Hexateuch,'" *Presbyterian Quarterly* 9 (1895): 505–28; W. M. McPheeters, "A Complaint against the Action of the Synod of South Carolina in Addressing an Official Communication to the Civil Commonwealth," *Presbyterian Quarterly* 12 (1898): 323–43; W. M. McPheeters, "The Independence and Spirituality of the Church Historically Considered," *Central Presbyterian* (12 April 1905); W. M. McPheeters, "Has the Church the Right to Have a Social Programme of Any Kind?," *CO* (3 March 1909); W. M. McPheeters, "An Unprecedented Action," *Presbyterian Standard* (15 March 1922).

focused McPheeters on a prominent minister in Arkansas who loudly defended evolution and denied biblical inerrancy from his pulpit and in the public press.[5]

That minister was Hay Watson Smith, pastor of Second Presbyterian Church, Little Rock, Arkansas. Born in North Carolina after the end of the American Civil War, Smith was, like McPheeters, the son of a Presbyterian minister. After receiving his undergraduate degree at Davidson College in 1890, he entered Union Seminary in Virginia but dropped out before the end of the term because of illness. Throughout the rest of the decade, he struggled with health and doubts about his ministerial calling; in the midst of that, he finished the course at Union Seminary and supplied various pulpits. By 1899 he was preaching again and received a call from Second Church in Little Rock; but because he had "begun to doubt some parts of the Calvinistic theology," Smith decided not to accept the call. Instead, he went to Union Seminary in New York City for a year of further study. While studying at Union, he received a call from a Congregational church in Brooklyn; he ended up serving for nine years in two different Congregational churches. In 1909, Smith returned to the South to serve as president of Selma Military Institute; two years later, Smith received a renewed call to return to his wife's hometown of Little Rock to supply the pulpit of Second Church. After serving as a supply for over a year and receiving a call to be the church's permanent pastor, Smith finally applied for admission to Arkansas Presbytery.[6]

In what would later be a contested move, Smith read a statement to the presbytery, laying out his views on a wide range of doctrinal areas, and asked to be received into the presbytery with the freedom to preach and teach his views. On the Scriptures, Smith claimed that he believed that the Bible was "the inspired revelation of God's will and character to men," but rejected "that theory of inspiration which

5. For Albert Sidney Johnson's role in the North Carolina evolution crusade, see Willard B. Gatewood Jr., *Preachers, Pedagogues, and Politicians: The Evolution Controversy in North Carolina, 1920–1927* (Chapel Hill, NC: University of North Carolina Press, 1966).

6. Scott, *Ministerial Directory*, 660; Hay Watson Smith, *Prestige and Perquisites* (Little Rock, AR: n.p., 1930), 3–5. The information that Smith gives in his pamphlet is slightly different from what is in the ministerial directory; I followed Smith's accounting of his education and ministry.

makes the Scriptures infallible in all matters of science, history, ethnology, etc." He also held that it was "impossible to accept" inerrancy, particularly when it came to the first eleven chapters of Genesis. When thinking about that opening section of Scripture, Smith affirmed that the theory of evolution was "the only one that explains and reduces to order a great mass of phenomena opening before us in the natural world. I accept that theory, therefore, to the extent that it validates itself in fact, and proves itself a good working hypothesis." Evolution, quite simply, was "God's method of bringing the world and its life into existence." He also addressed issues related to "total depravity" and the reprobation of the nonelect. While rejecting the Westminster Confession's teaching in both these areas, he hesitated to affirm exactly what he believed, save that God's mercy extended widely to include all humankind in God's invitation of grace. After indicating his openness to immersion as a mode of baptism, Smith closed his statement by observing that he could say nothing definite about doctrines such as the Trinity and the hypostatic union of Christ's two natures. "When we endeavor to penetrate below these [biblical] statements and facts, and to determine and define the metaphysical relations of Father, Son, and Holy Spirit, or of the human and the divine in Christ, postulating two natures and declaring just how they are related," he observed, "we are, in my judgment, entirely beyond our depth; we have passed from the ethical and religious to the metaphysical and philosophical." Smith did not reject these doctrines; he simply claimed, "I *know* nothing about them." Belief in these doctrines was not what made a Christian; faith in Jesus made someone a Christian. Hence, doctrinal speculation was relatively unimportant for those who were believers in Christ.[7]

At the time, no one objected to Smith's doctrinal position, and he was received into the presbytery and installed at Second Church in 1912. For the next ten years, Second Church experienced rapid growth, and Smith was viewed as one of the ablest ministers in Little Rock. Some local conservatives protested his views, but he was able to avoid becoming embroiled in any long-term controversies until 1923. At that point, Smith thrust himself into the growing national

7. Smith, *Prestige and Perquisites*, 7, 9, 13.

controversy over the teaching of evolution in public schools. After preaching two sermons defending evolution the year before, Smith published a lengthy pamphlet on the compatibility between evolution and Presbyterianism. Not merely a defense of evolution against the popular anti-evolution uprising led by fellow Presbyterian William Jennings Bryan, Smith's pamphlet was also a frontal assault on the doctrine of inerrancy. Arguing that the Bible "is inspired, but it is not inerrant," he went on to demonstrate that it was belief that the Bible was without error particularly in the first chapters of Genesis that had impeded scientific knowledge in the past and was currently obstructing intellectual progress in general society and in the Presbyterian Church. He also claimed that the five points of Calvinism were "static or obsolescent" and that the ordination vows that bound ministers to this doctrinal Calvinism were alienating the younger generation from the church. Presbyterians in America needed to follow Scots Presbyterians by championing progressive thought that would embrace "the theory of evolution, the modern study of the Bible, the need of a truer view of inspiration, and the necessity for the modernization of some parts of our theology." Only by seeking thoughtful theological progress would the church advance in the modern age.[8]

Needless to say, Smith's attack drew the notice of conservative Presbyterians and pulled him into a long-lasting controversy. Ouachita Presbytery presented an overture to the 1924 General Assembly, asking that court to adopt a statement to clarify the church's position on Smith's doctrinal views. In early 1927, Smith drew the ire of a Texarkana Presbyterian minister, F. Z. Browne, and the two men exchanged attacks in the Little Rock newspapers throughout the year. Browne accused Smith of dishonesty for remaining in the Presbyterian ministry with his views, to which Smith retorted that Browne and those like him had made a "fetish of tradition." Smith also had his church adopt a statement that repudiated Browne's charges and tweaked conservatives by warning that if they were to succeed "in their purpose of exclusion and intimidation, the Southern Presbyterian Church will

8. Hay Watson Smith, *Evolutionism and Presbyterianism* (Little Rock, AR: Allsopp and Chapple, 1923), 29, 75, 78, 81.

lose the power of self-modification and therefore of growth and progress from within. It will sooner or later degenerate into a belated sect,
without freedom, scholarship, or catholicity." Also convinced that the
general Presbyterian population was ignorant about evolution, Smith
published two other pamphlets that presented facts about evolution
from prominent scientists and that championed intellectual freedom
to explore new scientific theories.[9]

Finally, in 1929, the General Assembly received an overture from
Augusta Presbytery, asking it to investigate Smith's views as presented
in his pamphlets on evolution. It was in the midst of this debate that
McPheeters took over the controversy, offering a substitute motion
that called on the Assembly to instruct Arkansas Presbytery "to investigate the rumors that are abroad as to the soundness in the faith of
Rev. Hay Watson Smith." The resolution was crafted in order to make
the investigation broader than evolution; McPheeters and his allies
wanted to bring Smith to bar for his views on inerrancy, total depravity, and the deity of Christ as well. The General Assembly, perhaps
swayed by McPheeters's longtime service to the church, approved this
resolution through a voice vote that passed by a considerable majority.
But because of the ambiguity of the resolution's wording as well as
McPheeters's long-distance personal involvement with its prosecution,
conservatives would fail in their quest to discipline Smith.[10]

9. E. T. Thompson, *Presbyterians in the South*, 3 vols. (Richmond, VA: John Knox,
1963–73), 3:329–30; Hay Watson Smith, "Rev. Hay Watson Smith Gives Reasons for
Opposing Proposed Measure," *Arkansas Gazette*, 9 January 1927; F. Z. Browne, "Texas
Minister Replies to Dr. Smith on Evolution," *Arkansas Gazette*, 9 February 1927; Hay
Watson Smith, "Dr. Smith Replies to Texarkana Minister on Evolution," *Arkansas Gazette*,
12 February 1927 (all three articles in Hay Watson Smith Collection, PCAHC); Hay
Watson Smith, *The Charge, The Facts, The Resolution* (Little Rock, AR: n.p., [1927?]), 4, 6;
Hay Watson Smith, *Evolution and Intellectual Freedom: A Compilation of Opinions* (Little
Rock, AR: Jordan-Foster-Hamilton, 1927); Hay Watson Smith, *Some Facts about Evolution*
(Little Rock, AR: n.p., 1928).

10. Thompson, *Presbyterians in the South*, 3:330; MGAPCUS (1929): 27, 82–83; John
M. Wells to W. M. McPheeters, 30 May 1929; W. M. McPheeters to John M. Wells, 5 June
1929, both in J. McDowell Richards Papers, box 78, PHS. In this last letter, McPheeters
wrote, "It would be deplorable if in dealing with Dr. Hay Watson Smith the subjects of
evolution were made the main issue. Personally I have very decided views on evolution. I
regard that doctrine as at the bottom of most of our present day troubles in the Church
and out of it. On the other hand, I recognize the fact that it is exceedingly easy to obscure
the issue involved in the doctrine of evolution. So far as I can discover, not even men like

For McPheeters, this situation with Smith was the test case that the church needed in order to make a stand against the progressive theology making its way into the church. Though he wondered whether the church would do its duty and exercise discipline or "make the fatal mistake of seeking peace at any price," he also believed that the church needed to be alerted to the dangers of Smith's theology. He wrote widely in the regular newspapers and in pamphlets, arraigning his opponent's theology. In one widely circulated pamphlet, he suggested that Smith was unfaithful to his ordination vows by denigrating the Westminster Standards as an outmoded theological creed. In fact, "Dr. Smith explicitly rejects and even seeks to make odious in the eyes of the public, certain doctrines that have always been regarded as 'essential doctrines of the Presbyterian faith,' and that he himself says are 'essential to distinctive Calvinism.' " Simply because he might have declared his views to Arkansas Presbytery in 1912 did not mean that presbytery had been right in receiving him on this basis, McPheeters argued. Indeed, "why did Dr. Smith seek admission into the ministry of the Presbyterian Church" if he felt this way about Presbyterian doctrines? All that remained for Smith was to "exercise his right of withdrawal" from the church in order to preserve his "liberty of conscience."[11]

McPheeters hoped these maneuvers would be enough to convince Arkansas Presbytery, and the church at large, to discipline Smith. But when the Arkansas Presbytery commission reported in April 1930, it gave Smith a clean bill of theological health without even interviewing him directly about his views. In its report to presbytery, the commission focused its attention on Smith's original 1912 statement, which served as "the basis of the rumors" about his orthodoxy. Reading that statement in the most charitable light, particularly his statements on

---

Doctors F. L. Patton and B. B. Warfield had fought their way through that subject. That being the case, it seems to me it would be worse than a mistake to make that central in dealing with Dr. Smith."

11. W. M. McPheeters, *A Reply to a Communication of Rev. Dr. Hay Watson Smith* (Decatur, GA: n.p., 1930), 22–26. McPheeters was replying to a letter that Smith had written to the Columbia (South Carolina) *State* newspaper, published on 27 October 1929. Smith, in turn, had replied to a communication from McPheeters in that same newspaper, published on 22 September 1929.

the Trinity, the deity of Christ, and total depravity, the commission found "that he has not substantially changed his views since then, and that, in our opinion, the points of his divergence from our Standards are not of sufficient character to disqualify him from remaining a minister in good standing in the Southern Presbyterian Church." A number of protests were entered, including two separate protests from the dissenting members of the committee, Algernon Killough and James E. McJunkin. The protests centered on the fact that the commission had not investigated Smith's beliefs, but only the "rumors" about his beliefs.[12]

Immediately, McPheeters was in communication with McJunkin, pastor of Graham Memorial Presbyterian Church in Forrest City, Arkansas. The older minister instructed McJunkin to file a complaint to the synod about presbytery's action in regard to the Smith commission. Apparently, McJunkin and Killough did not take his initial advice and complained directly to the General Assembly. Not surprisingly, the 1930 General Assembly remanded the case to the Synod of Arkansas for its action. As ever, McPheeters was ready to advise McJunkin about the niceties of Presbyterian procedure. Yet the synod's Judicial Committee, during its fall 1930 stated meeting, used the unusual procedural pathway for the complaint—from the presbytery to the General Assembly to the synod—to reject it out of hand and not allow the complaint to be heard by the entire court. McPheeters was mortified: "It would be hard for me to express the pain, humiliation, and indignation caused me by the action of Arkansas Presbytery, in the first instance, and of the Synod in dismissing your complaint." He went on to observe that "I do not know what is to become of us, if the courts of Christ's church so far forget their responsibilities and their self-respect as to act in this fashion." Instantly, though, he returned to strategy: McJunkin needed to write a new complaint to the General Assembly, this time against the synod's action, with the hopes of getting a thorough investigation of Smith's views.[13]

12. *Minutes of the Arkansas Presbytery* 20 (Spring 1930): 21–23.
13. W. M. McPheeters to J. E. McJunkin, 12 April 1930; J. E. McJunkin to W. M. McPheeters, 9 June 1930; W. M. McPheeters to J. E. McJunkin, 17 June 1930; W. M. McPheeters to J. E. McJunkin, 14 October 1930; J. E. McJunkin to W. M. McPheeters,

Others were not sure that this was the best strategy. J. B. Hutton, pastor of First Presbyterian Church, Jackson, Mississippi, urged McPheeters and the Arkansas men simply to allow this matter to drop and "institute proceedings, de novo, before Arkansas Presbytery, at the spring meeting against Dr. Smith." If they were not willing to do this, then Hutton suggested that the men waive any complaint against the irregularities of the synod's action and make their complaint against the synod's finding itself, which would cause General Assembly to remand the case back to the synod for a retrial. This was the strategy that the conservatives settled on; they appealed to General Assembly for a fair hearing of their complaint before the Arkansas Synod. This time, the procedures worked in the conservatives' favor, and the 1931 General Assembly remanded the case back to Arkansas Synod with instructions to hear the case fairly.[14]

The Synod of Arkansas, at its fall 1931 stated meeting, received the General Assembly's instructions to consider McJunkin and Killough's complaint. The court decided that the Arkansas Presbytery had not fulfilled the intent of the 1929 General Assembly resolution in its failure to interview Smith directly and instructed the presbytery to reinvestigate the case. McJunkin was ecstatic, reporting to his mentor that "we feel that the presbytery cannot evade the matter any further, but will have to comply with the order of synod and allow us to question Dr. Smith in open presbytery." McPheeters responded immediately with possible strategies and thoughts. Surprisingly, the older man advised that "the more I think of it, the more I come to feel that it is neither necessary nor desirable that there be any examination of Dr. Smith personally." Fearful of Smith's own rhetorical prowess in any hostile interview conducted in his own church building, where presbytery was to meet, McPheeters held that "there is abundant evidence furnished by his own statements that his views are not in accord with the teachings of our Standards." In addition, he promised that he would

---

20 October 1930; W. M. McPheeters to J. E. McJunkin, 24 October 1930 (all in J. McDowell Richards Papers, box 78, PHS).

14. J. B. Hutton to W. M. McPheeters, 26 January 1931; W. M. McPheeters to A. M. Fraser, 10 June 1931 (both in J. McDowell Richards Papers, box 78, PHS).

write an indictment against Smith that could be used as the basis for the investigation.[15]

In the end, all the strategizing was for naught. Not only did the presbytery not follow synod's instructions to "examine Rev. Hay Watson Smith according to the *Book of Church Order*, using as a basis the Confession of Faith and the Catechisms of the Church with a view to ascertaining his beliefs," the court adopted a resolution that reaffirmed the findings of its 1930 commission. In addition, the resolution pointed out that presbytery had obeyed "the particular phrasing of the General Assembly's injunction, which reads 'to investigate the rumors abroad.'" Although the conservatives tried to offer a substitute motion to proceed with a direct examination of Smith, their substitute failed. Conservatives then tried their last stratagem: Killough preferred charges against Smith and requested thirty days to prepare his brief. But this was defeated as well when Smith's allies were able to pass a motion "that in light of the evidence before Presbytery, the Presbytery refuse to draw an indictment against Dr. Smith." This passed overwhelmingly. The conservatives' attempt to discipline Smith was crushed.[16]

McPheeters and his allies were stunned. McJunkin wrote that "I am so humiliated over the results of the meeting of this presbytery that I hardly know what to state to you and the rest of the dear brethren who have wrought and prayed in this matter. Mr. Killough and I are astounded and dazed at the way the presbytery ignored the Book of Church Order and the laws of the church, the orders of the superior courts, etc., especially the mandate of synod." McPheeters confessed that "I thought that nothing that Arkansas Presbytery could do would surprise me, but, if I understood your telegram correctly, I am surprised that even that presbytery should have the hardihood to wrest from you your unquestioned right to table charges against Dr. Smith."

15. J. E. McJunkin to W. M. McPheeters, 20 October 1931; W. M. McPheeters to J. E. McJunkin, 27 October 1931; J. E. McJunkin to W. M. McPheeters, 27 October 1931. See also J. B. Hutton to W. M. McPheeters, 28 October 1931; W. M. McPheeters to J. E. McJunkin, 3 November 1931; J. E. McJunkin to W. M. McPheeters, 6 November 1931; W. M. McPheeters to J. E. McJunkin, 7 November 1931 (all in J. McDowell Richards Papers, box 78, PHS).

16. *Minutes of the Arkansas Presbytery* 22 (Fall 1931): 7–9.

Though McPheeters was amazed by this turn of events, he knew that the next move was to complain yet again to the synod regarding the presbytery's failure to obey its instructions. But he would not have McJunkin as his point man in pursuing the complaint; McJunkin was forced to resign his church because his congregation took exception to his extracurricular activities in the Smith case. So the leadership of the complaint was turned over to Algernon Killough, pastor of the Presbyterian church in Marianna, Arkansas.[17]

When the Synod of Arkansas met for its fall 1932 stated meeting, it heard Killough's complaint. Though he tried to emphasize "that it was a case against the Presbytery of Arkansas, and not against Dr. Smith," the discussion that occurred after the case had been presented focused on the unfairness of the actions against Smith. And though Killough had circulated a pamphlet prepared by McPheeters showing the irregularities of presbytery's actions in both 1929 and 1931, it was not enough to sway the synod's mind. The complaint failed by a 4-to-1 margin. The only avenue left for conservatives was to protest to the General Assembly the following spring, in hopes that someone would observe the procedural irregularities and force Arkansas Presbytery to bring Smith to trial. When the case came before the judicial commission at the 1933 General Assembly, the presbytery and synod's actions were sustained and the complaint was denied. At issue for a number of the Assembly commissioners was the wording of the original 1929 resolution that McPheeters had offered and the Assembly had passed. One confidante wrote to McPheeters that "it struck me that they did about the only thing that could be done. I understand that the complaint was unfortunately worded in the instructions of the Synod to the Presbytery, which were to 'investigate the *rumors* about Dr. Smith's beliefs.' The claim was that this did not require an *examination* of Dr. Smith. It was in this way that the friends of Dr. Smith avoided a personal investigation of his beliefs." Also

17. J. E. McJunkin to W. M. McPheeters, 12 November 1931; W. M. McPheeters to J. E. McJunkin, 13 November 1931; W. M. McPheeters to J. E. McJunkin, 22 December 1931. McJunkin also reported the rumor, circulated throughout this affair, that Second Church intended to withdraw from the PCUS if Smith were brought to trial: J. E. McJunkin to W. M. McPheeters, 18 November 1931 (all in J. McDowell Richards Papers, box 78, PHS).

importantly, J. B. Hutton wrote in reflection on the Assembly's action, was "that the spirit of the Commission seemed to be impatient as to what they regarded as 'heresy hunting.'" The wording of the original resolution and McPheeters's long-standing personal involvement in the case eventually doomed conservatives' prospects. The case became more about conservatives' attitudes and actions than Smith's views.[18]

McPheeters was deeply embittered that the church had used the vagaries of its procedures to fail to discipline someone who appeared to be openly at odds with the church's doctrinal statements. Though he wrote a thorough impeachment of the botched handling of the case and circulated the pamphlet throughout the church, and though his friends tried to force the Assembly to reconsider the case in 1934, McPheeters eventually confessed that the case against Smith was lost.[19]

MCPHEETERS, THOMPSON, AND THE CHALLENGE OF PRES-BYTERIAN POLITICS

If the Smith case had been the only discipline case with which McPheeters was struggling, then perhaps he and other conservatives would not have had such a dark view of their church's future. But throughout his involvement with the Smith case, McPheeters had been fighting on another, more private front to bring discipline to the church. It was a ticklish situation because it involved a sister seminary and his alma mater, but he desired to see Ernest Trice Thompson, professor of church history at Union Seminary, brought to heel as well. Thompson, like McPheeters and Smith, was the son of a Presbyterian minister and a graduate of Union Seminary in Virginia. After serving a church in Texas, he returned to Union Seminary in 1922

---

18. *Minutes of the Eightieth Annual Session of the Synod of Arkansas* 11 (October 1932): 4–8; A. Killough to W. M. McPheeters, 19 October 1932, J. McDowell Richards Papers, box 78, PHS; A. Killough and J. E. McJunkin (and W. M. McPheeters), *Evidence Showing That the Findings of the Commission of Arkansas . . . Were in Violation of the Book of Church Order, Paragraph 183* (n.p.: [1932?]); R. A. White to W. M. McPheeters, 1 June 1933 (emphasis his); J. B. Hutton to W. M. McPheeters, 28 December 1933 (both in J. McDowell Richards Papers, box 78, PHS). McPheeters had also written an earlier pamphlet that contained much of the same evidence: W. M. McPheeters, *The Facts in the Case of Dr. Hay Watson Smith and Arkansas Presbytery* (Decatur, GA: Columbia Theological Seminary, 1931).

19. W. M. McPheeters, *Facts Revealed by the Records in the So-Called Investigation . . .* (Decatur, GA: n.p., 1934).

to teach English Bible. Three years later, he was shifted to the church history chair, which he would occupy until he retired from Union in 1963. Deeply influenced by the social gospel and the older liberalism of Friedrich Schleiermacher, Thompson above all desired to move the PCUS in a more progressive, tolerant, and ecumenical direction. Utilizing his writing talent, he accepted a number of assignments that would prove quite influential in the life of the church, including as book-review editor of the *Union Seminary Review* and commentator on the International Sunday School Union lessons for the *Presbyterian Standard*. He used these opportunities to introduce the church gently to then-current views of higher-critical scholarship, to promote social justice, to expand the borders of orthodoxy within the church, and to agitate the church for increased ecumenicity with the larger body of Christ.[20]

These activities placed him squarely opposite the position that McPheeters and his fellow conservatives occupied. It was not surprising, then, that McPheeters first noticed Thompson's openness to progressive biblical scholarship in the latter's Sunday school commentary. In December 1927, Thompson wrote in the *Presbyterian Standard* that some modern scholars held that when the Bible spoke of demon possession, it was observing the phenomenon that modern believers would recognize as mental illness. This openness to the way in which modern scholars "naturalized" the biblical material motivated McPheeters to write to Thompson. At the end of their exchange, McPheeters pointed out that Thompson had a responsibility as a PCUS minister and a professor in a denominational seminary to be careful in articulating his views: "Under these circumstances I would not feel at liberty to teach any view, even though I were personally convinced of its correctness, that I had reason to think was not the view of the Presbyterian Church US as expressed in our Standards, or in the unwritten interpretation of those Standards." He then opined that the church was not ready to accept "the view that the question of the reality of demoniac possession is an open question." The implication was clear—Thompson

20. For a thorough overview of Thompson's life and thought, see Peter H. Hobbie, "Ernest Trice Thompson: Prophet for a Changing South" (Ph.D. diss., Union Theological Seminary in Virginia, 1987).

was moving in directions that were outside the tradition of the church; if he kept doing so, he was opening himself and Union Seminary to attack from conservatives.[21]

While it appeared that the controversy would pass, Thompson again wrote about demon possession early in 1929 and again demonstrated his openness to the idea that the phenomenon represented "mental derangement." Again, McPheeters wrote to protest: "If one accepts as tenable the views contained in [this article], he is apt to find himself very much confused as to what statements in the Gospel narrative are to be taken as really expressing the teaching of Christ." At issue was the inspiration—and hence the authority—of Scripture. To cast doubt on the biblical presentation of supernaturalism was to cast doubt on the Scriptures themselves. This, in turn, would lead one to doubt whether Jesus himself was really "a wholly safe guide in regard to many other matters of fundamental importance." Directly after McPheeters had written this letter, he picked up the *Presbyterian Standard* to find that Thompson had questioned the traditional way of understanding the inspiration of the Bible. He wrote immediately, charging the younger professor with holding the views of "the Mediating School of Biblical Scholarship," which comprised "scholars whose evangelical antecedents prevent them from carrying their doctrine of Scripture to its logical conclusions; scholars who introduce into the Church of Christ the virus that ultimately destroys faith in the word of God though they themselves manage somehow to maintain their faith in Christ and in the teaching of a considerable portion of the Scripture." Even further, he characterized Thompson's positions as "contra-confessional and what is of much more importance, as contra-scriptural."[22]

Thompson fired back to both letters. He expressed his belief that "it is your attitude that makes such faith increasingly difficult for thoughtful men." Indeed, Thompson held that McPheeters was attempting to bind both the church and the minds of men "with the

---

21. Ibid., 212–13; W. M. McPheeters to E. T. Thompson, 26 March 1928, J. McDowell Richards Papers, box 80, PHS.

22. W. M. McPheeters to E. T. Thompson, 25 January 1929; W. M. McPheeters to E. T. Thompson, 28 January 1929 (both in J. McDowell Richards Papers, box 80, PHS).

chains of obscurantism." In a day when men and women read literature that raised questions about the truthfulness of the Bible, scholars had to provide answers; it would be disastrous to "shut people up to the particular interpretation of Bible language which we ourselves hold is apt to do more harm than good. It may be that they shall conclude that since they cannot hold the one interpretation which we will allow them they cannot hold to the inspiration of the Bible." McPheeters responded by challenging Thompson's specific interpretations: doubting the Mosaic authorship of the entire Pentateuch; dating the latest writing in the Old Testament in the Maccabean period; ascribing the canonicity of Old Testament books to their reception rather than to God's prior inspiration of them; and dating the formation of the Old Testament canon after Israel's exile. Each of these interpretations came from the "Mediating School," represented by scholars such as S. R. Driver, and McPheeters held that each struck at the inerrancy of the Scriptures. If people's faith in the Bible disintegrated, he worried, this "must ultimately prove fatal to the claims of the religion founded upon the book."[23]

McPheeters apparently backed off for a time, because of his and his wife's ill health as well as his desire to allow Thompson space to change his approach. But Thompson's writing once again activated McPheeters: this time it was Thompson's defense of the northern Presbyterian progressives' "Auburn Affirmation." This had plunged Thompson into a lengthy controversy with conservative John M. Wells in the pages of the *Presbyterian Standard*. The fact that Thompson was willing to defend those who held that the traditional views of biblical inspiration, the virgin birth, the substitutionary atonement, Christ's physical resurrection, and the reality of miracles were merely "theories" was enough to move McPheeters to action again. He wrote a lengthy letter to the Union Seminary president, B. R. Lacy, and placed the entire McPheeters-Thompson correspondence before him. After

23. E. T. Thompson to W. M. McPheeters, 1 February 1929; E. T. Thompson to W. M. McPheeters, 15 February 1929; W. M. McPheeters to E. T. Thompson, 28 March 1929; W. M. McPheeters to A. M. Fraser, 3 May 1929; E. T. Thompson to W. M. McPheeters, 6 July 1929; W. M. McPheeters to E. T. Thompson, 14 August 1929; E. T. Thompson to W. M. McPheeters, 19 August 1929 (all in J. McDowell Richards Papers, box 80, PHS).

highlighting the salient issues in the correspondence, he put the challenge to the seminary president. He recognized that Thompson was "within his rights in holding and teaching any views that he himself regards as not inconsistent with the teachings of Scripture and of our Confession until the difference of view between us touching these matters has been referred to some authority with the constitutional right to pass upon them." Lacy and the Union Seminary board had that right and, now being alerted to the issues, the responsibility to do so.[24]

If McPheeters expected Lacy to move expeditiously to investigate the matter, he was disappointed. Nearly a year later, he had heard almost nothing. In order to prod the president along, McPheeters wrote to him again, gently remonstrating that "as month has followed month without my hearing from you, I have at last begun to feel somewhat perplexed, and have begun to wonder whether you are going to content yourself with meeting my brotherly approach by accepting my letter merely 'as information.' Even at the risk of being misunderstood, may I say, that I hope that such is not your purpose." This prompted a response from Lacy, who claimed that he had talked with Thompson about the matter and thought it sufficient. But it was not sufficient for McPheeters; he immediately wrote back, seeking "some assurance that Dr. Thompson is going to refrain from advocating, either in his classroom or in the public press, these positions."[25]

Once again, Lacy tried to ignore McPheeters, causing the older man to write about his regret that "you do not seem to me to have viewed my approaches to you in the spirit in which they were made." Rather than viewing McPheeters as a friend, seminary colleague, and alumnus, Lacy viewed him suspiciously. And so the only option he had left was to send all the correspondence to four seminary trustees. Eventually, Lacy responded by noting that he had showed the older

24. The storm over Thompson and the Auburn Affirmation is covered in Hobbie, "Ernest Trice Thompson," 199–210; W. M. McPheeters to B. R. Lacy, 5 March 1931, J. McDowell Richards Papers, box 80, PHS.

25. W. M. McPheeters to B. R. Lacy, 19 January 1932; B. R. Lacy to W. M. McPheeters, 26 January 1932; B. R. Lacy to W. McPheeters, 1 February 1932 (all in J. McDowell Richards Papers, box 80, PHS).

man's letter to Thompson, who "categorically denies that you have correctly stated his position." He moved on to state strongly that in that light, "I do not see the necessity of answering your further questions in regard to what steps should be taken to silence Dr. Thompson." The seminary president would confer with the four trustees whom McPheeters had contacted before the next board meeting in order to devise a solution.[26]

Lacy decided to have the entire board of trustees meet with Thompson. Board member R. F. Campbell, pastor of First Presbyterian Church, Asheville, North Carolina, reported the results of the meeting to McPheeters. Though every member of the conference had great respect for McPheeters, "we did not find . . . in Dr. Thompson's published statements or in his correspondence with you anything that seemed to us likely to convince the Board or the Courts of the Church that he is out of line with his vows as an ordained minister or as a professor in the Seminary." B. R. Lacy also wrote to McPheeters in the aftermath of this conference, warning him that "regardless of what you or I or any leaders of the Church may say or do, this will be regarded by many in our Church and outside of it as an attack by one professor in a theological seminary upon a professor in a sister institution." The clear intimation was that McPheeters should drop the matter.[27]

The older professor was unmollified. Within six months, he had lost both the case against Hay Watson Smith and that against E. T. Thompson. Though he kept up the correspondence with Lacy throughout the summer of 1932, even threatening to take the matter to the General Assembly with charges against Thompson, McPheeters could only fulminate, "If our ministers are to be permitted to treat their ordination vows as a scrap of paper, my own feeling is that our

26. W. M. McPheeters to B. R. Lacy, 8 April 1932; B. R. Lacy to W. M. McPheeters, 15 April 1932; W. M. McPheeters to B. R. Lacy, 29 April 1932; B. R. Lacy to W. M. McPheeters, 5 May 1932 (all in J. McDowell Richards Papers, box 80, PHS). McPheeters sent out the correspondence to the trustees on 11 April 1932 (see his letters to R. F. Campbell, F. T. McFadden, W. McC. White, and J. J. Murray, 11 April 1932, J. McDowell Richards Papers, box 80, PHS).

27. R. F. Campbell to W. M. McPheeters, 17 May 1932; B. R. Lacy to W. M. McPheeters, 16 May 1932 (both in J. McDowell Richards Papers, box 80, PHS).

church will become a menace to public morals." He even drafted
and privately circulated a memorial about the Thompson affair, trying to raise support among conservative allies. Lacy caught wind of
McPheeters's continued activity and wrote to the Columbia Seminary
president, J. McDowell Richards, demanding that he rein in his Old
Testament professor. In response, McPheeters contemplated leaving the
seminary and forsaking his meager pension in order to continue his
attack on progressive thought in the church, but ill health prevented
him from doing so. When he died two years later, in 1935, he was
resigned to believe that there would be dark days ahead for his beloved
southern Presbyterian church.[28]

GLASGOW, THOMPSON, AND THE COALESCENCE OF CONSERVATIVE DISSENT

Though McPheeters died, his cause did not. By the late 1930s,
it had become increasingly clear to conservatives in the church that
the progressive element was driving the church's agenda. The progressives had successfully established the Permanent Committee on Social
and Moral Welfare, advanced in their attempts to revise the doctrinal
standards of the church, and reopened conversations on church union
with the northern Presbyterian church. In addition, the progressives
had once again raised the possibility of joining the Federal Council of
Churches in 1937; though that move had been defeated, it continued
to linger as a distinct possibility. And behind many of these liberal
successes stood E. T. Thompson.

Tom Glasgow, a ruling elder from Myers Park Presbyterian
Church, Charlotte, North Carolina, and McPheeters's nephew, was
concerned about the church's direction. At several General Assemblies, he had fought against what he saw as the liberal agenda, which
"favor[ed] Union, favor[ed] Federal Council and similar views—with

28. W. M. McPheeters to B. R. Lacy, 31 May 1932; B. R. Lacy to W. M. McPheeters,
4 July 1932; R. F. Campbell to W. M. McPheeters, 3 August 1932; R. F. Campbell to
W. M. McPheeters, 23 February 1933; W. M. McPheeters to R. F. Campbell, 28 February
1933; R. F. Campbell to W. M. McPheeters, 7 March 1933; J. McDowell Richards to B. R.
Lacy, 10 April 1933; W. M. McPheeters to J. McDowell Richards, 13 April 1933 (all in
J. McDowell Richards Papers, box 80, PHS).

a tendency toward some items of theological thinking which are at least a trend toward Modernism." By 1938, he had recognized that Thompson, and by extension Union Seminary, was a key leader for the more liberal wing of the church. He tried to warn the seminary's president, B. R. Lacy, that the most specific concerns about liberalism at Union centered on Thompson, "who seemed to be a very smart chap and a chap of definite liberal views." Over the next two years, Glasgow attempted to conference with Lacy about these matters; it did not happen, and the issues continued to fester.[29]

Convinced that the wellspring for future ministers was being polluted by theological liberalism and social progressivism, Glasgow took the issue to the floor of the 1940 General Assembly. He tried to convince the Assembly to set up a committee in order to investigate the teaching at the church's four theological seminaries. In particular, he focused his questions on how the doctrine of biblical inspiration was being taught at the seminaries. "I determined it was not improper to present another doctrinal matter of far greater importance to the Church, and affecting its vital power and existence—viz., the authority [and] inspiration of the Scriptures—not my position, but the historic position of our Church on that subject, which of recent years has been so freely questioned and impeached, both in and out of our and other churches," he later related to Lacy. To fellow conservative Judge Samuel Wilson, Glasgow was more direct: "The question on the doctrine of inspiration underlies the entire present unrest in our Church. It leans toward the Auburn Affirmation standing, and the transition from a Church operating under a final authority of God and His Word to a Church operating under the judgment and changing opinions of man." Glasgow's questions drew a direct and impassioned response from Union Seminary president Lacy as well as other Union graduates, who were sure that he was focused on Thompson.[30]

29. Tom Glasgow to B. R. Lacy, 9 June 1938, in Ernest Trice Thompson Papers, UPS. The best overview of the Glasgow-Thompson controversy can be found in Hobbie, "Ernest Trice Thompson," 294–356. See also Peter H. Hobbie, "Prophet under Fire: Ernest Trice Thompson and the Glasgow Case," *Affirmation* 6, 2 (Fall 1993): 129–45.

30. Tom Glasgow to B. R. Lacy, 27 May 1940; Tom Glasgow to Samuel M. Wilson, 28 May 1940 (both in Thompson Papers, UPS).

Glasgow refrained from a response at that point, though he felt that he could have "crucified some of [Union's] staff then and there, with information known personally to me concerning gentlemen present—more particularly Dr. E. Trice Thompson." It appeared that Glasgow had in mind a conversation that he had had with Thompson at the previous year's General Assembly, which Glasgow took as indicating Thompson's loose views on inspiration. As he repeated the conversation to others, Glasgow had Thompson claiming that "there are thousands of errors in the Bible" and refusing to affirm that the original scriptural documents were inerrant. Even more, these loose views were being passed on to Thompson's students. Glasgow noted to Lacy that "I have talked with your young [Union] graduates again and again—a tragic percent are 'blurred' on this vital issue." These former Thompson students did not reflect the older understanding of biblical inspiration that had been taught at Union Seminary by conservative heroes such as Robert Lewis Dabney, G. B. Strickler, and Thomas Cary Johnson. This "blurring" on inspiration led to a loss of spiritual power in these graduates, who were "very dear" to Glasgow.[31]

After the 1940 Assembly, Glasgow suggested that Lacy come to Charlotte to conference "off the record" over his concerns and determine how to move forward. Lacy agreed to come by way of Charlotte at the end of June, which delighted Glasgow: "I sincerely trust that nothing will interfere with this plan, and further, that it will be possible for you to allow sufficient time in Charlotte for a full and unhurried conference." In preparation for the meeting, Glasgow tried to dig up information that would be damning to Thompson, which in turn was reported to seminary president Lacy. The "off-the-record" meeting soon became a public one, with seminary trustees and a court stenographer present.[32]

---

31. Tom Glasgow to W. W. Glass, 11 June 1940; Tom Glasgow to B. R. Lacy, 27 May 1940; Tom Glasgow to E. T. Thompson, 28 June 1940 (all in Thompson Papers, UPS).

32. Tom Glasgow to B. R. Lacy, 27 May 1940; Tom Glasgow to B. R. Lacy, 31 May 1940; Tom Glasgow to W. W. Glass, 11 June 1940; W. W. Glass to Tom Glasgow, 14 June 1940. Glasgow also exchanged letters with Richard T. Gillespie (Richard T. Gillespie to Tom Glasgow, 5 June 1940). See further B. R. Lacy to Tom Glasgow, 20 June 1940; Tom Glasgow to B. R. Lacy, 22 June 1940 (all in Thompson Papers, UPS).

When Glasgow and Lacy finally met in Charlotte on 27 June 1940, Glasgow used the occasion to press the seminary president about Thompson's orthodoxy, reading sections of Thompson's writing that appeared deviant into the court stenographer's "record." Lacy, however, also came prepared to defend Thompson in a variety of ways: noting that the trustees had already investigated similar charges from Glasgow's uncle several years before and cleared Thompson; questioning Glasgow's understanding of biblical inspiration in the light of John Calvin and the Westminster Standards; and demanding that Glasgow divulge his sources of information, blaming fundamentalist Columbia Bible College as well as Charlotte minister Albert Sidney Johnson for stirring these matters up. He further challenged Glasgow to bring whatever charges he had against Thompson to his presbytery or the seminary's board of trustees. Above all, he challenged the accuracy of Glasgow's remembrances about his conversations with Thompson and his charges against the professor.[33]

The charges of inaccuracy particularly stung Glasgow because they touched his sense of integrity and raised questions about the nature of his criticisms of Thompson. He immediately wrote directly to Thompson, stating that "I unqualifiedly declare my conviction that it is accurate" and asking him to affirm that the conversation as Glasgow recalled it was in fact so. Glasgow went further: he wanted Thompson either to affirm or to deny whether he believed "that God originally and directly through His Spirit or in some other Divine manner did give to the authors of the Books of the Bible his original and inerrant divine revelation of his will to mankind." In reply, Thompson insisted that Glasgow had "missed the whole import of the discussion." As he remembered the 1939 conversation, Glasgow had claimed that "a single error in the Bible rendered the whole record uncertain, that under these circumstances the Bible could not be accepted as the Word of God."

33. "Conference at the Selwyn Hotel," 27 June 1940, Thompson Papers, UPS. Lacy continued to reiterate his position that Glasgow should bring these charges to the appropriate judicatories: see, e.g., B. R. Lacy to Tom Glasgow, 4 July 1940; B. R. Lacy to Tom Glasgow, 15 July 1940. Glasgow repeatedly denied links to other conservative forces in Tom Glasgow to B. R. Lacy, 6 July 1940. Glasgow and Lacy debated the use of the court reporter's transcript in B. R. Lacy to Tom Glasgow, 15 July 1940; Tom Glasgow to B. R. Lacy, 18 July 1940; B. R. Lacy to Tom Glasgow, 19 July 1940 (all in Thompson Papers, UPS).

Thompson had tried to say that there were a number of variations in the manuscripts to which scholars had access and that no one had ever seen the original manuscripts authored by the Scripture writers; as a result, "any informed man will have to admit the possibility of errors in the only Bibles that we possess." Beyond this, he only wished to affirm the Westminster Confession's statement on Scripture, to which he subscribed as part of his ordination vows.[34]

Glasgow felt that Thompson was continuing to evade his straight-forward questions and veritably shouted: "Dr. Thompson, you KNOW and KNOW FULL WELL, that this whole controversy turns around the question: 'What do YOU, Ernest Trice Thompson, MEAN when YOU say that YOU accept the statement on "inspiration" as set forth in the 1st chapter of the Confession of Faith, and what do YOU interpret these vows to mean!!' You carefully draft an apparently perfect answer that tells exactly NOTHING!" Glasgow was incensed that Thompson refused to meet with him privately—with a court reporter present—to answer his questions. "As a professor in a Theological Seminary or as just a plain, self-respecting man," he sneered, "if this is your attitude where your personal integrity is under fire, and your faithfulness to your sacred vows as a minister of the Gospel are impeached, I thank you for saving me the time and inconvenience of such a conference." The gloves were coming off, Glasgow warned. "I am closing the file in this matter and will proceed to take it to the Church at large, whose vital interests are at stake."[35]

Thompson replied in measured tones, noting that he took exception "to the general tone and the underlying spirit, which is to say the least not what one would expect from an elder in the Presbyterian Church, or from one Christian to another." He reaffirmed that Glasgow's recollection of their 1939 conversation "grossly misrepresents my position." He also noted that the reason why he refused to affirm or deny Glasgow's question was that the Westminster Standards were the "only doctrine" to which Thompson subscribed as a Presbyterian minister. He further objected "to your attempt to pin me to your

34. Tom Glasgow to E. T. Thompson, 28 June 1940; E. T. Thompson to Tom Glasgow, 4 July 1940 (both in Thompson Papers, UPS).

35. Tom Glasgow to E. T. Thompson, 9 July 1940 (emphasis his), Thompson Papers, UPS.

definition of the doctrine rather than to that set forth in the Standards, [and] to your vain attempt to set yourself up as a judge of orthodoxy in the Presbyterian Church in the United States." While Thompson was willing to say that "God gave to 'the authors of the books of the Bible his original and inerrant divine revelation of his will to mankind,'" he also pressed his point with Glasgow that "no informed man can deny the possibility of errors of various kinds in the only Bibles that we now possess." Thompson finally reiterated his determination that he would not meet with him, but encouraged Glasgow that "if you have reason to think that I am not fit to be a professor in a seminary in our church, or that I am untrue to my ordination vows, then it is your right, if not your duty, to bring charges against me" to the appropriate judicatory.[36]

By the time Glasgow replied to Thompson in mid-July 1940, he had a clear sense of what he needed to do. He indicated to Thompson that he was preparing a "report to the Church on the matter." Glasgow also suggested that in that report he intended to quote Thompson "direct from these writings which 'clearly reflect' your position toward the Scriptures as referred to AND CONSIDERED SACRED in our Confession of Faith. I shall let the reader judge as to whether that attitude is satisfactory for a Seminary professor." As a matter of fact, Glasgow was circulating such a report among conservative church leaders with notably pessimistic views about what it might accomplish. "Frankly, I am not sanguine with regard to the success of a prosecution," Glasgow confided to J. B. Hutton, minister at First Presbyterian Church, Jackson, Mississippi. "I believe the odds are at least 50–50 and probably a little better in favor of a successful prosecution if it is handled, frankly, fairly, and vigorously." His great hope was that a few ministers, especially in Thompson's presbytery, would come forward to lead the case. He confided to Samuel Wilson, a ruling elder from Lexington, Kentucky, that "I think it is absolutely futile for a Layman to undertake such a prosecution and further that the historic obligation and custom of the defense of the faith lies with the Ministry who are theologically trained and educated for that primary purpose." In

36. E. T. Thompson to Tom Glasgow, 15 July 1940, Thompson Papers, UPS.

fact, if the ministers did not step forward, "then the matter is already dead and I would not be disposed to in any way launch an individual attack where the Ministry was unwilling to take the historic obligation of the lead therein."[37]

Ministers did not step forward, however, and Glasgow increasingly felt the need to alert the church to the danger of Thompson's views. Six weeks later, Glasgow notified Thompson himself that "being unable to discuss the matters herein set forth with you personally, due to the fact of your declining to have such a conference, there seemed to me no course open but to lay the matter before the Church. This I have endeavored to do with honesty and with fairness in the pamphlet which I enclose herewith." The pamphlet, entitled *Shall the Southern Presbyterian Church Abandon Its Historic Position?*, represented a full-scale attack on Thompson's orthodoxy; it was mailed to all the ministers of the PCUS and the board of trustees at Union Seminary.[38] The main question that Glasgow set forward in his pamphlet was whether Thompson's "doctrinal views of the scripture and of our Standards conform to the historic positions of OUR Church." In his judgment, Thompson "openly and actively supports doctrines and interpretations of Scripture which are foreign to our interpretation of the Faith." In order to establish this, Glasgow focused his scrutiny on Thompson's Sunday school lesson expositions. Working through those lessons, he arraigned Thompson on several of the "fundamentals" that the 1939 General Assembly had declared were implied in the ordination vows: inspiration of the Bible; vicarious atonement; the virgin birth of Jesus; the reality of miracles; and the historicity of the Genesis account.

37. Tom Glasgow to E. T. Thompson, 18 July 1940 (emphasis his), Thompson Papers, UPS; Tom Glasgow to Samuel M. Wilson, 31 July 1940; Tom Glasgow to W. E. Everett, 31 July 1940; Tom Glasgow to J. B. Hutton, 13 August 1940; Tom Glasgow to Samuel M. Wilson, 14 August 1940 (all four letters in Samuel M. Wilson Papers, William T. Young Library, University of Kentucky, Lexington, Kentucky).

38. Tom Glasgow to E. T. Thompson, 30 August 1940; Tom Glasgow to B. R. Lacy, 30 August 1940; Tom Glasgow to E. T. Wellford, 3 September 1940 (all in Thompson Papers, UPS). This evidence corrects Hobbie, "Ernest Trice Thompson," 310, in which he suggests that Thompson did not know about and did not see the pamphlet until arriving at the Synod of Virginia meeting a week later.

"His beliefs REVOLUTIONIZE THE HISTORIC POSITIONS OF THE CHURCH and the interpretative approach thereto on these great doctrines and beliefs," Glasgow declared. As a result, he believed that Thompson "should be immediately removed from his position as a Professor."[39]

Progressives howled at the manner in which Glasgow aired his concerns against Thompson. D. P. McGeachy noted that "I am writing Mr. Glasgow and am trying to remind him in a brotherly way that, while he is entitled even to such views as he seems to hold, he certainly is not entitled to go at what he has in mind in the particular way he has chosen to follow." Calvin Grier Davis sniffed that "in the long run, it might prove to be a fortunate thing that the attack on Dr. Thompson from the heresy hunters of our church, which has seemed inevitable for several years, should have come from a man who was so poorly prepared to make it and who has harangued the commissioners to the General Assembly in so many meetings and for so many hours that many of them who might sympathize with his position have become disgusted." Much more cuttingly, Stuart Oglesby thought that "I would like to publish a psychological analysis of Tom Glasgow and his actions, but I wouldn't dare to." And Holmes Rolston worried that if Glasgow's attacks were sustained, "there will be little or no creative [theological] writing done within the Southern Presbyterian Church."[40]

39. Tom Glasgow, "Shall the Southern Presbyterian Church Abandon Its Historic Position?," in *A Statement For and Against Dr. Thompson* (Charlotte, NC: privately printed, 1941), 2, 3, 17 (emphasis his).

Glasgow eventually published all the documents for and against Thompson in this single pamphlet, *A Statement For and Against Dr. Thompson*. This larger pamphlet was mailed in May 1941 to all the commissioners to the 1941 General Assembly. In it, Glasgow included "Shall the Southern Presbyterian Church Abandon Its Historic Position?"; East Hanover Presbytery's "Report of the Committee on Glasgow Pamphlet"; Glasgow's reply to East Hanover Presbytery; an editorial that Glasgow wrote and that was rejected by *Presbyterian of the South*; an endorsement from J. B. Hutton Jr., a ruling elder from First Presbyterian Church, Jackson, Mississippi, who would factor into the controversy; and the vows of a Union Seminary professor. Because this became the final summary of the documents in this controversy, I will generally refer to this final version.

40. D. P. McGeachy to B. R. Lacy, 3 September 1940; Calvin Grier Davis to B. R. Lacy, 18 September 1940; Stuart R. Oglesby to B. R. Lacy, 3 September 1940; Holmes Rolston,

Several of the supporting synods of Union Seminary quickly rejected Glasgow's concerns. The Synod of North Carolina "deplore[d] the tendency for individuals to attack the character or orthodoxy of ministers and agencies of the church from their pulpits or by pamphlet, and would call upon those who may have any charges to bring against a minister or agency of the church to pursue the orderly processes clearly set forth in our book of church government." Likewise, the Synod of Virginia responded by electing Thompson as its moderator, the first time a minister had been elected to a second term in the history of the judicatory. It also rejected Glasgow's pamphlet, not only observing the irregular nature of the way in which he had brought his charges but also directing "attention to the action of the General Assembly expressing emphatic disapproval of the practice of circulating pamphlets, letters or articles attacking the orthodoxy or Christian character of ministers or courts of the church."[41]

In the Synod of Appalachia, however, there was more apprehension. As Union Seminary faculty member Donald Richardson reported, James Fowle, minister of the influential First Presbyterian Church, Chattanooga, Tennessee, expressed concern: "He expressed his feeling that Mr. Glasgow's pamphlet has simply brought into wider publicity a matter which for a long while had caused growing concern to many within the church. He thought that the Synod should insist on a thorough objective investigation." In this, Fowle was supported by Henry B. Dendy, minister at First Presbyterian Church, Weaverville, North Carolina, who had been "greatly concerned before the publication of the pamphlet and [felt] that this pamphlet had simply challenged the Church as to whether its concern should remain unexpressed." In response to these fears, the synod requested that Union Seminary investigate the charges against Thompson.[42]

"The Real Issue in the Tom Glasgow Pamphlet," *Presbyterian of the South* (23 October 1940) (all in Thompson Papers, UPS).

41. "Action of the Synod of North Carolina," 4 September 1940, in Thompson Papers, UPS; "News of the Church," *Presbyterian of the South* (18 September 1940): 7.

42. Donald Richardson, "Notes on Discussion in the Synod of Appalachia," in Thompson Papers, UPS.

Others expressed their concerns about Thompson's orthodoxy. W. S. Lacy supported Glasgow's charges, telling him that "you have done well in stressing his heresy and divergence from our Church as to inspiration. Not accepting the Bible as he should has resulted in his efforts to change or modify our catechisms and other standards. It is like Pandora's Box." Several presbyteries also asked for an investigation. Glasgow's Mecklenburg Presbytery petitioned the General Assembly to examine the orthodoxy of the seminaries in the light of the allegations against Thompson. Concord Presbytery likewise asked that the charges against Thompson be investigated by the appropriate bodies. Florida Presbytery supported Glasgow's charges and entered "our earnest protest against [Thompson's] teaching and request the Trustees of the said Seminary to remove him from the faculty in the interest of the purity and peace of our Church." In a similar vein, Central Mississippi Presbytery decided to set up a committee to investigate the charges and come to its own conclusion.[43]

In response to the charges raised in the pamphlet, Thompson requested his presbytery and the seminary's board of trustees to investigate his orthodoxy. This was a move that Lacy and Thompson had discussed throughout the summer in case Glasgow made some type of attack. Glasgow demanded that the record of these investigations be full and public: "As any appeal by either Dr. Thompson or the parties interested in the action of either the Trustees or the Presbytery of necessity must be 'on the record' as made at those investigations, it is, of course, important that the record be complete and in detail. I sincerely hope that this will be so handled without fail in order that there be no disappointment or just criticism concerning the inadequacy of the record."[44]

Glasgow would be disappointed in the results: Thompson's East Hanover Presbytery received the report of the committee investigating

43. W. S. Lacy to Tom Glasgow, 5 September 1940; Carl R. Pritchett to B. R. Lacy, 17 October 1940; S. L. Cathey to UTS Board of Trustees, 18 October 1940; "Action of Florida Presbytery in Session," 13 November 1940; J. B. Hutton Jr. to B. R. Lacy, 11 November 1940 (all in Thompson Papers, UPS).

44. B. R. Lacy to W. S. Royster, 7 September 1940, Thompson Papers, UPS; *Minutes of the East Hanover Presbytery* (Fall 1940): 19; Tom Glasgow to B. R. Lacy, 12 October 1940, Thompson Papers, UPS.

his orthodoxy near the end of November 1940 and completely exonerated him. In doing so, the committee dismantled both Glasgow's presuppositions and his charges: Glasgow thought that "a professor in one of our Theological Seminaries must accept the interpretation that has been placed upon our standards by those who have proceeded him in the Church"; that professors or ministers have "no right to hold or disseminate views that deviate, even in details, from the official standards of our Church"; that one could not accept "the assured results of textual criticism" without overthrowing biblical inspiration; and that there was only one acceptable method of biblical interpretation. Each of these presuppositions, the committee observed, was invalid; overthrow these assumptions and "the whole force of Mr. Glasgow's pamphlet is lost." Furthermore, they claimed that Glasgow's charges were faulty. The committee held that Glasgow took quotations out of context, drew improper inferences, demonstrated a lack of knowledge about allowable scholarly theories, and forced particular interpretations. In the end, the committee's conclusion was a ringing endorsement of Thompson: it deemed Thompson to be "in spirit as well as in mind thoroughly loyal to the Scriptures and to the Standards of our Church"; he was "entitled to the love and confidence of the Church"; and "his presence on the faculty of Union Theological Seminary is a distinct asset to that institution."[45]

Glasgow tried to publish articles in the various Presbyterian newspapers to keep pressure on Thompson, but found it difficult to place his articles. As a result, he was forced to self-publish pamphlets simply to respond to those who questioned his charges. In one reply to East Hanover Presbytery, he observed that its report seemed "to be more of a 'Brief in the Defense' of Dr. Thompson than an impartial report by an independent Committee on a judicial matter of a Church Court." He further charged that the presbytery's committee was a "stacked deck" and engaged in "a complete 'white-wash.'" He also continued to drum up support among conservative ministers and elders. At one point, he had hoped that the session of First Presbyterian

45. *Minutes of the East Hanover Presbytery* (Fall 1940): 44–51; "Committee Vindicates Dr. Thompson," *Richmond-News Leader* (25 November 1940), clipping in Thompson Papers, UPS.

Church, Chattanooga, Tennessee, would join him against Thompson. But in mid-January 1941, Park McCallie, an elder at the Chattanooga church, told Glasgow that the session had decided not to print its report on Thompson for widespread distribution. More troubling than Thompson's lack of orthodoxy, McCallie noted, was "the onus one would have to carry to get behind your own effort and boost it." Glasgow felt the disappointment of McCallie's lack of support keenly. "This decision," he observed, "will potentially seal the doom of any reasonable chance to establish the truth of this issue before the church."[46]

Glasgow's next-to-last hope was that the Union Seminary board of trustees would take action. Seminary president Lacy also knew that this would be an important process if the seminaries hoped to avoid an investigation by the General Assembly. As a result, the board's executive committee suggested that Glasgow be invited to come and present his case at the board's 11 February 1941 meeting. That invitation was relayed to Glasgow, albeit on short notice. His reaction was surprising: with an opportunity to present his case against Thompson to the judicatory that could do something about it, Glasgow decided not to come but instead asked that a court reporter be present at the meeting. That request was denied.[47]

In the end, it probably would not have mattered if Glasgow had been present or not. The board heard the narrative of events and charges and listened to Thompson's explanations. In the end, it adopted a statement "(1) reaffirming the allegiance of the Board to the Standards of the Seminary and of the Presbyterian Church in the United States and its determination to maintain those Standards;

46. Tom Glasgow, "Glasgow's Reply to East Hanover Presbytery," in *A Statement For and Against Dr. Thompson*, 34, 43; "Elder Decries Church Report on Thompson," *Richmond Times-Dispatch* (8 February 1941), clipping in Thompson Papers, UPS; J. Park McCallie to Tom Glasgow, 10 January 1941; Tom Glasgow to J. Park McCallie, 10 January 1941 (both in Thompson Papers, UPS).

47. B. R. Lacy to C. G. Rose, 31 January 1941; E. T. Wellford to Tom Glasgow, 3 February 1941; E. T. Wellford to B. R. Lacy, 3 February 1941; M. W. Norfleet Jr. to Tom Glasgow, 4 February 1941; Tom Glasgow to M. W. Norfleet Jr., 5 February 1941; Tom Glasgow to E. T. Wellford, 5 February 1941; B. R. Lacy to Tom Glasgow, 5 February 1941; Tom Glasgow to B. R. Lacy, 7 February 1941; B. R. Lacy to Tom Glasgow, 8 February 1941 (all in Thompson Papers, UPS).

(2) accepting as satisfactory the orthodoxy of Dr. E. T. Thompson and stating its purpose to retain him as a member of the faculty of the Seminary; (3) suggest[ing] to Dr. Thompson that in his public utterances and writings he exercise the greatest care to avoid any misinterpretation of his teaching." Lacy was convinced that the board's action had done little to satisfy Glasgow or those conservatives who supported him. "I don't think anything we can do will satisfy Tom Glasgow," Lacy observed to a seminary board member. "I look for him still to bring this matter to the floor of the General Assembly. I am glad to say that my Presbytery has appointed me a commissioner. I never enjoy being a commissioner at the Assembly and will certainly not enjoy it this year, but I do think it is well for me to be there in case Tom or any of his friends bring this matter to the front."[48]

Lacy's concern was prescient. The 1941 General Assembly would bring to an initial climax the division between progressives and conservatives that had been developing within the church for the past several years. Days before the meeting, each side canvassed the church with supporting materials. Glasgow sent out another pamphlet to all the Assembly commissioners containing all the documents pertaining to Thompson's case. He noted that several presbyteries had overtured the General Assembly on this matter; that this matter required the earnest attention of the presbyters; and that "the great fundamentals of the Church [must] be safe-guarded and protected against the devastating inroads which have been alleged and are earnestly believed to exist." Likewise, an open letter, originally published in the *Rockbridge County News* in Lexington, Virginia, was made into a handout for commissioners, defending Glasgow and his charges and claiming that "that report of East Hanover Presbytery strikes me as being a long step towards modernism. We have not yet reached the Auburn Affirmationists either in numbers or in doctrinal error, but we are

48. *Synopsis of the Minutes of the Board of Trustees of Union Theological Seminary, February 11, 1941* (Richmond, VA: Union Theological Seminary, 1941); "Seminary Board Rejects Glasgow Charges," *Presbyterian of the South* (26 February 1941), clipping in Thompson Papers, UPS; B. R. Lacy to C. G. Rose, 14 February 1941; B. R. Lacy to W. S. Royster, 15 February 1941 (both in Thompson Papers, UPS).

heading that way." Thompson himself also sent an open letter to the commissioners at Montreat, noting that Glasgow's actions violated Presbyterian procedure and ignored the vindicating actions of those parties who had oversight over him.[49]

The entire matter came to the General Assembly through a circuitous route. The various presbytery overtures desiring a committee to investigate the four seminaries and their teaching—and especially Thompson's teaching—were referred to the standing committee on theological seminaries. The majority of this committee recommended that the overtures seeking to investigate the seminaries and Thompson himself be answered in the negative. Noting the basics of Presbyterian polity, the majority observed that charges against a minister should be brought in his own presbytery and not enforced through the General Assembly, and that any charges against a seminary professor should be lodged with the appropriate seminary board. J. B. Hutton Jr., a ruling elder from Central Mississippi Presbytery, presented a minority report in which he argued that in fact such a General Assembly investigative committee would be constitutional because the Assembly had the power to bear witness against doctrinal error wherever it might be found. The debate on these matters went on for over five hours. In the end, the attempt to establish an investigative committee decisively failed, by a vote of 94 to 191.[50]

Thompson was not exactly vindicated, but he was victorious. After all, the Assembly refused to investigate his teaching (removing his name from the minority report before it) and to set up a committee to investigate the seminaries. As he remembered it later, "Freedom from the dead hand of the past, from the assumptions which underlay Mr. Glasgow's charges and which others shared that a theological

49. Tom Glasgow to Commissioners of the General Assembly, 15 May 1941; Addison Hogue, "An Open Letter" (15 May 1941); Tom Glasgow to E. T. Thompson, 16 May 1941; E. T. Thompson to the General Assembly of the PCUS, 22 May 1941 (all in Thompson Papers, UPS).

50. *MGAPCUS* (1941): 46–49; "Minority Report in re UnScriptural Doctrines Circulated Throughout the Entire Church . . ." (1941), Thompson Papers, UPS; "The General Assembly Proceedings," *CO* (4 June 1941): 13. Thompson incorrectly remembered this vote as 101–94; see Thompson, *Presbyterians in the South*, 3:338; Hobbie, "Ernest Trice Thompson," 347n25.

professor must not teach anything contrary to the Standards of the Church or the traditional interpretation of those Standards, had been upheld." Glasgow, too, recognized the importance of this fight. Reflecting on the entire battle in later memoirs for his children, he observed that "costly as it was, I have never regretted the whole matter. My action then has been the rallying point for historic Protestantism in the Southern Church." Coupling together the failure to discipline Thompson with the failures to prevent confessional revision and the redefinition of the church's spiritual mission, this was the moment that conservative dissent organized, fully coalesced and ready to fight for the church's future.[51]

RAISING CONSERVATIVE BANNERS

The Glasgow-Thompson controversy capped a decade in which conservatives had fought losing battle after losing battle in the life of their church. As conservatives saw it, the southern Presbyterian church was heading in the wrong direction, toward the same theological, social, and political liberalism as its northern cousin. Indeed, for these leaders, to fight for traditional Presbyterian doctrines was also to defend a range of other issues as well. As Tom Glasgow observed, the result of the Thompson controversy was that "those who stand for a whole Bible, wholly inspired, found a meeting place in the aftermath of that fight. In logical thought these seemingly technical matters go to the heart of Democratic government, free enterprise, separation of Church and State, and the great basic issues affecting your daily lives." This was not simply a church fight to Glasgow; rather, "in it and its final decision was your religious freedom and then your political and economic freedom. Without a sound theology, there can be no sound economic or political structure. The whole is tied together—obscurely, indirectly, but none the less inevitably."[52]

51. Thompson, *Presbyterians in the South*, 3:338; Tom Glasgow, *Did the Southern Assembly Err in the Case of Dr. Ernest Trice Thompson?* (Charlotte, NC: privately printed, n.d.); Tom Glasgow, "Personal Memoirs," Thompson Papers, UPS.

52. Tom Glasgow, "Personal Memoirs," Thompson Papers, UPS. Historian Peter Hobbie observed that "the 1941 General Assembly . . . marked a turning point in the church's march away from its narrow past and straitjacketed traditions. . . . After almost a year of intense struggle, Thompson, Lacy, church progressives, and friends of Union Theological

In order to defend the Bible and a constellation of conservative political and social perspectives, southern Presbyterian conservatives decided to found their own independent Presbyterian weekly periodical. Although conservative leaders had discussed such a journal off and on for six years, weeks after their defeat at the 1941 General Assembly, they gathered at Montreat to plan for a *Southern Presbyterian Journal*. In Glasgow's opinion, founding an independent, conservative journal was "the most vital matter confronting the church." Although organizers tried to get a prominent conservative churchman such as William Childs Robinson, professor at Columbia Seminary, or John M. Wells, former moderator of the General Assembly, to edit the magazine, they would eventually turn to two leaders in Asheville, Henry B. Dendy and L. Nelson Bell, to oversee the publication. There would not be a single more important decision in the rise of conservative dissent in the southern Presbyterian church.[53]

In the debut issue of the *Southern Presbyterian Journal*, which came in May 1942, Bell's opening editorial sought to justify the existence of the new monthly magazine. "There must be clear justification for the time, effort, and financial outlay involved in such an undertaking," he observed. What provided justification? "The civilization of which we are a part is perched precariously on the edge of an abyss," he noted. "The tragedy is that, in part, the Christian Church is to blame." The church had failed to preach the gospel "as truly and wholly the Word of God" and as a "Gospel of redemption" instead of "a program of social reform." In place of the historic verities, the church "has stepped out of its spiritual role, to meddle, as the Church, in political and economic matters and affairs of State." And yet if the church would preach the gospel faithfully, Bell believed that she could "provide the spiritual and moral stamina which is essential for world stabilization." The result would be "spiritual awakening and revival."[54]

Seminary had won a battle that would determine the future of Southern Presbyterianism and the eventual birth of the Presbyterian Church (USA)." Hobbie, "Prophet under Fire," 141.

53. Tom Glasgow to John M. Wells, 19 August 1941 (two letters with same date), John M. Wells Papers, PHS; Henry B. Dendy, "With Gratitude to God," *SPJ* (May 1945): 4–6; G. Aiken Taylor, "How the Journal Began," *PJ* (3 May 1967): 10–11.

54. L. Nelson Bell, "Why?," *SPJ* (May 1942): 2. Henry Dendy echoed the same themes of doctrinal purity and the spiritual mission of the church in "The Southern Presbyterian

It is important to notice that the conservatives' vision was not markedly different from that of their progressive opponents. Both sides believed that the gospel had something to say to American and global "civilization." As would become clear in the coming years, the *Southern Presbyterian Journal*, which served as the intellectual clearinghouse for conservative southern Presbyterians, offered very definite perspectives about the social, political, and economic crises of postwar America. The difference between progressives and conservatives centered on what was primary: did the church lead with gospel proclamation based on an inspired and inerrant Bible, which would result first in moral and then political and economic transformation, as conservatives believed? Or did the church lead with a prophetic word to the culture and a priestly activity of social concern, which would interest women and men in the gospel's spiritual and moral focus, as progressives held? These southern Presbyterian conservatives would raise their "banners" for Jesus as King over his church, the Bible as the inspired Word of God, the Westminster Confession as the best summary of what the Bible teaches, and the Great Commission to evangelize others as the lifeblood of the church. But they would also raise their banners for other things—anticommunism, segregation, and anticentralization—which would put them at odds with the progressive leaders in the PCUS and in step with larger political and social shifts in the American South.[55]

Journal Not Divisive," *SPJ* (September 1942): 2.

55. William Childs Robinson, "Our Southern Presbyterian Banners," *SPJ* (May 1942): 5–6.

5

"Red and Yellow, Black and White": Southern Presbyterian Conservatives and the Crises of Postwar America

Eighty-year-old J. E. Flow was a frequent contributor to the conservative *Southern Presbyterian Journal*. Raised in the segregated South, trained at Union Theological Seminary in Virginia, having served churches in Missouri, Oklahoma, and West Virginia, he had been an evangelist based in Concord, North Carolina, for the past eighteen years. But now, at the height of the agitation in 1954 to merge his beloved PCUS, popularly known as the southern Presbyterian church, with the northern Presbyterian church (PCUSA), he attempted to state a positive vision that would justify the separate existence of southern Presbyterianism beyond his own rapidly declining life. At the center of the vision were five commitments: the "old school" interpretation of Scripture and the Westminster Standards; the presbyterian form of church government; the grassroots principle of church oversight, symbolized in the role of diaconal care; the spiritual mission of the church; and "the purity and integrity of the White man of North America upon whose shoulders are laid the burdens of the world."[1]

1. J. E. Flow, "Positive or Negative?," *SPJ* (29 September 1954): 8–9. Strikingly, these issues, including segregation, have been cited in a recent essay by a participant in these

Flow's five commitments were near the heart of what most southern Presbyterian conservatives sought to preserve in the period between the fall of Berlin and the beginning of the Vietnam War. In this transitional period in the American South, southern Presbyterians felt the tremors of a changing world. Politically, the region's one-party system had been challenged by the Dixiecrat revolt in 1948 and would go for Goldwater in 1964. Even more, the nation would be rocked by the exposure of Communists in the higher levels of national government, beginning with Alger Hiss in 1948, but extending through Joseph McCarthy's House Un-American Activities Committee during the 1950s. Economically, the federal government's heavy military investment in the region during the World War II buildup and the continuing Korean War brought dollars and northerners into the region, exposing southerners to great numbers of both, often for the first time. While southerners appreciated the investment, they worried about centralized, bureaucratic overreach of the federal government and what it might mean for southern institutions. Socially, the civil-rights movement gained real momentum in the early 1950s when a young black minister from Montgomery, Alabama, Martin Luther King Jr., came to the forefront to serve as an organizational focal point for the often-diffuse movement. And religiously, southern Protestant denominations—whether Methodist, Baptist, or Presbyterian—were experiencing profound challenges to previously held orthodoxies concerning the nature of the Bible and the "fundamentals" of the faith.[2]

struggles: see Morton H. Smith, "The Southern Presbyterian Church and the Presbyterian Church in America," in *Interpreting and Teaching the Word of Hope*, ed. Robert L. Penny (Taylors, SC: Presbyterian Press, 2005), 206–12.

2. Craig S. Pascoe, Karen Trahan Leathem, and Andy Ambrose, eds., *The American South in the Twentieth Century* (Athens, GA: University of Georgia Press, 2005); Pete Daniel, *Lost Revolutions: The South in the 1950s* (Chapel Hill, NC: University of North Carolina Press, 2000); Numan V. Bartley, *The New South, 1945–1980* (Baton Rouge, LA: Louisiana State University Press, 1995); Dewey W. Grantham, *The South in Modern America: A Region at Odds* (New York: HarperCollins, 1994); Nadine Cohodas, *Strom Thurmond and the Politics of Southern Change* (Macon, GA: Mercer University Press, 1994); Dan T. Carter, *From George Wallace to Newt Gingrich: Race in the Conservative Counterrevolution, 1963–1994* (Baton Rouge, LA: Louisiana State University Press, 1999); David L. Chappell, *A Stone of Hope: Prophetic Religion and the Death of Jim Crow* (Chapel Hill, NC: University of North Carolina Press, 2004); Numan V. Bartley, *The Rise of Massive Resistance: Race and Politics in the South during the 1950s* (Baton Rouge, LA: Louisiana State University Press, 1969);

In response to this changing world, southern Presbyterian conservatives sought to buttress themselves by presenting a coherent, though disagreeable, antiprogressive ideology. In particular, they linked together many of these intellectual and cultural challenges into a comprehensive declension narrative: in their telling, Christian civilization in the United States, and especially in the South, was crumbling through compromises with Communists in Russia and China and machinations by aggressive liberals to promote racial integration. Both issues served as indicators of a larger trend—the attempt by progressives, both religious and political, to do away with necessary boundaries and forge centralized and ever-larger organizations that would serve a few elites and that would ultimately pave the way for the downfall of the world as they knew it.

For southern Presbyterian conservatives, one of the catalysts for uniting their fears of Communist intrusion, racial integration, and religious centralization was continued PCUS involvement with the Federal Council of Churches and its successor organization, the National Council of Churches. These Presbyterians saw progressive bureaucrats merging social, political, and religious concerns in the work of the councils; only a compelling and coherent response that similarly linked these concerns would sway church members. And yet such a response would also put these southern conservatives firmly in the middle of the developing national conservative political movement and make them a way-marker between the old and new Christian rights.[3]

David Stricklin, *A Genealogy of Dissent: Southern Baptist Protest in the Twentieth Century* (Lexington, KY: University Press of Kentucky, 2000); Peter C. Murray, *Methodists and the Crucible of Race, 1930–1975* (Columbia, MO: University of Missouri Press, 2004); E. T. Thompson, *Presbyterians in the South*, vol. 3, *1890–1972* (Richmond, VA: John Knox, 1973).

3. The literature on religion, race, anticommunism, and American conservatism is legion. Among the best studies over the past decade or so are Jonathan M. Schoenwald, *A Time for Choosing: The Rise of Modern American Conservatism* (New York: Oxford University Press, 2001); Kevin Kruse, *White Flight: Atlanta and the Making of Modern Conservatism* (Princeton, NJ: Princeton University Press, 2005); Matthew D. Lassiter, *The Silent Majority: Suburban Politics in the Sunbelt South* (Princeton, NJ: Princeton University Press, 2006); Joseph Crespino, *In Search of Another Country: Mississippi and the Conservative Counterrevolution* (Princeton, NJ: Princeton University Press, 2007); Joseph E. Lowndes, *From the New Deal to the New Right: Race and the Southern Origins of Modern Conservatism* (New

RED AND YELLOW: ANTICOMMUNISM

There was some amount of irony that southern Presbyterian conservatives took up the battle against Communism, integration, and centralization at all. After all, as evidenced by Flow's five commitments, they had long been committed to the ideal of the "spiritual mission of the church," which restricted the church's work to creed, liturgy, and service and made commentary on political and social matters taboo. For example, William Childs Robinson, professor at Columbia Theological Seminary, gloried in the church's commitment to the spiritual mission of the church and questioned whether the church should be involved in social and political matters. In a similar fashion, conservative leader L. Nelson Bell railed against "political churchmen": "We resent this further intrusion of Church leaders into the realm of international politics for three reasons. First, they are not competent in that particular field. Second, they have no right to use the prestige of the Church in this matter. Third, we think their advice is dead wrong." And it was this final point that often motivated conservative Presbyterian defenses of the spirituality of the church: the conservatives simply believed that progressive leaders were "dead wrong."[4]

Bell, for one, was far from shy about parlaying his religious status to engage in political commentary. Using his position as a ruling elder in the PCUS and as associate editor of the *Southern Presbyterian Journal*, Bell regularly supplied anticommunist columns throughout the 1940s and 1950s. He rationalized addressing what appeared to be a political issue in a religious periodical by claiming that "[Communism] is not a political issue at all; it is an ideology which is the antithesis of the freedoms which make effective politics possible." Indeed, Christians needed to recognize that "Communism is a hell-inspired and demonically controlled ideology which is an unceasing enemy of God,

---

Haven, CT: Yale University Press, 2008); Joseph Crespino, *Strom Thurmond's America* (New York: Hill and Wang, 2012).

4. William Childs Robinson, "The Spiritual Mission of the Church," *SPJ* (15 August 1950): 4; L. Nelson Bell, "Political Churchmen," *SPJ* (27 April 1955): 6–7. For similar sentiments, see also L. Nelson Bell, "Capitalism and Disorder," *SPJ* (15 October 1948): 5–6; L. Nelson Bell, "Bleeding to Death," *SPJ* (15 May 1950): 7.

His Christ, His Church and all of those blessings and freedoms which flow from Christianity." Or, to put it differently, Bell suggested that Communism "is a system of concepts which run far deeper than the variations of ideology found in the political realm. Communism is a religion." While Christianity led to personal freedom, love, service, and eternal salvation, Communism brought enslavement, hate, regimentation, materialism, and atheism to its followers. Further, Communists were determined to destroy Christian civilization in America. This was evidenced by the fact that "Communistic infiltration has been going on at an ever increasing rate of progress"; in universities, labor unions, and political organizations, Communists and their sympathizers were moving into positions of power and were parroting the "Moscow party-line." Ultimately, Communism was simply a tool in the devil's toolbox to destroy Christian civilization in America: "Be not deceived—Communism is so Satanic in its design, so intense in its execution, so opposed to everything Christians hold dear, that it must have its origin, implementation and supervision from the Evil One himself." In order to meet the challenge, Presbyterians needed to "face the facts and act as our fore-fathers acted" and recognize that "there can be no tolerance of Communism without inevitable loss as a result."[5]

Others joined Bell in warning of the Communist threat. M. A. Hopkins breathlessly warned that "Communism has always had as its one, persistent, consistent aim: World Revolution." Motivated by atheism, spurred on by deified leaders, Communists were radically devoted to their party and their ideals. Christians needed to excel the devotion of Communists to their cause in order to win the world to

5. L. Nelson Bell, "While Men Slept," *SPJ* (16 August 1948): 2–3; L. Nelson Bell, "For What It Is," *SPJ* (1 June 1950): 4; L. Nelson Bell, "Communism—A Religion," *SPJ* (15 November 1945): 3–4; L. Nelson Bell, "Challenge to What?," *SPJ* (15 February 1950): 4; L. Nelson Bell, "Beware," *SPJ* (1 June 1949): 5; L. Nelson Bell, "Be Not Deceived," *SPJ* (15 January 1949): 3; L. Nelson Bell, "The Method," *SPJ* (1 July 1953): 3–4. Bell and Dendy defended writing on Communism and political issues in a religious periodical several times: L. Nelson Bell, "Why We Are Concerned," *SPJ* (21 February 1951): 5; Henry B. Dendy, "National Policies and Christian Principles," *SPJ* (26 November 1952): 2. The first lengthy warning in *SPJ* about the Communist threat was Walter R. Courtenay, "The Red Horizon," *SPJ* (15 August 1947): 17–22.

Christ: "Communist fanaticism shames us Christians for our pale, anemic, lukewarm, half-hearted zeal and devotion to Christ." John R. Richardson likewise warned that Communists were infiltrating educational institutions and subverting the Christian morals of American youths. He also urged Presbyterians to hunt for Communist infiltration in their own church-related institutions: "We should not be so naïve as to think that such is impossible. It would be a salutary thing if the administrators of the Church's educational institutions should be the first to invite the House Un-American Activities Committee to make such an investigation."[6]

In fighting against Communist infiltration, pacifism and accommodation were not options for conservative Presbyterians. Nelson Bell abhorred those who attempted to win young people to the pacifist position: "We do not question the sincerity of these men, but we do deplore their objective. Given their own way, they would inadvertently, but none the less surely, deliver America and all that we hold dear, into the hands of the most diabolical system the world has ever seen." Indeed, "our temporizing with Communism within our land has been no less foolish than a child playing with a deadly snake." American failures in the early days of the Korean conflict were directly attributable to the mistaken assumption "that one can reason with Communism." Such an idea was nothing less than "wishful thinking." The only force that could ultimately defeat Communism was "an aroused Christian citizenship" that recognized "no ground for compromise."[7]

As part of this vigilance, Bell focused conservatives' attention on the rise of Communism in China and questioned American policies in the Far East. No doubt Bell's concern was motivated by his nearly twenty-five years of service as a missionary in China. Early on, he attacked the notion that Chinese Communism was more democratic than Russian Communism and defended Chiang Kai-Shek as

6. M. A. Hopkins, "Communism and World Missions," *SPJ* (1 April 1953): 9–11; John R. Richardson, "Subversive Influences in Education," *SPJ* (4 March 1953): 4–5. For more on conservative fears of Communist infiltration of college campuses, see William Billingsly, *Communists on Campus: Race, Politics, and the Public University in Sixties North Carolina* (Athens, GA: University of Georgia Press, 1999).

7. L. Nelson Bell, "No Time for Pacifism," *SPJ* (13 September 1950): 6–7; L. Nelson Bell, "There Is No Ground for Compromise," *SPJ* (20 December 1950): 4.

a republican liberator. In 1950, Bell portrayed Chiang as a Christian, "a babe in the faith" who needed American Christians to pray for him. Bell was also concerned that those missionaries who remained behind the "bamboo curtain" be protected in order to continue preaching the gospel. He consistently criticized American foreign policy toward mainline China as "abysmal," claiming that the situation in that country was the result of "the worst single diplomatic defeat in the history of the United States." The federal government must recognize that the number of actual Communist loyalists in China was quite small; one Bell friend claimed that China was actually "the one most anti-Communistic spot in Asia." Bell repeatedly urged the federal government not to recognize mainland China's Communist ruling party as a legitimate government, rather pleading that American policy be directed toward economic pressure on the Communist regime and strong support of the Nationalists, despite their own corruptions. Otherwise, American forces in Korea would face a "yellow peril" that would overwhelm our troops in the form of the "inexhaustible" Chinese Communist army. As late as 1952, Bell continued to support Chiang Kai-Shek and castigate the American government for not buttressing Nationalist forces in Formosa.[8]

When mainland China intervened in Korea on the side of the Communist forces, Bell continued to blame the federal government's foreign policy of appeasement and accommodation. By cowering in fear of Communist China and inviting it to press its claims regarding Formosa,

8. L. Nelson Bell, "Our China Policy," *SPJ* (1 December 1948): 4, 21; L. Nelson Bell, "Our China Policy," *SPJ* (1 May 1950): 6–7; L. Nelson Bell, "Our China Policy—Again," *SPJ* (1 July 1950): 4–5; Frank A. Brown, "Life under the Communists," *SPJ* (1 June 1949): 12–13; L. Nelson Bell, "Behind the Bamboo Curtain," *SPJ* (1 June 1950): 5–6; L. Nelson Bell, "The Most Anti-Communistic Spot in Asia," *SPJ* (1 November 1950): 7–8; L. Nelson Bell, "Shall We Recognize Communist China?," *SPJ* (11 October 1950): 3–4; L. Nelson Bell, "Far Eastern Affairs," *SPJ* (25 October 1950): 7; L. Nelson Bell, "We *Must* Change Our China Policy—And Quickly," *SPJ* (14 February 1951): 4; L. Nelson Bell, "While Rome Burns," *SPJ* (4 April 1951): 2–3; L. Nelson Bell, "The Yellow Peril May Be Red," *SPJ* (15 November 1950): 6–7; L. Nelson Bell, "More on China," *SPJ* (29 November 1950): 7–8; L. Nelson Bell, "The Forgotten Man," *SPJ* (31 December 1952): 5–6; L. Nelson Bell, "Shall We Recognize Communist China?," *SPJ* (24 February 1954): 4–5. In December 1942, the *SPJ* ran an article detailing Chiang Kai-Shek's alleged conversion: Melton Clark, "The Conversion of Generalissimo Chiang Kai-Shek," *SPJ* (December 1942): 15–16.

Americans demonstrated weakness that set in motion Chinese intervention and the slaughter of American troops. And when Truman dismissed Douglas MacArthur as head of American forces in Korea, it was further evidence that the federal government did not understand the Chinese Communist threat in the entire region. Nelson Bell defended MacArthur's analysis, even while recognizing that his insubordination needed presidential discipline. In the aftermath of MacArthur's departure, Bell characterized the government's leadership as "paralyzed . . . which is but a reflection of mass indecision." By late 1952, Bell was even advocating using the atomic bomb to bring the war to its conclusion: "If atomic warfare will end the war in Korea then the sooner it is started the better for all concerned."[9]

When the Korean conflict was concluded and when American policymakers supported China's entrance into the United Nations, Bell voiced his deep concern. "The number of trial balloons being sent up all over the country in favor of the recognition of Communist China and her admission to the United Nations is an ominous matter," he complained, "for it shows how wide-spread is the pro-Communist influence being exerted here in America and also how gullible some good Americans can be." He also questioned whether the United Nations could truly restrain aggressive global Communism. For evidence, he pointed to the way in which the United Nations had "engaged in obstruction, aggression, vilification, intrigue and conquest" during the Korean conflict. All this led to a de facto policy of appeasement and accommodation with Communism. In addition, because the United Nations was made up of countries that "either never knew God or have left the God of their fathers," it could never be a useful vehicle for America, a nation founded on "Christian principles."[10]

If Americans wanted to see the fruit of appeasement and accommodation, all they had to do was to observe how the federal government had interacted with Communist Russia. "When America recognized

9. L. Nelson Bell, "A Strong Delusion," *SPJ* (13 December 1950): 2–3; L. Nelson Bell, "Policies—Not Personalities," *SPJ* (25 April 1951): 3; L. Nelson Bell, "Paralyzed," *SPJ* (26 November 1952): 3.

10. L. Nelson Bell, "Communist China and the U.N.," *SPJ* (2 September 1953): 4; L. Nelson Bell, "Pollyanna and the U.N.," *SPJ* (7 October 1953): 2.

the present government of Russia, and exchanged diplomatic representatives in 1932, she took a downward step the consequences of which
continue to plague us as a people," Bell claimed. In addition, the
government followed a policy of expediency and fear of what Russia
might do, which made Russia "the master of international strategy."
What American leaders needed to do was to "demand the expulsion of
Russia and her satellites from the United Nations and ourselves break
off diplomatic relations with this government," recognizing that the
Russians desired "to destroy everything good on which our nation was
founded and for which she stands." Bell later darkly suggested that
"tens of thousands of unrecognized agents of Russia" had entered the
United States, seeking to subvert American freedoms.[11]

These Communist agents of subversion were finding places in
religious denominations and organizations. Helen Sigrist, allegedly
a former Communist Party member, warned that "churchmen are
especially easy to influence" by Communists because they are ideal-
ists; "Communists consider them the most naïve section of the world's
population." Another writer observed that Roman Catholic countries
in Europe were ripe for Communist takeover. "Rome has prepared the
soil for totalitarian Communism by its own totalitarianism," one writer
observed. "Rome has never allowed people to think for themselves, but
has instead taught and developed slavish obedience to her own decrees.
Communism has capitalized upon this pre-conditioning." American
Methodists were also viewed as opening the door for Communist
subversion. William Childs Robinson noted the reception that the
Methodist Federation for Social Action gave to Chinese Communist
leaders and to pro-Soviet spokesmen. When the Methodist bishops
from southeastern states denounced this action of the Methodist Federation, Robinson noted that this "pink fringe" had come into the
Methodist church through the reunion of the northern and southern
branches of the church in 1939.[12]

11. L. Nelson Bell, "Reaping," *SPJ* (10 January 1951): 6; L. Nelson Bell, "Righteousness
Exalteth a Nation (Not Expediency)," *SPJ* (8 October 1952): 3–4; L. Nelson Bell, "Let Us
Break with Russia Now," *SPJ* (26 November 1952): 2–3.

12. Helen Sigrist, "The Reds' Program for the Church," *SPJ* (26 March 1958): 9–11;
"Our Bulwark against Communism," *SPJ* (1 June 1949): 10; William Childs Robinson,

But these conservatives' greatest concern was that Communism had invaded Presbyterian denominations, north and south. When John Mackay, the 1953 moderator of the PCUSA, urged a face-to-face encounter with Russian officials in the hopes of bringing about reconciliation and forgiveness and claimed that McCarthyism was just as bad as Communism, southern Presbyterians assailed him. "In our judgment this is one of the most insidiously dangerous documents we have yet seen," Bell declaimed, "not only because of its implications, but also because of its source and the deference and weight which will be given it for that very reason." When the *Communist Daily Worker* applauded the northern Presbyterian actions, southern Presbyterian conservatives duly noted that fact. And Bell, for one, could not let go of the idea that northern Presbyterians advocated negotiating with Communists: "That radical and left-wing groups and individuals, along with the parlor pinks and fellow travelers should advocate this line of action is not surprising," Bell observed. "But when respected and influential representatives of the Protestant Church begin to advocate doing business with the Communists it is high time that Churchmen everywhere take notice and also action." It was another indication that these were not safe times.[13]

Fears of Red infiltration were not simply restricted to Yankee Presbyterians; even the "Southern Zion" was open to attack. Richardson Ayers claimed that Communism in the church was moving the PCUS toward "a great super, world church" that would deny the gospel itself; conservatives would have to suffer in order to preserve the gospel for future generations. Chalmers Alexander urged conservative believers to become "reactionaries," eager to defend the gospel and the American way of life. When loyalty oaths became the *cause célèbre* in the early

"Methodism's Pink Fringe," *SPJ* (1 March 1950): 6–7; William Childs Robinson, "Methodist Bishops of the Southeast Denounce Methodist Federation for Social Actions as Communistic," *SPJ* (30 August 1950): 4; "Journal to Be Published Weekly, Board Directs at Weaverville Meeting," *SPJ* (30 August 1950): 7; Chalmers W. Alexander, "Reactionary?," *SPJ* (6 September 1950): 2; L. Nelson Bell, "Well Spoken," *SPJ* (13 September 1950): 3.

13. L. Nelson Bell, "A Strange Pronouncement," *SPJ* (18 November 1953): 2–5; "Dangerous Reasoning—Continued," *SPJ* (25 November 1953): 2–6; "Communists Applaud U.S.A. Presbyterians," *SPJ* (2 December 1953): 9; L. Nelson Bell, "It Is Not 'Cynical' to Face the Facts," *SPJ* (20 January 1954): 4–6.

1950s, Nelson Bell, for one, defended them: "Churchmen and the Church should [not] . . . in any way hinder the honest efforts of our citizens to curb what was once a threat but which has now become a reality—the infiltration with a communistic propaganda and agents of the various phases of our national life." By the early 1960s, conservatives had begun to sniff out PCUS Communists in prominent positions. William C. Cumming warned that the Southern Presbyterian Peace Fellowship was "promoting various things that are exactly what the Communists want us to do, and that would make us helpless before them in their drive to enslave us along with the rest of the world."[14]

Not only were there fears of infiltration, but southern Presbyterians feared Russian domination in the aftermath of Sputnik's launch. Bell breathlessly opined that "the launching of the earth satellite by Russia is potentially the most significant event since the explosion of the first A Bomb over Hiroshima." He certainly feared Russian technological achievement, but he also worried about "an increased clamor for further rapprochement with Russia," which would lead to "the ultimate destruction of America and of the Free World." A couple of months later, though grateful that the Sputnik launches seemed to have shaken American complacency, Bell worried that a military buildup would hopelessly bankrupt America, through "piling up a national debt which there is no reasonable hope of paying off." In a similar fashion, H. V. Henderson Jr. feared the cost of "a race for technological superiority," which seemed to be the result of Sputnik. Others attributed Russia's technological leapfrog over the United States to more sinister forces. J. Park McCallie observed that "Satanic influences have aided atheistic Russia to beat so-called Christian America" in launching this satellite.[15]

In order to answer the claims of the Communists, Christian leaders needed to teach their young people "Christian economics."

14. L. Nelson Bell, "Those Loyalty Oaths," *SPJ* (18 June 1952): 2–3; William C. Cumming to G. Aiken Taylor, 9 July 1962, *Presbyterian Journal* Papers, PCAHC.

15. L. Nelson Bell, "A Rude Awakening . . . It Is Much Later than We Thought," *SPJ* (16 October 1957): 2–3; L. Nelson Bell, "Strengthening Our Defenses," *SPJ* (11 December 1957): 2–3; H. V. Henderson Jr., "What Price Preeminence?," *SPJ* (11 December 1957): 6–7; J. P. McCallie, "The Challenge of Sputnik," *SPJ* (26 March 1958): 8–9.

John R. Richardson observed that "the Communist economics cannot match Christian economics." And yet "unless young people are informed concerning the merits of Christian economics, some of them will embrace the Communist offer." Among the key principles of Christian economics included the right of private property, the principle of free enterprise, "the Christian interpretation of work," the idea of incentives, the sinfulness of waste, and "the proper observance of the Fourth Commandment," regulating rest, work, and worship. Underlying these principles were the ideals of individualism, limited government, and states' rights, all apparently "Scriptural principles." Seeming to eschew the "spirituality of the church," Richardson concluded that "the Christian church has a sacred duty to train our young people in Christian economics." All this was part of training them in a "Biblical world and life view." Nelson Bell followed this instruction by justifying the *Journal*'s inclusion of Richardson's essay: "Why should a Christian journal concern itself with economics? For the simple reason that the Bible gives us sound advice on money, its place and use." Only as Christian leaders embraced "biblical," capitalistic teaching and taught it to others, ever vigilant against those who would destroy the American way of life, would they be doing their duty to God and country.[16]

BLACK: ANTI-INTEGRATION

Although the Cold War and racial integration were the two key issues confronting southern conservatives during the 1940s and 1950s, relatively few PCUS conservatives directly connected the two.[17] Robert Gribble, longtime professor at Austin Presbyterian Theological Seminary, observed that "socialism, communism, radicalism, and all manner of subversive and malcontent forces . . . [all] particularly agitate the

16. John R. Richardson, "How to Teach Christian Economics to Young People," *SPJ* (23 April 1958): 7–14; L. Nelson Bell, "Responsible Economics or Chaos," *SPJ* (30 April 1958): 2–3.

17. See Jeff Woods, *Black Struggle, Red Scare: Segregation and Anti-Communism in the South, 1948–1968* (Baton Rouge, LA: Louisiana State University Press, 2004); George Lewis, "White South, Red Nation: Massive Resistance and the Cold War," in *Massive Resistance: Southern Opposition to the Second Reconstruction*, ed. Clive Webb (New York: Oxford University Press, 2005), 117–35.

race-question." William Childs Robinson held that Marxists wanted to do away with all distinctions and discrimination "in the life of the home, of industry, of races, and of social life that God has made." Thomas R. Miller made the link in stronger terms when he observed that when the PCUS supported *Brown v. Board of Education* in 1954, it "lin[ed] up on the side of Communism." The former president of Belhaven College, G. T. Gillespie, darkly suggested that the "violent agitation against segregation . . . coincides with the worldwide movement for racial amalgamation which has its fountainhead in Moscow." Joseph Jones, the minister of First Presbyterian Church, Fountain Inn, South Carolina, accused the National Association for the Advancement of Colored People (NAACP) of "aiding the advance of Communism" by "accomplishing the Communist objective of division, strife, hatred, enmity, chaos, and confusion." Paul Hastings protested the 1957 appearance of the black minister James Robinson as a speaker at Montreat, accusing him of belonging to various "Communist fronts" and defending the Communist Party.[18]

More often than not, rather than linking civil rights to Communist infiltration, southern Presbyterian conservatives simply defended segregation as a providential and pragmatic means to foster the prosperity of both races.[19] J. E. Flow observed that segregation was "the

18. Robert F. Gribble, "Column Left: March!," *SPJ* (15 July 1948): 3; William Childs Robinson, "No Distinctions . . . Except Those Made by God," *SPJ* (27 August 1952): 3; Thomas R. Miller to G. Aiken Taylor, 17 March 1961, *Presbyterian Journal* Papers, PCAHC; G. T. Gillespie, "Defense of the Principle of Racial Segregation," *PO* (14 March 1955): 5; Joseph S. Jones, "The Ku Klux Klan, the NAACP, and the Presbyterian Church," *SPJ* (31 July 1957): 7; Paul D. Hastings, "Strange Guests," *SPJ* (15 January 1958): 9–10. First Presbyterian Church, Greenville, South Carolina, also protested Robinson's appearance at Montreat; see "First Presbyterian Church of Greenville, S.C., Petitions Enoree Presbytery," *SPJ* (12 March 1958): 22.

19. The best student of religious defenses of segregation is David Chappell: see *A Stone of Hope*, 105–78; this summarizes much of his earlier essays, "The Divided Mind of Southern Segregationists," *Georgia Historical Quarterly* 82 (1998): 45–72, and "Religious Ideas of the Segregationists," *Journal of American Studies* 32 (1998): 237–62. Also important is Paul Harvey, *Freedom's Coming: Religious Culture and the Shaping of the South from the Civil War through the Civil Rights Era* (Chapel Hill, NC: University of North Carolina Press, 2005), 218–50; this summarizes material from his earlier essay, "Religion, Race and the Right in the South, 1945–1990," in *Politics and Religion in the White South*, ed. Glenn Feldman (Lexington, KY: University Press of Kentucky, 2005), 101–23. The key study of southern Presbyterians and race is Joel L. Alvis Jr., *Religion and Race: Southern Presbyterians,*

best way to preserve the peace and protect the lives" of both blacks and whites. He later suggested that Christians believed that "God Almighty made both of these [races] and He, and He alone, could have made them to differ from one another, and the difference is far more deep seated than the color of their faces." The natural conclusion was that because God had providentially ordered things this way, well-meaning Christians should encourage racial integrity. William Childs Robinson noted that God must have had some providential purpose in bringing blacks as slaves to America; and so, "while reading the lessons in Providence from the presence of the Negro in America may he also read the hand of Providence in the distinctness of the races." Nelson Bell agreed that "race distinctions" were "God ordained." And yet he also believed that segregation was not "a question of Christianity," but "a question of expediency." Instead of eliminating segregation, he opined that Christians should focus their efforts on doing away with "discrimination." That meant that blacks should be treated humanely while social boundaries and restrictions were still maintained. In fact, the way to lessen racial tensions was simply "to find individual occasions to do justice and show kindness to those who are of another race," while still maintaining racial integrity.[20]

There were several who attempted to justify segregation on biblical grounds. In an early essay on race relations, Nelson Bell observed that there was "a line which must be drawn and which must not be

1946–1983 (Tuscaloosa, AL: University of Alabama Press, 1994); also important are E. T. Thompson, "Southern Presbyterians and the Race Problem," *Austin Seminary Theological Bulletin* 83 (1968): 5–28; Dwyn M. Mounger, "Racial Attitudes in the Presbyterian Church in the United States, 1944–1954," *Journal of Presbyterian History* 48 (1970): 38–68; and James H. Smylie, "The Bible, Race, and the Changing South," *Journal of Presbyterian History* 59 (1981): 197–216. One study that focuses on the racial attitudes of Nelson Bell in the context of the new evangelicalism of the 1950s is Michael D. Hammond, "Conscience in Conflict: Neo-Evangelicals and Race in the 1950s" (M.A. thesis, Wheaton College Graduate School, 2002).

20. J. E. Flow, "The Federal Council on Human Rights," *SPJ* (1 February 1949): 18–19; J. E. Flow, "Different," *SPJ* (16 December 1953); L. Nelson Bell, "Christian Race Relations Must Be Natural, Not Forced," *SPJ* (17 August 1955): 4; L. Nelson Bell, "It Is Not a Question of Christianity, but Expediency," *SPJ* (15 February 1950): 6; William Childs Robinson, "Centennial of the End of the Slave Trade," *SPJ* (16 July 1958): 4–5; L. Nelson Bell, "Incidents Worth Emulating," *SPJ* (20 September 1950): 7; William Childs Robinson, "Wanted: Good Samaritans," *SPJ* (4 July 1956): 4.

crossed" and then referenced Acts 17:26, which suggested that "God also determined 'the bounds of their habitations.'" He also referred to Genesis 9 as possible evidence of "why God saw fit to make some men white and some black." W. A. Plecker also referred to Genesis 9 and 11, asking "what hindered God from giving the descendants of Ham the marked physical changes of color and features, with mental and moral difference as we find them today, all in keeping with Noah's prophecy, or curse, as being the servant of all?" Just to make it plain, Plecker identified the children of Ham with those were to be "servants of their brethren" and who "were headed for Africa." William H. Frazer claimed that "we believe in the 'social separation' of the races because we think that God believes in it." Apparently, part of the reason for the Old Testament exodus was to maintain Jewish racial purity (neglecting the fact that Moses had married a Midianite). Likewise, he claimed that God commanded racial separation, but could find only Acts 17:26 to support his claim. J. S. Robinson also believed that Acts 17:26 provided a good argument for segregation; after all, "the fact that God set the bounds of the nations shows that He knew that it was best for them not to intermingle socially." William Childs Robinson reflected on this same biblical text when he claimed that "God who has appointed the bounds of several habitations has given the churches no commission to wipe out the color line."[21]

More famously, G. T. Gillespie tried to make a biblical case for segregation. Originally a speech before the Synod of Mississippi in support of a resolution seeking to turn back the 1954 PCUS General Assembly's support of integration, his "defense of the principle of segregation" became the most widely circulated attempt to justify the practice biblically. And yet he opened his defense by admitting that the Bible "contains no clear mandate for or against segregation as between the white and Negro races." After this startling admission, he then surveyed biblical materials that he believed justified the practice.

21. L. Nelson Bell, "Race Relations—Whither?," *SPJ* (March 1944): 4–5; W. A. Plecker, "'Interracial Brotherhood Movement': Is It Scriptural?," *SPJ* (1 January 1947): 9; William H. Frazer, "The Social Separation of the Races," *SPJ* (15 July 1950): 6–7; J. S. Robinson, "Determining the Bounds of Their Habitation," *SPJ* (6 October 1954): 3–4; William Childs Robinson, "Christ Our Peace in Race Relations," *SPJ* (July 1945): 8. For the use of Genesis 9 in religious defenses of racial inequality, see Stephen Haynes, *Noah's Curse: The Biblical Justification of American Slavery* (New York: Oxford University Press, 2002).

In particular, he focused on the principle of "separation," especially through the early chapters of Genesis: the separation of Cain and Abel, the failure of separation before the Noahic flood, the reestablishment of separation afterward in Noah's sons, the divinely mandated separation at the Tower of Babel, and the separation of Abraham from the Chaldeans. Gillespie also focused on God's prohibition of intermarriage with the nations surrounding Israel, rereading this prohibition against the intermixture of religions as one against the intermixture of races. All of this suggested that God allowed the practice of segregation "by divine authority and express command." Further, "infractions of the command were punished with extreme severity." As a result, Gillespie concluded that "there is no ground for the charge that racial segregation is displeasing to God, unjust to man, or inherently wrong."[22]

Another defender of segregation from the Bible, Morton Smith, then professor of Bible at Belhaven College in Jackson, Mississippi, also utilized many of these same texts. After admitting the essential unity of humankind, Smith stressed human diversity, appealing to Acts 17:26 and the Tower of Babel story in Genesis 11, from which he suggested that "the principle of separation of peoples or of segregation is not necessarily wrong per se. In fact, it seems clearly to be God's order of things." But he appealed to other texts as well. He looked at Deuteronomy 7:3, which, along with Genesis 6, Ezra 9–10, Malachi 2:10–16, and 2 Corinthians 6:14, argued against "intermarriage with other peoples" (again ignoring that this was based on spiritual, not racial, reasons). He tried to answer the integrationist's use of Galatians 3:28 by sighing that "it can hardly be maintained that he meant to imply that there were no real and continued distinctions within the group that he lists." Rather, both Jesus and the apostle Paul exemplified the principle of "unity in diversity and . . . diversity in unity." Hence, it was only fair to conclude, Smith believed, that the Bible gave good grounds to practice segregation and especially to avoid any intermarriage between the races.[23]

22. Gillespie, "Defense of the Principle of Racial Segregation," 6–8; G. T. Gillespie, "A Southern Christian Looks at the Race Problem," *SPJ* (5 June 1957): 11.

23. Morton H. Smith, "Bible Study for Circle Bible Leadership on 'Jesus and Citizenship': Lesson 8—Brotherhood and Race," *SPJ* (3 July 1957): 17–21.

The great fear that these conservative believers had if segregation ended was undoubtedly interracial marriage.[24] As early as 1944,
Nelson Bell worried about those who crossed the racial and biological
line and produced "half-breeds." He would later observe in 1949 that
"the inevitable end" of civil-rights agitation both inside and outside
the PCUS was "intermarriage between the races." A year later, he
warned that racial "extremists" were "advocating the elimination of
racial lines [and] they privately admit the ultimate necessity of the
intermingling and intermarriage of the races." In a 1955 editorial that
received wide notice in the church and secular press, Bell continued
to wring his hands over interracial marriage: "We feel constrained to
say that the greatest enemies of a solution of the [racial] problem are
those integrationists who say that the ultimate solution of the race
issue lies in the intermarriage of the races."[25]

Bell was not alone in his anxieties over interracial marriage.
J. David Simpson baldly claimed that "non-segregation means eventual inter-marriage" and wondered what would happen if white young
people had to bear the "cross and burden" of "resisting and repelling
every natural urge of affection ripening into the desire for marriage
between the negro and white as the years go by."[26] William H. Frazer,
too, was worried about "miscegenation," which would lead to "a weakening of the resistance to certain diseases by the hybrid off-spring"
and impede the progress of the (white) American citizen. What was
necessary to preserve racial integrity was segregation, G. T. Gillespie

24. For this, see Jane Dailey, "The Theology of Massive Resistance: Sex, Segregation,
and the Sacred after *Brown*," in Webb, *Massive Resistance*, 151–80.

25. Bell, "Race Relations—Whither?," 4–5; L. Nelson Bell, "What Next?," *SPJ* (15 February 1949): 2; Bell, "It Is Not a Question of Christianity, but Expediency," 6; Bell, "Christian
Race Relations Must Be Natural, Not Forced," 5.

26. J. David Simpson, "Non-Segregation Means Eventual Inter-Marriage," *SPJ* (15 March
1948): 6–7. Simpson goes on to write, "Yes, I repeat, non-segregation of the races is to my
mind unscriptural; whereas, segregation of the races is to my mind definitely scriptural.
Marriage between sharp racial lines of color and characteristics such as is found in the
red, brown, black, white and yellow races is unscriptural; marriage within the confines of
separate races is definitely scriptural and is enjoined upon the Social order. Amalgamation,
miscegenation, and hybrid races unscriptural; races kept inviolate as to mixture, preserved
pure in strain and their integrity kept, is positively taught of the Scriptures. I repeat again,
non-segregation means eventual inter-marriage." Ibid., 7.

believed; he held that "the pattern of segregation . . . uniformly provided an effective check against the process of amalgamation." In a later essay, Gillespie believed that the "crux of the whole racial problem" boiled down to one simple question: "Is it desirable that social relations leading normally to intermarriage and ultimate racial amalgamation should be encouraged and approved; or is it more desirable, in the interests of all parties and society as a whole, that racial intermarriage should be discouraged or prohibited, and that each race should be enabled to preserve its own racial integrity?" And J. S. Robinson protested that the church in its official consideration of racial matters failed to "touch the heart of the segregation question as it relates to the South, namely, social life and intermarriage."[27]

Arguments against racial intermarriage drew heavily from "modern" anthropology and commonsense animal breeding. Gillespie, for one, argued that "black groups each have their own distinctive physical and cultural characteristics" that would not merge easily with "white groups." Recognizing that the saying "birds of a feather flock together" held a measure of truth, he suggested that "the intelligent farmer does not allow his dairy and beef breeding stock to run in the same pasture, otherwise he would down grade his herds, and have only a herd of scrubs or mongrels." The same principles, he held, applied "with even greater force to the mating of human beings of widely different types and cultural backgrounds." As a result, any policy or practice that involved "the gradual integration and ultimate amalgamation of the white and colored races in the United States" would represent "a colossal blunder, a betrayal of unborn generations, and a monstrous crime against civilization."[28]

And so situations in which whites and blacks would socialize during formative ages were to be regulated closely. Early on, Nelson Bell expressed doubt concerning "the wisdom of bringing our young people together with Negro boys and girls in the Young People's Conferences." This was because "at these conferences, the social and recreational

27. Frazer, "The Social Separation of the Races," 7; Gillespie, "Defense of the Principle of Racial Segregation," 5–6; Gillespie, "A Southern Christian Looks at the Race Problem," 8; Robinson, "Determining the Bounds of Their Habitation," 3–4.

28. Gillespie, "A Southern Christian Looks at the Race Problem," 9–10.

aspects are stressed along with the spiritual. These contacts in the most impressionable years, and under the stimulus of an overstressed racial consciousness, can well lead to tragic and disastrous results," namely, intermarriage. In 1950, the Montreat Retreat Association—the historic camping and assembly grounds for the PCUS—voted to allow adult groups to come to Montreat on a "non-segregated basis," but decided to discontinue allowing black children to participate in the Young People's Conferences. As Bell later explained, the Montreat Association was "the first in our church to officially hold up a hand and say, 'Stop,' to our young people and we mean it." When the issue of desegregation heated up in the church in 1954, Bell warned that accepting black young people to Montreat conferences would lead to "unrestricted social relationships for all the Negro and white young people employed in Montreat." That same year, Bell worried over the fact that another western North Carolina Christian conference center was pairing off "a Negro boy and a white girl, or a white boy with a Negro girl, for the playing of games and for square dancing." Such was a "travesty" and a "gross injustice," Bell exclaimed, for who knew where such relationships might lead?[29]

In addition, Christian education materials published by the denominational board needed to be rigorously reviewed to ensure that Presbyterian youths were not being "brainwashed" in favor of integration. Paul Hastings detailed the claims of two books written by staff members of the PCUS Board of Christian Education. These books raised the explosive question of interracial marriage, promoted Christian fellowship between the races, and encouraged interracial conferences. These books also warned young people that the older generation would not agree with them on interracial relationships and suggested that they might have to disobey parents in order to

29. L. Nelson Bell, "Racial Tensions: Let Us Decrease—Not Increase Them!," *SPJ* (15 February 1947): 3; Bell, "It Is Not a Question of Christianity, but Expediency," 6; L. Nelson Bell, "Race Relations and Montreat," *SPJ* (15 June 1950): 2; L. Nelson Bell, "Race Relations and Montreat," *SPJ* (15 July 1950): 5; "Montreat Cottage Owners Ask That Segregation Be Maintained at Montreat," *SPJ* (28 July 1954): 12; L. Nelson Bell, "Montreat and Desegregation," *SPJ* (15 September 1954): 3; L. Nelson Bell, "Take Care," *SPJ* (16 June 1954): 3. See also Mary-Ruth Marshall, "Handling Dynamite: Young People, Race, and Montreat," *American Presbyterians* 74 (1996): 141–54.

act on Christian conviction. In addition, the authors commended the NAACP and other "race mixing organizations," books by Mary McLeod Bethune and Lillian Smith, authors with known Communist or deviant lifestyles, and poetry by Langston Hughes, who wrote "the most blasphemous thing I have ever read concerning our Lord Jesus Christ." According to Hastings, all of this demonstrated "the lack of judgment of such 'Crusaders,' and the way they are used by the most radical individuals and groups in the country." Conservative parents needed to be on the watch to keep their youth pure.[30]

In order to defend their "southern way of life" further, some southern Presbyterian conservatives associated themselves with Citizen's Councils, dedicated to "states' rights and racial integrity." In 1957, the session of First Presbyterian Church, Jackson, Mississippi, defended "citizens groups" against a negative portrayal by the General Assembly's Committee on Christian Relations: "This session would point out that there are numerous citizen's councils and groups throughout the South which are composed of Christian citizens of the highest type, and that these groups not only do not resort to or condone violence, but, on the other hand, are actually deterrents to the use of violence." When Carleton Putnam, far-right author and speaker, came to Jackson, Mississippi, for a Citizen's Council rally in 1961, the planning committee included prominent Presbyterian ministers and elders. The following year, conservative minister Albert Freundt claimed that Oxford, Mississippi, clergy were wrong to call the state to repentance for the rioting and vandalism surrounding James Meredith's admittance to the University of Mississippi. Southern Presbyterian conservatives believed that these types of citizens' organizations were preferable to the lawless and mob-sponsored activities of the Ku Klux Klan, which Nelson Bell denounced as "un-American and un-Christian" and on par with the Communists.[31]

30. Paul D. Hastings, "Are We Going to Let Our Young People Be Brain Washed like This?," *SPJ* (4 September 1957): 5–6.

31. "Statement Adopted by the Session of the First Presbyterian Church of Jackson, Mississippi," *SPJ* (19 June 1957): 10; "These Distinguished Community Leaders Served on the Carleton Putnam Dinner Committee in Jackson," *The Citizen* (November 1961): 42–45; Albert H. Freundt Jr., "Oxford Clergy Wrong Calling for 'Repentance'!," *The Citizen* (October 1962): 4–6; L. Nelson Bell, "Hoodlums," *SPJ* (15 August 1949): 5. See

Other conservatives used public forums to advocate gradual racial progress that allowed southerners to sort out the issues without federal intervention. Nelson Bell recognized that "segregation by law could not be legally defended," and yet "forced integration cannot be defended, either on legal or moral grounds"; each position infringed on the "legal right of the individual." Rather, all those involved in the racial problem needed to recognize that "it *must* be solved on the basis of local conditions, and in the light of what would be the natural contacts and alignments." Coercion from outsiders, whether religious or governmental, only exacerbated the situation: "*Until the attempts to force an unnatural solution* are stopped there will be no right solution." Bell's desire for a natural, not coerced, resolution of racial problems found articulation in a statement that he signed with a number of other southern Presbyterians. In "An Appeal to Fellow Christians," leading southern Presbyterians agreed that "to force social contacts, in the name of Christianity, where such contacts are not desired, can compound our problems, not solve them." Rather than promoting "zeal to break down racial barriers," Christians should love others in "those daily contacts with people of other races where courtesies, consideration and love should be shown to everyone, regardless of color." Racial relationships had to be natural, Bell believed, not forced.[32]

Southern Presbyterian conservatives, however, found themselves in the minority on racial segregation in the official courts of their church. In 1954, the PCUS General Assembly adopted a report that affirmed "that enforced segregation of the races is discrimination which is out of harmony with Christian theology and ethics" and that urged southern Presbyterian colleges, campgrounds, and churches to be open to all, regardless of race. In addition, it applauded the U.S. Supreme Court's recent decision in *Brown v. Board of Education* and called on southern Presbyterians "to lend their assistance to those charged with

---

also Peter Slade, *Open Friendship in a Closed Society: Mission Mississippi and a Theology of Friendship* (New York: Oxford University Press, 2009), 108–9.

32. Bell, "Christian Race Relations Must Be Natural, Not Forced," 3–5 (emphasis his); "An Appeal to Fellow Christians," *SPJ* (11 April 1956): 7–9. The "Appeal" was signed by men on both sides of the theological divide: progressives such as J. McDowell Richards, Frank Caldwell, Marion Boggs, and Ben R. Lacy Jr. signed the document, as well as conservatives Bell, J. Wayte Fulton Jr., C. Darby Fulton, and G. Aiken Taylor.

the duty of implementing the decision." PCUS conservatives howled loudly at the General Assembly's decision. Nelson Bell once again observed that "there is a great difference between abolishing segregation as a Christian principle and *imposing non-segregation*. The latter could prove both un-Christian and utterly unrealistic." Paul Hastings was blunter, claiming that the advice of the General Assembly "shocked the members at the grassroots of the Church." He decried the General Assembly's attempt at "imposed social change" when it recommended integration of PCUS ministries.[33]

Soon, conservative churches and presbyteries began to protest the Assembly's action. For example, the session of First Presbyterian Church, Jackson, Mississippi, "unanimously declare[d] their conviction that in this matter the General Assembly did err." Further, the church's session also warned that it would "not follow the recent advice of the General Assembly urging non-segregation. And declares that segregation of the races is not discrimination and declares that this Church shall, with good-will toward all men, maintain its traditional policy and practice of distinct separation of the races." Mount Zion Presbyterian Church, Rose Hill, North Carolina, agreed: "We deny that segregation of the races in the church is un-Christian or that it is contrary to the teaching of the Scripture." As a result, "whether any man agree with us or not, for us it is wrong to accept the counsel of the General Assembly in this instance. We therefore reject it." Tuscaloosa Presbytery protested as well: fearing that the General Assembly's advice would lead to "race mongrelization, which result would become a 'stench in the nostrils' of all true lovers of race purity," these leaders "unequivocally" rejected it. Meridian Presbytery "deplore[d] the action of the General Assembly in its recommendation regarding segregation, and . . . refuse[d] to accept said recommendation as wise, or binding on our consciences."[34]

33. *MGAPCUS* (1954): 187–97; Bell, "Take Care," 3 (emphasis his); Paul D. Hastings, "The Issues Become Clear," *SPJ* (30 June 1954): 7–8. Joel Alvis is simply wrong in claiming that the PCUS report did not have *Brown v. Board of Education* in view; instead, it is explicitly mentioned there. Alvis, *Religion and Race*, 57.

34. "First Church of Jackson, Miss. Declares Itself on Segregation," *SPJ* (7 July 1954): 8; "Mount Zion Presbyterian Church," *SPJ* (4 August 1954): 16; "Tuscaloosa Presbytery Protests against Assembly's Advice," *SPJ* (4 August 1954): 17; "Presbytery of Meridian against Union," *SPJ* (3 November 1954): 18.

By the 1955 General Assembly, several presbyteries along with the Synod of Mississippi had petitioned that body to "reconsider and rescind" the previous year's actions because "serious errors in judgment" had been made in adopting the report supporting desegregation. In addition, when the Council on Christian Relations, the successor to the old Permanent Committee on Social and Moral Welfare, presented its report on "Unity in the Church with Diversity," a minority report was submitted that charged the previous General Assembly with causing disunity in the church by erroneously "declaring segregation to be a sin and in seeking to obligate the members of both races in the Presbyterian Church in the United States to work for the integration of the races, inasmuch as the Scriptures do not sustain the view that segregation in itself is wrong or un-Christian." But the minority's views were not aired; after a short debate, the question was called, and the Assembly voted to consider and approve the original report of the council.[35]

Between the actions of the General Assembly and the "mind-washing" tactics of the PCUS Board for Christian Education, the "sledgehammer" approach of denominational leadership was increasingly frustrating some southern Presbyterians. Central Presbyterian Church, Jackson, Mississippi, presented an overture to the Central Mississippi Presbytery that complained that "the efforts to have the churches accept integration have been carried to the extreme" by the denomination. In the three-year period between 1954 and 1957, the church was "pressurizing" the churches to a particular position without recognizing that those in the Deep South had "attitudes toward the race question [that] run deep with much feeling." Central Church asked the Assembly to back off on the racial issue, allow for local leaders to deal with matters in their own way and time, and provide for moderation and "love and fairness for all." The presbytery adopted this resolution overwhelmingly.[36]

35. *MGAPCUS* (1955): 36–40, 76–79, 166–70; John R. Richardson, "The 1955 General Assembly," *SPJ* (22 June 1955): 5–6. The Synod of Mississippi had adopted the overture of Central Mississippi Presbytery: see *Minutes of Central Mississippi Presbytery* (Spring 1955): 62–63.

36. *Minutes of Central Mississippi Presbytery* (Fall 1957): 15–16.

Others were trying to find moderate positions that might get southern conservatives beyond the racial crisis of the 1950s. In the aftermath of the 1957 Little Rock crisis, Nelson Bell tried to make distinctions that were lost on some of his allies. He claimed that "desegregation and integration are not synonymous terms"; in fact, "forced segregation is un-Christian because it denies the rights which are inherent in American citizenship." Further, he observed that those Christians who set aside "the discriminations and humiliations and restrictions of the past" in race relations should not be deemed liberal or unfaithful to the southern past. This was increasingly an issue as Bell's son-in-law, Billy Graham, preached the gospel to nonsegregated audiences. Bell was forced in the coming days to defend Graham's practices, telling one writer that Graham "feels that so far as the preaching of the Gospel is concerned, he must preach to all on an unsegregated basis. With his world-wide ministry, any other policy would destroy his opportunity to reach three-fourths of the millions of the world." Like Graham's, Bell's desire to see the gospel promoted around the world trumped racial integrity. Finally, he blamed extremists on both sides of the issue for present tensions, both staunch integrationists and "men who are determined to maintain white supremacy by fear and lawlessness." He suggested that the blacks who sought to integrate the Montgomery bus line were "reasonable" and that those who opposed them were engaged in "legalized discrimination." These white extremists needed to give way to leaders who would engage in consultations with black leaders in "mutual consideration and Christian love." Though he saw himself as defending segregation, he did so in the mildest of terms.[37]

Other southern Presbyterian conservatives would reject Bell's moderate position. Mississippi minister W. A. Gamble excoriated Bell

37. L. Nelson Bell, "Some Needed Distinctions," *SPJ* (5 June 1957): 2–3; L. Nelson Bell to Mrs. Willard Steele, 10 June 1958; L. Nelson Bell to W. A. Gamble, 18 February 1956 (both in L. Nelson Bell Papers, BGC). See Steven P. Miller, "Billy Graham, Civil Rights, and the Changing Postwar South," in Feldman, *Politics and Religion in the White South*, 157–86. To Edward Jones, Bell claimed that "Billy does not believe in integration any more than you and I do. The point is that he feels, along with me, that legal or forced segregation is unchristian and that segregation should be on a voluntary basis." L. Nelson Bell to Edward Jones, 21 October 1958, L. Nelson Bell Papers, BGC.

for suggesting that legalized segregation was unjustifiable. Not only was Bell illogical, Gamble held, but he took a position that stood "against the Constitution of every Southern state." Further, his position denied the one recourse that Mississippians had taken in race relations, namely, legalized segregation. In addition, "it cannot be forgotten that the removal of segregation laws, and the consequent mingling of the races more and more, will inevitably result in miscegenation," Gamble claimed; he then darkly accused that "the person who opposes segregation by law should seriously consider the part he may have in developing a mongrel population, a development I believe God disapproves."[38]

In a similar fashion, G. T. Gillespie defended legalized segregation as a pattern that had evolved over time and had served both races well. Though admitting that it was "far from perfect," he also held that "the evils and injustices which have arisen under the system of segregation have been purely incidental and have not been due to any fallacy in the principle of segregation, but to the weakness and perversities of individual members of both races." Even then, such evils and injustices existed in only "a few localities"; in fact, there was "no indication of any serious disturbance of the friendly relations existing between the rank and file of Negroes and whites throughout the South." As a result, Gillespie defended massive resistance to the implementation of *Brown v. Board of Education*, for only as segregation was maintained "as a permanent feature of our public policy" would both races know "present and future welfare."[39]

In an effort to keep the moderate and hard-line segregationist PCUS wings together, the *Southern Presbyterian Journal* board of directors adopted a statement of policy in August 1957. It represented a movement away from Bell's developing moderate position and leaned toward a stricter version of segregation. The statement accused those who promoted "enforced integration" of favoring it for political reasons and "partisan advantage"; it claimed that the situation as it existed in the American South was too complicated for outsiders to solve;

38. W. A. Gamble to L. Nelson Bell and Henry Dendy, 10 February 1956, L. Nelson Bell Papers, BGC.

39. Gillespie, "A Southern Christian Looks at the Race Problem," 9.

it also held that "racial integrity as it has developed in the Providence of God" was worth preserving, so that "voluntary segregation in churches, schools, and other social relationships is for the highest interests of the races, and is not un-Christian"; and finally, the document affirmed "that interracial social relationships, rather than being the ideal to which the church should work, are actually compounding the problems they seek to solve." This strong statement in favor of racial integrity sought to answer the racial crisis of the 1950s in the terms of massive resistance, instead of gospel charity.[40]

WHITE: ANTICENTRALIZATION

As southern Presbyterian conservatives read the signs of the times, all they could see was the continuing attempt to knock down historical barriers and to move toward centralization in the larger society as well as the church. "Slowly the tides of tyranny move towards centralization," Robert Gribble observed. "Once necessary for the waging of successful (?) war, over-all planning now seeks perpetuation. Loss of states' rights, by concession here and yielding there, becomes alarming reality." Nelson Bell reprobated the trend toward "a managed national economy" as "un-Christian, uneconomical, and a scandal of inefficacy." In particular, this centralizing trend was blamed on a "little band of determined liberals," which was "well organized, persistent and very vocal." What these men desired was "one world," in which a "great world-wide community of peoples and nations" would be gathered together; but what they forgot was that "the world, as such, knows not God nor his Christ." Organizations, movements, or ideologies that sought to break down distinctions and barriers between religions, states, or races were profoundly dangerous. As a result, to oppose centralization and totalitarianism, whatever the political or religious form, fueled conservatives' rhetoric and actions.[41]

40. "Statement of Policy on Race Relations," *SPJ* (28 August 1957): 3.

41. Gribble, "Column Left: March!," 4; L. Nelson Bell, "Is a Managed Economy Christian?," *SPJ* (3 January 1951): 2; Chalmers W. Alexander, "A Little Band of Determined Liberals," *SPJ* (15 August 1950): 13; L. Nelson Bell, "One Worldness," *SPJ* (10 February 1954): 3–4.

Southern Presbyterians especially saw in the Federal Council of Churches and its successor organization, the National Council of Churches, an attempt to forge a progressive, bureaucratic, centralized approach to political, economic, racial, and spiritual problems. From the very first issue of the *Southern Presbyterian Journal* in 1942, southern Presbyterian conservatives opposed the Federal Council and advocated withdrawal from the organization. "Any participation toward unity with an organization so thoroughly out of harmony with the beliefs and practices of the Southern Presbyterian [church]," Daniel Iverson observed, "would be worse than a compromise." Vernon Patterson charged that the Council desired to force all the churches to comply with the Council's radical social and economic programs in its hopes to forge "a world government, initiated by and therefore probably dominated by, a world church." The Council also sought a program of racial integration that would make conservatives "shudder at the tremendous possibilities that may result." Nelson Bell noted that "one of the characteristics of the present liberal theological movement is the desire for power, power to control the activities and agencies of the Church in line with programs conceived by those in authority." He later observed that the National Council meetings represented prepared programs, "developed beforehand by some of the ablest men in the ecclesiastical world, men who are irrevocably committed to a particular philosophy of the Church, social action and world affairs." J. E. Flow protested the Federal Council's early attacks on segregation, claiming that southern blacks were "naturally, a careful, jovial, and contented people" who embraced segregation themselves until agitated by northerners. "If we have to choose between segregation of the races and race riots," Flow observed, "we prefer segregation of the races, or even 'Jim Crowism.'"[42]

Not only did the ecumenical movement desire to hinder the work of individual denominations, but it also represented a socialistic

42. Daniel Iverson, "The Aims and Purposes of the Federal Council," *SPJ* (May 1942): 21–23; Vernon W. Patterson, "Bases of a Just and Durable Peace," *SPJ* (June 1942): 6–7; L. Nelson Bell, "Out of the Bag," *SPJ* (June 1944): 6–7; L. Nelson Bell, "Over the Left Field Wall—A Foul," *SPJ* (10 December 1958): 2–3; J. E. Flow, "The Federal Council and 'Race Segregation,'" *SPJ* (15 May 1946): 10.

predilection for managed solutions to social problems. In 1942, Charles C. Dickinson protested the Federal Council's support of the National Committee to Abolish the Poll Tax, which linked the PCUS with "radical organizations" and brought "politics into our church courts." Robert Vining suggested the following year that the Federal Council stood "vigorously opposed to capitalism." An examination of its documents would reveal "an underlying and deep-seated hostility" to the prevailing American economic system. In the late 1940s, L. E. Faulkner noted that the Federal Council represented "one of the most effective promoters of planned and managed economy which includes, of course, regimentation, collectivism, and different forms of national socialism." More ominously, the Federal Council also supported President Truman's "mis-named Civil Rights program" and "non-segregation of races." In fact, a comparison between the Communist Party platform and the Federal Council's would reveal striking commonality in goals and methods. In a similar fashion, the Continuing Church Committee declared in 1947 that "the Social views of the Federal Council, specifically urging the elimination of all racial segregation is both unwise and improper" and that "the economic views of the Federal Council are basically Socialistic and, if developed and accomplished as now proposed, will destroy the very foundations of Free Enterprise and Constitutional Government." William Childs Robinson begged the church to protest against the "superdenominational councils committing our Church against the American system of free enterprise." Nelson Bell questioned why the Federal Council spent so much time on economic and racial matters to the exclusion of weighty moral matters, such as gambling, alcohol use, and sexual immorality. The only thing he could conclude was that "those who actually control and direct the activities of the Federal Council have an interpretation of Christianity and a philosophy of life which is seriously impaired and which is therefore dangerous."[43]

43. Charles C. Dickinson, "Political Activities of the Federal Council of Churches," *SPJ* (December 1942): 12; Robert L. Vining, "The Federal Council: Foe of Capitalism," *SPJ* (August 1943): 5–7; L. E. Faulkner, "The Federal Council of Churches Encourages Regimentation," *SPJ* (15 November 1948): 14; L. E. Faulkner, "The Case against the Federal Council of Churches," *SPJ* (1 June 1950): 14–17; "The Findings of the Annual Meeting of

Not only was the Federal (and later the National) Council promoting socialist ideals and racial integration, it was also harboring and encouraging Communists. As early as 1943, Robert Vining charged that "certain aspects of Communism have made a strong appeal to some of the staff of the Federal Council." In 1948, Nelson Bell warned that leaders of this organization were spewing out "pro-Communist propaganda." A few months later, the Federal Council was faulted for placing America and Russia on the same level when it came to foreign policy. In 1950, the *Southern Presbyterian Journal* republished a strongly worded column from the Dallas *Morning News* that accused the Council of representing "socialist infiltration."[44]

The crowning evidence of the Communist threat represented by the National Council of Churches came when it advocated China's admission into the United Nations in 1958. For PCUS conservatives, this demonstrated beyond a shadow of a doubt the Council's softness on Communism. Nelson Bell cried that this action "must have brought great comfort and joy to Moscow and Peking." The *Southern Presbyterian Journal* also ran a series of exposés by Vernon Patterson and Horace Hull meant to reveal the National Council's deep commitments to Communist ideals: one such article concluded that its program "could not have more nearly conformed to the Communist 'line,' if it had originated in the Kremlin"; another charged that the leaders of the Council "have been and are *promoting a socialist revolution in America*. They will not be turned aside from this." Bell would

---

the Continuing Church Committee," *SPJ* (1 September 1947): 3; William Childs Robinson, "Capitalism: In Theory and Practice," *SPJ* (1 April 1949): 5; L. Nelson Bell, "A Dangerous Philosophy," *SPJ* (1 May 1950): 2–3. Faulkner, vice president and general manager of Mississippi Central Railroad Company, also made the same connections between centralization and race in "The Federal Council of the Churches of Christ in America: Let's Look at the Record," *SPJ* (15 April 1947): 12–13; "The Federal Council vs. Capitalism," *SPJ* (15 December 1948): 17–18; "The Voice of the Federal Council of the Churches of Christ in America Speaks for Your Church and You," *SPJ* (1 January 1949): 14–15; "The Federal Council of Churches Acts as a Political Action Committee," *SPJ* (15 September 1949): 23; "Our Storehouse of Freedom Is Being Robbed," *SPJ* (1 March 1950): 8–9; "The National Council of Churches," *SPJ* (4 June 1952): 6–7. See also Flow, "The Federal Council on Human Rights," 15–17.

44. Robert L. Vining, "The Federal Council and Communism," *SPJ* (September 1943): 21–23; L. Nelson Bell, "What Accord?," *SPJ* (15 May 1948): 3; L. Nelson Bell, "Our 'Spokesman' Again," *SPJ* (16 May 1949): 3; "Newspaper Columnists Expose Radical Teachings of Federal Council Leaders," *SPJ* (1 April 1950): 6–7.

soon demand that "there is no course left to Christians who disavow this leadership than to take effective measures through their respective church courts *and at the same time* discontinue the payment on any funds which might be channeled to the National Council for its use." Only by withholding money could conservatives remain free from the taint of "radical left-wing policies" advocated by the Council. Bell along with Henry Dendy would later observe that "we believe the National Council, as now led and operated, to be a menace to the welfare of the Church and of the nation."[45]

Yet even if they could cut off the National Council of Churches, conservatives could not be freed from progressive social actions taken in the name of their church. Particularly problematic for many PCUS conservatives was the way in which the National Council's positions were filtered into the denomination through the PCUS Council on Christian Relations. Conservatives had long seen the committee as providing a voice for progressive ministers and argued that it should be abolished, but these demands became more insistent after 1954. "There is growing dissatisfaction with the Council on Christian Relations," the *Southern Presbyterian Journal* observed in 1958. "Entirely too many of its recommendations come from sources outside our own church, particularly from the National Council of Churches." The previous year, the session of First Presbyterian Church, Jackson, Mississippi, had voted to de-fund the Board of Church Extension,

45. Bell, "Over the Left Field Wall," 2–3; Vernon W. Patterson, "The National Council Urges the Churches to Aid Communism," *SPJ* (25 February 1959): 9–10; Vernon W. Patterson, "The National Council's 'Social Gospel,'" *SPJ* (22 April 1959): 9–10 (emphasis his); L. Nelson Bell, "The National Council of Churches: Repudiation Necessary," *SPJ* (31 December 1958): 2–3 (emphasis his); "Who or What Is Divisive?," *SPJ* (21 January 1959): 2. Patterson and Horace H. Hull's other articles included: Vernon W. Patterson, "Misrepresentation by the National Council," *SPJ* (18 February 1959): 7–8; Horace H. Hull, "The National Council of Churches: How It Developed," *SPJ* (11 March 1959): 5–7; Horace H. Hull, "The National Council of Churches and It's [*sic*] Predecessor the Federal Council," *SPJ* (18 March 1959): 5–6; Horace H. Hull, "The Serpent Sheds Its Skin," *SPJ* (25 March 1959): 5–6; Horace H. Hull, "Pertinent Questions and Answers on the National Council of Churches," *SPJ* (1 April 1959): 5–7; Horace H. Hull, "The N.C.C.C. in the Mundane Sphere," *SPJ* (8 April 1959): 7–8; Horace H. Hull, "Can You Change a Leopard's Spots, Or, Can the National Council Be Reformed?," *SPJ* (15 April 1959): 7–9; Vernon W. Patterson, "Withdrawal the Only Recourse," *SPJ* (15 April 1959): 11–13; Horace H. Hull, "The National Council's 'Group Dynamics,'" *SPJ* (22 April 1959): 6–8.

under which the Council existed. Now the *Journal* and others sought to abolish the Council for bringing in "race mixing propaganda of the worst sort, written by some of the most radical crusaders and extremists in America, many of them having been connected with communist front organizations." A few months later, the *Journal*'s board of directors also protested how the programs of the National Council were "flooding our church" and even being taught to kindergarten Sunday school children.[46]

Against this centralized moralism, southern Presbyterian conservatives championed a more individualized Christian ethic. They repeatedly claimed that they were not denying that the church needed to "speak out" on moral or social issues. Rather, they held that they were challenging whether the venue for the church's witness was through "corporate Church action." As Nelson Bell observed, "When, in the name of the Church, she steps out into the world to make deliverance of any kind other than in the spiritual realm, she has either lowered or abdicated her mission." On the other hand, individual Christians had the duty to engage in social activity, affecting the society of which they were a part. "In other words," Bell went on to summarize, "it is the duty of the Church through her ministry and even through corporate actions, to teach Christians their duties as Christians. We believe her mission focuses at this point and stops right there." And yet when the PCUS did this—instructed Christians in their duties in matters of race, economics, alcohol, and labor—conservatives consistently held that these matters were "essentially secular in nature, and only incidentally related to the function or mission of the church as a religious institution." Once again, it appears that PCUS conservatives objected more strongly to the progressive message and centralized moralism of their denomination than to the need to engage social issues per se.[47]

46. "Christian Action and Coercion," *SPJ* (5 March 1958): 2–3; "Statement Adopted by the Session of the First Presbyterian Church of Jackson, Mississippi," 8–10; "To Our Beloved Church: An Affirmation and Appeal," *SPJ* (3 September 1958): 2–4.

47. L. Nelson Bell, "How Shall We Speak?," *SPJ* (28 May 1958): 2–3; John R. Richardson, "The 98th General Assembly," *SPJ* (14 May 1958): 13.

A CONSERVATIVE WORLDVIEW

The connection between the National Council of Churches and the progressive leaders of the PCUS, with their advocacy of managed solutions to complex social and political issues in the name of Jesus, would continue to push conservatives to articulate "hard truths," presumed to have been drawn from a "biblical worldview." This need to react enabled PCUS conservatives to link racial traditionalism, anticommunism, and libertarianism into a powerful argument for conservative dissent, stressing what was wrong with their church and their country. And this argument moved people to political activism both within and outside the church.[48]

In 1958, Dan McEachern publicized a new organization called "Presbyterian Laymen for Sound Doctrine and Responsible Leadership." The need for this group arose from the fact that "these laymen are convinced that the *liberal ministers* in our Church are taking our Church, in many of its programs, down strange roads which are in violation of the Standards of the Church and contrary to the desires of an overwhelming majority of the members of our Church." Yet when McEachern laid out his evidence for this charge, he pointed to a number of issues: the funding of the Council on Christian Relations by the Fund of the Republic, an organization that also funded "the NAACP and other race mixing organizations"; booklets published by the Council that represented "race mixing propaganda of the worst sort" and that "were written by some of the most radical men and women in the country" who "belonged to a number of Communist front organizations"; the invitation to James Robinson, a minister who had previously served the NAACP and "who freely admitted to having belonged to a large number of Communist front organizations," to speak at the Women's Conference; and the 1957 PCUS emphasis on Christian Citizenship, "which consisted mainly of a race mixing program." The theological objections (alleged violations of church

48. Samuel S. Hill, "Northern and Southern Varieties of American Evangelicalism in the Nineteenth Century," in *Evangelicalism: Comparative Studies of Popular Protestantism in North America, the British Isles, and Beyond*, ed. Mark A. Noll et al. (New York: Oxford University Press, 1994), 284–85; Schoenwald, *A Time for Choosing*, 6.

doctrinal standards) merged seamlessly with social and cultural protests (contravening conservative social mores).[49]

McEachern's organization was not the only laymen's organization that organized to battle both social and theological liberalism. A group from Selma, Alabama, led by local businessman John Ames, started in 1959 to "protest in everyway possible" against the fact that "the liberals have taken over the organized leadership of the church." As evidence for this, Ames cited the election of E. T. Thompson as moderator of the 1959 General Assembly. Thompson was elected by the "liberal machine" working to destroy the PCUS "as a spiritual organization," instead making it into "a political and social service organization." One of Thompson's nomination speeches was delivered by a man who was leading the effort "to bring about the integration of the public schools in Atlanta and the state of Georgia." And of course, Thompson himself was a notorious theological liberal, as demonstrated by Tom Glasgow, and a social liberal, as shown by his promotion of the PCUS support of *Brown v. Board of Education.* He had "led the liberals of the church in their efforts to bring about the integration of the races, not only in the church but in the public schools and the community life." Ames's group desired to raise conservatives' consciousness on these issues before it was too late; but like McEachern's, Ames's theological objections to the theology of Thompson and other liberals merged seamlessly with concerns over racial justice.[50]

This merger of doctrinal, political, racial, and economic conservatism represented the worldview of southern Presbyterian conservatives. In their minds, it was not possible to separate the strands; the same Bible that taught of Jesus' death, burial, and resurrection was the same Bible that legitimated segregation, championed individualism, and castigated Communism. The disagreement with PCUS progressives, then, was not whether the Bible spoke to social issues; rather,

49. Dan H. McEachern, "Shocked into Action," *SPJ* (8 October 1958): 10–11 (emphasis his).

50. "Southern Presbyterian Group Says 'Liberal' Ministers Running Church," *Mobile Register* (20 October 1959): 1; *Presbyterian Laymen for Sound Doctrine and Responsible Leadership* 1 (c. 1959); *Presbyterian Laymen for Sound Doctrine and Responsible Leadership* 2 (c. 1959). Copies of the *Presbyterian Laymen* can be found at the PCAHC.

the disagreement was whether the Bible supported traditionalist or progressive approaches to those issues. In addition, the two sides differed on the way of achieving social ends: progressives generally favored institutionally driven change through pronouncements, while conservatives desired personal, "natural," gradual change through evangelistic outreach and conversion. Those differences would come to be represented more clearly in the decade ahead.

6

"Can Two Walk Together Unless They Be Agreed?" Defeating Reunion with Northern Presbyterians

In 1952, when William C. Cumming went to Westminster Presbyterian Church, Texarkana, Texas, the PCUS was in the middle of a long debate over whether it should reunite with the northern PCUSA. Like many other conservative ministers, he was concerned about the proposed reunion. And his reasons for concern were typical, repeated over and over from 1937 until reunion was finally defeated in 1955. The northern church, Cumming argued, was lax on doctrine, and the evidence of this laxity was seen in the 1924 Auburn Affirmation—a document that affirmed a diversity of interpretations of doctrinal fundamentals—and in the ill treatment of northern Presbyterian conservative J. Gresham Machen in the 1930s. "As has been said, 'The Auburn Affirmation made the U.S.A. church safe for the Modernists,' and it might be added that it made it unsafe for anyone who dares to raise his voice in protest or tries to do anything about the disloyalty of the official leadership of the church," he wrote. The implication for southern conservatives was obvious: enter at one's own risk.[1]

1. William C. Cumming, "The Real Reason for Rejecting Reunion," *SPJ* (5 January 1955): 8. On the Auburn Affirmation and the PCUSA's treatment of Machen, see Sean Michael Lucas, *J. Gresham Machen* (Darlington, UK: Evangelical Press, 2015).

Even as southern Presbyterian conservatives fought with progressive ministers and elders, they recognized that they had no chance to reform the PCUS if their body joined with the PCUSA. After all, the "liberal group" in the PCUS had seized control of the church's machinery, exonerated theological liberals such as Hay Watson Smith and E. T. Thompson, worked to centralize power in church offices in Richmond and Atlanta, issued progressive social prounouncements, and revised the WCF. And yet there was a sense among conservatives that the grassroots of the church was essentially opposed to the progressive leadership and could be rallied if given enough time and information. On the other hand, if the progressives' hands were strengthened by the liberal element in the northern church, there would be no place for conservative witness in the church's future.[2]

And for these conservatives, such a future was impossible to imagine. On the one hand, the core doctrines of the gospel had to be preserved if future generations would come to Christ. Throughout the debate on reunion with the PCUSA, conservatives insisted that continued adherence to the fundamentals of the faith would be undermined if the plan of union were approved. They wrote countless articles defending "the fundamentals"—biblical inerrancy, the virgin birth of Jesus, his substitutionary death on the cross and bodily resurrection from the grave, the reality of miracles and the supernatural, and the hope of Jesus' literal and physical return.[3] These fundamentals were central to the gospel that gave individuals hope; divergence from them brought only death. As Nelson Bell observed, "Christianity—the Church—have prospered only as God, His Son, and His Word

2. Tom Glasgow, "Distressing," *SPJ* (1 August 1949): 3. Conservative belief in the "grassroots" was an axiom during this period: see, for example, Tom Glasgow to W. E. Everett, 31 July 1940, in Samuel M. Wilson Papers, Special Collections, University of Kentucky, Lexington, Kentucky.

3. See, by way of example, J. E. Flow, "The Word of God," *SPJ* (6 December 1950): 4; B. Hoyt Evans, "The Reliability of the Scriptures," *SPJ* (1 October 1952): 6–7; William Childs Robinson, "The Westminster Standards on the Bible," *SPJ* (31 December 1952): 3–4; L. Nelson Bell, "Some Reasons Why Evangelical Christians Believe in the Virgin Birth," *SPJ* (13 September 1950): 2–3; L. Nelson Bell, "What Did He Do?," *SPJ* (27 March 1951): 2; L. Nelson Bell, "Some Reasons Why the Evangelical Believes in the Resurrection," *SPJ* (7 October 1953): 2–3; L. Nelson Bell, "Neglected—A Great Doctrine," *SPJ* (27 December 1950): 4.

are given the place of unswerving loyalty and devotion on the part of those who bear His Name. The immediate future is fraught with the gravest dangers and the greatest of these is that men may compromise in their basic loyalty to the Christ of the Bible." Christianity itself was at stake in this battle.[4]

These religious issues, however, would find their place in a larger defense of a southern conservative cultural system in which anticommunism, anti-integration, and anticentralization served important roles as complicated defenses of the inspiration of the Bible. To separate these issues was impossible, both intellectually and by the force of events themselves. For example, J. E. Flow's five-point program that justified the continued existence of the southern church was presented in 1954 in the context of the fight against reunion—and joined next to a defense of Scripture and the Westminster Confession was "the purity and integrity of the White man of North America upon whose shoulders are laid the burdens of the world." And yet even if conservatives desired to move toward a more moderate position on issues of race and how that might relate to the possibility of reunion, the United States Supreme Court's decision in *Brown v. Board of Education* made such moderation difficult, especially when the same 1954 PCUS General Assembly that sent down the plan of union for presbytery votes also issued a report that recommended working for the integration of southern churches and schools. Suddenly, the controversy over reunion became more than a fight to preserve a southern church; it became a battle to preserve the southern way of life.[5]

STEPS TOWARD REUNION

The original impetus for reunion, which was decisively defeated in 1955, had actually begun twenty-six years before. At the 1929 General Assembly, several presbyteries had asked the denomination to "take active steps toward organic union of all Presbyterian bodies in the United States." Somewhat surprisingly, the Assembly overwhelmingly agreed to

4. L. Nelson Bell, "Two Philosophies and a Widening Chasm," *SPJ* (1 December 1954): 3.
5. J. E. Flow, "Positive or Negative?," *SPJ* (29 September 1954): 9. The PCUS did have a nongeographic synod for African Americans, Snedecor Memorial, but it was so small that it hardly factored into conservatives' self-image as a "white church."

do this, setting up an Ad Interim Committee to explore how to bring this to fruition. This committee did its work and reported to the General Assembly each year; the ebbs and flows were such that it did not appear to conservatives that reunion with the northern Presbyterians or organic union with other Presbyterian or Reformed bodies was a serious threat. While there was an attempt to allow for "federated churches" in 1936, in which a church could potentially have dual affiliation and that could open the door for union, this was defeated. In 1937, the committee recommended that "no action be taken touching any plan of union, since the plan of federal union advocated by our General Assembly has not met with acceptance on the part of our sister churches, and since they have not proposed any substitute therefor." In place of this recommendation, an audacious substitute was moved: that the committee be replaced with a Permanent Committee on Cooperation, with instructions "to explore the possibilities of cooperation or union with the other Presbyterian bodies and to report each year its progress to the General Assembly." Again, surprisingly, the substitute was passed without discussion or debate.[6]

Perhaps the other issues of the 1937 Assembly, especially confessional revision and attempts to reenter the Federal Council, distracted conservatives who stood against reunion. If so, the following year's general gathering shook them awake. The Permanent Committee on Cooperation reported that it had made great progress in reunion conversations with the northern Presbyterians. The developing proposal focused on creating stronger regional synods under a single General Assembly; this would allow the southern church to maintain some measure of local control within a single denominational body. As the

6. E. T. Thompson, *Presbyterians in the South*, 3 vols. (Richmond, VA: John Knox, 1963–73), 3:559–62; *MGAPCUS* (1937): 39, 123. One can follow the discussion on federated churches in the pages of *CO*: Samuel H. Sibley, "Constitutional Amendment Touching Federated Churches," *CO* (21 August 1935): 10; H. Tucker Graham, "Dual Membership," *CO* (18 September 1935): 15; James I. Vance, "Judge Sibley's Article," *CO* (18 September 1935): 15; George Summey, "Constitutional Amendment Touching Federated Churches," *CO* (25 September 1935): 10–11; Henry M. Woods, "Constitutional Amendment Touching Federated Churches," *CO* (23 October 1935): 24; C. T. Caldwell, "That Constitutional Amendment!," *CO* (13 November 1935): 10–11; J. M. Wells Jr., "The Proposed Amendment to the Book of Church Order," *CO* (26 February 1936): 15; C. H. Maury, "Presbyterians, U.S. and U.S.A. in South," *CO* (22 April 1936): 22.

report noted, "the members of the [Presbyterian Church in the] U.S.A. committee were explicit and emphatic in asserting that they would be quite ready and glad for all powers possible, consistent with maintaining the integrity of the reunited Church, to be taken from the Assembly and given to the Synods." At the 1938 General Assembly, meeting in Meridian, Mississippi, conservatives led by Tom Glasgow moved to shut the committee down. Glasgow felt that advocates for reunion had tried to influence the General Assembly's standing committee, which reviewed the permanent committee's work, in improper ways. He later reported how he had dealt with these progressive leaders: "A hot discussion developed in which I had to sit Dr. [E. T.] Wellford down pretty severely as he was badly out of order. Our committee decided to recommend that the whole Union Committee be thanked and released and another appointed." The personal acrimony of the committee's meeting spilled out on the Assembly's floor; Glasgow related, "I got the floor again and spoke for 45 minutes, giving the assembly all the details of our committee meetings. I was interrupted again and again from the floor but asked and gave no quarter. I believe it was the most trying debate I was ever in." The Assembly decided by a narrow vote to follow Glasgow; it dismissed the previous committee and set up a new expanded committee with broader regional participation.[7]

The result was little different. If anything, steam picked up for reunion with the northern church. The report of the new permanent committee to the 1939 General Assembly noted that the two committees representing the northern and southern churches agreed to look with favor on a reunion on the following terms: on the basis of the doctrinal standards of the two churches (which were soon to be the same standards as the result of the work of the PCUS Committee on Confessional Revision); the northern Presbyterian brief statement of faith, adopted in 1913; provision for newly reorganized synods that would provide local oversight and control; and the unity of the church maintained by a single General Assembly with merged boards for

7. *MGAPCUS* (1938): 56; "Reports to the General Assembly," *CO* (11 May 1938): 6; Tom Glasgow, "Personal Memoirs," E. T. Thompson Papers, UPS. Wellford was the minister at First Presbyterian Church, Newport News, Virginia; he was also chairman of the board of trustees at Union Theological Seminary, Richmond, Virginia.

missions, publication, and pensions. In addition, the northern Presbyterians would agree to maintain the southerners' segregated synod
for their African-American churches. Rather than taking action on
the report, the 1939 General Assembly referred it to the presbyteries
for their advice and direction.[8]

Not only did this action set in motion the possibility of drum-
ming up greater support for the idea of reunion, but it also activated
conservatives to begin opposing reunion. Edward Ford, a minister
from Thibodaux, Louisiana, offered what would become the single
most common argument against reunion. He pointed to failure of
northern Presbyterians to observe sound doctrine—as evidenced by
the 1924 Auburn Affirmation and the defrocking of conservative
minister J. Gresham Machen—as the reason not to reunite. The South
Carolina Presbytery passed a resolution not to reunite for the same
reason: "Just recently we recall the invasion of the Auburn Affirmationists resulted in virtual victory of the invaders." Likewise, ruling
elders from across the denomination protested reunion on the same
grounds, noting that the northern "Auburn Affirmationists" "have
filled and are filling leading pulpits, chairs in theological seminaries, and positions on the boards of the church." While the northern
church might not view the inspiration of Scripture or virgin birth of
Jesus to be fundamental, "we believe that the great doctrines rejected
by these men are vital and essential doctrines." Not only this, but the
northern church leaders "have disciplined men like Dr. J. Gresham
Machen and other stalwart upholders of the faith, and have shut
their eyes to the many Modernists who fill their pulpits and the
chairs of their seminaries." The *Mississippi Visitor* editorialized that
the northern church was a mixed bag doctrinally: "They have room
for the Auburn Affirmationists, but no room for men like J. Gresham
Machen." As a result, the southern church should remain separate
and continue to live.[9]

8. "General Assembly Report," *CO* (5 April 1939): 5.
9. Edward A. Ford, "The Question of Reunion," *CO* (24 May 1939): 12; D. J. Woods,
"Action of South Carolina Presbytery," *CO* (6 March 1940): 10; "Representative Elders of
All Synods Appeal to Fellow Elders to End Union Controversy and Save Their Church,"
Mississippi Visitor (October 1939): 1; "Let the Presbyterian Church Live," *Mississippi Visitor*

Robert Fry also noted that northern Presbyterians demonstrated "a marked difference in the interpretation of ecclesiastical authority" compared to southerners. The power of the General Council and church boards in the northern church stood in contrast to the alleged "grassroots" approach of the PCUS. The great evidence that this power could be abused was the Machen case, which had led to the creation of the Orthodox Presbyterian Church in 1936. In a fiery pamphlet, Tom Glasgow echoed these arguments. He observed that the only ministers to be expelled from the PCUSA were the Machen conservatives, who refused to "support all institutions and causes officially approved by the Northern Assembly. . . . Failing to conform to the orders of the Leaders of the Church, these Ministers were summoned before their presbyteries for trial." Such abuse of ecclesiastical authority—conservatives' being disciplined but liberals protected—was an obvious reason not to reunite. In fact, Glasgow urged, presbyteries needed to instruct the General Assembly to direct the committee to "refrain from all negotiations pursuant to union" with any church and especially the northern Presbyterian church.[10]

As debate continued to unfold over the potential of reunion, issues other than simply theological or ecclesial ones came to the forefront. Glasgow's brother, popular minister Samuel McPheeters Glasgow, noted that the southern church's special testimony was "the unique spiritual nature of the church," a witness that would be lost in reunion. Tom Glasgow followed that up by noting how the northern Assembly made political pronouncements on a range of cases dealing with racial violence in the South, including the case of the Scottsboro nine and the advocacy of antilynching laws. These cases demonstrated that the northern church consistently failed to recognize

---

(July 1939): 3. In a separate issue, the *Mississippi Visitor* gave a historical overview of the entire background for the Auburn Affirmation and why it was problematic: see "Against What Did the Auburn Affirmationists Protest?," *Mississippi Visitor* (February 1940): 3–4.

10. Robert Excell Fry, "The Problem of Reunion," *CO* (12 July 1939): 10; Tom Glasgow, *Is Union Wise between the Northern and Southern Presbyterian Churches—Now?* (Charlotte, NC: privately printed, 1939), 2–3; Tom Glasgow, "Shall We Continue to Seek Union with the U.S.A. Church?," *CO* (19 July 1939): 13. J. M. Wells Jr. also pointed to the Machen case as an example of unbridled Yankee force and a reason not to reunite: "Strife or Progress?," *CO* (2 August 1939): 10.

that "the Church is a spiritual body and that these matters lie within
the province of the civil or state authorities and not the Church." J. W.
Campbell also objected to the way in which the northern church inter-
jected itself into "the political convictions" of southerners, pointing to
the "anti-lynching bill" as "a political slur at the South." In February
1940, a group of ruling elders released "A Letter from Ruling Elders
to the Ruling Elders of the Presbyterian Church in the United States."
Their open letter addressed not only the theological and ecclesial
issues involved, but also "the race question": "We must keep our hands
free to settle it as our judgment, here on the ground, deems wise and
best and right. . . . You cannot afford to let control of the best way to
handle this question pass from you." Theological looseness and racial
openness both made the northern church suspect.[11]

Southern Presbyterian progressives were not silent. One of the key
promoters of reunion, Dunbar Ogden, minister at Napoleon Avenue
Presbyterian Church in New Orleans, published a pamphlet promoting reunion. Collecting articles originally published in the *Christian
Observer*, Ogden dealt with the common objections to reunion. To
those who suggested that the Auburn Affirmation indicated the theological drift of the northern church, Ogden breezily claimed that "it
is a well-known fact that in these past fifteen years there has been a
decided movement toward theological conservatism. The modernism which then influenced sections of the U.S.A. Church is now
discredited." Those who used the expulsion of J. Gresham Machen
as evidence of bureaucratic overreach needed to understand that the
cause of Machen's deposition—the erection of a new independent
Presbyterian mission board—was profoundly un-Presbyterian and
would have been dealt with as such in the southern church as well.

11. Samuel McPheeters Glasgow, "Union or a Continuing Church?," *CO* (6 September
1939): 10; Tom Glasgow, "Union or Unity," *CO* (20 September 1939): 22–23; J. W. Campbell, "Do We Want Union?," *CO* (29 November 1939): 15; "A Letter from Ruling Elders
to the Ruling Elders," *CO* (28 February 1940): 15, 22. Among the elders who signed the
open letter were three key conservative leaders: J. Park McCallie (from First Presbyterian
Church, Chattanooga, Tennessee); Samuel M. Wilson (from Lexington, Kentucky); and
W. Calvin Wells (from First Presbyterian Church, Jackson, Mississippi). This open letter
was the same letter that had been published in October 1939 with sixteen signatures from
leading ruling elders in each synod.

And those who worried about the proposed union of the northern church with the Protestant Episcopal Church should recognize that it was all simply conversation that might never be realized. As a result, he argued, the Assembly should instruct its Permanent Committee on Cooperation to continue conversations toward a potential reunion.[12]

Not surprisingly, Ogden's pamphlet drew a sharp response from southern Presbyterian conservatives. William Childs Robinson observed that Ogden's special pleading did not do away with the fact that reunion would be on the northern church's terms, leading to an organic union in which the southern Presbyterian witness would "be brushed aside and we are to become a part of the larger body." Ogden also failed to recognize, Robinson observed, that the principle in the Machen case was that he had been required to act against his conscience in a matter not regulated by Scripture and had been convicted without a fair trial, which was an example of a "legislative exercise of power." Further, the basis of reunion—the common doctrinal standards of both churches—did not reassure at all in light of the Auburn Affirmation. "We would be giving away our corporate testimony to the doctrine of the atonement found in our Standards and in the Brief Statement, by joining a Church in which this large group of ministers, many of them highly honored by their Church, maintain that this doctrine of the work of Christ is not necessary for Presbyterian ordination," Robinson concluded. Clearly, for conservatives, reunion could not happen.[13]

Robinson would go on to lodge other arguments against union with the northern Presbyterians. He understood Jesus' words in John 17, which appear to commend unity among his followers, as not ruling out the propriety of denominational divisions: "We officially declare that the visible unity of the Church is not destroyed by denominational divisions, but that all of these denominations which maintain the Word and the sacraments in their fundamental integrity

12. Dunbar Hunt Ogden, *Reunion of the Presbyterian Churches, U.S.A. and U.S.* (n.p.: privately printed, [1939?]), 23–24.

13. William Childs Robinson, "Reunion of the Presbyterian Churches, U.S.A. and U.S.: Pamphlet by Rev. Dunbar Hunt Ogden," *CO* (24 January 1940): 11, 22. Ogden replied to Robinson in "That Pamphlet on Reunion," *CO* (21 February 1940): 14–15.

are true branches of the Church of Jesus Christ." Even more, the history of the church demonstrated that early on the church had remarkable organizational diversity and that its unity was doctrinal, not organizational. All of this made it difficult to conceive of union with a church that "passes such legislation as the Spring resolution," an 1861 resolution that demanded loyalty to the national government and forced the division of the Presbyterian church on the eve of the American Civil War. Conservative theologian George Summey agreed. Unity did not require church union; in fact, "outward union, forced against some of these conditions, would be anything but unity." Such conditions would include differences in doctrine, church order, or even "racial conditions." Clearly, there were vast differences in doctrine between the northern and southern churches; Summey pointed to the "prevalence of so-called 'liberal' types and interpretation of doctrine; [and] the huge emphasis placed upon a so-called 'social gospel'" as well as the top-down judicial processes that showed up in 1837, 1866, and more recently in the Machen case. To move into union with such a church would lead simply to "absorption," with the loss of independence and local control.[14]

By the time the 1940 General Assembly arrived, it was clear that a majority of presbyteries favored continuing dialogue toward reunion with the northern Presbyterian church. Forty-five presbyteries asked that the Permanent Committee on Cooperation and Union be continued as it was; only twenty-nine mustered opposition, while another ten asked that the committee focus only on cooperation. On the floor of the Assembly, there was lengthy debate over the permanent committee's report, which came through the Standing Committee on "Foreign Relations" (that is, relationships with other churches). Conservatives repeatedly attempted to kill any possibility of union, culminating with a substitute motion from Judge Samuel Wilson, a ruling elder from Lexington, Kentucky. Wilson's substitute resolved that the plan of union previously proposed in 1939 was to be "disapproved and rejected." His motion also sought to dismiss the recently

14. William C. Robinson, "Organizational Unification and Its Arguments," *CO* (27 March 1940): 14; George Summey, "Unity or Union," *CO* (17 April 1940): 11.

expanded committee. After lengthy debate, Wilson's substitute was overwhelmingly rejected, 212–65. In the final report, the Assembly agreed to continue the permanent committee with two major purposes: "to stress co-operation with other Presbyterian bodies" and "to continue to explore in search of suitable ways and means of bringing into one body all the branches of our Presbyterian family." But conservatives were able to force language into the recommendation that urged the committee "to safeguard the purity of doctrine, the properties of the churches and endowments, the theological seminaries and other educational institutions, the administration of Home Missions, the direction of Foreign Missions supported by the respective Synods, and the content of Sunday school literature." While advocating continued exploration of reunion, southerners also expressed hesitation and doubt.[15]

PLAN FOR UNION

The attempt to reunite the northern and southern Presbyterian churches began in earnest in 1943, when the Permanent Committee on Cooperation and Union presented the first draft of a proposed plan of union to the church. Although it was referred back to the permanent committee, the plan put conservatives on notice. When the plan of union was sent to the churches and presbyteries for their comments in 1944, southern Presbyterian conservatives raised argument after argument against the plan. The fact that they now had the *Southern Presbyterian Journal* as a communication medium made the task of persuading the church easier.[16]

First and foremost, southern Presbyterian conservatives desired to preserve a church that defended the "fundamentals" of the faith, and they warned repeatedly that the northern Presbyterian church was a theologically liberal church. Even before the first plan of union was proposed, Robert Vining warned against any union that would lead to

15. "The General Assembly Proceedings," *CO* (29 May 1940): 18–19; *MGAPCUS* (1940): 66.

16. A quick sketch of reunion discussions between 1943 and 1947 can be found in Thompson, *Presbyterians in the South*, 3:565; *MGAPCUS* (1943): 61; *MGAPCUS* (1944): 79. See also L. Nelson Bell, "One Elder Looks at the General Assembly," *SPJ* (June 1943): 7.

a "surrender of Christian truth." He then sought to demonstrate that any "profession of loyalty to its doctrinal standards by the Presbyterian Church, U.S.A., seems empty in view of its official actions in recent years." Nelson Bell agreed, noting that "the official actions of the majority of these brethren during the past ten years clearly indicate that they do not consider soundness of doctrine as of prime importance." Once again, the key piece of evidence was the northern church's 1924 Auburn Affirmation as evidence of the northern church's theological unreliability. Daniel Gage subjected the Auburn Affirmation to a detailed analysis and concluded that it pointed to the northern church's entrenched theological indifferentism. Bell observed that "until the Auburn Affirmation is officially repudiated by the Northern Church, it remains a fact that what we consider essential doctrines of Christianity are not considered essential for ordination in that Church." In 1946, Bell again suggested that "the Auburn Affirmation, unrepudiated and unrepented of, lies as an insurmountable barrier to plans for union. Within these five points, declared unessential by the Affirmationist, lies the very heart of the Gospel message." Chalmers W. Alexander cited the Auburn Affirmation as the key doctrinal barrier between the two churches and gave a lengthy exposition of it for laymen.[17]

Conservatives sought other lines of evidence about the northern church's doctrinal deviancy. When northern Presbyterians elected noted theological liberal Henry Sloan Coffin as moderator in 1943, southern Presbyterian conservatives seized this as evidence of the church's unsoundness. W. Calvin Wells observed that the proposed plan of union would demote ruling elders, move ordination in an episcopal direction, and introduce women elders into the church.

17. Robert L. Vining, "Church Union," *SPJ* (February 1943): 18–20; Daniel S. Gage, "The Auburn Affirmation," *SPJ* (August 1942): 16–18; L. Nelson Bell, "What Is Progress?," *SPJ* (April 1943): 20–21; L. Nelson Bell, "Can Union Unite?," *SPJ* (May 1944): 4; L. Nelson Bell, " 'Interpreting' and the Auburn Affirmation," *SPJ* (15 February 1946): 3–5; Richardson Ayers, "The Real Issue in Union," *SPJ* (15 March 1946): 8–9; Chalmers W. Alexander, "Unite with the Northern Presbyterian Church? No!," *SPJ* (15 July 1947): 9–11. Other articles citing the Auburn Affirmation as sufficient grounds for not reuniting with the PCUSA: William C. Robinson, "The Liberal Attack upon the Supernatural Christ," *SPJ* (1 May 1946): 4–5; D. B. Gregory, "Remaining Obstacles to Union," *SPJ* (1 June 1946): 6–7; J. E. Flow, "One Union Too Many," *SPJ* (1 August 1950): 11–12; Paul D. Hastings, "The Main Objection to Union," *SPJ* (15 July 1953): 8.

William Childs Robinson noted that Henry Van Dusen, professor of systematic theology at Union Seminary in New York City, not only denied the virgin birth of Jesus, but also claimed that Jesus was not the eternal Son of God. Later, Robinson pointed out that northern Presbyterian minister Illon Jones denied the historicity and objectivity of Christ's resurrection and later became vice president at the PCUSA San Francisco Theological Seminary. More often than not, however, conservatives simply asserted that the northern church contained "various parties within the Church as divergent as theological poles can separate them"; such a broad church and such theological liberalism argued against reunion.[18]

But there were also telltale signs of doctrinal deviancy within the southern church itself. Conservatives reacted strongly when Columbia Seminary professor Samuel Cartledge published his *A Conservative Introduction to the Old Testament* in 1943, which seemed to promote more progressive understandings of biblical inspiration. One conservative writer observed that doctrinal confusion in the church was deepened "when a professor of another leading Seminary spreads further confusion by declaring the known and accepted Liberal interpretation of Scripture as actually being the 'Conservative' position thereon." Nelson Bell demanded that Columbia Seminary force Cartledge to publish a retraction of the offensive material in his book. A third writer observed that "a low view of inspiration on the part of the professor will inevitably bring many of his students to the same position." The fact that these liberal positions were now becoming accepted in some portions of the southern church was even worse: "It is little comfort to the thoughtful mind should it be pled that some of our Church Courts now support this interpretation of Scriptures. This support, such as it is, comes after years of infiltration [as] students, coming under this liberal teaching, have entered pulpits throughout the Church." All the more reason to raise the wall against union with the northern

18. Henry B. Dendy, "The Moderator of the U.S.A. Church," *SPJ* (July 1943): 4; Bell, "Can Union Unite?," 4; William C. Robinson, "Is Southern Presbyterianism Ready to Receive a Theological Liberalism Which Does Not Accept the Deity of Christ?," *SPJ* (August 1944): 9; Robinson, "The Liberal Attack upon the Supernatural Christ," 5; W. Calvin Wells, "Church Union," *SPJ* (April 1944): 16–17.

church; if liberals in the southern church gained strength through union, then conservative Presbyterians would have no hope of rescuing their church.[19]

And so, over and over, conservatives hammered the doctrinal issue. William Crowe observed in 1944 that "when Southern Presbyterians speak of organic union, they are talking about a unity in belief; whereas, in the North, in discussing the same subject, the thought in mind is unity in government." Likewise, Nelson Bell argued that the southern Presbyterian conservative "insists that from the time of Paul the message has ever been the same, while the liberal, cutting loose from the absolute authority of the Bible, has a message varying with the time and teaching of liberal thinkers." Daniel Iverson agreed, claiming that "doctrinal purity has really become an issue in Protestant Christianity today, and it is of vital concern in matters pertaining to union." Richardson Ayers pointed out that the "first and foremost" question before the church was one of "belief," which led back to the essential doctrines questioned in the Auburn Affirmation. Herbert Springall noted that "the basic, central problem is to find, if possible, a common denominator for the interpretation of the most important truths of the Christian faith as set forth in the Standards of both denominations. The true source of all difficulties is spiritual, not mechanical; it is belief, not action; doctrine, not administration."[20]

This conservative defense of biblical doctrines merged with a defense of conservative politics and social practices. In fact, conservatives made the point that liberal theology led to progressive social action. Vernon Patterson noted that "the natural result of this doctrinal declension [in the northern Presbyterian church] has been an increasing emphasis upon social and political activities, humanistic rather than spiritual." Included in those social activities were "inter-racial

---

19. "What Is Truth?," *SPJ* (July 1943): 4; L. Nelson Bell, "A Bent Sword," *SPJ* (July 1943): 5; "Needed—A Clear Distinction," *SPJ* (August 1943): 2; "A Sacred Trust," *SPJ* (September 1943): 2.

20. William Crowe, "Is Organic Union of the Presbyterian Churches to Be Disired [*sic*]?," *SPJ* (July 1944): 13–14; L. Nelson Bell, "A Layman Looks at Liberalism," *SPJ* (15 September 1945): 3; Daniel Iverson, "Unionitis," *SPJ* (1 March 1946): 13; Ayers, "The Real Issue in Union," 8–9; Herbert S. Springall, "What Would Be the Gain in Union?," *SPJ* (1 April 1946): 23.

programs aiming at complete social equality between the races." He summed up the northern church's programs as "anti-capitalistic and socialistic, and some are near-communistic." Nelson Bell agreed, matter-of-factly stating that "extreme liberal theology, placing as it does its main emphasis on the establishment of a better social order, has only too often found itself expressing sympathy with, and even approval of, many things in the Communistic program."[21]

Because the northern church had embraced "liberal" theology, which led to progressive social and political programs, PCUS conservatives feared that merger would also lead to liberalized racial and political practices in the South. In response, a group of conservative leaders met at Montreat in 1944 to form the "Continuing Church Committee," which would "promote a vigorous and aggressive education program" about the plan of union. In assessing proposed union with the northern church, these leaders observed that there were important differences in the way in which the churches viewed "the proper function of the church in dealing with social, political, and racial problems," which "would undoubtedly give rise to hurtful controversy in the church." Two years later, Randolph Lee noted that the northern church was on record for racial inclusiveness; and yet "it is not the business of the Church to push a program that seems to have as its end the amalgamation of the races." William Childs Robinson protested the plan of union, as it developed, because it did not provide for segregated presbyteries and synods. He disputed any plan that would encourage blacks "to think that we expect the amalgamation of the races," and especially when that plan was determined by "USA 'Liberals,' who do not have the Negro question as acutely before them as we do."[22]

Indeed, southern conservatives repeatedly cited the fear of northern coercive action in a reunited church. R. L. McNair warned that

21. Vernon W. Patterson, "Organic Union with Spiritual Unity?," *SPJ* (15 February 1946): 9; L. Nelson Bell, "Protestants-Catholics and Communism," *SPJ* (15 July 1946): 2.

22. John R. Richardson, "How the Continuing Committee Got Its Name," *SPJ* (15 January 1948): 2–3; "Continuing Church Committee Holds Meet[ing] in Atlanta," *SPJ* (15 December 1945): 5–6; Randolph Lee, "An Open Letter," *SPJ* (15 March 1947): 4; William Childs Robinson, "Are the U.S.A. Liberals to Determine the Terms of Union?," *SPJ* (15 March 1946): 5–6.

"on a question of local interest or opinion, our vote would count for practically nothing. . . . Prominent[] among these is the present race question." He feared "the possibility of opening to all races our schools and colleges, our seminaries and even our orphanages, to say nothing of our churches and conventions." In 1949, Bell warned that merger with the northern Presbyterians might lead to a coercive approach to racial reconciliation, upsetting "the gradual and wise" progress that southerners were making on their own. A few years later, William H. Frazer argued that one of the key reasons for preserving the PCUS was "its sensible attitude toward racial relations." That meant demonstrating respect and Christian love toward blacks while avoiding "social intermingling of the races." W. C. Tenney opposed union with the northern church because it "has in practice adopted views and policies in the field of economic and social relations at variance with those of the Southern Church." Especially troubling was that church's continued entrance into "the field of politics in the formulating and advocating [of] particular employer and labor policies and laws, and civil rights legislation about which honest and intelligent persons differ in judgment."[23]

Throughout the debate, conservatives warned that union with the northern church could mean secession by some from that newly united church. Nelson Bell questioned whether "advocates of union at any price realize that they can persist until they cause a split in our own church." H. Tucker Graham confidently predicted that "as there 'will always be an England behind the white cliffs of Dover,' so will there always be a Southern Presbyterian Church. Hence it is crystal clear that those who are promoting union are unconsciously fostering disunion." J. E. Flow agreed, observing that regardless of what happened with the union vote, "there will still be a Southern Presbyterian Church. It may be greatly depleted and poor in this world's goods, after being robbed of its property, but it will be a church that stands for the faith once delivered to the saints, and there will be Ruling Elders in it who are

23. R. L. McNair, "Is Organic Union Desirable?," *SPJ* (15 May 1946): 5; L. Nelson Bell, "Shadows of Things to Come?," *SPJ* (15 July 1949): 3; William H. Frazer, "Why I Favor Preserving the Southern Church," *SPJ* (23 July 1952): 7–8; W. C. Tenney, "The Plan of Union," *SPJ* (3 March 1954): 7–8; "Disturbing," *SPJ* (10 March 1954): 1.

not willing to sell their birthright for a mess of pottage." In thinking about all of the church's property in colleges, seminaries, missionary holdings, and conference grounds, R. L. McNair suggested that if a division came, "the only fair and honest proposition would be made in the offer to allow the Southern Church—the rightful owner of all of it—to hold it, and for those who go out to relinquish it, since they would be no longer any part of the original organization." Chalmers Alexander warned that division would occur because conservatives "do not have the least intention in the world of merging with the heresy-tainted Northern Presbyterian Church. If merger does take place, we intend to sever our connection with the Presbyterian Church." The Continuing Church Committee was prepared for just that contingency, for "it was dedicated to the preservation of the Presbyterian Church, U.S., and to conserve its priceless heritage."[24]

But there was hope that the moment for division would not be yet. By 1948, it had become clear to progressive leaders seeking to shepherd reunion that they did not have enough votes in order to accomplish their goal. As a result, the Permanent Committee on Cooperation and Union recommended "that for a period of five years the entire plan of reunion with the Presbyterian Church, U.S.A., be held in abeyance, and that during this time the committee confine its activities to explore avenues of acquaintance and cooperation only." On the surface, this period of delay seemed to suggest that the plan of union would be shelved in order to drum up more support for it. Conservatives wrongly believed, however, that the tabling of the plan meant that no one from either side should or would agitate the issue. Nelson Bell typified this confusion: "By the recent action of the General Assembly discontinuing all activities for union for a period of five years, this issue has been set aside and the emphasis of the church again brought to focus on its primary work and mission. As an evidence of good faith it was announced on the floor of the

24. L. Nelson Bell, "It Could Happen," *SPJ* (1 January 1946): 3; H. Tucker Graham, "Union or Disunion?," *SPJ* (1 March 1947): 28; J. E. Flow, "Where Are We Going?," *SPJ* (15 April 1946): 30–31; McNair, "Is Organic Union Desirable?," 6; Alexander, "Unite with the Northern Presbyterian Church? No!," 11; Richardson, "How the Continuing Committee Got Its Name," 2–3.

General Assembly that the annual meetings of the Continuing Church Committee which have been held each Summer in Montreat would be discontinued for the next five years." Bell thought that evangelism and revival would replace conversations about reunion for five years; he was to be proved sadly mistaken.[25]

Almost immediately, Bell tried to clarify his understanding of the Assembly's decision to hold the plan in "abeyance." He wanted it to be clear that "this action was aimed to *restrict* the activities of our Permanent Committee on Cooperation and Union for a period of five years." Twice more in the same article, Bell emphasized that the intent of the action was to "limit" and "restrict" the reunion activities. He also recognized that if the committee did not restrict its activities, the result would be potentially disastrous for conservatives: "Those who oppose union under present conditions have no idea of permitting the misinterpreting of this Assembly action so as to bring about a 'fait accompli' five years hence." That, however, was exactly what progressives intended, as became clear in the following months. By March 1949, it was obvious that the union committee had no intention of embracing a moratorium on its activity, but was engaged in a wide range of activities to increase relational ties with northern Presbyterians. Bell was left to sputter, "We do not believe many of the proponents of union who were present at the last Assembly will stand by quietly and see our Church precipitated into controversy afresh when they know a violation of both the spirit and intention of the Assembly's action" by the committee was taking place.[26]

At the 1949 General Assembly, conservatives tried to force the Assembly to agree with their understanding of the "moratorium" on the plan of reunion. This attempt failed miserably, which left Tom Glasgow

25. *MGAPCUS* (1948): 30, 63; L. Nelson Bell, "The Continuing Church Committee," *SPJ* (15 June 1948): 3; L. Nelson Bell, "The General Assembly: One Layman's Appraisal," *SPJ* (15 June 1948): 5. For evidence that the tabling of the plan of union was for the purpose of cultivating support, see Thompson, *Presbyterians in the South*, 3:566–67.

26. L. Nelson Bell, "Restrictive—Not Directive," *SPJ* (15 July 1948): 2 (emphasis his); L. Nelson Bell, "Unthinkable," *SPJ* (1 March 1949): 2–3; "Dr. Bell's Letter to Dr. Ogden and Dr. McCain," *SPJ* (1 March 1949): 4–5. McCain responded to Bell in "Agitation as to Union," *SPJ* (16 May 1949): 9. That other conservatives shared Bell's understanding is obvious from "The Continuing Church Committee: A Statement," *SPJ* (1 October 1948): 2–3.

to observe, "This action of the recent Assembly again confirms the fact that there was no meeting of minds in the Atlanta moratorium resolution and hence no moratorium declared." And so conservatives revved up their opposition once again. They held a meeting at Second Presbyterian Church, Birmingham, Alabama, where William Childs Robinson and Wilbur Cousar outlined many of the flaws in the proposed plan to reunite with the northern Presbyterians. Not only this, but Robinson and Cousar noted how the leading theologians in the northern church leaned "toward naturalism as against supernaturalism" and approached the Bible on a "rationalistic basis," as evidenced in their Sunday school literature and other publications. Of course, southern progressives were at work doing the same as well as furthering avenues of "acquaintance and cooperation" with the northern church. And PCUS progressive leaders also desired to see this merger include more denominations; in 1950, the Assembly invited "other Presbyterian and Reformed bodies asking them to consider a larger union of all churches of the Presbyterian family." In the event, the United Presbyterian Church of North America (UPCNA), a small northern Presbyterian denomination, pursued this invitation. By 1952, the drive for reunion had become a three-way union among the mainline northern and southern Presbyterian branches and the UPCNA.[27]

Even as these union talks continued, southern Presbyterian conservatives tried to find a legal basis for taking their church property with them if they needed to leave a united church. Henry Davis, a South Carolina lawyer, tried to spell out the legal principles involved in a local southern Presbyterian congregation's ownership of church property. He urged individual congregations to incorporate for the purpose of holding title to their properties for themselves and not for the denomination, and "I challenge any merged Church to take [your property] away from you. . . . This is the Presbyterianism that has been understood and practiced in the South since the first Presbyterian Church was established therein." J. E. Flow noted that the PCUS *Book of Church Order* itself placed the ownership of property with the local congregation. At

27. Tom Glasgow, "The End of a Moratorium Which Never Existed," *SPJ* (1 July 1949): 2–3; "Enthusiastic Meeting at Birmingham," *SPJ* (15 November 1949): 3; *MGAPCUS* (1950): 37, 86–87.

the same time, Tom Glasgow suggested that the whole issue of church property was not an ecclesiastical matter at all, but merely a civil affair subject to the laws of the various states. Nelson Bell warned that the northern and southern branches of the Presbyterian church had different understandings of church property; merger would bring all the southern Presbyterian church property under the northern Presbyterian understanding of holding property in trust for the denomination. The obvious implication for southern Presbyterians: if a church wanted to maintain control of its church property, it should fight reunion; and if that fight failed, it should make every effort to enter a "continuing Presbyterian church" with its property.[28]

In order to prepare better for such an eventuality, on 20 August 1952, the Continuing Church Committee met and formed itself into an "Association for the Preservation and Continuation of the Southern Presbyterian Church." Not only would this association work toward preserving the PCUS and preventing reunion, but if reunion happened, it would provide the structures for a new Presbyterian body that would serve as the continuation of the old church. It centered its "unique testimony" on the fact that the PCUS was "historically a confessional church"; the association was "dedicated, therefore, not so much to a preservation of a Church, but rather to the preservation of a clear witness." And yet in the editorials that followed the announcement of this association, it seemed as though the continuing witness would include other matters: not just purity of doctrine, but also the local ownership of church property, the spiritual mission of the church, and "the matter of 'race relations' that divides the two branches." After all, the northern church "demands the abrogation of segregation, and

---

28. Henry E. Davis, "A Legal Principle," *SPJ* (20 September 1950): 16; J. E. Flow, "Majority Rule," *SPJ* (18 October 1950): 6; Tom Glasgow, "The Title to Church Property," *SPJ* (15 November 1950): 10–11; L. Nelson Bell, "Presbyterian Doctrines of Church Property," *SPJ* (1 June 1950): 3–4; Henry B. Dendy, "Prominent U.S.A. Presbyterian Leaders Declare Their Stand on Church Property Issue," *SPJ* (29 November 1950): 6–7. Other significant treatments on church property before the 1954–55 vote included: L. Elmo Holt, "The Presbyterian Doctrine of Church Property: A Reply," *SPJ* (20 August 1952): 6–9; C. Ellis Ott, "The Status of Church Property in the Southern Presbyterian Church," *SPJ* (27 August 1952): 9–10; William C. Robinson, "Historical Observations on Local Church Property," *SPJ* (15 April 1953): 3–4.

the allowing of races to intermingle without any adherence to racial lines," while the southern church believed that Christian love could exist between the races only with the preservation of "racial integrity." It was this merger of biblical belief and social relations that made the threat of "absorption" by the northern church so fearful.[29]

THE YEAR OF DECISION

By the time the presbyteries had the opportunity to vote on union with the northern church in 1954, all the arguments had been rehearsed and rehashed numerous times. But as they actually considered the plan, they did so in the aftermath of a General Assembly meeting that had encouraged the denomination and its members to work for the desegregation of southern society. All these issues—fears of ecclesiastical centralization and totalitarianism along with racial liberalization and progressive theology—served to crystallize conservative dissent in an unexpected way. Although proposals for cooperation and union, along with racial integration, had been supported by the General Assembly with strong majorities, union with the northern Presbyterian church was defeated by a majority of presbyteries. Nelson Bell, for one, would not have been surprised by that final result. As the final version of the plan had been sent to the presbyteries for study in 1953 before it would be finally approved by the General Assembly for the final vote the next year, he noted, "It is estimated by observing men that possibly as many as forty Presbyteries will vote *against* the proposed union, while only twenty-three adverse votes are required to defeat the plan." In the event, forty-three presbyteries voted against the plan, but it required both hard work by conservatives and the unpredictable ordering of events to make it happen.[30]

Fears over church-led efforts to work for the end of segregation were stoked in early 1954 when the *Southern Presbyterian Journal* published a copy of a letter written by the assistant secretary of the PCUSA board

29. "Meeting of the Association for the Preservation and Continuation of the Southern Presbyterian Church," *SPJ* (3 September 1952): 1; "An Announcement," *SPJ* (3 September 1952): 16; William C. Robinson, "The Church Union Issue," *SPJ* (1 October 1952): 3–4; W. H. Frazer, "Desire for Union," *SPJ* (24 September 1952): 3.

30. L. Nelson Bell, "The Dilemma," *SPJ* (12 August 1953): 3 (emphasis his).

of Christian education. On the surface, the letter was an information piece, alerting pastors that young people who qualified, regardless of race, could get funds for college if they were willing to attend a college "predominantly of the other race." Henry Dendy, however, read this letter as evidence that "there is afoot a movement to subsidize students for the specific purpose of breaking down segregation." As such, it was a program of "infiltration" and an unchristian effort on the part of the northern Presbyterians "to promote the breaking down of a pattern of life on a basis of racial origin." Then, a couple of months later, when the PCUSA stated clerk, Eugene Carson Blake, appeared "on behalf of" the northern church before the Fair Employment Practices Commission, once again the *Journal* highlighted the racial aspects of this event: the commission existed "to force an employer" to hire "a Negro"; if someone else was hired, the employer could be sued to show that "he had not discriminated against a Negro"; even more, the fact that the stated clerk appeared to discuss these matters gave "a picture of coming events if union of the Churches transpires. Here we see the autocratic and authoritarian powers of church leaders. Here, also, we see a total disregard for our feelings and judgments in a specific matter." The conclusion was straightforward: "Brothers—stay out of this proposed union."[31]

Two weeks before the General Assembly was to convene in Montreat, the United States Supreme Court delivered its decision in *Brown v. Board of Education*, in which it proclaimed that "separate-but-equal" education facilities were "inherently unequal" and should have no place in American society. With that decision, the Court dismantled the legal basis for segregation in education even while it would require several years and legislative action to integrate the public schools in a meaningful fashion. In response to this decision, the Standing Committee on Christian Relations, the annually appointed committee that reviewed the work of the Council on Christian Relations, issued "A Statement to Southern Christians." In the statement, the committee recommended that the Assembly adopt this statement: "Having in mind the recent decision by the Supreme Court of the United States concerning segregation, the Assembly commends the principle of the

31. Henry B. Dendy, "Behind the Scenes," *SPJ* (20 January 1954): 6–7; "Disturbing," 1.

decision and urges all members of our churches to consider thought-fully and prayerfully the complete solution of the problem involved. It also urges all our people to lend their assistance to those charged with the duty of implementing the decision." There was great outrage on the floor of the Assembly from conservatives, led by Tom Glasgow, who tried to have the report tabled. But the attempt to table the report failed by a 165-to-239 vote, and it was passed by nearly the same margin.[32]

When the Permanent Committee on Cooperation and Union finally presented the plan of union to the General Assembly for its approval, debate on the floor lasted four hours. Part of the reason for this was that conservatives, led by *Journal* supporter and ruling elder Chalmers Alexander, had packed the standing committee that reviewed the report and brought a majority report that recommended that the question of union "be answered in the negative" and that "the Committee on Cooperation and Union be dissolved and its members be thanked for their faithful service." There was a minority report, and it was ultimately substituted for the majority report—all the con-servative heavyweights rose to speak against the minority report and against union: Robert Strong, G. Aiken Taylor, Tom Glasgow, John Reed Miller, and John R. Richardson. In the end, the plan of union passed the Assembly by a vote of 283 to 169.[33]

Undoubtedly, the debate over the report on *Brown v. Board* and desegregation set the context of much that followed, not only at the Assembly itself, but also in the way in which the debate over the plan of union was conducted during this year of decision. While it claims too much to assign the reason for reunion's failure simply to *Brown v. Board*, the General Assembly's support of it added together with the larger context of southern Presbyterians' fears over the northern church's support for integration certainly provided a powerful apolo-getic against reunion. To be sure, there were some churches that linked

32. *MGAPCUS* (1954): 54, 194; John R. Richardson, "The 94th General Assembly," *SPJ* (9 June 1954): 6. For two books on *Brown*, see James T. Patterson, *Brown v. Board of Education: A Civil Rights Milestone and Its Troubled Legacy* (New York: Oxford University Press, 2001), and James C. Cobb, *The Brown Decision, Jim Crow, and Southern Identity* (Athens, GA: University of Georgia Press, 2005). The quotation from the *Brown* decision is from Patterson, *Brown v. Board*, 67.

33. Richardson, "The 94th General Assembly," 10.

the two together: for example, the session of First Presbyterian Church, Goldsboro, North Carolina, considered both the plan of union and the resolution against segregation in the same meeting and defeated both. Likewise, the session of North Avenue Presbyterian Church, Atlanta, adopted a resolution opposing reunion because they feared the loss of "the more conservative theological and social emphasis of our denomination."[34] And yet the key reasons that conservatives had for defeating reunion were the doctrinal deviancy of the northern church, the differences over the ownership of church property, and the administrative centralization of the PCUSA.

Conservatives knew that it was unlikely that they would defeat union at the Assembly; they needed to defeat it in the presbyteries. Likewise, the progressives knew that they were unlikely to get the required three-fourths of the presbyteries to agree to unite with the northern churches. But both sides worked hard to present the case for and against the plan of union. When the presbyteries began to meet for their fall 1954 gatherings, Nelson Bell and John R. Richardson hit the road to make the case against union. The pastor of Westminster Presbyterian Church in Atlanta, Richardson, worked presbyteries in Georgia; Bell went to Knoxville Presbytery in Tennessee and Lexington-Ebenezer Presbytery in Kentucky. At his stops, Bell conducted debates with Frank Caldwell, the esteemed liberal president of Louisville Presbyterian Theological Seminary, on the issue. Those

34. "Report of Session to the Congregation of the First Presbyterian Church, Goldsboro, NC," *SPJ* (21 July 1954): 15; "North Avenue Presbyterian Church," *SPJ* (4 August 1954): 1. See also "Resolutions and Overtures," *SPJ* (25 August 1954): 15; "Presbytery of Meridian against Union," *SPJ* (3 November 1954): 17–18; "Still They Come," *SPJ* (24 November 1954): 13.

For examples of those who "blame" the defeat of reunion on *Brown* (and hence conservative racism), see Thompson, *Presbyterians in the South*, 3:574; David M. Reimers, "The Race Problem and Presbyterian Union," *Church History* 31 (1962): 203–15; Erskine Clarke, "Presbyterian Ecumenical Activity in the United States," in *The Diversity of Discipleship: The Presbyterians and Twentieth Century Witness*, ed. Milton J. Coalter, John M. Mulder, and Louis B. Weeks (Louisville, KY: Westminster John Knox, 1991), 161. Two books suggesting that race was part of the context in which reunion was defeated, but was not necessarily the main issue, are Joel L. Alvis Jr., *Religion and Race: Southern Presbyterians, 1946–1983* (Tuscaloosa, AL: University of Alabama Press, 1994), 57–62, and Bradley J. Longfield, *Presbyterians and American Culture: A History* (Louisville, KY: Westminster John Knox, 2013), 191–95. My view generally agrees with Alvis and Longfield.

debates went well: "He was very much a gentleman throughout the entire discussion," Bell noted about one stop, "and those who heard seem to think that the audience was overwhelmingly on our side."[35]

As important as these debates were, far more important for conservatives was the *Southern Presbyterian Journal*. Article after article emphasized the doctrinal and polity issues at stake. The transcending issue in the entire discussion was "conflict over Truth, God's authoritative and infallible Word of Truth," Robert Henderson held. The question, Nelson Bell observed, was "whether the Presbyterian Church shall be a *confessional* or an *inclusive* church." Robert Strong agreed, observing that "the difference may perhaps best be defined by saying that in the North are found interpretations of the doctrinal standards that seriously deviate from ours." There was one provision in the plan of union that was "so dangerous that it should cause every member of our Southern Presbyterian Church to vote against union," Paul Hastings argued: the duties and power given to the General Council, "an un-Presbyterian organization, foreign to the historic polity of Presbyterianism and calculated to completely alter the constitutional processes of the church."[36]

Even as these debates were being played out at the presbytery level, conservatives began to band together across lines. Right-leaning moderates published a statement in the *Christian Observer* that argued against union. Signed by centrists such as A. W. Dick from Second Church in Memphis, Marc Weersing from Central Church in Jackson, Mississippi, J. Wayte Fulton from Shenandoah Church in Miami, and Vernon Broyles from North Avenue Church in Atlanta, the document aligned these men with the *Journal* conservatives who had been leading the fight for the past fifteen years. Likewise, Bill Hill, pastor of West End Presbyterian Church in Hopewell, Virginia, first wrote in the *Journal* on this issue in an open letter to a northern big-steeple pastor.

---

35. Thompson, *Presbyterians in the South*, 3:574; L. Nelson Bell to John R. Richardson, 30 September 1954, 5 October 1954, and 12 October 1954 (all in L. Nelson Bell Papers, box 69, folder 12, BGC).

36. Robert Henderson, "Above the Issue of Organic Union . . . the Battle for Truth," *SPJ* (29 September 1954): 7; L. Nelson Bell, "It Is Historic Presbyterianism Which Is at Stake," *SPJ* (7 July 1954): 3; Robert Strong, "On Church Union," *SPJ* (25 August 1954): 6; Paul D. Hastings, "It Is Not Presbyterian," *SPJ* (15 September 1954): 8.

Their differences on union, Hill observed, were matters of conviction "concerning the authority of the Word of God and the teaching of Scriptures." Hill went on to admit to being "ashamed that there are some few in the South who are opposing Union on the grounds of an imagined connection with 'segregation' or 'integration.'" Still, for Hill at least, the main issue was doctrinal.[37]

These allies and the strong antiunion votes coming from the fall presbytery meetings gave conservatives more courage as the new year came. By late January 1955, the result was certain: there was no way that union could get the three-fourths needed to pass; union was defeated. The *Journal* rejoiced: "To a great host across the church this news has brought a sigh of relief, for the proposed union has been most unpopular with the great majority of people in the pew." The reasons for the unpopularity of the plan were the ones that the magazine had pointed out for over seventeen years: the "grave and deep differences in polity, doctrinal interpretation, philosophies of administration and procedure" among the three churches and especially between the southern church and the PCUSA. And yet even the joy at defeating reunion was tempered with the reality that "the desire of an inclusive church" on the part of some had not gone away. Conservatives knew and feared that there would be other attempts at reunion in the future. The question would be how to make sure that the same outcome—the continuation of the southern Presbyterian church—would result even if the church at large decided to give up its distinctive witness.[38]

By the time the 1955 General Assembly came, it was clear how large the conservatives' victory was: forty-two presbyteries for reunion, forty-three presbyteries against. Even the resolution to dismiss the Permanent Committee on Cooperation and Union, however, had language that would be used to great effect by pro-union forces: "That the General Assembly authorize and encourage its Boards and other agencies to

37. "Some Thoughts on Union," *SPJ* (22 December 1954): 2–3; William E. Hill, "A Reply to Dr. Harrison Ray Anderson," *SPJ* (22 December 1954): 3–4.

38. L. Nelson Bell, "Look Forward!," *SPJ* (26 January 1955): 2–3; Henry B. Dendy, "Let Us Have Peace," *SPJ* (9 February 1955): 2; Paul D. Hastings, "The Committee on Cooperation and Union Must Be Dissolved," *SPJ* (27 April 1955): 19–20.

explore and carry out, subject to the approval of the General Assembly, as much joint and cooperative activity within the sphere of their responsibility as may advance the cause of Christ." In the years ahead, this language would be used to continue work on all sorts of unitive projects, from joint Sunday school curriculum and hymnals to union presbyteries and synods. By the time reunion discussions fired back up in 1969, the churches would be much closer doctrinally, administratively, and relationally; reunion would eventually become a reality for the northern and southern branches of the Presbyterian church.[39]

All of that was in the future, however. For most conservatives, the aftermath of the reunion battle was a bit of a letdown. Having spent so much time arguing against reunion, conservatives struggled to figure out what they were actually for. Nelson Bell, for one, recognized this sense of malaise in the conservative leadership: "Now that union has been defeated, I think that all of us are feeling a definite 'let-down.' I sense this in letters and also in conversations and also in my own personal feelings." Part of the depression was the result of "the situation in the leadership of our Church, in our seminaries, colleges, boards, and agencies. This has been true in the past and it is not any worse now than it was before." What was required was for conservatives, "through prayer and under God's leadership, to try to bring about a change in the situation." God's leadership would apparently involve raising up new organizations and new prophets to evangelize the South and strengthen PCUS conservatives for the challenges of the days ahead.[40]

39. *MGAPCUS* (1955): 70.

40. L. Nelson Bell to Board of Directors of *SPJ*, 4 March 1955, L. Nelson Bell Papers, box 72, folder 7, BGC.

7

"The Only Hope for America": Southern Presbyterians, Billy Graham, and the Mission of the Church

Many readers of the *Southern Presbyterian Journal* must have smiled in recognition and hope when they received the 15 February 1950 issue of the magazine. On the cover was an attractive young man, age thirty-one, with piercing eyes and a slight smile on his face, wearing his signature double-breasted suit with garish tie and protruding pocket handkerchief. The only indication of the identity of the young man was a simple line: "Billy Graham; see pages two and three." It was all that was necessary—for, as the rest of the magazine explained, American newspapers had become preoccupied with the preaching ministry of the young evangelist. *Journal* editor Henry Dendy was not restrained in his thoughts about Graham: "As we heard him preach there came to us the definite conviction that God had raised up, in this our needy time, a servant on whom rests the mighty power of the Holy Spirit such as is rarely seen."[1]

Billy Graham did not simply represent a gifted preacher who led significant evangelistic meetings; he embodied the hopes of many conservative Protestants, regardless of denomination, for spiritual renewal in America in the 1950s. As Dendy's praise suggested, southern

1. Henry B. Dendy, "Billy Graham," *SPJ* (15 February 1950): 2.

Protestants especially felt that theirs was a "needy time," for the world as they knew it was under attack. Plagued by social agitation from within over racial integration and from without by infiltrating Communists, worried by the centralizing thrusts of the National Council of Churches and the federal government, and convinced that the younger generation was moving toward spiritual bankruptcy and moral confusion, conservative Protestants in the South believed that the only answer was revival. In Graham's ministry, southern Protestants believed that God was once again visiting his people and turning America to himself.[2]

   While Graham and his team sought to lead interdenominational meetings and while he held his church membership in the Southern Baptist Convention, southern Presbyterian conservatives felt extremely invested in Graham's ministry in the 1950s. Certainly they were invested because of the countless connections that Graham had with southern Presbyterians, from his own upbringing within the Associate Reformed Presbyterian Church to his marital connections to the Nelson Bell family, former PCUS missionary and leading conservative voice. But the connections went deeper. As a result both of their ideology, which merged political, cultural, and religious conservatism seamlessly together in their southern brand of modern American conservatism, and of their biblical and theological reflection, Graham represented a symbol of hope for both their nation and the PCUS. Convinced that their church was veering off-track by not focusing appropriately on the church's true spiritual mission of evangelism, southern Presbyterian conservatives used Graham's evangelistic

---

2. On Graham's importance and impact within southern Protestantism, see Steven P. Miller, *Billy Graham and the Rise of the Republican South* (Philadelphia: University of Pennsylvania Press, 2009); Steven P. Miller, "Billy Graham, Civil Rights, and the Changing Postwar South," in *Politics and Religion in the White South*, ed. Glenn Feldmann (Lexington, KY: University Press of Kentucky, 2005), 157–86; David L. Chappell, *A Stone of Hope: Prophetic Religion and the Death of Jim Crow* (Chapel Hill, NC: University of North Carolina Press, 2004), 139–52.

   For Graham's importance to conservative American Protestantism, see Joel A. Carpenter, *Revive Us Again: The Reawakening of American Fundamentalism* (New York: Oxford University Press, 1997), esp. 211–32. The best biography of Graham remains William Martin, *Prophet with Honor: The Billy Graham Story* (New York: William Morrow, 1991); but see also Grant Wacker, *America's Pastor: Billy Graham and the Shaping of a Nation* (Cambridge, MA: Harvard University Press, 2014).

success and international prominence to bolster their position and make plain their deep differences with progressive fellow-churchmen. They earnestly believed that as the church returned to its fundamental commitment to evangelism, not only would they know God's revival blessings, but God would use them to reverse America's downward decline by bringing spiritual renewal to the entire nation.[3]

Graham's example would inspire many within the southern Presbyterian church to carry on with evangelistic endeavors. Some churches, such as First Presbyterian Church, Jackson, Mississippi, had long held evangelistic meetings with men such as Sam Jones, G. Campbell Morgan, and Billy Sunday; when Graham came to Jackson in 1952, it was natural for the church to be a major supporter of the campaign. Others would take on the mantle of full-time evangelist. Wade Smith, a former First Church Jackson deacon, would eventually train for the ministry and go into full-time evangelism. Most important among the "lesser prophets" who would arise would be Bill Hill, longtime pastor of West End Presbyterian Church, Hopewell, Virginia. In 1958, Hill would go into evangelism full time in an effort to promote revival in the "Southern Zion." And in order to foster such a revival time, he would form a network of evangelists who specialized in Billy Graham–style evangelistic meetings. The Presbyterian Evangelistic Fellowship (PEF) would serve over time as an important means of salvation, not only for the Redeemer nation, but for the world.[4]

WHAT AMERICA NEEDS

As southern Presbyterian conservatives looked at America, they had a generally pessimistic view. In the very first issue of the *Southern Presbyterian Journal*, Nelson Bell declared, "The civilization of which we are a part is perched precariously on the edge of an abyss. This is obvious to all, whether in or outside of the Church. The tragedy is that, in part, the Christian Church is to blame." And the reason

3. On the theme of America as a Redeemer nation, see the classic work of Ernest Lee Tuveson, *Redeemer Nation: The Idea of America's Millennial Role* (Chicago: University of Chicago Press, 1968).

4. Sean Michael Lucas, *Blessed Zion: First Presbyterian Church, Jackson, Mississippi, 1837–2012* (Jackson, MS: First Presbyterian Church, 2013), 68–69.

was simple: "It has left its God-given task of preaching the Gospel of salvation from sin through the Lord Jesus Christ." Later, Bell would sound the same themes. "To all who will consider the handwriting is surely on the wall. To America there must come a spiritual awakening, a revival of faith in the Son of God and a turning to Him in confession of sin," he proclaimed. W. Twyman Williams asked whether "we really think that as a nation we are less drunken, less immoral, less corrupt in government and in business, more law-abiding, more God-fearing" than the European nations that had borne the brunt of two world wars. The only conclusion possible was that God's judgment was coming upon America. Bell assessed America's moral decay by noting that "sin in every form is flouted before our eyes. We are a licentious people, an increasingly intemperate people. The Sabbath is more and more a holiday instead of a holy day. Only too often we have a form of godliness but deny the power thereof. There is corruption and bribery and intrigue in high and low places." Elsewhere he observed, "Soft, loving pleasure, speaking often in terms of religion but living in ease and wallowing in impurity and lust, America is increasingly becoming prey to the inward decay which has again and again destroyed nations."[5]

The only way to reverse this American decay and avert God's judgment was revival. L. Nelson Bell was consistent in his belief that revival was the chief need for America's churches and civilization. In 1946, he declared, "Without controversy, we all can certainly agree that our great need is a heaven-sent revival. . . . When this revival comes we will find ourselves drawn to each other because we are closer to Him." America needed "a great spiritual and moral awakening which will in turn give that fiber of soul and character which will reflect itself in public and private life and again make our nation great, as God counts greatness." Others agreed with Bell's assessment of both America's problem and God's solution. Samuel McPheeters Glasgow observed that "the church must have a Revival or sag into deeper depths of failure and false assurance." Kenton Parker held that

---

5. L. Nelson Bell, "Why?," *SPJ* (May 1942): 2; L. Nelson Bell, "Revival or Else," *SPJ* (15 July 1949): 5; W. Twyman Williams, "Our Nation Next?," *SPJ* (17 January 1951): 4; L. Nelson Bell, "Impending Judgment," *SPJ* (14 March 1951): 3.

unless God brought spiritual revival to America, it would experience "some sort of terrible catastrophe compared with which the French Revolution would look like child's play."[6]

In order to bring such spiritual renewal to America, several ingredients were needed. Chief among them was whole-souled surrender to the power of the Holy Spirit. Kenton Parker urged people to "hear God's voice as He speaks in judgment, and yet in love, agonize in prayer as we let His Spirit search our hearts, and look to HIM for a gracious Revival." Nelson Bell asked whether "our failures as Christians and as a Church [are not] due to our repeated attempts to accomplish a supernatural task with natural means alone." There was "supernatural power available to all who come seeking Him in humility and truth. The possibility of world-wide revival will merge into the certainty of such a spiritual awakening when we as Christians and as the Church, go forth in that power alone." In a 1950 article, Bell passionately claimed, "We must have a revival. . . . We need more than anything else the power which comes alone from the outpouring of God's Holy Spirit." Only as God's people humbled themselves and sought God in repentance and confession would the Spirit's power come and revival occur. This was exactly where the church-union movement got things wrong: "It is our conviction that a desperately sick world needs the testimony, not of a great ecclesiastical body, but of a Spirit-filled and directed message."[7]

Another ingredient for religious revival in America was a willingness to set aside denominational boundaries in order to foster evangelistic success. What was required was a "bigness of soul and spirit which welcomes true evangelism and evidence of spiritual power wherever it may be found." Nelson Bell chided his Presbyterian readers for failing to pay attention to the gospel ministry of "sideline" Protestant

6. L. Nelson Bell, "The Greatest Need of All," *SPJ* (15 November 1946): 3; L. Nelson Bell, "Are We Big Enough?," *SPJ* (16 January 1950): 2; Samuel McPheeters Glasgow, "Evangelism and Revivals," *SPJ* (15 March 1950): 2; J. Kenton Parker, "Revival or Revolution," *SPJ* (15 March 1950): 3.

7. J. Kenton Parker, "Post-war Planning," *SPJ* (January 1945): 3 (emphasis his); L. Nelson Bell, "The Work of the Holy Spirit: Natural or Supernatural?," *SPJ* (15 September 1949): 4; L. Nelson Bell, "Our Greatest Need," *SPJ* (15 February 1950): 4; L. Nelson Bell, "It Is Historic Presbyterianism Which Is at Stake," *SPJ* (7 July 1954): 3.

churches: "We have looked into the preaching of many of the pastors of these smaller churches and we find that most of them are preaching the Gospel of Jesus Christ," he noted. "We find that God is blessing their ministry and honoring their witness to Him and His Word. We find a fire and a zeal too often lacking in our own pulpits." The lesson here was that "revival will come when Episcopalians and Pentecostalists, Presbyterians and Baptists, Nazarenes and Methodists and others are willing to get down before God and pray for an outpouring of His Holy Spirit." As Christians linked arms in prayer and evangelism, America would be changed.[8]

Equally important, perhaps, was a belief that God still used mass evangelism and other evangelistic strategies to win people to the Christian faith. Hayes Clark noted that "this work of evangelism may be done by individuals speaking to individuals or by mass revival movements." Thankfully, "the day of mass evangelism has not passed but is just now coming into its own through the 'Youth Crusades.' The dire need of the hour is a mass evangelism of others through an 'Adult Crusade.'" Nelson Bell pleaded with people to "stop this talk of the day of mass evangelism being past. God yet uses any and every method which exalts Him and His Word. Certainly America needs the impact of this message—the message of salvation for sinners. Let us use and promote any method which brings men to know Him." John R. Richardson also defended such evangelistic methods, noting that "the most devoted servants of Christ have never felt ashamed to engage in street-corner evangelism."[9]

In addition, personal evangelism was necessary in order to save America from ruin. Vernon Patterson held that God's purpose in his world would be accomplished "by witness to Christ, to call out from all nations a people for God. It is not humanizing, socializing, or civilizing the world. It is not 'remaking the world order.' It is not even Christianizing the world. It is evangelizing the world until the body of Christ is complete." T. E. P. Woods gave instruction on how

8. Bell, "Are We Big Enough?," 3.
9. Hayes Clark, "Evangelism Today?," *SPJ* (15 February 1946): 26; L. Nelson Bell, "Revivals," *SPJ* (1 February 1949): 3; John R. Richardson, "Street Corner Evangelism," *SPJ* (15 October 1948): 2.

to do personal evangelism from initial contact to closing questions meant to lead someone to Christ. By using a plan for evangelism, ordinary people might use ordinary means at ordinary times. And yet Austin Seminary professor R. F. Gribble observed that God used such evangelism for extraordinary purposes. Sometimes Christians failed to witness because they sensed various hindrances, such as presuming that people were saved when they were not and assuming that people knew the gospel when they did not. Believers needed to surmount those hindrances, evangelist Preston Sartelle argued, by developing "a new sense of urgency of the Christian message for all who are lost." There were other tools, however, that Christians might use. For example, J. Park McCallie suggested that Laymen's Evangelistic Clubs were such a tool for encouraging men in personal work. "There is no joy comparable to the joy of winning men to Christ by witnessing," he observed. "Now is the time of all times to do it, when men are faced with the fact that society cannot save itself, but is headed for self-destruction."[10]

Not only this, but conservatives urged their followers to ask God to send more evangelists and laborers into the harvest. C. T. Caldwell declared that "the failure of evangelism is not in the harvest but in the fact that we work in the fields with just about half enough force. . . . We must have more ministers" to do this work of evangelism. John R. Richardson agreed and urged the theological seminaries to make sure that future ministers were ready for that task: "Our first step in strengthening our theological education is to put the emphasis on evangelism where the New Testament places it." In the end, as Presbyterians "exalt the truth as it is in Christ Jesus both in our preaching and in our Church life, we shall be close to, if not actually in a revival." As Cary Weisiger put it hopefully, "Presbyterians can be revived."[11]

10. Vernon W. Patterson, "Evangelism—Hope of the Present and Challenge of the Future," *SPJ* (August 1942): 13; T. E. P. Woods, "Personal Evangelism," *SPJ* (March 1945): 23–24; R. F. Gribble, "Pointers for Personal Evangelism," *SPJ* (15 March 1950): 4–5; Preston Orr Sartelle, "Hindrances to Personal Evangelism," *SPJ* (15 August 1947): 9; L. Nelson Bell, "If the Gospel Message Is True Then It Is Urgent!!!," *SPJ* (15 October 1952): 5; J. Park McCallie, "Evangelism," *SPJ* (13 October 1954): 5.

11. C. T. Caldwell, "Evangelism: Another Angle," *SPJ* (January 1945): 2; John R. Richardson, "Stronger Theological Education," *SPJ* (January 1945): 4; Cary N. Weisiger III,

Even as they hoped and proclaimed that revival was possible, southern Presbyterian conservative leaders wondered why revival had not yet come. One elder suggested that the problem could be found in the general worldliness of the church: "The plain, blunt truth is that we church people, year after year, slowly but surely, have been compromising more and more with worldliness until the Holy Spirit simply does not see fit to use us as the human instruments through which to bring about a great revival in the church." Not only were church people exhibiting worldliness that prevented revival, but so were church leaders. Nelson Bell claimed that "if the pastors and officers will set the example necessary and with this example earnestly pray for the guidance of God's Spirit we believe revival and blessing is sure to follow. Worldliness in the church is a symptom of spiritual sickness. Let us seek the cure of the disease, [and] the symptoms will then disappear." And so both ministers and people needed to pursue repentance and renewed faith in Christ if revival was going to come and America be saved. As Preston Sartelle noted, "It becomes absolutely necessary to have an awakening and restoration in Christian lives before we can have a successful and sustained evangelistic outreach." Such awakening meant that Christians needed to "put off sin and put on Christian living and service."[12]

Tied to the issue of worldliness was a spirit of indifference and complacency within the church that hindered the outpouring of the Spirit. "Why is there so much back-patting and so little getting down on knees and crying out to God for a spiritual awakening?" Nelson Bell asked rhetorically. "We believe it is because indifference and complacency have infected Christians and churches as a canker and we believe only a work of the Holy Spirit can bring about the revival which is necessary." Such indifference was demonstrated in the fact that so few Christians were willing to pay the price for revival. "If we are to have a revival," Bell held, "it will have to begin in our own hearts and we will have to open them to the cleansing and filling of

---

"Can Presbyterians Be Revived?," *SPJ* (15 October 1946): 5.

12. Chalmers W. Alexander, "Do We Really Want a Great Revival?," *SPJ* (15 January 1949): 9; L. Nelson Bell, "Worldliness: A Symptom," *SPJ* (15 September 1949): 3; P. O. Sartelle, "What Is Revival and Why?," *SPJ* (15 January 1949): 5.

the Holy Spirit." Such a price would include "a total surrender of our minds, our wills, and our bodies." If Christians would pay the price, revival could and would come.[13]

For PCUS conservatives, the most significant reason for the lack of revival was the church's failure to maintain a consistent doctrinal witness. "The great doctrinal truths presented under the influence of the Holy Spirit [are] the source of the evangelistic power we seek," one writer noted. Repeatedly, southern Presbyterian conservatives made this same clear connection between doctrinal faithfulness and spiritual renewal. "The one thing which can revitalize the Church, under the power of the Holy Spirit, is a restatement of the content of Christianity itself," Nelson Bell observed. "The weakness and the failures of the Church in our age are due to a departure from the things which constitute the Gospel message." At the end of the day, it seemed to be self-evident that "when one becomes committed to the modernistic position he has lost his power to win souls" and hence to see revival. In 1952, to make this point clear, a group of ministers and laymen took out a full-page advertisement in the *Southern Presbyterian Journal*. The text of the advertisement made the connection between revival and clear doctrine: "The greatest need of the Church and the greatest need in America is a revival of Christian faith and practice; the weakness of the Church centers in her attempt to cater to men, through diluting the Christian faith and watering down the Christian message; the power of the Church stems from the presence of the Holy Spirit and revealed in a body of truth which men are to believe and by which they live."[14]

Central to this message was the church's traditional emphasis on the inspiration and authority of Scripture. C. T. Caldwell noted that "if one does not believe in the inspiration and inerrancy of the Bible he cannot speak with authority and zeal for anything it says," especially the evangelistic message of Scripture. Nelson Bell believed

13. L. Nelson Bell, "We'd Like to Quit," *SPJ* (6 December 1950): 7; L. Nelson Bell, "Where Shall It Start?," *SPJ* (13 May 1953): 6; L. Nelson Bell, "Can We Have Revival?," *SPJ* (24 June 1953): 2.

14. C. T. Caldwell, "The Bearing of Orthodoxy on Evangelism," *SPJ* (1 November 1945): 2; L. Nelson Bell, "God's Underground," *SPJ* (2 May 1949): 5; "Neo-Christianity," *SPJ* (21 January 1953): 3; "Union Will Not Bring Revival," *SPJ* (24 September 1952): 16.

that "maximum spiritual power is in part conditioned on faith in the plenary inspiration of the Scriptures." Because many in the PCUS were teaching a low view of biblical inspiration and authority, the church was lacking in spiritual power. This failure of faith in the Bible's authority characterized most of the Protestant churches in America, explaining both the low tide of spiritual power and the sense of national decay. And yet the answer was not simply apologetics that demonstrated the inspiration of Scripture; the final and sole solution was actually revival. That faith in the inerrant Scripture was both the basis for and the result of revival was not a tautology for conservatives. Rather, it was the way that God worked: "The solvent which will end controversy and restore to our church the emphasis which is paramount and central will be a genuine revival in our own hearts and in the courts of our church as well," Bell held. "That is the solution and we do not believe there is any other." In fact, when revival comes, "it will be the most glorious thing which could happen to us, and to the world."[15]

PROPHET OF THE NEW SOUTH

For many southern Presbyterians during the 1950s, Billy Graham represented their great hopes for a national revival. In fact, Graham was a prophetic figure for southern Protestants generally; as his father-in-law, Nelson Bell, put it: "There can be no question but that God has raised up for this generation a man of truly prophetic vision, for Billy Graham has a sense of divine call and destiny as impelling, in some measure, as the prophets of old." Southern Presbyterians began following Graham's ministry as early as 1948 while he served with Youth for Christ International. When Graham was five years removed from Wheaton College and his marriage to Nelson Bell's daughter, Ruth, his evangelistic meetings in Des Moines, Iowa, were the first to be highlighted in the *Southern Presbyterian Journal*. They were declared the greatest meetings since 1914 when Billy Sunday had preached in that town, and Graham's team was credited with bringing 725 people

15. Caldwell, "The Bearing of Orthodoxy on Evangelism," 2; L. Nelson Bell, "The Hole in the Dyke," *SPJ* (9 July 1952): 3; L. Nelson Bell, "Danger Ahead!!!," *SPJ* (22 July 1953): 3; L. Nelson Bell, "What Is the Solution?," *SPJ* (27 May 1953): 1; L. Nelson Bell, "What Will a True Revival Do?," *SPJ* (30 March 1955): 3.

to faith in Christ and an additional 417 "young people under the age of 35" to commit for full-time missionary service. One local business leader gushed, "This is the greatest thing that has happened in my 32 years as a Christian. I've never seen anything like it."[16]

The turning point for Graham's career was his 1949 evangelistic campaign in Los Angeles, during which William Randolph Hearst famously instructed his newspapers to "puff Graham"; it was also the sign to southern Protestants that Graham had arrived as the surrendered servant who would bring revival to America. *Southern Presbyterian Journal* editor Henry Dendy characterized the meetings as "one of the most remarkable and fruitful city-wide revivals in modern times" because Billy Graham "captured the imagination of the entire city and under the blessing of God's Spirit has been the means of literally winning thousands for Christ." Originally scheduled to last only three weeks, the campaign continued into its eighth week and was used to convert "some of Los Angeles' best known citizens," including Stuart Hamblen, a prominent radio host. Even mob boss Mickey Cohen sent for Graham and "spent two hours talking to him about his soul." Surely this was evidence that "the day of revival is not over"; all southern Presbyterians should pray "that these revival fires may spread over our land, not only to the salvation of countless souls but also to stem the tide of iniquity which is engulfing our nation." Southern Presbyterians had to reason that if God could use Graham in a godless place such as Tinseltown, then surely God could use him throughout America, north and south.[17]

Two such cities were central places in the South's self-identity: Columbia, South Carolina, and Atlanta, Georgia, which Graham visited during 1950. He spent three weeks at Columbia, where he packed out the University of South Carolina football stadium with

16. L. Nelson Bell, "I Saw Harringay," *SPJ* (26 May 1954): 8; L. Nelson Bell, "Youth for Christ," *SPJ* (July 1945): 3; "Youth for Christ," *SPJ* (1 November 1948): 14.

17. Henry B. Dendy, "Revival in Los Angeles," *SPJ* (1 December 1949): 3; L. Nelson Bell, "Back of Revival," *SPJ* (2 January 1950): 4. The best accounts of the Los Angeles campaign and its importance to Graham's career are Martin, *A Prophet with Honor*, 112–19, and Carpenter, *Revive Us Again*, 211–32; also important is George Harsch, " 'Puff Graham': American Media, American Culture, and the Creation of Billy Graham" (Ph.D. diss., University of Southern Mississippi, 2005).

over forty thousand people. It was reported that "around 2,000 people were converted at this final Sunday afternoon service. It was said that strong men stood and wept under great emotion at the sight of the hundreds who came forward to accept Christ." From there, Graham came to the unofficial capital city of the South, Atlanta, at the end of 1950 in order to call the city "to repentance and to turn to Christ, 'the only answer to world needs today.'" In one message, he exhorted city leaders, "Prepare to meet God, oh, America," highlighting the spiritual, moral, and social deterioration of the nation: divorce, alcoholism, juvenile delinquency and crime, sexual sin, and sexually motivated crime. "I think we are done for in this country unless we have a great revival—a great spiritual revival," Graham said. His crusade once again was successful; and for the first time, all the nation could see it—from Atlanta, Graham gave his first "Hour of Decision" broadcast on the American Broadcasting Company's television stations.[18]

As Graham's ministry advanced, southern Presbyterians believed that they saw revival fires falling elsewhere, especially on the younger generation. Cary Weisiger III reported that spiritual emphasis week at Grove City College in Pennsylvania was unusually blessed, leading him to speculate that "perhaps what we are seeing today is an upsurge of religious revival unknown on our campuses for fifty years." Others, such as Kenton Parker, agreed; after noting Graham's evangelistic success at Boston University and a recent spiritual uptick at Wheaton College, he suggested, "I feel that this is one of the most interesting 'signs of the times' and may be the beginning of a great outpouring of the Spirit upon us as a people." Even H. H. Thompson, director of evangelism for the PCUS, hoped that there was "every reason to believe the Church is deeply stirred in the matter of evangelization and that surely God is speaking to His Church at this time." Could

18. Henry B. Dendy, "The Billy Graham Evangelistic Campaign in Columbia, S.C.," *SPJ* (1 April 1950): 2; "Rev. Billy Graham in Atlanta, Ga.," *SPJ* (1 March 1950): 21; "Billy Graham Scheduled for Coast to Coast Broadcast This Fall on ABC," *SPJ* (20 September 1950): 21; J. E. Flow, "Billy Graham in Atlanta," *SPJ* (29 November 1950): 2–4; see also Martin, *Prophet with Honor*, 128–30, 136–39. Henry Dendy also noted when Montreat College hosted a Graham broadcast, rejoicing that "the announcer gave a graphic description of Montreat and its relationship to our Southern Presbyterian Church." Henry B. Dendy, "Montreat on ABC," *SPJ* (27 December 1950): 4.

it be that God was using Graham to turn the South and the nation as a whole to Christ?[19]

Graham's triumphs throughout the South were reported with regularity in the pages of the *Southern Presbyterian Journal*: Fort Worth was transformed, with 12,500 nightly filling the Will Rogers Coliseum; Houston, the murder capital of the country, saw its Graham crusade extended an extra week; Chattanooga built a new auditorium to hold the Graham meetings; Dallas filled the Cotton Bowl with seventy-five thousand people to hear Graham preach; and Montreat was set abuzz by Graham's appearance at the 1952 PCUS church-extension conference. Coinciding with his preaching at Montreat, an entire issue of the *Journal* was dedicated to his ministry. There was a retrospective of his southern preaching campaigns, with Presbyterian pastors and elders testifying to the good that Graham had done in their respective towns. Repeatedly, his success throughout the South was attributed to "the presence and power of God's Holy Spirit." Typical was the praise from John Reed Miller, pastor of First Presbyterian Church, Jackson, Mississippi: "I have never heard a more dynamic, Spirit-filled and gifted evangelist than Billy Graham. I am convinced that he is God's man to bring the revival in America for which all of us have been praying. . . . I gave all-out support to Billy Graham—and how grateful I am that I did! There has been a spiritual awakening throughout my entire church." And one minister, reflecting on the effect of Graham's ministry at the church-extension conference, sighed, "In the past, Billy Graham has been used to reach a city for Christ. Here at Montreat this summer God has used him to reach an entire denomination."[20]

19. Cary N. Weisiger III, "Spiritual Emphasis Week," *SPJ* (15 March 1950): 3; J. Kenton Parker, "College Revivals," *SPJ* (15 March 1950): 4; Deedie-May Austin, "Many Believe a Great Revival Is Near at Hand," *SPJ* (15 March 1950): 5. See also "Students and the Gospel," *SPJ* (1 June 1950): 9–10.

20. "Billy Graham in Fort Worth," *SPJ* (11 April 1951): 5; "Successful Graham Campaign Continues for Extra Week," *SPJ* (18 June 1952): 11; "Billy Graham Crusade, Chattanooga, Tenn.," *SPJ* (25 February 1953): 11–12; Henry B. Dendy, "75,000 Hear Gospel in Dallas Meeting," *SPJ* (2 July 1953): 10–11; "Church Extension Conference Will Feature Billy Graham," *SPJ* (28 May 1952): 10; Henry B. Dendy, "A Man with God's Message," *SPJ* (13 August 1952): 2; "The Campaigns," *SPJ* (13 August 1952): 12; "Billy Graham at Montreat," *SPJ* (3 September 1952): 3; Lucas, *Blessed Zion*, 116–17.

Soon it seemed clear that God intended to use Graham to reach the world for his sake. After a triumphal session of preaching to American troops in 1953 during the height of the Korean conflict, Graham prepared to conquer London with the gospel in 1954. Six months before the beginning of the London meetings, the *Journal* editor requested "importunate prayer" for Graham's ministry in England, "a practically pagan country." In the weeks leading up to the 1 March start, details of the campaign's preparation were reported to southern Presbyterian readers so that they might gain a sense of the magnitude of the spiritual battle, "a bold, valiant, and well organized challenge to win England back to Christianity." The entire campaign was given full reportage in the *Journal*, and the verdict became increasingly clear as the weeks rolled: London was experiencing "a work of God not paralleled before in our generation," one in which 36,431 people would fill out decision cards. And there was great hope that the revival would not stop there; Nelson Bell pleaded for southern Presbyterians to "covenant to pray for a world-sweeping revival which will solve the problems of individuals and of nations. Too long we have limited Him by our puny faith."[21]

While southern Presbyterians continued to maintain an abiding love for and interest in Graham and his ministry, the London campaign was the height of their hopes for spiritual renewal. Here was a prophet who was wholly surrendered to the power of the Holy Spirit,

21. Walter G. Sugg Jr., "Visit of Evangelist Billy Graham to Far East," *SPJ* (6 May 1953): 17; the 4 March 1953 issue of *SPJ* had a picture of Graham preaching to the troops on the front cover. Henry B. Dendy, "Pray for England," *SPJ* (4 November 1953): 2; "Pray for London Campaign," *SPJ* (17 February 1954): 2; "London Altered for Opening Meeting of Billy Graham Crusade," *SPJ* (3 March 1954): 16; Henry B. Dendy, "Billy Graham: The London Campaign," *SPJ* (17 March 1954): 3; Henry B. Dendy, "A Work of the Spirit," *SPJ* (24 March 1954): 3; Bell, "I Saw Harringay," 10. See also Martin, *Prophet with Honor*, 173–85.

Other articles on the London crusade included: William W. Beckner Jr., "An American Physician and the London Crusade," *SPJ* (24 March 1954): 5–6; "Report from London," *SPJ* (31 March 1954): 6–7; "News from London," *SPJ* (1 April 1954): 6; "From London Again," *SPJ* (14 April 1954): 5–6; Henry B. Dendy, "It Is No Secret," *SPJ* (21 April 1954): 4; "More about the London Campaign," *SPJ* (28 April 1954): 4–5; "Amazing Grace," *SPJ* (5 May 1954): 3–4; "Billy Graham at Cambridge," *SPJ* (12 May 1954): 3–4; "The London Campaign: Revolt in Britain," *SPJ* (19 May 1954): 6–10; L. Nelson Bell, "Harringay Impressions," *SPJ* (2 June 1954): 3–6; L. Nelson Bell, "This Is the Lord's Doing," *SPJ* (9 June 1954): 3–5; L. Nelson Bell, "London Campaign—Aftermath," *SPJ* (16 June 1954): 5–6.

faithfully preaching God's Word and evangelical doctrines, coop-
erating with those of evangelical conviction across denominational
lines in mass evangelism for the good of the nation and the world.
Graham presented the true solution to the problems that both the
church and nation faced; as Nelson Bell put it, "The way out of our
dilemma is to pray for such a mighty work of the Holy Spirit across
America that we shall again center our interest, time, and money on
winning souls to Jesus Christ. This controversy [on church union]
can be used of the Lord to clarify our thinking on vital matters of
both faith and polity. But it could also be used of Satan to disrupt,
divert, and divide."[22]

Southern Presbyterian conservatives would get blow-by-blow
updates about Graham's ministry through 1957. They rejoiced when
he succeeded in Scotland and at London's Wembley Stadium, and
they grieved when he was maliciously attacked by liberals such as
Reinhold Niebuhr and by extreme right-wingers such as Carl McIntire
and Bob Jones.[23] As Graham and his team prepared for the campaign
in New York City in spring 1957, Henry Dendy once again sent out
the word for conservative southern Presbyterians to pray: "This is a
situation which calls for earnest prayer, for importunate prayer, for
agonizing prayer. A true revival in New York could stir the nation and
the world. This must be a work of God's Holy Spirit." Plans for the
event were laid out in some detail: the personal-counselor program;
the radio coverage; the staff of associate evangelists; the large number
of ushers and choir members. And its successes were duly noted as
Graham filled Madison Square Garden on opening night with over
eighteen thousand people.[24]

22. L. Nelson Bell, "The Way Out," *SPJ* (30 June 1954): 3.

23. For example, "Billy Graham Team Close Month Long Crusade in New Orleans," *SPJ*
(17 November 1954): 6–8; "Pray for Glasgow," *SPJ* (16 February 1955): 3; L. Nelson Bell,
"Glasgow—Now," *SPJ* (9 March 1955): 3–4; L. Nelson Bell, "The Miracle of Wembley,"
SPJ (1 June 1955): 20–21; George Burnham, "Billy Graham in India," *SPJ* (1 February
1956): 5; Robert Strong to L. Nelson Bell, 24 August 1956; L. Nelson Bell to Robert Strong,
3 September 1956 (both in L. Nelson Bell Papers, box 69, folder 24, BGC); L. Nelson Bell,
"The *Christian Beacon* and the Communists Attack Billy Graham," *SPJ* (6 April 1955): 3–5.

24. Henry B. Dendy, "The New York Campaign," *SPJ* (20 February 1957): 4; "Plans for
Billy Graham New York Crusade Surpass All Expectations on Eve of Opening Meeting,"

By July 1957, however, a different note was being sounded. Graham's policy of inclusion of liberal Protestants created great difficulty for some conservative leaders within and outside Presbyterianism. Nelson Bell hammered "extreme fundamentalists" who dared to "smear" Graham for allowing liberal northern Presbyterian minister John Bonnell to have a leadership role in his campaign. By Labor Day 1957, Bell was once again defending Graham, this time for his policy of encouraging those who made spiritual decisions to return to the church of their choice, whether Bible-believing or otherwise. And in private correspondence, he had to defend Graham's views on racial integration because he invited Martin Luther King Jr. to give an invocation during the crusade. These three issues—Graham's inclusion of liberal ministers in leadership; his policy of returning individuals to their churches from which they came; and his general practice of nonsegregated campaigns, begun in 1952 but receiving greater attention after the New York campaign—all combined to make it less appropriate to mention him as frequently in the pages of the *Southern Presbyterian Journal*. There would be continued defense of Graham, especially of the New York campaign and his 1958 San Francisco evangelistic meetings, but by 1959 the publicity given to his ministry would have significantly decreased.[25]

As Graham's ministry became global, southern Presbyterian conservatives tended to turn their focus in other directions. It seemed that the day of revivals was passing by—not only did the Graham events not arrest the moral decline, but the South was experiencing challenging times with the civil-rights struggle. That did not stop

---

SPJ (10 April 1957): 16–18; L. Nelson Bell, "Madison Square Garden: The Old Gospel in a New Arena," *SPJ* (29 May 1957): 2–3.

Nelson Bell defended Graham against charges of "slipping" theologically because of his inclusion of John Bonnell in the Scotland campaign. This issue would come again in New York City. See, for example, John R. Richardson to L. Nelson Bell, 4 April 1955; L. Nelson Bell to John R. Richardson, 13 April 1955 (both in L. Nelson Bell Papers, box 69, folder 12, BGC).

25. L. Nelson Bell, "The New York Campaign—Sifting the Wheat," *SPJ* (3 July 1957): 3; L. Nelson Bell, "But Wisdom Is Justified of Her Children," *SPJ* (4 September 1957): 2–3; L. Nelson Bell to Mrs. Willard Steele, 10 June 1958; L. Nelson Bell to William Rogers, 17 June 1958 (both in L. Nelson Bell Papers, box 47, folder 8, BGC); Miller, *Billy Graham and the Rise of the Republican South*, 66.

some churches from continuing evangelistic ministries or from supporting Graham's ministry. For example, under John Reed Miller and
Don Patterson's leadership, First Church, Jackson, Mississippi, hosted
Graham's brother-in-law Leighton Ford in 1956 and would support
Graham in his meetings in the city in May 1975. But even this congregation's leadership would eventually move away from evangelistic
meetings toward a greater focus on international missions and local
theological education.[26]

BILL HILL AND SOUTHERN PRESBYTERIAN EVANGELISM

By the time Aiken Taylor became the editor of the *Presbyterian
Journal* in 1959, he would continue to note Graham's evangelistic triumphs and would continue to defend Graham privately. But he would
also introduce and support other homegrown varieties of Graham's
ministry.[27] Of these, none were more important than William (Bill)
E. Hill Jr. Born into a Presbyterian minister's home in 1907, Bill Hill
was related to several prominent southern Presbyterian families: his
great-grandfather was Thomas Reese English, who was a scion of
South Carolina Presbyterianism; his grandfather taught English Bible
and pastoral theology at Union Seminary; his sister married Aubrey
Brown, who would be the longtime editor of the progressive *Presbyterian Outlook*; and his cousins included the McGeachy and Cousar
clans, many of whom would be significant missionaries and ministers.
Hill's father was a noted theological moderate and ministered at several
of the more significant cosmopolitan pulpits in the southern church:
West End Presbyterian in Atlanta; First Church Fayetteville, North
Carolina; and finally, Second Presbyterian in Richmond. If anyone
should have imbibed the ethos of progressive southern Presbyterianism—both its elitism and paternalism expressed through the social
gospel—it would have been Bill Hill.[28]

26. Lucas, *Blessed Zion*, 117–18.
27. For examples of G. Aiken Taylor's defense of Graham in correspondence, see G. Aiken
Taylor to William A. Macaulay, 30 January 1961, *Presbyterian Journal* Papers, box 197,
folder 5; G. Aiken Taylor to Gordon Clark, 6 November 1967, *Presbyterian Journal* Papers,
box 150, folder 15 (both at PCAHC).
28. Otto Whittaker, *Watchman, Tell It True* (Manassas, VA: Reformation Education
Foundation, 1981), 18; W. W. Moore, "Dr. Thomas Reese English," *Union Seminary*

And for a time, Hill was a strong proponent of the social gospel. After receiving the requisite southern Presbyterian education at Davidson College and Union Seminary, he served two churches in Hopewell, Virginia: West End Church and First Presbyterian Church. There he attempted to meet the challenging social and economic conditions with a version of the social gospel that coupled it together with evangelistic methods and preaching. Starting in 1929 and each year after that, Hill would hold evangelistic meetings in his congregation and challenge them to bring unconverted friends and family to hear the gospel preached. He also emphasized door-to-door visitation, not simply visiting church members, but visiting everyone in given city blocks, sharing the gospel with them, and inviting them to church. With the onset of the Great Depression, he would also begin to wage war against social ills in industrial Hopewell, especially against prostitution and gambling and for unionized labor. A turning point came when Hill attended an anniversary celebration at Moody Bible Institute in Chicago; the messages there uncovered the problems of theological liberalism and the social gospel, offering some of his seminary professors and favorite ministers as examples. He soon came to realize that the social gospel was actually undercutting his emphasis on mass and personal evangelism. By the 1940s, he was committing himself more fully to biblical inerrancy, premillennialism, and especially evangelism as the way forward for his congregations. He sided more and more with conservatives in Hanover Presbytery and in the PCUS generally.[29]

As Hill continued to look for evangelists for his congregation's annual revival meetings, he discovered a significant lack of adequate Presbyterian evangelists. He found himself resorting to using Baptists and nondenominational preachers who could effectively preach the message of salvation to his congregation. As he began to reflect on this need, he also wondered whether the Lord was leading him to

Review 26 (1914–15): 311–21. Information also came from the appropriate entries in E. C. Scott, ed., *Ministerial Directory of the Presbyterian Church, U.S., 1861–1941* (Austin, TX: Von Boeckmann-Jones, 1942), and E. D. Witherspoon Jr., ed., *Ministerial Directory of the Presbyterian Church, U.S., 1861–1967* (Doraville, GA: Foote and Davies, 1967).

29. Whittaker, *Watchman, Tell It True,* 104–9, 131–58.

full-time evangelism. For a number of years, Hill had led three to six evangelistic meetings each year in various churches around the country. By 1957, he was wrestling with the sense that his time at West End was concluding. Significant in that regard were two conferences on evangelism that he led for the North Alabama Presbytery and the Synod of Alabama; after these meetings, which confirmed a sense of divine calling to transition into a Billy Graham style of ministry, he notified his elders at West End Church that he was leaving the pastorate to move into itinerant evangelism.[30]

And so in July 1958, Bill Hill went into full-time evangelism. When he did so, he believed that he was the only PCUS minister dedicated to this style of ministry. Over his first five years as an evangelist, he preached in ninety-eight evangelistic meetings in nine states. He also became recognized among conservatives as a representative of exactly what they had prized when they promoted Billy Graham: a forthright presentation of the gospel with the expectation that a changed individual would in turn live differently and make an impact in his or her neighborhood, workplace, and family. For younger southern Presbyterian conservatives, there was also his commitment to evangelizing African Americans and his insistence that his ministries be integrated, a commitment that was of long standing from his days in Hopewell. In Hill, conservatives had someone who was passionately committed to evangelism and revival, but who spoke about it theologically in ways that Presbyterians could appreciate.[31]

Hill would come increasingly into the pages of *Presbyterian Journal* defending evangelism and revival in terms that would have been familiar to most readers. For Hill, revival was a "spiritual awakening . . . in which churches are under conviction, homes and families are changed, the moral tone of the community is lifted." The reason that such revivals were necessary was that churches and Christians were conformed to the world. In order to move forward into the world with spiritual power, God needed to send revival. This was particularly the case if evangelism was going to occur and people were to be won to

---

30. Ibid., 297–300.
31. Ibid., 327; "The Presbyterian Evangelistic Fellowship," *PJ* (2 March 1966): 7. For Hill's commitment to integrated ministry, see Whittaker, *Watchman, Tell It True*, 205–7, 291.

Christ. "Before the Church can become really zealous for evangelism, something else must take place—spiritual renewal, or if you please, revival," Hill declared. Bible study, prayer, and fervent preaching of the doctrines of the Bible were necessary to bring about spiritual renewal, which would produce real evangelism and social change.[32]

Like Billy Graham, Hill urged that revival and evangelism were necessary to save the American way of life. Democracy itself depended on "Protestant, Bible-believing countries, where people are self-disciplined, morally and emotionally mature." As one looked around at America, however, one saw the opposite: signs of decline that would be followed by "deadlock, violence, paralysis, pseudo-democracy, total government control and ultimately dictatorship." How could America be saved from such a disastrous end? Only by turning back to the Bible and the Bible's plan of salvation. And that could happen only if God sent revival: "Can America turn back to the eternal principles of the Word of God, the faith of our fathers? Only a real spiritual awakening will do it. . . . Without this, by all tokens of history, democracy is doomed in America and in the world, once more to sink into oblivion for generations to come." Revival would bring about the desired change.[33]

And it would produce the evangelism that the church desperately needed. For Hill, "biblical evangelism is simply a matter of bringing others into a saving relationship with Jesus Christ." It was not to be confused with social change, although biblical conversion and widespread revival would bring about significant societal transformation. It was not the same as religious education, although those converted by biblical evangelism would need education. Rather, biblical evangelism declared a message that was "first a call to repentance toward God, and second to faith in the Lord Jesus Christ." This message was declared especially by pastors in the regular ministry, but also by full-time evangelists. As these men were set apart for full-time evangelistic ministry, the church as a whole would be strengthened in the task of evangelism. But that task would become a high priority only when

32. William E. Hill Jr., "Revival—A Dirty Word?," *PJ* (4 July 1962): 5–6.
33. William E. Hill Jr., "Democracy's Doom," *PJ* (21 March 1962): 7–8.

"the ground is prepared by spiritual revival." Revival and evangelism went together for the advancement of the church.[34]

As Hill championed the cause of evangelism and revival in the PCUS, he came to realize that he could not continue to do this work on his own. Early in 1964, Hill led a series of Evangelism Prayer Conferences, which not only encouraged prayer as the basis for citywide evangelism, but also highlighted the need for more evangelists in the PCUS. That summer, several conservative leaders who were passionate about the cause of evangelism gathered to pray and deliberate about what to do. The result was the creation of PEF. In order to have a fellowship that was more than one evangelist, these leaders agreed to join together financially to support Dick Little as the second full-time worker. By 1966, PEF had added John Fain and Ben Wilkinson as associate evangelists. They had also merged with the Atlanta-based Evangelism Services Association to create a regional organization for evangelism. Eventually, they would also host a significant conference at Montreat each summer that would outdraw many of the programs sponsored by denominational leaders.[35]

Hill's significance for southern Presbyterian conservatives was in the success of his evangelistic campaigns. Here was someone with unblemished Presbyterian connections who demonstrated the truth of what conservatives had said all along: gospel preaching, born out of confidence in the inerrant Bible, was the means for bringing about spiritual renewal, both in the PCUS and in America at large. Against the liberal leadership that continued to push the social gospel and religious education as the way forward for the church, conservatives could point to Hill and PEF, along with Billy Graham, as the truer path. As PEF continued to have success among conservatives, Hill's voice would become increasingly significant as the crisis in the church came to a head.

THE "SPIRITUAL" MISSION OF THE CHURCH

Southern Presbyterians' consistent support for Billy Graham and his style of evangelism as well as their ongoing longing for spiritual

---

34. William E. Hill Jr., "Evangelism: Bogus or Biblical?," *PJ* (9 September 1964): 7–8.
35. Whittaker, *Watchman, Tell It True*, 368–70; "Presbyterian Evangelistic Fellowship," 7.

renewal pointed to a deeper issue, one to which conservative leaders returned again and again: namely, the spiritual mission of the church. At the heart of that mission were a spiritual focus and an evangelistic imperative—telling men and women about their sin and the offer of salvation in Jesus. "What is the mission of the Church?" Nelson Bell asked rhetorically in 1945. "It should go without argument that the mission of the Church is to proclaim Christ as the Savior of sinners, the one and only hope of salvation." Wilbur Cousar later declared, "What is the centrality of the Church's Mission? The Great Commission provides a concentrated, yet comprehensive, answer. It says that the church's supreme mission is to evangelize." Samuel McPheeters Glasgow agreed that "the primary mission of the church of Christ and its consuming passion must always be, bringing lost men and women and children to the only Savior." William Childs Robinson noted that the southern church had always gloried "in the spiritual mission of the Church" that followed from its commitment to "the sole Headship of our Lord Jesus Christ. As He is our King it is the Church's duty as part of His Kingdom to do only those things He has commissioned His Church to do, that is, worship God, preach the Gospel, proclaim the law of Christ, given in His Word."[36]

PCUS conservatives contrasted their understanding of the church's mission with progressive voices within and outside their church. For example, Nelson Bell used a *Presbyterian Outlook* article to highlight the divergences between evangelicals and liberals: "Emphasis on education more than on preaching the Word; emphasis upon Christian ethics rather than on the one source of such ethics—the atoning work of Christ; emphasis on human achievement rather than on the new birth." Later, reflecting on a 1948 ecumenical meeting in Amsterdam that served as the lead-up to the World Council of Churches, Bell observed that there was a deep cleavage in the PCUS understanding of the church's mission. If the church had "a spiritual mission, then the primary and predominating work of the Church

---

36. L. Nelson Bell, "The Mission of the Church," *SPJ* (June 1945): 5; R. Wilbur Cousar, "The Centrality of the Church's Mission," *SPJ* (16 May 1949): 7; Samuel McPheeters Glasgow, "A Watchman," *SPJ* (13 August 1952): 5; William Childs Robinson, "The Spiritual Mission of the Church," *SPJ* (15 August 1950): 4.

is to preach the unsearchable riches of Jesus Christ to men who are lost for all eternity and whose only hope lies in faith in that which he has done for them." On the other hand, some churches taught that the human condition was "essentially good" and that human beings needed "primarily the opportunity to make good." These churches saw their mission to be "work[ing] for reforms which will make possible the achieving of happiness, peace, prosperity, and health."[37]

Other southern Presbyterian conservatives similarly distinguished between their understanding of the church's mission and the liberals' understanding. "In our modern age two general positions have been set forth as to what the position is in relation to the social problems of the world," R. P. Robertson observed. The liberals held that "the Church's primary emphasis is that of easing suffering, correcting social and economic problems." Conservatives understood that "the primary message of the Church is the proclamation of the Gospel; that it is the prime duty of the church to make clear to a world dying in sin that the only hope is in the Christ of the Gospel." These questions were the primary ones facing the church: Would the church primarily be a social and educational agency, or would the church be an evangelistic agency? How did social change happen, and how might America be transformed—through education or evangelism?[38]

Conservatives consistently set forward this fundamental difference in their understanding of the mission of the church as the major divide between themselves and their progressive counterparts— conservatives placed confidence in evangelism and progressives in education and social reform. For example, Bell contrasted "a Spirit-sent and directed revival," which would produce "a personal experience with the living Christ," with merely "educat[ing] young people into church membership" and "invit[ing] others to 'join the Church.'" He noted that "education has its place but personal salvation is a personal

37. L. Nelson Bell, "Christianity and Realities," *SPJ* (15 August 1946): 4; L. Nelson Bell, "Both Deep and Wide," *SPJ* (1 December 1948): 4. For a brief exploration of this divide in other southern Protestant denominations, see Charles Reagan Wilson, "Making the South: Religion in a Twentieth-Century Region," in *The American South in the Twentieth Century*, ed. Craig S. Pascoe, Karen Trahan Leathem, and Andy Ambrose (Athens, GA: University of Georgia Press, 2005), 209–22.

38. R. P. Robertson, "What Is the Message of the Church," *SPJ* (1 February 1949): 19.

experience and it comes through a work of the Holy Spirit in the individual heart and no other way." At one point, Nelson Bell noted pithily, "Remember, men are born into the kingdom, not educated into it." This was because "this doctrine of the new-birth is diametrically opposed to the natural teaching of our time, a teaching which stresses improvement in environment, social opportunities and privileges, education and other natural processes as the answer to man's dilemma. Following closely in this naturalistic substitute for God's supernatural work is the emphasis on education as a means within itself."[39]

For southern Presbyterian conservatives, this commitment to evangelism as the church's spiritual mission was finally a commitment to the authority of God's Word. This was modeled by Graham's own method, as Tom Glasgow noted. "Without debate," he wrote, "Billy Frank Graham is today the nation's greatest and most widely sought after evangelist. And what is his message? 'Thus saith the Lord,' the exclusive story of Salvation by a Crucified Savior from the Old Book and supporting the Whole Book." Henry Dendy, reflecting on Graham's 1953 Asheville, North Carolina, campaign, observed that he "preaches with power and with authority because his life and his message are saturated with the Word of God and empowered by the Holy Spirit." This was "an example to preachers of our time, for his work is a living testimony": the mission of the church was spiritual in nature and centered on the preaching of the gospel from the inspired Word of God. And, Dendy noted during the 1954 London campaign, Graham's spectacular success was "because of this faithful adherence to the Scriptures. . . . Let him change his beliefs and his message to that of modern theological liberalism and he would be shorn of his power as surely as Samson was shorn of his power when his hair was cut short." By trusting unreservedly in God's Word, Graham and, by extension, conservative southern Presbyterians were the ones who had power to accomplish the church's true mission: the saving of souls.[40]

39. Bell, "Our Greatest Need," 4; "Problems of Youth," *SPJ* (15 June 1950): 3; "Revivals," 3; Bell, "Revival or Else," 5; Bell, "The Work of the Holy Spirit," 4.

40. Tom Glasgow, " 'Culture' or 'Christ,' " *SPJ* (1 June 1950): 9; Henry B. Dendy, "Billy Graham in Asheville," *SPJ* (25 November 1953): 7; Dendy, "It Is No Secret," 4. For similar observations, see Flow, "Billy Graham in Atlanta," 4; Dendy, "A Work of the Spirit," 2.

But things became complicated for these southern Presbyterian conservatives in that evangelism was never simply about disembodied souls; there was an expectation that renewed individuals would make an impact in their local contexts. "We feel every effort of the Church should be directed towards the winning and nurturing of Christians— new-born individuals in Christ," Nelson Bell declared. "A changed social order will come through such individuals and in no other way." R. L. McNair admitted that "the saved man will become the best citizen. Saved men will restore order." Wilbur Cousar claimed that "the regenerated Christian, 'born from above,' is to be the infiltrating agent of righteousness in a corrupt world. He is to daily practice the virtues of his new found faith and to condemn the vices of his contemporary society." It was true, Bell later declared, that evangelical Christians who represented "the great soul-winners of each generation" all too often discounted and failed "to appreciate that the individual Christian and the Church have a social responsibility. Men need the Gospel, but they need food and clothing too. Men need Christ's redeeming power in their lives, but they also need the removing of injustices and discriminations." In fact, personal transformation would lead to social reform: "Social reforms must come through and from redeemed lives."[41]

This confidence that evangelism could produce genuine social transformation made drawing the lines on what constituted the spiritual mission of the church or how it played out in local contexts difficult and sometimes apparently arbitrary. From the reports on Graham's evangelistic meetings, one could conclude that the spiritual mission of the church would clearly have a social impact. For example, in Fort Worth, it was claimed that "the Billy Graham Crusade is literally a religious revival set up to fight crime, political corruption, immorality and all the other ills of our generation." And a reporter from Houston noted that the police saw crime statistics decline during the meetings. Moreover, Graham never hesitated to use his preaching ministry to hammer Communism. As historian William Martin noted, Graham

41. L. Nelson Bell, "The Application of Social Principles," *SPJ* (1 October 1946): 3; R. L. McNair, "Evangelism," *SPJ* (October 1944): 7; Cousar, "The Centrality of the Church's Mission," 7; L. Nelson Bell, "A Plea for Christian Unity," *SPJ* (18 March 1953): 5; L. Nelson Bell, "The Work of Redemption Primary and Central in the Gospel," *SPJ* (3 June 1953): 2.

claimed that "not once will you hear from this platform an attack, by implication or otherwise, against any religious or political group. The only one I mention from the platform occasionally is Communism, which is anti-God, anti-Christ, and anti-American." Such rabid anticommunism mixed together with Graham's gospel message made it hard to know where the church's spiritual mission ended and the nation's political mission began.[42]

Perhaps the greatest difficulty for southern Presbyterians in stewarding the church's spiritual mission and in promoting revival derived from their consistent focus on its potential benefits for America. In this regard, southern Presbyterian conservatives and progressives had a great deal in common. While conservatives were quick to point out areas in which liberals sought to transform society through programs of reform and education, they never differed with progressives concerning the ultimate goal—namely, the transformation of America. This was the unstated presupposition of both parties within the church during this period: that American civilization was essentially Christian; that the church was neglecting its duty by not speaking out on the internal corruption of the country and by failing to bring about meaningful change; and that the church was the fundamental instrument in reversing this trend and so saving America. The difference was that conservatives believed that the church's mission of evangelistic outreach, typified by Billy Graham and others like him, represented the only hope for America because only through personal transformation would national and international transformation be possible.[43]

Still, this emphasis on evangelism would serve to connect southern Presbyterian conservatives to their past and would be the key thing that they desired to preserve going forward. Such a commitment to the spiritual mission of the church would prevent them from taking the side of civil-rights protesters, but would also encourage them to preach the gospel both domestically and internationally. Notably, when

---

42. "Billy Graham in Fort Worth," 5; "Successful Graham Campaign Continues for Extra Week," 11; Martin, *Prophet with Honor*, 165; Wacker, *America's Pastor*, 231–34.

43. Here I am reflecting the insight of D. G. Hart, *The Lost Soul of American Protestantism* (Lanham, MD: Rowman and Littlefield, 2002), and D. G. Hart, *Deconstructing Evangelicalism: Conservative Protestantism in the Age of Billy Graham* (Grand Rapids: Baker, 2004).

the time for division between PCUS conservatives and progressives came, "obedience to the Great Commission" would be one of the three things that these conservatives wanted known about themselves. It was to save the lost souls of Americans and others that a continuing church would emerge.

8

Concerned Presbyterians: Southern Presbyterian Conservatives and the Crises of the 1960s

As southern Presbyterian conservatives looked at their world and their church during the late 1950s and 1960s, they grew increasingly concerned. All around them were signs that freedoms historically taken for granted by white Protestants were being abridged, moral certainties were being undone, and the rising generation was in danger of forsaking the old paths. While conservatives had voiced these fears from the end of World War II on, their concerns and anxieties heightened with the successes of the civil-rights movement, the continued opposition of Communists, the move toward women's equality in the context of church offices, and the sexual and moral license of their children. Nelson Bell warned, "Today we are witnessing the death of a nation. . . . America is doomed—heading for the certain judgment of a holy God." Most southern Presbyterian conservatives agreed with Bell's gloomy prediction.[1]

And so these conservatives tried to find moral certainty in an age gone mad, but it was hard to find. Increasingly, they listened to reactionary voices that promised ways forward that would preserve the southern way of life. Noted segregationist Robert Ingram, founder

1. L. Nelson Bell, "Watching a Nation Die," *PJ* (12 February 1964): 11.

of St. Michael's Episcopal School in Houston, not only spoke to the Jackson, Mississippi, Citizen's Council in 1962, but also championed Christian day schools as a means of circumventing the integrationist directives contained in *Brown v. Board of Education*. His work was also featured in the pages of the *Southern Presbyterian Journal*. Likewise, when right-wing propagandist Dan Smoot was at the height of his popularity in purveying Cold War hysteria, Aiken Taylor, the editor of the renamed *Presbyterian Journal*, distributed copies of Smoot's report upon request. Although Taylor recognized that sometimes Smoot exaggerated and twisted his information "beyond propriety," he also told a supporter that he had been "an admirer" of Smoot's for a number of years. William Buckley's nascent *National Review* was warmly commended by Nelson Bell, as was his book *God and Man at Yale*. Jesse Helms, erstwhile news commentator for WRAL-TV in Raleigh, North Carolina, and future United States senator from North Carolina, regularly found a place in the pages of the *Journal*. And even Barry Goldwater was viewed as a potential fellow traveler, one who knew that extremism in the defense of liberty was no vice. To be sure, not all southern Presbyterian conservatives shared every particular view of these right-wing political commentators and activists, but they were all heading the same direction with similar diagnoses and solutions for preserving American civilization.[2]

The striking thing was that for a worldview that repeatedly emphasized the spiritual mission of the church, these religious conservatives could not see that their "private" or "individual" advocacy for political and social policies and positions blurred the lines of the nonsecular mission of the church. By providing religious rationales for

2. "Religious Leader for Segregation," *Jackson Clarion Ledger* (13 May 1962); John R. Richardson, "Freedom's Holy Light," *SPJ* (26 June 1957): 5; G. Aiken Taylor to Mrs. George E. Johnston, 25 February 1964; G. Aiken Taylor to C. M. Jones, 20 March 1964; G. Aiken Taylor to W. A. L. Sibley Jr., 29 May 1964 (all in *Presbyterian Journal* Papers, box 183, folder 5, PCAHC); "The 'National Review,'" *SPJ* (14 December 1955): 8. For an example of Jesse Helms's editorials reprinted in the *Journal*, see "Leadership in Some Direction," *PJ* (7 February 1962): 6. Bell made obvious although implied reference to Goldwater in "What 'Extremists'?," *PJ* (12 August 1964): 13; see also Taylor, "That Word 'Extreme,'" *PJ* (2 September 1964): 14. For Ingram, see Joseph Crespino, *In Search of Another Country: Mississippi and the Conservative Counterrevolution* (Princeton, NJ: Princeton University Press, 2007), 67.

political and social issues, they desired to speak to all of life in the same way as their liberal counterparts. Hence, being a "concerned Presbyterian" was a matter of being fearful about not simply the theological or ecclesiastical direction of the southern Presbyterian church, but also its racial, social, and political direction. Defending "our Southern Zion" meant defending the entire conservative cultural system.

RACE, CIVIL RIGHTS, AND THE SOUTHERN (PRESBYTERIAN) WAY OF LIFE

There was a marked shift in the direction of the conservative southern Presbyterian magazine in 1959. Not only did the board of directors drop *Southern* from its title, making it simply the *Presbyterian Journal*, but they also brought in a new editor, G. Aiken Taylor.[3] Born in 1920 to missionary parents in Brazil, Taylor returned to the United States when he was fifteen to complete his education. He graduated from Presbyterian College in South Carolina in 1940 and spent the war years in the army as a captain and company commander in the 142nd infantry. After the war, he graduated from Columbia Theological Seminary and then Duke University with a Ph.D. with a focus on John Calvin and religious education. When he was at Columbia, Taylor had served a church in Smyrna, Georgia, and while he was at Duke, he had served the Northside Presbyterian Church, Burlington, North Carolina. It was there that he became involved with a notorious discipline case, involving Charles M. Jones and the Chapel Hill Presbyterian Church; because he went with those who opposed Jones based on biblical principles, instead of preserving silence, he believed that it cost him his "lifelong dream" of teaching at Columbia Seminary.[4]

And yet it was through his principled stand that Taylor came to the attention of conservative leaders. He was one of the key speakers on the floor of the 1954 Assembly against reunion with the northern

3. Discussions about dropping *Southern* from the masthead had begun in 1956: "1956 Report of the Committee to Study the Southern Presbyterian Journal," L. Nelson Bell Papers, box 73, folder 3, BGC.

4. "Biographical Sketch," in G. Aiken Taylor Papers, box 114, folder 2; G. Aiken Taylor to Marshall Dendy, 7 June 1960, *Presbyterian Journal* Papers, box 197, folder 3 (both at PCAHC). For the Chapel Hill case, see Mark Pryor, *Faith, Grace, and Heresy: The Biography of Rev. Charles M. Jones* (Lincoln, NE: Writer's Showcase, 2002).

church; his articles and speeches around that time drew notoriety. He left Burlington, North Carolina, and went to serve the Presbyterian church in Alexandria, Louisiana, for five years before he was approached to take on the editorship of the *Journal*. One of his questions in taking on this role was whether he would have to agree with and promote the *Journal*'s aggressive position on racial segregation. Growing up on the mission field had caused Taylor to have a much different attitude about segregation than most southerners. He told Nelson Bell, "I don't like agitation on the social question from either side. I am not an integrationist, neither am I a segregationist. My position on this issue is that a view point of whatever kind should not be made the criterion for determining the place or the worth of a man . . . or a church paper." In reply, Bell assured Taylor that there was a range of opinions on segregation among the board of directors for the magazine and that he would not be required to hold to a particular party line. That said, the older man also counseled him not to push his more moderate racial views either: "I feel you would be utterly foolish to come to the Journal as editor and make race an issue—certainly at this juncture. There are so many more important things which need to be faced." As it would happen, Taylor's position on race, as evidenced in his writing and editorial practice, would largely harmonize with Bell's own: downplaying forced segregation, dismayed by outside agitators who stirred up the racial issue, and concerned not to let racial politics divert attention from the more important doctrinal and social issues of the day.[5]

The first notice of race relations after Taylor became editor actually came from Nelson Bell. Once again, he sounded all the notes about "interracial marriage" and "mulattos" that he had sounded before. But there was a new note as well: "We believe that we who live in the South must come to terms with changes which, while having taken place gradually, are now actualities. To those who have made educational and economic progress to the place where they need public services, these should be granted, not grudgingly but as a matter of course." In

---

5. Paul Hastings to G. Aiken Taylor, 17 March 1954, G. Aiken Taylor Papers, box 114, folder 22, PCAHC; G. Aiken Taylor to L. Nelson Bell, 29 May 1959; L. Nelson Bell to G. Aiken Taylor, 15 June 1959 (both in L. Nelson Bell Papers, box 75, folder 16, BGC).

addition, Christians needed to view blacks as those who had souls "as precious in God's sight as that of any other person." Evangelism was being hindered by the racial agitation; justice needed to be done. At the same time, conservatives needed to make sure that such moderation would not divide the church. Taylor urged the church to vote down the overtures coming to the 1960 General Assembly seeking to reopen reunion conversations with the northern church. Among his reasons were pronouncements by the northern church on race issues: "Some of the pronouncements, such as those on race relations, have been sufficiently explosive to produce a wide-open split in a Church such as ours." Racial moderation did not mean advocacy for integration, nor did it commit individuals to agitate the church on the issue.[6]

Even with Taylor and Bell's moderation on racial issues, there were those in conservative ranks who were determined to maintain racial integrity. W. A. Gamble, stated clerk of Central Mississippi Presbytery and sometime contributor to the *Journal*, was infuriated by the recent moderation on racial issues. Board member John R. Richardson tried to calm Gamble down by writing, "We realize there has been some dissatisfaction. I am grateful, however, to tell you that I feel that in basic convictions all connected with the Journal have not changed nor will change in the future" on the issues of racial integrity. As a way of backing that reassurance, the *Journal* board issued a statement insisting "that the integrity of each race should be a matter of paramount importance and grave concern that much today which purports to be 'Christian race relations' has nothing to do with Biblical Christianity but works toward the destroying of racial integrity as it has developed in the Providence of God." As a result, the board reaffirmed "voluntary segregation in churches, schools, and other social relationships," which was all for the "highest interests of the races." In fact, "forced interracial social relationships, rather than being the ideal to which the church should work, are actually compounding the problems they seek to solve. Racial integrity is something to be preserved, not broken down."[7]

6. L. Nelson Bell, "One Southerner Speaks," *PJ* (13 April 1960): 9, 18; G. Aiken Taylor, "Church Union an Issue," *PJ* (20 April 1960): 11.

7. John R. Richardson to W. A. Gamble, 12 August 1960 and 15 August 1960, both in L. Nelson Bell Papers, box 69, folder 13, BGC; "Journal Day Attracts Throng of Supporters,"

This defense of racial integrity did not mean that violence was an acceptable vehicle for sustaining it. East Alabama Presbytery declared itself against the mob violence that engulfed the 1961 Freedom Riders in Birmingham and Montgomery: "We express our deep regret and emphatic disapproval of mob violence for whatever cause." Likewise, Nelson Bell was appalled by the lawlessness on the part of both sides of the civil-rights struggle in Birmingham in 1963. "One of our chief concerns is the effect these demonstrations are having on young people, both Negro and white," he declared. "Many white boys and girls, encouraged no doubt by their parents, have participated in counter demonstrations involving insults and violence. At the same time many Negro young people are being led into a psychological blind-alley— following the idea that 'rights' can be secured by mob action." Not mob violence, but adherence to the law was the way forward; "where laws perpetuate injustices, they must be changed."[8]

And yet on the other side, the pursuit of racial justice did not legitimize lawbreaking either. When the 1965 General Assembly endorsed a range of civil-rights activities, including peaceful demonstrations and sit-ins, over sixty commissioners filed a dissent. Nelson Bell presented it to the Assembly, arguing that "some of the methods sanctioned in the document are 'contrary to or go beyond the jurisdiction of the Church.'" Even if the church desired to support "worthy goals" such as racial justice, Aiken Taylor noted, that did not mean that it could do so through "radical measures" or "extremism or vindictiveness." Later in 1965, Bell worried again that peaceful demonstrations were a small step from civil disobedience and that "the step from civil disobedience to riots and violence is even shorter." Willfully breaking laws, even for a worthy goal, was wrong: "No nation should permit injustice and discrimination to be a part of its accepted way of life.

PJ (31 August 1960): 5.

8. "Presbytery Expresses Regret over Incidents," *PJ* (14 June 1961): 22; L. Nelson Bell, "A Plea for Communication," *PJ* (26 June 1963): 8. On the Freedom Riders, see Raymond Arsenault, *Freedom Riders: 1961 and the Struggle for Racial Justice* (New York: Oxford University Press, 2006). It is noteworthy that the moderator of the PCUS distanced himself from the March on Washington in August 1963 for fear that "mass demonstrations . . . often generated race hatred and served mostly to gratify radical extremists." "Churches' Part in March a Mistake Says McCorkle," *PJ* (11 September 1963): 19.

But no nation can survive which placidly allows people to make of themselves prosecutors, jurors, and executioners—and this applies to *all* citizens." Brice Dickson held that civil disobedience actually made race relations "more precarious" than ever, creating social unrest that encouraged Communists around the world. Ends did not justify the means: breaking the law, whether to support segregation or integration, was never right.[9]

Sometimes defending racial integrity, or at least defending the South's approach to racial issues, required an active engagement of those who disagreed. In 1963–64, Hattiesburg, Mississippi, was an important center for voter-registration efforts in which northern Presbyterian ministers worked. The three Hattiesburg Presbyterian ministers—William J. Stanway, Newton Cox, and Ed Jussely—sought to engage their Yankee counterparts, both in the local press and by their willingness to debate the issue on their home turf. As a result, these three ministers along with two ruling elders went to Charleston, Illinois, to speak to Presbyterians there about the racial situation throughout the Deep South. Even more, they communicated their commitment to the spiritual mission of the church: "the church as an organization has no business taking part in political and sociological affairs." That was not to say that the gospel did not have social implications; it most assuredly did. But the Hattiesburg Presbyterians pointed to Scripture to show that it neither justified civil disobedience nor countenanced northern Presbyterians' "invasion" of Hattiesburg to promote racial justice. If northern Presbyterians desired to help blacks, they should preach the gospel to them, which would in turn promote their social and economic well-being.[10]

9. "Assembly Endorses 'Civil Rights' Action," *PJ* (12 May 1965): 7; G. Aiken Taylor, "Evaluating the 105th Assembly," *PJ* (12 May 1965): 14; L. Nelson Bell, "Danger Signals," *PJ* (29 September 1965): 15; L. Nelson Bell, "The Road to Lawlessness," *PJ* (24 August 1966): 15 (emphasis his); Brice T. Dickson, "What about Civil Disobedience?," *PJ* (14 June 1967): 12; Samuel T. Harris Jr., "The Problem of Civil Disobedience," *PJ* (6 December 1967): 8–10.

10. G. Aiken Taylor, "The Heart of the Matter," *PJ* (11 March 1964): 10; [Leonard Lowrey,] "The Church and Its Purpose," *Hattiesburg American* (22 February 1964). For more on this historic debate, see Robert Patrick Rayner, "On Theological Grounds: Hattiesburg Presbyterians and the Civil Rights Movement" (M.A. thesis, University of Southern Mississippi, 2009), 55–67. An account of the 1963–64 Hattiesburg voter-registration movement

Other churches were not as interested in dialogue. Second Presbyterian Church, Memphis, Tennessee, drew national attention for its refusal to admit mixed-race groups to corporate worship services. One of several Memphis churches targeted in early 1964 by the local chapter of the NAACP for its "kneel-ins," Second Church reacted the most negatively. The groups were refused admittance, and church officers patrolled the narthex and the front of the church, looking for those who would seek to "integrate" the services. The Second Church kneel-ins drew media attention not only because of their racial component, but also because the congregation was scheduled to host the PCUS General Assembly in 1965. As a result, several presbyteries and synods, along with the liberal *Presbyterian Outlook*, protested allowing the Memphis church to host the Assembly; by February 1965, the Assembly's moderator, Felix Gear, a former pastor of Second Church, had decided to move the coming meeting to the denomination's assembly grounds in Montreat.[11]

Conservatives felt that the attention given to the situation at Second Church, Memphis, was slanted and unjust. At one point, Aiken Taylor claimed that this church was receiving negative attention merely "to embarrass the pastor's brother, Senator Richard Russell," a noted segregationist who was fighting against civil-rights legislation. Later, he observed that Second Church was being singled out because it was "a great evangelical congregation with a tremendous . . . evangelistic and missionary testimony." As a result, young liberals in the PCUS were trying to "alienate and divide, to punish and to destroy" the reputation of this church. It did not help, of course, that one of the main Second Church ruling elders who opposed the kneel-ins, Horace Hull, was a longtime leader on the *Presbyterian Journal* board of directors. Others tried to defend Hull and his position. Nelson Bell claimed that Hull was really a racial moderate; his position was that "the question of seating Negroes in the congregation should not be forced by the

can be found in Mark Newman, *Divine Agitators: The Delta Ministry and Civil Rights in Mississippi* (Athens, GA: University of Georgia Press, 2004), 46–67.

    11. A full account of the Memphis kneel-ins can be found in Stephen R. Haynes, *The Last Segregated Hour: The Memphis Kneel-Ins and the Campaign for Southern Church Desegregation* (New York: Oxford University Press, 2012).

proposed meeting of the General Assembly." Yet Hull's actions were decisive not only in preventing Second Church from admitting black worshipers, but also in eventually splitting the church and creating a new congregation, Independent Presbyterian Church.[12]

Conservative Presbyterians also protested the National Council of Churches' "Delta Ministry" that started in 1964 and continued through 1967. The Delta Ministry focused on poverty and racial injustice in the Mississippi Delta, although it also worked on voter registration in south Mississippi towns such as Hattiesburg and McComb. As conservatives, they disliked the arrival of "outside agitators" into their areas to stir up the racial situation; as Presbyterians, they did not care for the fact that their own tithes and offerings were being used to support outsiders' coming into the South to work for racial justice. As the program progressed, the *Journal* wagged its head at every alleged association of the Delta Ministry with Communists and unionizers, signaling the leftward political and racial purposes of the program. When the Delta Ministry leaders encouraged African Americans to stage a "live in" at the deactivated Greenville, Mississippi, Air Force base, it was another sign of the lawless aims of the program.[13]

Not only did conservative Presbyterians not appreciate attempts to force integration in congregations and in their daily lives, but also they disagreed with the desegregation of presbyteries. The 1964 General Assembly had determined to do away with Snedecor Memorial Synod, the nongeographical synod that served as the court of original jurisdiction for African-American ministers. As a result, the Assembly instructed the presbyteries to receive the black ministers and churches. John Reed Miller, pastor of First Presbyterian Church, Jackson, Mississippi, moved

12. G. Aiken Taylor, " 'Young Turks' in Action," *PJ* (24 June 1964): 12; G. Aiken Taylor, "An Emergency?," *PJ* (10 February 1965): 12; L. Nelson Bell to J. McDowell Richards, 14 November 1964, J. McDowell Richards Papers, PHS; Haynes, *Last Segregated Hour*, 108–9, 113, 190.

13. G. Aiken Taylor, "World Missions and the 'Delta,' " *PJ* (10 February 1965): 12–13; "NCC Names Delta Ministry 'Evaluators,' " *PJ* (9 February 1966): 4–5; "Delta Project Leader[s] Suggest More US Aid," *PJ* (23 February 1966): 5; G. Aiken Taylor, "Incident in Mississippi," *PJ* (9 March 1966): 12–13; "Panel Urges Support of Delta Ministry," *PJ* (8 February 1967): 4–5. For a telling of the Delta Ministry, see James F. Findlay Jr., *Church People in the Struggle: The National Council of Churches and the Black Freedom Movement, 1950–1970* (New York: Oxford University Press, 1993), and Newman, *Divine Agitators*.

to replace *instruct* with *request*, arguing that the resolution as worded "would be construed as improper coercion and would result in harmful reaction at the local level." Yet the "instruction" was passed, only to be rescinded the following year for a more gradual approach. And yet even that proved to be too much for some presbyteries. Tuscaloosa Presbytery rejected the Assembly's instruction to receive black Presbyterian congregations within its bounds, as did Central Mississippi Presbytery. It would not be until 1969 that Central Mississippi Presbytery would receive black ministers into its membership.[14]

Conservative Presbyterians had a deep distrust of civil-rights leader Martin Luther King Jr., and worked to prevent his influence within the PCUS. When the Board of Christian Education's Division of Christian Relations invited King to speak at its August 1965 conference at Montreat, racial conservatives sought to rescind the invitation on the floor of the General Assembly. And the *Presbyterian Journal* gave full coverage to his appearance, highlighting his responses to questions about his involvement with Highlander Folk School in Tennessee, which conservatives had connected to Communism, and about whether the civil-rights movement had Communist connections. For the next three years, whenever King was mentioned, it was always in connection with his supposed Communist leanings, making in a more subtle fashion the same connections between integration and Communism that had been so effective in the previous decade. When King was killed in 1968, Aiken Taylor admitted frankly, "Martin Luther King was not a man we admired" because of his alleged Communist connections as "documented" by the FBI. His death was the result of the principles of civil disobedience that he had defended: "Those who have advocated (or excused) civil disobedience share the blame for the death of Dr. King." Justice would not come through injustice, no matter how effective or eloquent the messenger.[15]

14. G. Aiken Taylor, "The Assembly in Detail," *PJ* (13 May 1964): 19; "Tuscaloosa Presbytery Rejects Assembly Order," *PO* (25 May 1964): 3; "Jackson Church Is Refused Admittance," *PO* (26 September 1966): 3.

15. "Attempt to Block King Defeated by Assembly," *PJ* (5 May 1965): 8; L. Nelson Bell, "One Commissioner's Reactions," *PJ* (19 May 1965): 13, 18; "2 Speakers Headline 'Historic' Weekend," *PJ* (1 September 1965): 4–5; "M. L. King Suggests Red in UN, Cease Fire,"

Conservatives would demonstrate their distrust of King and his legacy even more publicly. In 1969, the PCUS General Assembly approved a recommendation to hold a memorial service for King the next year when the Assembly met in Memphis. Conservative leaders thoroughly disliked the idea that King would be memorialized for "his martyrdom and as a positive expression of love for all the members of the body of Christ." As a result, Concerned Presbyterians made stopping the memorial service one of their goals for the following year. They sponsored an overture from Tuscaloosa Presbytery that sought to demonstrate that King was a theological liberal who came to prominence through "the climate of violence which he helped to create." Far from being a martyr or an example, King was a divisive figure; honoring him would not "promote peace, healing, or reconciliation in the denomination." However, the overture failed to stop the memorial service in Memphis; and so, conservatives brought a personal resolution that detailed King's alleged heterodoxy as well as his supposed association with Communists and called the Assembly to express regret that the memorial service happened. Signed by seventeen leaders, including W. Jack Williamson, H. S. Williford, Robert Strong, and John R. Richardson, the resolution was answered strongly in the negative by the Assembly and the moderator ordered that the resolution itself be expunged from the minutes. Still, conservatives made their feelings about King widely known: he was not a force of reconciliation and good for them.[16]

And especially when the messenger was unworthy or threatening, church and society should withstand the message. That was Taylor's take on James Forman's "Black Manifesto," first presented at Riverside Church in New York City in May 1969. Throughout the summer of 1969, the manifesto was presented in several congregations; the manner of presentation—with the interruption of services especially in congregations that had television broadcasts—caused churches to

---

PJ (22 September 1965): 5–6; G. Aiken Taylor, "This Is the Not the Way to 'Justice,'" *PJ* (17 April 1968): 12.

16. Concerned Presbyterian Memo to Presbytery Chairmen, et al., 24 July 1969, http://www.pcahistory.org/findingaids/concerned/Memo-July1969.pdf; *MGAPCUS* (1970), 37, 136–37.

take precautions in case black militants were to arrive. Meanwhile, the PCUS Council on Church and Society urged the church to take seriously the reparation demands of the black militants and to understand the context from which these demands came. But Taylor and other southern Presbyterian conservatives saw the manifesto and the PCUS response as Marxist—focused on the redistribution of wealth—and unworthy of serious attention. The messenger and the message were too radical to be heard.[17]

Even as the 1960s came toward a close, Nelson Bell continued to advocate what he took to be racial moderation. "*Forced* segregation was wrong, *forced* integration is equally wrong," he reiterated. And yet behind his continued commitment to the idea that "Christian race relations proceed from love, not force," he had actually traveled a long way from the late 1940s and early 1950s. He recognized that the Supreme Court had no choice but to void Virginia's statute against interracial marriage; he observed that churches had no business enforcing "closed door" policies, banning blacks from corporate worship, a practice that was "un-Christian." He also admitted that society needed to provide "the right of equal opportunity" to all its citizens, a commitment that could only be the result of Christian morality shaping social policies. All these positions were far beyond what Bell could have imagined twenty years before. And yet he continued to believe to the end of his days that the civil disobedience practiced by civil-rights leaders such as Martin Luther King worsted the cause of race relations. Bell could not see that if it were not for the willingness of King and others to disobey Jim Crow laws in order to gain racial justice, then racial moderates such as Bell would have never come to defend equal opportunity regardless of race or color.[18]

17. "More Services Interrupted by Militants," *PJ* (28 May 1969): 6; "Church Offices Given Up to 'Manifesto' Militants," *PJ* (28 May 1969): 6; "Presbyterian US Unit Pronounces on Manifest," *PJ* (9 July 1969): 7–8; G. Aiken Taylor, "Shall We Capitulate?," *PJ* (9 July 1969): 12.

18. L. Nelson Bell, "Fruits of Mistakes," *PJ* (9 August 1967): 13, 20 (emphasis his); L. Nelson Bell, "Civil Disobedience," *PJ* (22 May 1968): 9. On this point, I agree with David L. Chappell, *A Stone of Hope: Prophetic Religion and the Death of Jim Crow* (Chapel Hill, NC: University of North Carolina Press, 2004).

COMMUNISM AND THE NATIONAL COUNCIL OF CHURCHES

While Taylor and Bell sought to moderate southern Presbyterian conservatives on race, they both continued conservatives' full-throated opposition to Communism. Even before he became editor of the *Presbyterian Journal*, Taylor was known for his anticommunist views. Writing in *Christianity Today* in 1958, he observed that Communism failed because it was a "godless" political and economic philosophy. That was the point at which it differed from Christianity: "Communism believes the supreme good to be the betterment of Man; Christianity wants only to glorify God." Because humans, and not God, were at the center of communistic philosophy, it was focused on materialism as the chief end of humans, and it justified a coercive approach to rectifying imbalances in wealth distribution. As a result, Communists failed to raise their vision "beyond the horizon" to consider God or his ways in the world. It was fundamentally an atheistic worldview.[19]

Taylor's views on Communism harmonized nicely with the territory already staked out by Nelson Bell before 1960. Together, they filled the editorial pages with warnings about Communism throughout the next decade. Chief among the warnings was that America's policies toward Communist Russia were hopelessly naive. At the end of the Eisenhower years, Bell warned that "the gradual shaping of international policies to conform to our increasing (probably unconscious) trust in the words and motives of the Kremlin continues." This was undoubtedly the result of Khrushchev's visit to the United States; after that, "it seems that at every point Russia is succeeding in softening up opposition and in furthering her long-range plans for eventual world domination," all without firing a shot. But it was also the result of long-term policies pursued by the United States government, going back to 1932 when it extended official recognition to Soviet Russia. This was an endorsement of Communism's "spirit of Anti-Christ" for which God would hold America accountable.[20]

19. G. Aiken Taylor, "Why Communism Is Godless," *Christianity Today* (22 December 1958): 13–14.

20. L. Nelson Bell, "The Kremlin Smiles," *PJ* (13 April 1960): 9; L. Nelson Bell, "The Seed Sprouts," *PJ* (27 April 1960): 10; L. Nelson Bell, "When It Comes," *PJ* (20 July 1960): 7.

America's naiveté about Communism did not change with a transition in administrations; the Kennedy administration, too, was "deluded into the belief that in some way we can do business with Communism." The only way to deal with Communism, according to Bell, was to "quarantine" it from the free world, withdrawing "diplomatic recognition at every level." To those who thought severing all diplomatic relations with Communists was foolish, Bell retorted that the "breaking off of diplomatic relations with Russia offers us the advantage of crystallizing world opinion on our side." Neutral and uncommitted nations would no longer turn to Soviet Russia but would be "galvanized" by this action. In 1964, as Bell traveled in the Far East, he saw the effects of Communism on the churches; in China, especially, the church organizationally had disappeared, gone underground, and had its buildings confiscated by the Communist leadership. The same had happened in North Korea as well; these two nations "bear mute testimony to what Communism really is," namely, a godless and aggressive ideology determined to wipe out Christianity throughout the world.[21]

Not only were federal government policies naive, but the American public was as well when it came to the ways of Communists. In 1961, Bell warned that Communist groups operated by "filtered infiltration," in which "a button is pushed in Moscow" that communicated something to a dedicated Communist, who then passed it along to a fellow traveler. This individual spread the ideas to a liberal church leader, who took up the issue and confused the local church member. The church member never connected the dots back to Moscow, and yet America's danger was found "with that small, dedicated and disciplined group which takes its orders from Moscow, and with the dupes who foolishly try to protect them." In fact, Communists "are making every effort" to infiltrate America and other free nations, which was a fact that Americans were ignoring "to our own undoing." This ignorance was seen in one 1961 newspaper editorial that claimed that the Communist Party was drastically weakened: anyone who believed

21. L. Nelson Bell, "It Is to Survive," *PJ* (14 June 1961): 9; L. Nelson Bell, "Have We Waited Too Long?," *PJ* (11 October 1961): 11; L. Nelson Bell, "Christians and Red China," *PJ* (24 June 1964): 13.

that, Aiken Taylor observed, was "either badly deluded or deliberately deceptive." When the Belgian and American governments rescued nearly two thousand hostages from the Congo in 1964, Communists and fellow travelers raised protests. Such protests caused Nelson Bell to observe that "despite years of experience we Americans continue to indulge in the wishful hope of 'containment' and 'negotiation.' It was those who try to unmask Communistic intrigue who found themselves under fire, not from open Communists but from fellow Americans who should know better. One of Communism's great victories has been leading so many Americans to look on anti-Communism as 'right-wing extremism.' "[22]

This naiveté was problematic because Communists succeeded and gained power when people unwittingly embraced the Communist worldview and sought to implement it. Nelson Bell warned that "if Communism ever takes over in America it will not be Russians taking over America, but Americans taking over America in the manner experienced by many other countries—Cuba, for instance. These Americans will be those who have shared in sabotaging the ideas and ideals by which and on which America was founded." Thus, criticizing free-market capitalism or the House Un-American Activities Committee was evidence of Communist infiltration; likewise, the subversion of American youth through art and music, school textbooks, and college professors also was a way that Communists were winning "without firing a shot." American Christians needed to pay better attention to the way in which Communist propaganda worked its way into daily life: "Day by day more and more Americans are having their minds conditioned for further compromise with, and even capitulation to, Russia." Kenneth Keyes agreed and cited the example of his own son, whose "mind had been poisoned by the devilish propaganda of International Communism" while he was a student at Duke University.[23]

22. L. Nelson Bell, "Filtered Infiltration," *PJ* (22 March 1961): 13; L. Nelson Bell, "Lost Perspective," *PJ* (17 May 1961): 5; G. Aiken Taylor, "Communism Weakened?," *PJ* (12 July 1961): 9; L. Nelson Bell, "A Glimpse behind the Curtains," *PJ* (16 December 1964): 13.

23. L. Nelson Bell, "That Vital Omission," *PJ* (16 August 1961): 5–6; L. Nelson Bell, "Truth vs. Propaganda," *PJ* (20 September 1961): 11; L. Nelson Bell, "Counsel of Doom," *PJ* (15 November 1961): 11; Kenneth S. Keyes, "The Vital Role of the Layman in the Church Today," *PJ* (10 January 1962): 6.

While southern Presbyterian conservatives were profoundly anxious about worldwide Communism, they were especially alert to signs
that it had infiltrated the churches. In one 1960 editorial, Aiken Taylor
quoted the secretary of public affairs for the National Association of
Evangelicals, Clyde W. Taylor, noting that "it can be seen why certain
liberal churchmen have frequently called for social revolution. While
it may be true that they have not adopted the Marxist-Lenin phase of
socialism, there has been a tendency to promote a 'social' gospel which
has been related at points to the (ideological) objectives of Communism."
An example of how liberal churchmen supported Communism was
the Fellowship of Reconciliation's 1960 statement against the Mutual
Security Pact with Japan; the net effect was to support the "massive,
Red-sponsored riots in that far-eastern country." These kinds of actions,
"extreme social concern(s) associated with radical religion," were why
"clergymen are sometimes called communist-sympathizers." Another
example was from a 1961 issue of the *Presbyterian Outlook*, the liberal
southern Presbyterian magazine, that approvingly quoted D. L. Munby,
a British economist and vice-chair of the World Council of Churches.
Munby favored "a much greater degree of equality than exists even in
the most Socialistic of the Western European nations"; this association was further proof of the connections between liberal theology and
Communist-like economic and social policies. In fact, it was an axiom
that "liberal religion almost always stands to the left politically, economically and socially as well as theologically"; presumably, the axiom
was just as true for the marriage of conservative theology and politics.[24]

Of course, for southern Presbyterian conservatives, the most
obvious source and purveyor of Communism in religious circles was
the National Council of Churches. Its adherents were the ones who
were most critical of anticommunism: "Not even the Communist
Party itself is as vocal in condemnation of 'right-wing extremists' as

24. G. Aiken Taylor, "Communism in the Churches," *PJ* (30 March 1960): 10; G. Aiken
Taylor, "Why Clergymen Are Called Communists," *PJ* (27 July 1960): 11; G. Aiken Taylor,
"Do You Know Communism . . . When You See It?," *PJ* (25 October 1961): 10; G. Aiken
Taylor, "Conservatives and Politics," *PJ* (2 January 1963): 10. Nelson Bell observed in 1966
that "the materialistic and humanistic philosophy of the extreme theological liberal is but a
step from Marxian dogma." "Protestants, Catholics, and Communism," *PJ* (14 December
1966): 13.

are the official organs of several major denominations and especially of the National Council of Churches." But conservatives saw them as the ones most responsible for the acceptance of Communism in the churches. In 1961, the session of Northminster Presbyterian Church, Greenville, South Carolina, adopted a resolution that charged the council with having "repeatedly espoused Communist causes" and giving "aid and comfort to the Communist enemy." Private individuals expressed the same sentiments. Robert R. Wallace claimed that "the National Council of Churches is basically rotten and stands for everything that I do not. We do not even talk about the same God. Therefore, that Socialistic, Communistic, Left-Wing, Liberal Integrationist outfit cannot do nor say ANYTHING that is acceptable to me." Not surprisingly, conservatives scrutinized everything that the National Council of Churches proposed with a searching eye for Communist-inspired propaganda and positions.[25]

One example of this scrutiny was Taylor's commentary on a 1963 address given by Joseph Sittler to the annual meeting of the National Council of Churches. Sittler, Lutheran professor of theology at the University of Chicago Divinity School, set out "a theology for the NCC," a "new Christology" that emphasized the unity of all humanity in Christ; the dividing line between those who knew they were in Christ and those who did not was obedience to Jesus himself in love for neighbor. Taylor saw all this as dangerous theology and social policy: "The effect is really to reduce religion from a transaction basically between man and his Maker to a transaction basically between man and man. In the last analysis, God becomes my neighbor and religion becomes Socialism. Stripped of the theological language this is Marxism, pure and simple." And it was the theological undergirding of the National Council of Churches: social gospel transformed into Marxist ideology and practice to be doled out to the constituent churches, including the PCUS.[26]

25. G. Aiken Taylor, "Anti-Communism and the Anti-Anti's," *PJ* (10 January 1962): 10; "Overture in Regard to the National Council of Churches" (13 March 1961); Robert R. Wallace to G. Aiken Taylor, 19 November 1963 (emphasis his) (both in *Presbyterian Journal* Papers, box 183, folder 3, PCAHC).

26. G. Aiken Taylor, "A Theology for the NCC," *PJ* (25 December 1963): 7–8.

As the 1960s progressed, conservatives came to believe that "Marxism has become virulent at certain levels of the 'ecumenical' movement." Examples included National Council of Churches proclamations about leveling the incomes of Americans to raise nearly a quarter of the population to a national average; NCC leaders' expressed promises about "greater and more radical revolutions" after the racial crisis passed; and student leaders' declarations that Christians needed to cooperate with Marxists in order to meet the world's needs. When the 1966 National Council of Churches study conference applauded "open and frank commendation of Communism," it simply confirmed what conservatives had known all along. With the addition of the fact that the National Council was heavily invested in the Delta Ministry in Mississippi and other racial-equality movements through its Commission on Religion and Race, it became obvious to conservatives that the leveling philosophy of Marxism was being propagated at several levels through the organization.[27]

Many of these issues came together through the National Council's opposition to the Vietnam War. The *Presbyterian Journal* did not editorialize on Vietnam until the 1966 PCUS General Assembly adopted the National Council policy statement on the war, issued the previous December. The policy statement urged the United States to enter into negotiations with Communist North Vietnam and the Viet Cong as quickly as possible and asked the United Nations to intervene and establish such negotiations if practicable. When the Assembly voted to adopt the policy, it seemed to conservatives that the church not only had involved itself in a purely secular matter, but had sided dangerously with the Communists, seduced to do so by the National Council. And it provided encouragement to those who protested the war as "victims of clever propagandists" and who were "caught up in a movement which strikes at the very roots of a stable society."[28]

27. G. Aiken Taylor, "The Churches Join the *Revolution*," *PJ* (29 January 1964): 10; G. Aiken Taylor, "They Laud Communism," *PJ* (30 March 1966): 13.

28. G. Aiken Taylor, "The Assembly Acted . . . ," *PJ* (11 May 1966): 9; G. Aiken Taylor, "The 1966 Assembly: An Evaluation," *PJ* (11 May 1966): 12; L. Nelson Bell, "Recipe for Anarchy," *PJ* (11 January 1967): 13. For treatments of southern Presbyterians, the National Council, and Vietnam, see Rick L. Nutt, *Toward Peacemaking: Presbyterians in the South and National Security, 1945–1983* (Tuscaloosa, AL: University of Alabama Press, 1994),

Southern Presbyterian conservatives were equally concerned by the civil unrest demonstrated by the younger generation in their opposition to the Vietnam War. Brice Dickson observed that "our Communist enemies in Viet Nam and around the world are greatly encouraged by the Church resolutions for unilateral peace and for the other groveling demands for peace at any price. The draft card burnings and the seminars on 'legal avoidance' of military duty reflect the breakdown of the moral fiber of our people." Nelson Bell agreed, noting that the protests created conditions under which Communism thrived and were often used by Communists to their own ends. When the National Council of Churches joined with the American Civil Liberties Union in 1967 in defending three draft resisters, it was yet more evidence that the organization was working against American society and for Communism. It was of a piece with "NCC officials openly support[ing] Communist causes and attack[ing] the anti-Communist position of the U.S. government." And this was an organization that had the backing of the PCUS, one that was working for the destruction of civilization in America and for the "hell-inspired and demonically controlled ideology" of Communism.[29]

THE ROLE OF WOMEN IN THE CHURCH

Compared to the struggles over civil rights and Communism, the debates over women's ordination were relatively tempered and short-lived. The discussion began as a result of the proposed 1954 reunion with the northern Presbyterian church.[30] Since 1930, it had been permissible to ordain women to the offices of elder and deacon in the northern church. In the PCUS, however, neither office was open to women, which made it a potentially significant difference to be resolved if reunion were to

---

and Jill K. Gill, *Embattled Ecumenism: The National Council of Churches, the Vietnam War, and the Trials of the Protestant Left* (DeKalb, IL: Northern Illinois University Press, 2011).

29. Dickson, "What about Civil Disobedience?," 12; L. Nelson Bell, "A National Emergency," *PJ* (24 May 1967): 15; "NCC Joins in Defense of Draft Resisters," *PJ* (13 December 1967): 5–6; G. Aiken Taylor, "Is Communism No Longer an Evil?," *PJ* (14 February 1968): 12–13; L. Nelson Bell, "For What It Is," *PJ* (21 February 1968): 13.

30. For a detailed account of women's issues in the Presbyterian tradition, see Lois A. Boyd and R. Douglas Brackenridge, *Presbyterian Women in America: Two Centuries of a Quest for Status* (Westport, CT: Greenwood, 1983).

happen. And yet conservatives did not even mention the issue in the pages of the *Southern Presbyterian Journal* until September 1953, when the editors offered commentary on the final version of the plan of union. They simply noted that the policy of women serving as elders "has no Scriptural basis and is not allowed in our church." In December 1954, when reunion was nearly defeated, the *Journal* ran its first article critical of the northern Presbyterians' policy of women as officers in the church. Thomas K. Mowbray, pastor of Powell Presbyterian Church, Spartanburg, South Carolina, recognized that modern society had granted women many opportunities; in fact, "women today are more the equals of men than ever before. Society has been richly blessed because of their emancipation." And yet the Bible limited church offices to men: "In New Testament history, only men are seen to have been called to permanent official work in the church; and the qualifications demanded (1 Tim 3; Titus 1) contemplate men ONLY." To allow women officers was to be disobedient to God and to court his displeasure.[31]

In the event, reunion was defeated, but this did not mean that the issue of women as officers went away. In response to several overtures, the 1955 General Assembly appointed a study committee to determine the biblical position of women in the church. As that committee prepared its report, William Childs Robinson offered his own biblical study of the place of women in the church. He noted that the church is "the house of God" and as such God has ordered his household so that "our Lord has given the place of regular government to men both by the example of those He has called and by the conditions for such offices." With that lone restriction, "God has used women in highly significant and useful places." In fact, Phoebe functioned as a "deaconess" and other women "prophesied," which led the apostle Paul "to draw the line against women participating in authority to preach or administer the sacraments." In the final analysis, for Robinson and other conservatives, women and men shared a common standing before God in Christ, but had different places in the order of church and home.[32]

31. "A Study of the Plan of Union," *SPJ* (2 September 1953): 5; T. K. Mowbray, "Women Elders in the Church," *SPJ* (1 December 1954): 9 (emphasis his).

32. Thompson, *Presbyterians in the South*, 3 vols. (Richmond, VA: John Knox, 1963–73), 3:478; William C. Robinson, "A Biblical Study of the Place of Women in the Church," *SPJ*

When the Assembly's study committee returned in 1956 with a recommendation that women be admitted to the offices of both elder and deacon and when the Assembly voted in favor of the change subject to the majority vote of the presbyteries, conservatives turned their attention to the "women's issue" with full force. Thomas Casey appealed to 1 Timothy 2:8–15 to demonstrate that "the *only* way then in which the woman is not to exercise authority is in the explicit official capacity of Elder and Deacon." This restriction was based on "the priority of Adam's creation, and the priority of the woman's defection" in the garden of Eden. One pastor, Gabriel Abdullah, suggested that male leadership in the church was rooted in the fact that the "masculine Triune God" had made man in his own image; the implication of this was that only males were made in God's image, women serving simply "to alleviate man's loneliness." Regardless, it was clear to these conservatives, based on the biblical material, that women should not serve as officers in the church.[33]

One of the issues that conservatives had to answer was why it was acceptable to have women missionaries, teaching and leading internationals, but not to have women as elders, teaching and leading in southern Presbyterian churches. William Childs Robinson argued that the New Testament was filled with examples of women serving in missionary work: the women who supported Jesus' ministry in Luke 8; the women who gave the first witness to the resurrection; the four daughters of Philip mentioned in Acts 21; and Priscilla, the wife of Aquila, mentioned in Acts 18 and Romans 16. All of these demonstrated a "full and explicit approval of a *female* missionary." But there was not an explicit New Testament warrant for women serving as elders in the church. "It is up to proponents of the innovation [of women elders] to offer '*clear* Bible evidence' to the effect that God has authorized a woman to be an elder in the Church."[34]

(25 April 1956): 7–8; William C. Robinson, "The Sufficiency of Scripture and Women Elders," *SPJ* (15 August 1956): 2–3.

33. Thomas L. Casey, "Women as Elders," *SPJ* (19 September 1956): 12–13; Gabriel Abdullah, "On the Position of Women in the Church," *SPJ* (26 September 1956): 13.

34. William Childs Robinson, "In the New Testament We Find Female Missionaries, but Not Women Elders," *SPJ* (17 October 1956): 3–4 (emphasis his).

Conservatives did not simply rely on the biblical material to argue against women officers. They also raised questions about the increasing wave of feminism and the mixed results of women's equality. Edward Thornburg observed that "the rising tide of marital difficulties and delinquency [was] due directly or indirectly to the absence of the wife and mother from the home." And while "women have definitely proved to be at least the equal of men in most occupations," it was still the case that "they have failed to prove in a great number of cases that they could be both homemaker and breadwinner." Likewise, William Childs Robinson blamed the agitation for women in office on "the behests of a modernistic equalitarianism or the clamor of current culture." Whether it was caving in to the culture or something more insidious, this agitation for women officers was not worthy of the church.[35]

The 1956 proposal for allowing women to serve as elders and deacons was defeated in the presbyteries, but that did not put an end to the issue. If anything, the cultural shifts of the next five years created a stunning dynamic in which the PCUS would completely reverse itself and approve the ordination of women to the offices of elder, deacon, and minister. The process toward the ordination of women began in 1959, when the Assembly authorized an Ad Interim Committee on Adult Work that was studying a number of structural issues connected to the Board of Christian Education and the Board of Women's Work. When this committee reported in 1962, it urged that "the General Assembly take immediate steps to initiate the process by which women may become ordained officers in the Presbyterian Church, US, and be extended the same privileges as are now extended to our male membership, thus implementing the spiritual doctrine of 'the priesthood of all believers' and in this way strengthen and enrich the spiritual life and program of our Church." This recommendation—to prepare a concrete proposal for presentation to the 1963 General Assembly—had the support of the Board of Women's Work and two recent General Assembly moderators.[36]

35. Edward C. Thornburg, "Women in the Church Today," *SPJ* (31 October 1956): 7; William Childs Robinson, "The Distinctions God Has Made Equality: Modernistic or Calvinistic?," *SPJ* (9 January 1957): 5.

36. "Ordination Asked for Church Women," *PJ* (28 February 1962): 3; Thompson, *Presbyterians in the South*, 3:479.

While all the biblical material that had previously been used would seem to be in play, *Journal* editor Aiken Taylor recognized that the ground had shifted in the debate: "Of all the opinions calculated to make one unpopular in the Church, none bears a more iron-clad guarantee than the opinion that Ordination belongs peculiarly to men." Because one could "not settle this debate by quoting Scripture," the best one could say against women's ordination was that it was "out of character," a female usurpation of the roles and functions given to males. Conservatives did make a half-hearted attempt to argue against women's ordination. McFerran Crowe observed that "the passages in the New Testament which tell of the ordination of elders and deacons simply do not mention women at all. Men are *assumed*. There is no possibility of missing the apostle's intention. He meant men." Even if one argued that Romans 16:1, which described Phoebe as a deaconess, allowed for women to serve as deacons, that was no argument that women were to be admitted to positions "of authority and government." Aiken Taylor noted that Galatians 3:28, which held that there was "neither male nor female" in Christ, "refers to the Christian's relationship in Christ, not to the duties of Christians within the Church." The qualifications of elders, Taylor held, stressed "the masculine nature of the office." Bill Williams claimed that "praying and prophesying" in 1 Corinthians "had nothing to do with conducting public worship services or governing the church." Rather, the apostle "was only making room for the woman to give a glorifying utterance to God when He should move in her heart either with a special revelation or with the inspiration to special prayer." While these arguments would continue to be used by conservatives, the relatively few articles in the pages of the *Journal* on the issue suggested that they knew they were fighting a losing battle.[37]

By the 1964 General Assembly, it was clear that women's ordination was a *fait accompli*. It had passed through the presbyteries by

37. G. Aiken Taylor, "Ordain Women?," *PJ* (11 April 1962): 10; McFerran Crowe, "Ordain Women?," *PJ* (4 September 1953): 7, 9; G. Aiken Taylor, "Equal but Different," *PJ* (18 September 1963): 10–11; Bill Williams, "A Bible Study on the Position of Women," *PJ* (4 December 1963): 5. Crowe extended his treatment of the biblical materials in "Ordain Women? Part II," *PJ* (11 September 1963): 7–8, 19–21, and "Ordain Women? Part III: The Broad Sweep of Scripture," *PJ* (18 September 1963): 7–8, 21.

a 53–27 margin and was debated and passed by the 1964 Assembly, making it an official part of Presbyterian church government. None of this was noted by the *Journal*, in part because there were other, more important issues before the church. Though southern Presbyterians were nearly the last among the mainline denominations to embrace women's ordination, the fact that they did by such a large margin and so rapidly was a larger signal about the character of the church. Conservatives should have seen it as a signal of where "the grassroots" really were—the "silent majority" in the church had quietly shifted in a more progressive direction on a biblical issue.

CHILDREN OF THE SIXTIES: GENERATIONAL TRANSITIONS AND TENSION

As southern Presbyterian conservatives dealt with race, class, and gender—through the issues of the civil-rights movement, Communism, the National Council of Churches, and women's ordination—they did have a larger concern. As Presbyterians, these leaders believed in the generational nature of the church, which required nurturing the next generation in the truths of the gospel and the Reformed faith. And so they expressed concerns about American culture and the Presbyterian church during the 1960s because they were worried about the effects on the next generation as it took its place in the church's leadership. During the postwar years, with the emergence of Billy Graham and the Youth for Christ revivals, conservative leaders had some confidence that the faith was being passed on. When the sixties arrived, however, they began to experience deep concern that the next generation did not want a faith that looked like that of their parents. This was a significant issue—the generational conflict over the future of the faith—that drove conservative leaders to move toward new institutional structures that would stand for the old-time religion and conservative social mores.

Early in Aiken Taylor's tenure as editor of the *Presbyterian Journal*, he ran an article by Billy Graham on "a Christian philosophy of Education." Graham observed that so many young people lost their faith when they went to college because they were exposed to "progressive education," in which educators insidiously, "stealthily, and methodically" inculcated into their students a godless approach to learning that was "responsible for the mass departure from American principles, American ideals and Biblical morals." This godless approach denied that there were timeless standards of morality and that there was a spiritual aspect to humanity. This twofold denial served to damage America's political and religious life. Such a diagnosis meant that Christians should support Christian schools, Bill Hill argued. "While we sleep, our children—our boys and girls—perish on the rocks of unbelief, of atheism, cynicism, humanism, of the confusion of a scientific age, of a pagan world of education," he declared. "We have left them to the mercy of a pagan education given by the state, which at best pushes God off into the corner and at worst ignores His existence."[38] It is striking that while several southern cities established segregation academies after the decision in *Brown v. Board of Education*, the issues of Christian education were first broached in the *Presbyterian Journal* in the late 1950s and focused on increasing evidence of the secularization of public schools. Three years before *Engle v. Vitale* and five years before the 1964 Civil Rights Act gave the federal government power to desegregate public schools, Hill and other conservative Presbyterians advocated Christian education for a common reason: the desire to pass on the faith to the next generation.[39]

Increasingly, conservatives wrung their hands over the loss of faith at denominational-related colleges and schools. Nelson Bell cited a report from the *National Review* in which twelve denominational-related

38. Billy Graham, "A Plea for a Christian Philosophy of Education," *PJ* (2 December 1959): 5–6; William E. Hill Jr., "The Christian School—Why Not?," *PJ* (2 December 1959): 14. Hill followed up with three more articles on Christian schools: "Democracy and Christian Schools," *PJ* (22 June 1960): 7–8; "How to Start a Christian School in a Local Church," *PJ* (29 June 1960): 7–8; "What a Christian School Will Do for a Church," *PJ* (6 July 1960): 7–8. Hill's church, West End Presbyterian Church, Hopewell, Virginia, started a Christian school in 1947.

39. For another account of a Christian school that started for similar reasons, see Sean Michael Lucas, *Blessed Zion: First Presbyterian Church, Jackson, Mississippi, 1837–2012* (Jackson, MS: First Presbyterian Church, 2013), 121–23. Importantly, when First Presbyterian Church, Hattiesburg, Mississippi, was invited to participate in a Citizen's Council academy in 1965, it declined: *Session Minutes, First Presbyterian Church, Hattiesburg, Mississippi* (12 July 1965). For an account of school desegregation in Mississippi, see Crespino, *In Search of Another Country*, 173–266.

schools, including the PCUS-related Davidson College, had been surveyed and that claimed that over three-fourths had "reacted against
their religion because of what they have been taught in courses dealing
with religion." Not only was this bad news for Christian parents who
sent their children to such colleges to preserve them in the faith, but it
was bad for the future of the church as well: "The Church desperately
needs true Christian education, but the testimony of entirely too many
students themselves is that in some places Christian education has
gone sour." In the college classroom, young people needed someone
who was committed to "communicating Christian truth" with full
confidence that "he himself believes what he is talking about." When
the students heard this kind of Christianity, they would respond with
faith because they "respect convictions."[40]

Of course, most Presbyterians would not have access to Christian schools or choose to send their children to Presbyterian colleges. Yet most parents hoped that Presbyterian college ministries
would serve as a place of faith on a secular campus. As Aiken Taylor
noted, however, it was in the campus ministries "where advanced
ideas in ecumenism and other new religious forms most often find
their earliest implementation." And so on many southern campuses,
PCUS campus ministry was being merged with Methodist, Baptist,
and Disciples groups into a single, nondenominational ministry that
would downplay differences and that would utilize National Council
of Churches materials. Increasingly, these nondenominational groups
were involving themselves in left-wing politics, attacking the John
Birch Society, and promoting Communism. Even when the PCUS
campus ministries continued on their own, they tended to be much
more liberal theologically and socially than the congregations from
which the students came. In these ministries, students were exposed
to social-gospel issues—poverty, illiteracy, racism, economic justice—
but heard little gospel preaching or teaching, which was denigrated as
"fundamentalist." Little wonder that these PCUS campus ministries,
called "Westminster Fellowships," struggled, and it was little surprise

40. L. Nelson Bell, "Christian Education Gone Sour," *PJ* (6 November 1963): 5–6;
L. Nelson Bell, "Young People Respect Convictions," *PJ* (27 November 1963): 11.

when the PCUS Board of Christian Education voted in 1966 to phase these ministries out in favor of the joint campus ministries shared with other mainline denominations.[41]

And yet solid evangelical campus ministries were important because American culture was becoming sex-crazed and was threatening to take young people off track morally, physically, and spiritually. Nelson Bell observed that "young people are but a reflection of their elders[, which] creates for our nation a problem—the problem of God's certain judgment on the sex obsession we have permitted and only too often fostered." Later he wrung his hands over "the boldness of men who wield a sex-obsessed influence over many people," from the psychiatrist who urged the use and distribution of contraceptives to the college professor giving sexual advice in minute detail. Especially problematic were the lewd books, available at any newsstand, that were filled with "fornication, adultery, and perverse acts with an obsession which denotes minds steeped in the depths of depravity." Bell admitted, "We are frightened for the seeds of sex obsession are now bearing the fruit of promiscuity and those who should be trying to stem the tide of immorality are pouring oil on the flames of lust." What made it worse was when Presbyterian campus ministers encouraged sexual liberation under the guise of "realistic" approaches to sexuality. Aiken Taylor pointed to a Presbyterian campus minister in Colorado who argued that premarital sex was permissible for those who had a "covenant of intimacy" already established; this was yet another instance of the situational ethics taught from pulpits and classrooms across the country. Even a synodical newspaper offered expert opinion that created space for premarital sex, which was "the wisdom of this world and not God's revealed truth."[42]

41. G. Aiken Taylor, "Student Work Already Merged," *PJ* (4 January 1961): 10; G. Aiken Taylor, "Remember Student Work at Synod," *PJ* (6 June 1962): 11; G. Aiken Taylor, "A Typical Student Gathering?," *PJ* (18 July 1962): 8; G. Aiken Taylor, "Two Views of Student Work," *PJ* (20 January 1965): 12; G. Aiken Taylor, "COCU a Fact in Student Work," *PJ* (16 November 1966): 12.

42. L. Nelson Bell, "Remember Sodom!," *PJ* (21 June 1961): 11; L. Nelson Bell, "Filthy Dreamers," *PJ* (22 April 1964): 11; L. Nelson Bell, "Open Sewers," *PJ* (26 January 1966): 13; G. Aiken Taylor, "A New Sexual Ethic?," *PJ* (29 April 1964): 10; L. Nelson Bell, "The Sex Revolution," *PJ* (24 April 1968): 13.

Southern Presbyterian concerns skyrocketed, however, as student demonstrations began in earnest in the mid-1960s. Not only were students at state colleges running wild, but even students at denominational schools seemed to have cast off all restraint. Whether it was at Ohio State University, where thousands of students protested in the streets, or at "some Church-related institutions" such as Davidson College, where students demanded permission to keep alcohol in their rooms and "those aspects of education which identify the school as more than secular" were eliminated, the future appeared dark as young people rejected biblical morality. What was worse was that the adults on campus—faculty and administrators—"weakly capitulated to the demands of the students, no matter how far afield these may be." When Students for a Democratic Society (SDS) disrupted the 1968 Democratic National Convention in Chicago, southern Presbyterian conservatives were horrified to learn that the University Christian Movement, the joint campus work of the National Council of Churches, had urged students to take part in the protests. Worse yet was the defense of SDS's actions by leaders at the 1969 Montreat youth conference and their urging of the destruction of the state and the redistribution of wealth. Was this the way in which the next generation was to engage the issues of the day? Was this how the church would include them in the work of the gospel?[43]

The only response that the PCUS leadership could offer was "experimental" worship as a way of connecting with young people. One such 1968 service offered at Montreat received a full review in the pages of *Presbyterian Journal*: electric guitars and folk music, especially Bob Dylan's anthem "Blowin' in the Wind," a dialogue in place of the sermon that focused on social-gospel causes with no Bible references at all, and a lack of traditional liturgical structures. The evening service was more of the same: a jazz trio, a movie that focused on race and poverty, a message that called for economic and political justice, a litany that focused on social sins, the Lord's Supper accompanied by "We Shall Overcome," and the service's ending with "sacramental

43. Jesse Helms, "Mob Rule," *PJ* (8 July 1964): 14; L. Nelson Bell, "Campus Revolution," *PJ* (16 June 1965): 13; L. Nelson Bell, "More to Come," *PJ* (9 October 1968): 13, 23; Clydie [Paul Settle], "007 Rides Again," *PJ* (27 August 1969): 6.

applause." Aiken Taylor was appalled: "We couldn't help wondering if there was really any essential difference between the agony-and-ecstasy unfolding before our battered senses, and the wild festivities which met Moses when he came down from the mountain with the tablets of stone in his hand." The entire service was nothing other than "idolatrous sacrilege," and it was all offered as the way to reach young people. Nelson Bell worried that "the Montreat conferences will rather have the ultimate effect of misleading hundreds of precious young people—channeling their faith and activities into something far removed from personal Christianity, into social activism of a type which is basically materialistic and secularistic."[44]

In case southern Presbyterians thought these experimental forms of worship used at Montreat were simply a one-time attempt to broaden the church, it soon became clear that this was not the case. Several months later, at the PCUS Youth Quadrennial hosted in Atlanta, the same kinds of experimental worship were used: the congregation scrawled thoughts in graffiti as part of the worship service; people threw rubber balls at imitation stained-glass windows; profanity was used in the context of worship. In none of the worship services were prayers offered in their traditional form. As troubling as these practices were, worse was the theology undergirding them: worship "is that which relates me to my neighbor, which makes me feel good, which gives me identity. It is an effort to become immersed in the world." This was nothing less than "religion in its final, ultimate stages of secularization," Aiken Taylor declared. "Here was the Church with its spiritual umbilical cord severed, with no otherworldly objectives, with nothing to which to relate except man himself." It was the church at rock bottom.[45]

As the 1960s came to a close, Nelson Bell expressed the fears of a great number of southern Presbyterian conservatives. "Where is the Church leading her young people today?" he asked. After a decade

44. G. Aiken Taylor, "A Sunday at Montreat," *PJ* (21 August 1968): 7–13, 22; G. Aiken Taylor, "Worth Asking: What Is Sacrilege?," *PJ* (21 August 1968): 16; L. Nelson Bell, "Montreat: Retrospect and Prospect," *PJ* (4 September 1968): 7.
45. G. Aiken Taylor, "When Worship Is Not," *PJ* (22 January 1969): 12; G. Aiken Taylor, "Clydie Should Have Gone," *PJ* (22 January 1969): 7–9; G. Aiken Taylor, "To the Bottom and Starting Back," *PJ* (5 February 1969): 12.

of theology that denied the need for individuals to repent from sin and to believe in Jesus, but that instead urged people to enter into the world where God was already active and join the revolution, the church appeared to be leading its youth away from the faith. "As we have seen young audiences stand cheering and applauding black militants and representatives of the Communist-leaning Students for a Democratic Society there have been tears in our eyes and our hearts have felt like lead." The issues of race, gender, and society raised by the 1960s were not being answered by reference to what the Bible said and by a life of faith and obedience to Jesus, but were blurred by sincere yet unbiblical approaches. Even worse, the church's best and brightest were being turned away from faith in Jesus and instead wandering off into a "world come of age." The movement for a solution to the problems in the church, one that would eventuate in the creation of a church committed to evangelical and evangelistic Presbyterianism, started not simply to preserve a witness to the authority of Scripture or the Reformed faith. Whether recognized or not, the movement for a continuing church started in the belief that the next generation would be eternally lost if something was not done.[46]

46. L. Nelson Bell, "Whither the Youth?," *PJ* (27 August 1969): 15.

9

"The Faith of Our Fathers": The Central Issue for Southern Presbyterian Conservatives

By the end of the 1960s, southern Presbyterian conservatives had seen their denomination move significantly leftward. Although there had been a significant progressive presence in the church from the beginning of the century, especially represented in the seminaries and agencies, by this period the progressives had become the majority in the presbyteries and synods as well. On social and political issues, the PCUS offered increasingly liberal slants on civil rights, the war in Vietnam, and gender equality. Yet for conservatives, these social and political left turns had a deeper root: they sprang from a rejection of the authority of the Bible and an abandonment of the Reformed faith as summarized in the Westminster Standards.

That diagnosis was not new: it had been the constant refrain from the 1920s on—namely, that in abandoning the inspiration and inerrancy of the Scriptures, theological liberals could not maintain biblical authority. Once God's Word was replaced with human beings' words, then religion would become sociology and politics, with no power to change the human heart or society. In 1966, Roy LeCraw boiled down the controversy in the church, writing, "The central issue is this: Is the Bible really God's infallible, inerrant witness to men, written by the hands of men who were directly under the inspiration and guidance of the Holy Spirit? Or is it merely a record of man's religious instincts, bearing witness to his 'growing awareness' of God but containing many allegories, myths and sayings which are only human in thought and application?" Three years later, Nelson Bell put it similarly: "The basic divergence has to do with attitudes toward the Bible—on the one hand the full integrity and authority of the Scriptures, and on the other, varying degrees of rejection, from belief that the Bible contains the Word of God (but is not the Word of God), down to the view point that the Bible is no longer relevant to today's world." Conservatives believed that they stood for the Bible while progressives did not, and the results were plain to see.[1]

Flowing from this commitment to biblical authority were other theological commitments to the sinfulness of human beings and the redemption of sinners through Jesus' death, burial, and resurrection. A belief that the Bible was God's Word meant that one believed what the Bible said about human beings, about who Jesus was, and about what Jesus did. In other words, for these conservatives, a commitment to the Bible meant a commitment to the gospel, which in turn produced a commitment to evangelism and world missions. It also meant a commitment to biblical morality—not the situational ethics of modern existentialism, but the timeless ethic found in Scripture. Theological liberalism had abandoned these commitments and replaced them with the "new theology, new morality and new evangelism."[2]

That was why many conservatives were beginning to conclude that they could not remain in the southern Presbyterian church much longer. While the progressive leadership urged conservatives to remain in a future united Presbyterian church, Jack Williamson, a ruling elder from Greenville, Alabama, observed that there was a significant barrier to doing so: "We still believe the faith of our fathers. . . . As confessional Church members we have taken vows as to our faith and calling." To compromise the faith once received was something that

1. Roy LeCraw, "The Issue Is the Bible," *PJ* (31 August 1966): 12; L. Nelson Bell, "What Are the Divisions?," *PJ* (3 September 1969): 7. This was a constant theme for Bell: see "For This We Contend," *PJ* (8 January 1964): 9; "Were They Wrong?," *PJ* (2 April 1969): 15.
2. L. Nelson Bell, "Not 'New'—But Very Different," *PJ* (26 May 1965): 7.

conservatives could not do. The purity of the church and the future ministry of the gospel were at stake.[3]

BIBLICAL AUTHORITY AND THE REFORMED FAITH

As conservative dissent developed in the PCUS in the period between World War II and the Korean conflict, the doctrinal issues of biblical authority and confessional loyalty were constant themes—in particular, they were front and center in the long-running debates over reunion with the northern Presbyterian church. As the 1960s progressed, conservatives continued to offer the same diagnosis of the denomination's ills and the same solution. The problem with the PCUS was its move away from a full-throated affirmation of biblical authority and its concomitant denial of biblical truths; the solution was to return to biblical authority in every area of ministry and life. As Aiken Taylor observed, "Today's departures from the faith—in the name of orthodoxy—are many. However, the reasons why there are such departures are relatively few . . . and invariably associated with some basic attitude toward the Bible or the church." And those attitudes could be summarized in "three mistaken notions": revelation was an event; the Bible was a witness to and instrument of revelation; and the church was mission.[4]

The first mistaken notion was that revelation was an event. "The modern theologian says that God is all the time doing things and every act is a revelation of Him. When we rightly interpret His acts they become revelations to us," Aiken Taylor summarized. Of course, a major problem was whether humans could actually deduce from events what they needed to know about God. Another difficulty was that often events were preceded by or followed with propositional truths that set the context or offered interpretation for the events; the new understanding of revelation as event, however, called the propositions something other than revelation. This was illogical, Taylor argued: instead, Christians had to recognize that "revelation is first and foremost intellectual propositions" that interpreted the mighty acts of God.[5]

3. W. Jack Williamson, "But No Capitulation," *PJ* (10 September 1969): 7.
4. G. Aiken Taylor, "'Biblical' Theology," *PJ* (25 October 1961): 5.
5. Ibid.; G. Aiken Taylor, "Revelation Is More than Event," *PJ* (4 September 1963): 8–9.

Also problematic was the view that the Bible was not itself God's revelation, but only a witness to and instrument of that revelation. This language, drawing from the work of Karl Barth, separated revelation itself from the Bible. For Barthians, revelation was always the self-revelation of God in Jesus Christ. And so the Bible could witness to this revelation and be an instrument for this revelation, but was never to be identified directly with revelation. One effect of this belief was that religious experience would be severed from religious knowledge. Another was that the actual words of the Bible were not themselves revelation, but rather reflected "the fruit of some one's reflection upon God's mighty acts in the world." Hence, it was not necessary to be careful about the biblical words or even to study them; they served as one, albeit the supreme, witness among several. In addition, by not identifying the Bible with God's revelation, "this view solves the problem of the man who wishes to accept the Scriptures as 'true'—when he thinks he cannot receive them as infallible." Such a view allowed theologians and individuals to suggest that "the text (the actual words) of Scripture [is] unimportant. What counts is what those words say to my heart." If it were necessary to deny what the actual words said, that would be acceptable because the Bible simply witnessed to the truth of God in the revelation of Jesus. It was merely a human witness, as fallible as other human witnesses, that God condescended to use to encounter his people.[6]

The final mistaken notion in the new theology was the idea that the church was mission. The church did not "do" missions; rather, it *was* mission. Taylor dismissed this idea as "an essentially pantheistic existentialism" that inevitably led to the denial of "world missions" and global evangelization. This claim held that "all men are under the Lordship of Christ, but some are in mission, some are not yet in mission—while the mission itself embraces all men." In addition, everything that every human being did contributed to the mission of Christ in the world, which buried "the primary task embodied in the Great Commission." Rather than tell others about Jesus and

6. Taylor, "'Biblical' Theology," 6; G. Aiken Taylor, "What the Bible Says," *PJ* (21 March 1962): 11; G. Aiken Taylor, "It Is!-It Isn't!-It Is! It Isn't!," *PJ* (15 January 1964): 8, 11.

the way of salvation through faith in him alone, the church on mission engaged in "a welter of good causes from orphan support to new kitchen equipment." Instead of sending missionaries who were specifically called to a particular field to share the gospel, each Christian's secular calling contributed to God's mission and every sphere in which the individual found himself provided the opportunity to assist in forming an authentic human community. The result was a loss of evangelistic fervor and a denigration of world missions as traditionally understood.[7]

These three mistaken notions about the Scriptures and theology actually represented a new religion that was different from Christianity, according to conservatives. Nelson Bell observed that this new religion offered a new theology, new morality, and new evangelism. The new theology argued that human beings were not sinners, lost apart from Jesus Christ and exposed to God's judgment. Rather, human beings were fundamentally good, alienated from God and his world, and needing political, social, and economic justice. The new morality rejected the absolutes of the Bible and instead argued that one's existential situation guided the individual in the application of love for the purpose of human flourishing. The result, though, was that ethics was relative and that Christians accepted "the mores of unregenerate man so that fornication, adultery, and homosexuality" might be allowable, depending on what love dictated. The new evangelism did not confront human beings with their need of a Savior, but rather comforted human beings in their alienated context and sought to speak of the "meaning of Jesus Christ" for life in the secular world today. "The inevitable conclusion," Bell observed, was "that the 'new' theology, morality and evangelism—followed to their inevitable conclusion—lead to a religion which is not Christianity." Cut adrift from the Bible as the only source of divine authority in the world, the new religion had "a form of godliness which denies the power thereof."[8]

7. G. Aiken Taylor, " 'Mission' a Threat to World Missions," *PJ* (1 August 1962): 10–11; G. Aiken Taylor, "That Word 'Mission,'" *PJ* (13 February 1963): 10–11; G. Aiken Taylor, "World Missions at the Crossroads," *PJ* (7 April 1965): 12; G. Aiken Taylor, "This Is World Missions?," *PJ* (26 January 1966): 12.

8. Bell, "Not 'New'—But Very Different," 7–8.

What was the solution? "The only corrective to such nonsense is a firm stand upon the Scriptures as the inspired, totally authoritative Word of God—the only definitive source of religious truth," Taylor declared. Those who affirmed that the Bible was the inspired Word of God, that the Bible was God's revelation, would be doctrinally sound and spiritually effective; those who did not affirm biblical inspiration and authority would go off the rails doctrinally and spiritually. And that was because the Bible told people about God, Jesus, salvation, and gospel. "If one does not believe the Scriptures then there is little reason to accept his protestations of faith in the Gospel," Taylor suggested. The only way that one would come to know the gospel was through the Scriptures. And the only way to know Christ was to know the Bible: "You will not get to know Jesus Christ apart from getting to know the Bible—or at least the Message of the Bible." The Bible is the "way to Christ. It is the divinely appointed means of grace whereby we find Christ, meet Christ, learn of Christ—and in which we commune with Christ."[9]

That was why conservatives made tight connections between biblical inspiration and inerrancy, doctrine, and evangelism. If the Bible was God's Word, then what it said about God, human beings, Jesus, and salvation was God's Word; if what it said about the human condition was true, then it served as the basis and warrant for evangelism and missions. But if it was not true, then the gospel was not true, the doctrines were not true, and evangelism was unnecessary and unwarranted. Indeed, "to argue for a fallible Bible can only lead up the blind alley of lost zeal and power." Not only this, but to deny biblical authority—represented in the doctrines of biblical inspiration, infallibility, and inerrancy—would lead one to conclude that there was no system of doctrine in Scripture at all. All truth would become relative and functional, contextualized and temporary. The result would be that the "infection of unbelief" would spread "until it penetrates the whole body" of Christ's church.[10]

9. Taylor, "What the Bible Says," 11; G. Aiken Taylor, "Why It Matters . . . ," *PJ* (12 December 1962): 10; G. Aiken Taylor, " 'Believe the Gospel' Includes Miracles," *PJ* (12 December 1962): 10; G. Aiken Taylor, "Christ *and* Scripture, or Christ *in* Scripture?," *PJ* (26 August 1964): 12.

10. L. Nelson Bell, "What Comes Out of a Fallible Bible?," *PJ* (9 January 1963): 11, 22; G. Aiken Taylor, "When There's a Stand to Take," *PJ* (16 December 1964): 12.

A BATTLEGROUND IN THE LOCAL CHURCH

One area in which conservatives worked to point out the negative effects of progressive understandings of biblical authority was in the church literature produced for the local church. During the 1960s, the PCUS Board of Christian Education produced two major projects: the Layman's Bible Commentary and the Covenant Life Curriculum (CLC). Together, these two projects represented an attempt to make the fruits of critical scholarship accessible to laypeople in a form that they could understand and use. Not surprisingly, both the commentaries and the curriculum came under attack by conservatives as they tried to show how this literature strayed from historic understandings of biblical authority and doctrine.

The Layman's Bible Commentary was published in twenty-five volumes between 1959 and 1964 and represented a major effort to provide a single source of commentary for Sunday school teachers and Bible study leaders in the southern Presbyterian church. As with any other series, some volumes drew more comment than others. Aiken Taylor's overall assessment was that the series reflected a "theological schizophrenia" that plagued the PCUS in general: while many of the commentaries took a traditional approach to issues of authorship, they also approached "the Biblical evidences of the supernatural and the miraculous with great caution." Some of the volumes demonstrated a "tacit universalism," while others showed "a slavish acceptance of the findings of radical higher criticism." A few volumes were simply "trash" because of their reliance on source criticism and the evidence of general unbelief. Still others were excellent, representing generally traditional perspectives and heartfelt devotion. In the end, though, because of the mixed character of the series, conservatives needed to protest the more radical volumes. Starting in 1962, Taylor urged conservatives to petition the General Assembly to direct the Board of Christian Education to suspend publication until better editorial safeguards could be put in place to guide the books theologically. In the event, at least one church session, Westminster Presbyterian Church, Shreveport, Louisiana, did petition the Assembly along the lines that Taylor wished, and two presbyteries adopted such overtures. When the issue was debated at the 1962 General Assembly, the overtures to request greater editorial oversight were defeated by a nearly 4-to-1 margin. Losing the vote on redirecting the Layman's Bible Commentary was not surprising; rather, Taylor hoped that the outrage created by the commentary series would affect other literature produced by the PCUS.[11]

Far more problematic was the CLC, which was the new Sunday school and Bible study curriculum produced by the PCUS Board of Christian Education in cooperation with other mainline Protestant denominations. From the development of the foundation papers to the actual production of the curriculum, *Journal* editor Aiken Taylor spent a great deal of time on the CLC. In May 1960, he was invited to go to Richmond and dialogue with Board of Christian Education leaders on the foundation papers, which would serve as the guiding documents for developing the new curriculum. Major flaws that he saw at that point were deficient understandings of revelation and Scripture. In particular, he complained that the foundation papers defined revelation exclusively as "mighty acts of God in history," events that disclosed something about God as individuals encountered deity. "A serious flaw appears in the thought that Revelation is not 'objective' for all time and whether or not acknowledged,—but that the disclosures of God only 'become' Revelation as they are received as such." Likewise, in this understanding, the Bible was not itself divine revelation, but a witness to and instrument of revelation. This devalued the Bible and replaced it with other witnesses to God's revelation, especially the church in its witness to God's mighty acts in the world. And the result of this understanding of the Bible promised "a radical departure from the historic Reformed tradition

11. G. Aiken Taylor, "The Layman's Bible Commentary: A Review Article," *PJ* (7 December 1960): 7; G. Aiken Taylor, "The Layman's Bible Commentary," *PJ* (8 November 1961): 5–6; G. Aiken Taylor, "The Layman's Bible Commentary," *PJ* (11 December 1963): 5–6; G. Aiken Taylor, "The Layman's Bible Commentary," *PJ* (16 December 1964): 7–9; G. Aiken Taylor to W. G. Foster, 16 November 1961, in *Presbyterian Journal* Papers, box 195, folder 8; Lewis M. White to Marshall C. Dendy, n.d., in *Presbyterian Journal* Papers, box 197, folder 5 (both at PCAHC); G. Aiken Taylor, "Signs of Hope," *PJ* (21 February 1962): 10; "The Crucial Debate," *PJ* (13 June 1962): 5–9, 18–20. Nelson Bell also commented in "A Tarnished Debate," *PJ* (27 June 1962): 10.

of theology and the Evangelical understanding of the Gospel of Jesus Christ."[12]

When the foundation papers were released to the church as a whole, Taylor offered lengthy commentary on them in the *Journal*. In particular, he reiterated his objection to the understanding of the Bible and its relationship to divine revelation offered by the CLC. In the new curriculum, revelation did not mean God's self-disclosure through "propositional truths," but only in "mighty acts," events, and especially the life, death, and resurrection of Jesus Christ. Hence, revelation was an event, "an incident experienced by one or more persons at a particular time in history." When biblical characters experienced such a revelation event, then it became the Word of God to them. The Bible itself was not divine revelation, but the record of and witness to such revelation. It might be the supreme witness to revelation, but it was not the only one: the church, too, served as a witness to revelation. In the same way that the church could be fallible as it witnessed to the mighty acts of God, so the Bible might be fallible as well. This understanding of divine revelation and its relationship to Scripture "allows for mistakes in the Bible" while still claiming that the book also contained "the truth of God." In addition, this understanding of revelation allowed for continuing revelation "as today's witnesses better interpret the will of God than those who interpreted it centuries ago." The upshot was that parts of the Bible "could be declared obsolete on the grounds that those witnesses of revelation supplied a less perfect interpretation of the will of God than modern witnesses (the Church today)."[13]

While Taylor's criticisms of the foundation papers seemed to cause the Board of Christian Education to pause, it soon became clear that the new curriculum would not express the Westminster Standards' position on the inspiration of the Scriptures. Evidence of this came in two ways. One piece of evidence was that Christian

12. "National Council Says 12 Denominations Jointly Plan Curriculum," *PJ* (15 March 1961): 7; G. Aiken Taylor to Marshall C. Dendy, 27 May 1960; G. Aiken Taylor to William P. Anderson, 4 October 1960 (both in *Presbyterian Journal* Papers, box 197, folder 3, PCAHC).

13. G. Aiken Taylor, "The New Curriculum: Introduction," *PJ* (15 March 1961): 7–8, 20; G. Aiken Taylor, "The New Curriculum: Revelation," *PJ* (22 March 1961): 5–7. See also G. Aiken Taylor, "The New Curriculum: Bible and the Church," *PJ* (29 March 1961): 7–9; "The New Curriculum: What Will Be Taught," *PJ* (12 April 1961): 10–11, 21–22.

education board members claimed that the "assured results of modern scholarship" would characterize the new curriculum, meaning that traditional understandings of biblical inspiration and authority would not be found. Another line of evidence was found in materials already produced by writers in other curricula produced by the board. Two such examples included the claim that the creation account had been passed down by oral tradition until it was finally written in Genesis and the assertion that the Gospels had been written in the postapostolic age out of materials gathered by apostolic communities reflecting each group's particular interest. While these were common positions in critical scholarship, it was shocking to conservatives to find them in Sunday school literature for children. Would this be the direction of the new literature once it finally appeared?[14]

When the first book of the CLC came out in the summer of 1963, Taylor and other conservatives were stuck. William Kennedy's *Into Covenant Life* was orthodox and generally faithful to the Reformed faith. To criticize it would open conservatives up to accusations of unfairness; to praise it would potentially send the confusing signal that progressive denominational leaders could produce trustworthy materials even after two years of criticism in the pages of the *Journal*. As Kennedy's book was published, conservative leaders debated how to respond. Some, such as Milton Scott, wanted the *Journal* to repudiate the CLC regardless of its content or approach. Others, such as Tom Glasgow and Nelson Bell, supported Taylor's general position, which was to praise that which was praiseworthy and criticize portions of the CLC that contradicted the Bible and the Reformed faith.[15] In the

14. William Rose to G. Aiken Taylor, 8 September 1962 (with a copy of a letter from Holmes Rolston to William Rose), in *Presbyterian Journal* Papers, box 197, folder 2; G. Aiken Taylor to Kenneth Keyes, 4 October 1962, in *Presbyterian Journal* Papers, box 151, folder 14 (both at PCAHC); G. Aiken Taylor, "Where Did the Bible Come From?," *PJ* (12 September 1962): 5–6, 22.

15. See Tom Glasgow to Board of Directors of *PJ*, 14 July 1963; Tom Glasgow to G. Aiken Taylor, 15 July 1963; Tom Glasgow to G. Aiken Taylor, 20 July 1963; Tom Glasgow to Board of Directors of *PJ*, 20 July 1963; Tom Glasgow to G. Aiken Taylor, 24 July 1963; Tom Glasgow to G. Aiken Taylor, 25 July 1963; Milton Scott to G. Aiken Taylor, 2 August 1963; Milton Scott to Tom Glasgow, 3 August 1963; Milton Scott to Tom Glasgow, 22 August 1963 (all in *Presbyterian Journal* Papers, PCAHC); L. Nelson Bell to Tom Glasgow, 24 July 1963, L. Nelson Bell Papers, BGC.

end, the *Journal* board sided with Taylor's tactical strategy, which freed him to write, "We have seen Dr. Kennedy's study course. Its content seems faithful to the Scriptures and to the Reformed faith. We believe it deserves a thorough and fair trial." The response from some, such as Robert Wallace, was immediate: "I was amazed, shocked and disappointed . . . that you would recommend the churches to use this church literature." Yet Taylor continued to insist that a more moderate tactical approach would allow him to influence future installments of the curriculum as it appeared.[16]

When the 1964 CLC books appeared, Taylor's tone became more critical even as he tried to balance his criticisms with praise. While admitting that Arnold Rhodes's book *The Mighty Acts of God* was doctrinally "impeccable," Taylor noted how the book followed "the critical, or liberal, line" on historical issues, using the documentary hypothesis for the Pentateuch, working with a late date for Daniel, and claiming that the creation account borrowed from Babylonian epics. If a church were to use this book, he suggested, then "traditional viewpoints of date, authorship and context will begin to disappear." Likewise, Nelly McCarter's *Hear the Word of the Lord* was a generally "helpful treatment of the subject matter." The main problem with the book was that while McCarter sought to convey the highest possible respect for the inspiration and authority of Scripture, he did so "without indicating perfection or infallibility" and admitted that his position was frankly Barthian. Finally, the installment offered by William Ramsey, called *The Meaning of Jesus Christ*, was "the most useable of the new texts." Yet "it is weaker than the others at the basic point of the meaning of revelation and the authority of the Scriptures." Moreover, the book suggested that Jesus had come to messianic consciousness at his baptism, a position that "hardly agrees with Scripture."[17]

The board of the *Journal*, however, still displayed significant fractures over how to approach the curriculum and its view of Scripture.

16. G. Aiken Taylor, "Using the C.L.C.," *PJ* (4 September 1963): 8; Robert R. Wallace Sr. to G. Aiken Taylor, 3 September 1963, *Presbyterian Journal* Papers, box 197, folder 2; G. Aiken Taylor to Robert J. Ostenson, 25 September 1963, *Presbyterian Journal* Papers, box 197, folder 13 (both at PCAHC).

17. G. Aiken Taylor, "The C.L.C. for '64," *PJ* (3 June 1964): 9–11.

Two months after Taylor's review of the 1964 texts, the board issued a statement, published in the *Journal*, that "it is evident that the latest volumes in the Covenant Life Curriculum in effect take away from the Church a Bible which is the very substance of God's revelation, inerrant and infallible in faith and practice." In place of this traditional understanding of Scripture, the new curriculum substituted a view of the Bible that saw it as "a collection of material from largely unidentifiable sources which is at best only the record of impressions and of hearsay evidence concerning God's 'acts' in history." This statement drew the ire of the Board of Christian Education and involved Taylor and the *Journal* board in an embarrassing sequence in which it was discovered that the editor had failed to characterize one writer's views on Scripture fully. Not only did the entire sequence put conservative leaders at odds with one another, it gave the progressive establishment an opportunity to deny that it held to a Barthian view of Scripture and revelation, a denial that was not fully truthful itself.[18]

Perhaps these difficulties caused conservatives to pull their punches a bit when the next volumes appeared. Taylor continued to pursue his strategy of affirming what he could praise and criticizing what he could not in an effort to steward his influence for future releases in the curriculum; he even told Clayton Bell, Nelson Bell's son then serving in Dothan, Alabama, "If I were a pastor today I would certainly use the CLC in my church." As a result, E. T. Thompson's church history survey and Sara Little's study of creeds and catechisms received much praise, as did the junior-high curriculum written by William Ramsay and John Leith. Taylor continued to stress that the major flaws in the curriculum were the low view of biblical authority

18. "The C.L.C.—After One Year," *PJ* (26 August 1964): 12–13; L. Nelson Bell to Board of Directors of *PJ*, 9 October 1964; L. Nelson Bell to Board of Directors of *PJ*, 3 November 1964 (which includes Board of Christian Education to Pastors and Elders of PCUS, 29 September 1964) (both in L. Nelson Bell Papers, box 72, folder 7, BGC); L. Nelson Bell to G. Aiken Taylor, 29 October 1964, L. Nelson Bell Papers, box 75, folder 16, BGC; "A Board Answers a Board," *PJ* (9 December 1964): 14–15. Ironically, in light of the controversy, Taylor gave an explanation of his omission before the controversy in "Unfair to CLC?," *PJ* (9 September 1964): 12; see also G. Aiken Taylor, "C.L.C., Scripture, and the Record," *PJ* (14 October 1964): 12; G. Aiken Taylor, "Why They Cannot Do It," *PJ* (14 October 1964): 13; G. Aiken Taylor, "That CLC Matter," *PJ* (4 November 1964): 12–13.

and the assumed universalism: "One huge fallacy exists in all the CLC books we have read; namely, the assumption that *all* are in Christ, hence, *all* are free from the law of sin and death, hence, Christian ethical behavior is possible for *all*."[19]

But the most problematic of all the CLC texts was Shirley Guthrie's *Christian Doctrine* (1968). The son of a Presbyterian minister and former student of Karl Barth at Basel, Guthrie had taught theology at Columbia Seminary since 1958. For all the evident Barthianism in the underlying doctrinal foundations of the CLC, Guthrie's *Christian Doctrine* was the book that made clear its indebtedness to Barth for its dialectic methodology. Taylor recognized this in his review of the book when he noted that "this theme of 'both-and' runs throughout the text. Over and over again Dr. Guthrie attacks a historic interpretation of the Christian faith, then affirms it just before the lid is slammed shut." But there were "numerous excursions into heresy" in the book: the denial of the lost condition of human beings, the fall of Adam, and humans' intrinsic evil while still affirming "original sin"; the affirmation of the fundamental goodness of humans and nature; and especially the denial of final judgment. Taylor observed, "There is no spiritual condemnation in the traditional sense in this book. Nobody will be damned. In 'judgment' God is man's Savior." In the end, the book was unusable because Guthrie "suggests positions that are radically different from the historic Reformed and evangelical position." The book had dozens of places "where the plain teaching of Scripture is denied." It represented theology that was "padded, twisted, re-arranged—with subtle ridicule of orthodoxy." The only reason for any church to use this book would be so that "the 'old time religion' [would] disappear from [the] congregation."[20]

19. G. Aiken Taylor to B. Clayton Bell, 27 February 1965, *Presbyterian Journal* Papers, box 196, folder 15; G. Aiken Taylor to Wallace M. Alston Jr., *Presbyterian Journal* Papers, box 197, folder 9 (both at PCAHC); G. Aiken Taylor, "Only If . . . ," *PJ* (24 August 1966): 15 (emphasis his).

20. G. Aiken Taylor, "This Is Christian Doctrine?," *PJ* (10 July 1968): 7–8; G. Aiken Taylor, "What about the 1968 CLC Text?," *PJ* (10 July 1968): 12; G. Aiken Taylor, "Use That CLC Text?," *PJ* (11 September 1968): 12. Although Columbia Seminary president J. McDowell Richards wrote to Taylor to protest his review of Guthrie's book, even he admitted that Guthrie expressed "clear disagreements with the Reformed faith" and offered

Of course, by 1968, very few conservative congregations were using the CLC. For example, First Presbyterian Church, Jackson, Mississippi, had not used the denominational Sunday school literature since 1957, when it switched to the materials produced by Gospel Light, a strongly evangelical alternative. When the new curriculum was being previewed in 1963, church elders had attended the workshops offered by the Board of Christian Education. The church session, however, decided not even to study the feasibility of using the materials because of the program's shaky theological foundations. Aiken Taylor recognized this to be the case from reading his own mail. As he related to one inquirer, "The truth of the matter is that today literally hundreds of churches are turning away from the CLC to better literature." Others never started using it in the first place; one example was Robert Wallace, pastor at Salem Presbyterian Church, near Winnsboro, South Carolina. Objecting to Taylor's generally moderate approach to the literature, Wallace declared, "I have, at my own expense, ordered and received and read everything that has been released in reference to, or as a part of the CLC, and knowing who put it out, I want nothing whatever to do with it, and will not have anything to do with it. We are using Bible-centered, Christ-centered, sound in the doctrine literature, and are happy with it, and want no part of anything put out by liberals and integrationists and socialists and left-wingers." Biblical authority in the life of a local church was too precious to trust anything offered by the denominational bureaucrats who were taking the church in undesirable directions.[21]

That did not stop the progressive leaders from trying to force conservative congregations to use denominational literature. Jack

statements that appeared to endorse universalism: J. McDowell Richards to G. Aiken Taylor, 26 July 1968, *Presbyterian Journal* Papers, PCAHC. Nelson Bell agreed with Taylor's criticisms: see "What's Wrong with This Book?," *PJ* (16 April 1969): 8–10. Ironically, Guthrie had first been recommended to join the faculty by William Childs Robinson: J. McDowell Richards to L. Nelson Bell, 5 November 1956, J. McDowell Richards Papers, box 41, PHS.

21. Sean Michael Lucas, *Blessed Zion: First Presbyterian Church, Jackson, Mississippi, 1837–2012* (Jackson, MS: First Presbyterian Church, 2013), 121–22; G. Aiken Taylor to Mrs. Gilbert F. Dukes, 28 August 1967, *Presbyterian Journal* Papers, box 196, folder 12; Robert R. Wallace Sr. to G. Aiken Taylor, 19 November 1963, *Presbyterian Journal* Papers, box 183, folder 3 (both at PCAHC).

Williamson reminded his fellow conservatives that each church had the liberty and freedom to teach its children the Bible as it saw fit. That liberty was threatened when presbyteries inquired whether a prospective minister would use Presbyterian literature in his Sunday school. "That is an improper question," Williamson charged. "It is the constitutional right and responsibility of each local church session to choose the educational materials used by that particular church." Even the 1968 General Assembly had reaffirmed that principle; conservatives should not be cowed into using material that did not affirm the Bible and the catechism.[22]

Progressives had other ways to bring pressure on conservatives who did not approve or use the curriculum. In early 1969, the Board of Christian Education filed a formal complaint with the General Assembly's newly created Grievance Committee about Taylor and his editorials criticizing the CLC materials. The board asked this Grievance Committee "to put an end to the systematic effort of this teaching elder which serves to impugn the integrity, reliability and soundness of this Board, its staff and educational program, creates suspicions through this campaign of distrust, distortion, and negativism," and rejects the use of denominational materials. In the end, after some irregularities in process, the Grievance Committee found Taylor guilty of "journalistic irresponsibility and unwarranted criticism" of the board. In addition, Northeast Texas Presbytery sent an overture to the Assembly asking it to censure Taylor for injuring the peace, purity, and unity of the church; the Assembly did not comply because it was not Taylor's court of original jurisdiction. Still, these attempts to silence the *Journal* editor as the main critic of the new curriculum, rather than considering whether his criticisms had merit, demonstrated a new effort by progressives to require loyalty to the church's program over commitment to the faith of the fathers.[23]

The significance of these battles over Sunday school literature brought the fight for the faith of the fathers into the Sunday school

22. W. Jack Williamson, "Be Watchful and Strengthen," *PJ* (11 September 1968): 8.

23. "A Complaint," *PJ* (8 January 1969): 10–11; "To the General Assembly," *PJ* (8 January 1969): 11; L. Nelson Bell, "'Hot Potatoes' and 'Due Process,'" *PJ* (5 March 1969): 12–13; "Free Press, Speech Rights Reaffirmed," *PJ* (14 May 1969): 6.

classrooms of the local church. Conservatives were convinced that if liberals succeeded in pushing their critical approaches to the Bible and Christian doctrine in the church's classrooms, then the faith of the fathers would be lost to the next generation. Biblical inspiration and inerrancy, the deity of Jesus, the reality of miracles, and more besides were threatened as the CLC materials were produced. In the end, conservatives abandoned the denominational literature rather than allowing critical scholarship to undermine the faith of God's people.

A BATTLEGROUND IN THE PRESBYTERIES

Another place where conservatives struggled to preserve the faith of the fathers was in the presbyteries. While conservatives regularly complained about the ability of presbyteries' Commissions on the Minister and His Work to block conservative ministers from receiving ministerial calls, there were times when they were able to use that same authority to block more progressive ministers from entering conservative presbyteries. The most notorious instance was in Central Mississippi Presbytery, a situation occupying a number of years and a great deal of energy that dealt with the call of the Rev. Abel McIver "Mac" Hart to Trinity Presbyterian Church in Meridian, Mississippi. This case drew national attention because Central Mississippi Presbytery was perhaps the most conservative presbytery in the PCUS; and as a result, it had served as a thorn in the flesh of progressive denominational leaders for decades. As the Hart case unfolded, liberal southern Presbyterians would use it as evidence that Mississippi Presbyterians needed to be reined in and disciplined.[24]

Born in 1928 in Staunton, Virginia, Mac Hart had graduated from Davidson College and Columbia Seminary when he was licensed and ordained by Mississippi Presbytery in 1953 in order to serve the Fayette and Union Church churches. He left that presbytery in 1956 to

24. For conservatives' complaints about the Commission on the Minister and His Work, see G. Aiken Taylor, "Commissions on the Minister and His Work," *PJ* (2 March 1960): 10; G. Aiken Taylor, "Commissions on the Minister and His Work (Part II)," *PJ* (9 March 1960): 10–11; G. Aiken Taylor, "Those Commissions," *PJ* (27 April 1960): 10; G. Aiken Taylor, "The Commission and Fairness," *PJ* (9 November 1966): 12. Much of this telling of the Mac Hart case follows my version in *Blessed Zion*, 109–14.

serve two churches in Wynne, Arkansas. He had married the daughter of prominent southern Presbyterian moderate Felix Gear, who taught at Columbia Seminary. He was returning to Mississippi in order to serve Trinity Church, Meridian, as its pastor, a step up from the yoked parishes that he had previously served.[25]

When the matter came to the Central Mississippi Presbytery's Commission on the Minister and His Work, the commission reported at the April 1962 stated presbytery meeting that it did not concur in the church's call to Hart. In response, presbytery adopted a procedural motion that Hart be examined with a view to his admission. After his theology examination, led by John Reed Miller, pastor at First Presbyterian Church, Jackson, Mississippi, the presbytery voted 52–32 not to sustain Hart's theology examination. As a result, the presbytery voted 55–27 not to sustain his transfer examination as a whole. A complaint was filed against the action of the presbytery in not sustaining Hart's examination; eleven ministers and sixteen elders eventually signed the complaint. The presbytery appointed a committee that would answer the complaint on the presbytery's behalf.[26]

The complaint was filed with the Synod of Mississippi's Judicial Commission. John Reed Miller attended that meeting and defended the presbytery's actions before them. But in the synod's report, the judicial commission directed that the matter "be remanded to the Presbytery on the basis of the findings of this Commission, with instructions that Rev. A. M. Hart be re-examined, and that a full, complete, and properly authenticated transcript of such examination and all of the proceedings relating thereto, be filed with this Commission." Miller led the presbytery in responding to the synod's judicial commission by noting that "it was improper for Synod to entertain the Complaint . . . inasmuch as such a matter as the examination of a minister for admission to a presbytery is not within the jurisdiction of a Synod." One of the foundational principles of Presbyterian government was that "Presbytery alone has power to receive, dismiss, examine, and judge ministers." And so the presbytery complained

25. E. D. Witherspoon Jr., ed., *Ministerial Directory of the Presbyterian Church, U.S., 1861–1967* (Doraville, GA: Foote and Davies, 1967), 232.

26. *Minutes, Central Mississippi Presbytery* (19 April 1962): 64–65.

to the entire synod about the action of its judicial commission; the presbytery approved this action by a vote of 57 to 29.[27]

The entire matter got extremely complicated, even by Presbyterian standards, as a result of a memorial that was filed by eleven Central Mississippi Presbytery ministers with the Synod of Mississippi that met in June. While the context of the memorial was the Hart case, the ministers made much broader charges: the presbytery "has expressed and sanctioned many attitudes and ideas and actions which have promoted schism"; it had preferred those ministers "trained in denominations or seminaries known to be opposed to the life and work of the Presbyterian Church in the U.S."; it made the work of the churches in finding pastors difficult "by unwise and unconstitutional approaches to the prospects." The conclusion was simple: "The totality of these co-existing conditions is schism, the abuse of power, and failure in the loyalty to the Church—its life and mission." This memorial would occupy the synod's attention for well over a year: presbytery appointed a committee to craft a response at its October 1962 meeting, and this committee met with the synod in October and again in March 1963. The committee attempted to show that the accusations made by these ministers were both baseless and improper: such accusations should have first been filed in the court of original jurisdiction, the presbytery itself. While synod deliberated over these arguments, Central Mississippi Presbytery formally charged the eleven signers of the memorial with making false and unsubstantiated charges against the presbytery and disregarding the provisions of the *Book of Church Order* by not lodging complaints with the presbytery first.[28]

By the summer of 1963, the Synod of Mississippi had decided against the presbytery and ordered Hart to serve the Trinity Church in Meridian on a supply basis until he could be received by the presbytery; the synod also sided with the writers of the memorial in agreeing that presbytery was overstepping its authority in a number of areas.

27. *Minutes, Central Mississippi Presbytery* (19 July 1962): 76–78; "Presbytery Reversed," *PJ* (27 June 1962): 15; "Mississippi Presbytery Defies Synod Order," *PO* (6 August 1962): 3.

28. *Minutes, Central Mississippi Presbytery* (19 July 1962): 81–82; "Central Mississippi Presbytery Files Charges against Eleven," *PO* (6 May 1963): 10.

The synod directed Central Mississippi Presbytery to reexamine Hart with a "full, complete, and properly authenticated transcript" of the examination to file with the synod. Once again, the presbytery filed a notice of complaint against the action of the synod, this time appealing to the General Assembly to preserve the rights of the presbytery in determining its own membership. The 1964 General Assembly denied the complaint of the presbytery and concurred with the Synod of Mississippi: essentially, the denial meant that the presbytery was forced to reexamine Hart with a view of completing his call to the Trinity Church.[29]

At a called meeting in July 1964, the presbytery once again examined Hart. Once again, it found his theological perspectives to be wanting: by a vote of 54 to 18, it did not sustain that portion of his transfer examination. When the final vote came on whether to sustain his examination as a whole, the presbytery voted 49 to 16 not to sustain. While a transcript was made and forwarded to the Synod, the presbytery voted not to allow Hart to view the transcript before authentication and not to include the transcript in the presbytery's minutes. Once again, Miller was the chairman of the committee that would respond to the synod if any questions came. As it happened, questions did come: when the Synod of Mississippi met in November 1964, the majority of its judicial commission ruled that Central Mississippi Presbytery had "erred in conducting an examination which was improper, arbitrary and oppressive in that bias and prejudice was manifest in both the form and content of many questions." The judicial commission also had a minority report claiming that the majority on the commission had reached an incomplete and improper decision. When the synod received the two reports, the report of the minority from the judicial commission was adopted. In response, the synod moderator, William J. Stanway from First Presbyterian Church, Hattiesburg, Mississippi, appointed a new judicial commission to receive and review the entire case; a minority of the synod filed a complaint, which would go to the General

29. *Minutes, Central Mississippi Presbytery* (20 June 1963): 123–26; "Mississippi Commission Pleads for Peace and Unity," *PO* (24 June 1963): 4; *Minutes, Central Mississippi Presbytery* (9 July 1964): 21–22.

Assembly's Permanent Judicial Commission, about irregularities in voting on this matter.[30]

What were the issues that prevented Hart from being admitted as a member of the presbytery? While later remembrances of some progressive Presbyterians suggested that Hart had been rejected because he favored racial integration, it is striking that those questions did not come up in contemporary reports from the progressive *Presbyterian Outlook*. Rather, the issue that the *Outlook* noted was that Hart appeared to deny the historicity of Adam as presented in Genesis 1–3. When asked directly about Adam's historicity, Hart said, "If the scripture teaches the historicity of Adam and Eve, then yes. I would [so affirm] if I were convinced that this were so." When pressed on this, Hart retreated to say that the answer to the question of Adam's historicity depended on the exegesis of the passages involved; he refused to give a direct affirmation beyond saying that "in whatever sense the Genesis account uses Adam[,] . . . [Romans 5:12–14] speaks of Adam as a representative and a beginning of the human race. I think this is the sense in which the passage used it; I think this is the sense in which the Confession of Faith uses it." This was one example among many, for conservatives, that seemed to suggest that Hart would not stand for biblical authority and doctrine in common with the majority of Central Mississippi Presbytery. By late 1965, it had become clear that Hart would not be received into Central Mississippi Presbytery; he left Meridian and accepted a call as associate minister at the notably progressive Second Presbyterian Church, Little Rock, Arkansas.[31]

30. *Minutes, Central Mississippi Presbytery* (9 July 1964): 23–24; "Central Mississippi Presbytery Again Rejects Hart," *PO* (27 July 1964): 3; "Mississippi Discharges Hart Case Commission," *PJ* (17 November 1965): 6; "Mississippi in New Tangle," *PO* (15 November 1965): 3.

31. "On the Historicity of Adam," *PO* (26 July 1965): 4. On the suggestion that Hart was rejected because he supported racial integration, see R. Milton Winter, "Division and Reunion in the Presbyterian Church, U.S.: A Mississippi Retrospective," *Journal of Presbyterian History* 78, 1 (2000): 76; Joel L. Alvis Jr., *Religion and Race: Southern Presbyterians, 1946–1983* (Tuscaloosa, AL: University of Alabama Press, 1994), 67–68; William G. McAtee, *Transformed: A White Mississippi Pastor's Journey into Civil Rights and Beyond* (Jackson, MS: University Press of Mississippi, 2011), 51. This is not to suggest that race did not provide a subtext of the Hart case; yet even McAtee noted that at none of the presbytery examinations at which he was present did racial integration come up. Ironically, Mac Hart

Still, the concerns behind the memorial continued to work their way through Presbyterian processes. The Synod of Mississippi urged the Central Mississippi Presbytery to work toward conciliation on the issues raised by the memorialists. As a result, the presbytery appointed a committee, chaired by First Church elder Stokes Robertson Jr., to consider the problems within the presbytery. The report offered at the May 1965 presbytery meeting was adopted unanimously and addressed many issues of procedure: election to the Permanent Committee on Nominations; how debate might happen and might be closed; methods to ensure a diversity of opinion on presbytery committees; and withdrawing the memorials and charges that had been issued. It appeared by the end of 1965 that perhaps all the issues connected to the Hart case had been concluded.

And yet at some level, they were just beginning. The 1966 General Assembly, through its Permanent Judicial Commission, sustained the complaint of the minority of the synod who held that there were a number of irregularities and urged the Central Mississippi Presbytery "to review carefully its procedures of examination to the end that future difficulties of this kind may be averted." But the Assembly did not stop there. It created a Pastoral Visitation Committee of five members with former moderator Charles King as chair to investigate the reasons for unrest in the Synod of Mississippi. When the committee reported to the next year's General Assembly, it noted that there was "a strong anti-Assembly attitude" in the synod, rooted in the belief that "the Assembly, in its policies and pronouncements and in the literature of certain of its agencies, has departed from the faith set out in its standards." The pastoral committee also observed that opposition to the Assembly and its agencies was "most acute" in Central Mississippi Presbytery. It claimed that the reason for this was that "a considerable number of ministers . . . have received training in theological seminaries outside the bounds of our denomination." In the light of its findings, the pastoral committee recommended that the 1967 General Assembly require the synod to ensure that Central Mississippi

---

would be the executive presbyter of Hanover Presbytery in Virginia when conservatives such as Bill Hill and Kennedy Smartt left the PCUS in 1972–73.

Presbytery have appropriate examinations, that its Commission on the Minister and His Work not deprive a church of its pastoral choice, that it elect commissioners to the Assembly representing the diversity of the presbytery, and that it continue to support financially the work of the Assembly's agencies and boards.[32]

The 1967 Assembly voted to approve the committee's recommendations, even though the committee chairman, Charles King, warned that "the Presbyterians of Mississippi will not be forced. I appeal to the Assembly to go about this in the spirit of trust and hope, and not by trying to bind these people." King's words were prescient; when the Synod of Mississippi met in November 1967, it "declined to implement General Assembly instruction in regard to Central Mississippi Presbytery." The synod pointed out that the issues arising out of the Mac Hart case had been appropriately adjudicated and were now concluded. Even more, the synod did not have the power to limit or direct a presbytery in matters about its own membership, which constitutionally were within its own authority. And when the Central Mississippi Presbytery met, it, too, reacted negatively to the Assembly's demands, receiving the admonitions "as information" and rejecting a motion suggesting that it was willing "to receive and communicate with such visitors from the General Assembly as the Assembly sees fit."[33]

Not surprisingly, the 1968 General Assembly viewed these actions negatively. It approved recommendations from its continued pastoral committee to the Synod of Mississippi demanding that the synod appoint a "strong pastoral committee" that would visit Central Mississippi Presbytery "to persuade the presbytery to correct the injustices" raised by the Mac Hart case and "to study the causes of the 'unhappiness, disunity and hostility among Presbyterians in the synod.'" For conservatives who had repeatedly rehearsed the

32. "Synod Actions: Mississippi," *PO* (27 June 1966): 4; "Synod of Mississippi Visitation," *PO* (29 May 1967): 7–8.

33. "Assembly Directs Mississippi Actions," *PJ* (21 June 1967): 4; "Assembly Demand Not Implemented," *PO* (13 November 1967): 3; "What the Synod of Mississippi Did," *PO* (20 November 1967): 4–9; "Mississippi: 'We'll Stick by Constitution,'" *PJ* (15 November 1967): 5–6; "Central Mississippi Presbytery 'Receives Information,'" *PO* (12 February 1968): 4.

J. Gresham Machen–PCUSA case from the 1930s in the previous decades, all of this looked like a replay of centralized progressive authority coming to crush conservative dissent. In the end, though, the Synod of Mississippi did appoint a pastoral committee that worked with the General Assembly's pastoral committee to calm the waters in Central Mississippi Presbytery. In fact, the Assembly's committee was able to report in 1969 that "we feel things are moving in the right direction." And while Central Mississippi Presbytery did not yet represent fully the diversity of views in the church, "we are encouraged to believe the process of reconciliation has really begun." The Assembly did not receive this encouragement, however, instead continuing its pastoral committee and enlarging its direction and powers.[34]

By the end of the 1960s, not only was reconciliation not beginning, but the fissures that would produce separation were growing larger. Central Mississippi Presbytery was one of the few regional church courts that conservatives dominated. When the General Assembly began to flex its authority in trying to force the presbytery to broaden its representation on committees and in its commissioners to the Assembly, and especially in appearing to mandate the financial support of the work of the national agencies and boards, southern Presbyterian conservatives saw this as the beginning of the end. They had rehearsed the stories of Machen and the "mandate of 1934" too many times not to recognize the handwriting on the wall. As long as conservatives could maintain the faith of the fathers in the few presbyteries that they controlled, there was some hope of rescuing and reforming the church. As liberals made it clear that this could no longer continue, conservatives were faced with a stark choice: maintain loyalty to the Reformed faith or the denomination.[35]

---

34. "Recommendations for Mississippi Problem," *PO* (3 June 1968): 11; "Mississippi Visitation Committee," *PO* (17 March 1969): 4; "Mississippi Visitors Get More Directions," *PJ* (14 May 1969): 10. The *PO* did print a letter from Robert Tascott, pastor of Covenant Presbyterian Church, Jackson, Mississippi, that offered a dramatically different viewpoint from the Assembly's committee: "Mississippi Story," *PO* (14 April 1969): 2.

35. For Machen and the "mandate of 1934," see Sean Michael Lucas, *J. Gresham Machen* (Darlington, UK: Evangelical Press, 2015), 98–109. In case conservatives forgot those lessons, Robert Strong reminded them in "A History Lesson," *PJ* (12 February 1969): 9–11.

A BATTLEGROUND IN THE DENOMINATION

The issue of biblical authority and doctrinal fidelity did not manifest itself merely in the educational literature for the local church and in the ministers who were coming through presbyteries. It also affected the way in which the denomination as a whole approached the issue of world missions. Not only did the new view of revelation and Scripture mean that the church was itself God's mission as it entered the world, but the revised understanding of biblical authority also led to universalism and secularization that undercut the work of worldwide evangelization.

In 1962, Aiken Taylor began to raise concerns that the church had unwittingly moved toward universalism. By *universalism* he meant "the wishful thought that God will save all men: that all men will find Him in another world if they don't meet Him here." While the Bible clearly denied universalism and affirmed the exclusive nature of salvation through Jesus, that did not stop modern theologians, even within the PCUS, from affirming God's universalistic purpose. In two volumes of the Layman's Bible Commentary, writers affirmed that God would save all human beings, either in this present age or in the age to come. And even when it was not explicitly affirmed, there was present in the life of the church a "practical universalism" that was hampering the missionary movement. In 1962, when PCUS missionaries gathered for a consultation, a desire was expressed for a statement on universalism. In the end, a statement was presented that actually affirmed universalism in so many words; as Taylor summarized it, "without Christ men would perish; but He is now Lord of all and by His death He has saved all even though some do not yet know it."[36]

By the mid-1960s, the great danger to world missions had become secularization. Following the lead of John A. T. Robinson's book *Honest to God* (1963) and Harvey Cox's *The Secular City* (1965), progressive theologians argued that Christians needed to enter into "a world come of age" to find that God was already present in the world and its struggle. Rather than finding God in the corporate worship and

36. G. Aiken Taylor, "Universalism—What Is It?," *PJ* (20 June 1962): 7–8, 19; G. Aiken Taylor, "Consultation Evades 'Universalism' Issue," *PJ* (7 November 1962): 13.

ministries of the church, Christians needed to enter into the struggle for justice for the poor and equality for the downtrodden because that was where God was. The church's mission was not worship or evangelism, but social justice and human community. A variation on secularization was the "death of God" movement that enjoyed a bit of interest in 1966 when *Time* magazine highlighted the work of Emory professor Thomas J. J. Altizer. He suggested that human beings had lost a sense of God's transcendence, living as functional atheists; for them, God was "dead." Not only this, Jesus as the God-figure had died and remained dead; hence, God was actually dead. When Jesus died, God entered into self-extinction and released his Spirit into the world. As a result, theology needed to reformulate its understanding of God, emphasizing the idea of "incarnation": God's Word came into each existential moment that humans experienced; God's Spirit was present in the world clothed in the struggle for social justice and revolution; and human beings needed to be open to God's Spirit wherever he was to be found.[37]

Taylor believed that this "secular theology" might prove to be "the most dangerous development in the Church in this century." Nelson Bell agreed: those who articulated this version of theology, going so far as to suggest that "God is dead," were simply "fools, dead men spiritually. They are talking about a God they do not know, in their spiritual ignorance, pride and audacity committing what may well prove to be the ultimate blasphemy." Not only was the secular theology dangerous theologically, it was also problematic for world missions. By redefining fundamental theological understandings, this secularized theology challenged Christians' understanding of what God's purpose was in the world. In this understanding, world missions was not about evangelism, telling men and women that they were sinners whom Christ invited to come to him, but about social justice: "Where the Christian wants to 'make human life truly human' by introducing a lost sinner to Jesus Christ, the secularist tries to 'make human life

---

37. G. Aiken Taylor, "They Secularize the Gospel," *PJ* (18 August 1965): 10–11. A helpful summary of this "secular theology" can be found in Stanley J. Grenz and Roger Olson, *Twentieth-Century Theology: God and the World in a Transitional Age* (Downers Grove, IL: InterVarsity Press, 1993), 156–69.

truly human' by 'freedom' drives, 'justice' agitation, 'anti-poverty' programs—giving man the 'status' that an affluent social order and a benevolent government can supply." The theology of secularization called on the church to identify itself with the world, "to make its mission a program of social, economic, and political action—to evangelize by 'serving men.'" To be sure, when lost people came to faith in Jesus Christ, it did make a social difference; but that was always a by-product of the central mission of the church, which was evangelistic appeal and Christian discipleship.[38]

When the church returned to the Bible and the Westminster Standards, it would discover that the church's mission involved world evangelization with the message of sin and redemption through Jesus Christ. Malcolm MacDonald observed that "you can't discard the authority of the Word of God for the pronouncements of individuals and agencies, nor can you substitute the reason of man for the revelation of God and seek to supplant what Jesus said about the Gospel of personal redemption for a program of socialistic and world reform and at the same time find joy and happiness in religious living and life." Ernest Mason agreed: the traditional Reformed belief was in "the necessity of personal salvation and the nurturing of the individual soul," not in the social salvation of the earth through the elimination of "all the social, economic and political ills of society." The kingdom of God came first to the hearts of men through personal salvation, Nelson Bell averred; it did not become "an earthly reality by social engineering, either by the Church or by secular government."[39]

The secularization of theology and growing commitment to universalism caused conservatives to view the direction of the PCUS Board of World Missions negatively. By 1966, Taylor was noticing troubling trends: a shift in promotional-material focus for world missions

38. G. Aiken Taylor, "Watch Out for 'Secularization,'" *PJ* (18 August 1965): 12; L. Nelson Bell, "God Lives!," *PJ* (27 April 1966): 7–8; G. Aiken Taylor, "The Harm in Secularization," *PJ* (9 March 1966): 12–13; G. Aiken Taylor, "'Concern' Is 'Mission'?," *PJ* (24 August 1966): 14.

39. Malcolm MacDonald, "The Mission of the Church," *PJ* (20 April 1966): 11–12; Ernest E. Mason, "The Fallacy of the Social Concept of Salvation," *PJ* (25 January 1967): 10; L. Nelson Bell, "The Kingdom of God," *PJ* (25 January 1967): 13.

away from preaching the gospel to social service with a special focus on world brotherhood and poverty relief, added together with a loss of a distinctive call to overseas evangelization. The following year, Taylor highlighted the "stride further left" that the Board of World Missions took in authorizing ecumenical missionaries credentialed by the National Council of Churches and working toward united missions efforts with the northern Presbyterians in Mexico as well as Roman Catholics in Central and South America. When the church issued its materials for the mission study for 1968, it recommended the National Council of Churches materials on world religions that generally affirmed universalism and hedged on Christian exclusivism. Each move was evidence that in the case of the agency that was closest to the church's mission and identity—world missions—the church was forsaking the faith of the fathers.[40]

Perhaps this was part of the reason why conservative churches were increasingly supporting non-PCUS missionaries and using non-PCUS speakers for their mission conferences. "The making of a major tragedy is created when concerned and evangelical Presbyterians begin to feel that if they want to support a work in primary obedience to the Great Commission, they have to look outside official denominational channels," Aiken Taylor noted. And yet what other choice did conservatives have? As he later observed, "It would not be an exaggeration to say that the principal religious issue in our time continues to be *the mission of the Church*." If the church's mission was to preach the gospel of Jesus and to make disciples in every nation under the authority and warrant of God's Word, then church leaders had to find a way to accomplish that mission, either with or without the denomination. Increasingly, however, the Presbyterian desire for connectional ministry in which a denominational body could be obedient to the Great Commission without obstacles and with a common understanding would challenge conservative loyalty to the PCUS.[41]

40. G. Aiken Taylor, "Whither World Missions?," *PJ* (17 August 1966): 9; G. Aiken Taylor, "World Missions Board Accelerates Change," *PJ* (25 January 1967): 12–13; G. Aiken Taylor, " 'Mission' Study for 1968," *PJ* (15 November 1967): 10–11, 16.

41. G. Aiken Taylor, "World Missions in the Limelight," *PJ* (19 February 1969): 12; G. Aiken Taylor, "Don't Compromise the Mission!," *PJ* (17 December 1969): 14 (emphasis his).

THE DIFFERENCE IN THE CHURCH

At the 1968 Journal Day conference in Weaverville, North Carolina, Jack Williamson observed, "I believe that secularized Protestantism is celebrating its own funeral by rejecting its doctrinal heritage of *Sola Scriptura*—the formal principle of the sole authority of the Bible as the Word of God." That was the dividing line between conservative and progressive southern Presbyterians: would the church maintain its grip on the faith of the fathers, especially its commitment to biblical authority, or would the church reject that faith for a newly secularized religion? Conservatives still had some hope that the church could be reformed and restored to the older faith because the church still was in principle a confessional body. "Church officers vow to receive and adopt them [i.e., the doctrinal standards] and we must continue to insist with relentless fervor that this subscription be made in simple honesty," Williamson urged. Ben Wilkinson agreed that the loyalties of officers were to "Christ, the Head of the Church; the Bible, the Word of God; the Confession of Faith and catechisms; then the Church—and in that order. The ordination vows we take were formulated by design in their order of importance." Tom Glasgow also pointed to the importance of the ordination vows that committed the officers to the doctrines of the Standards. "By these solemn vows," he noted, "all ministers and officers of our Church are pledged to a defense of the Confession and the purity of that faith." If ministers and elders could be held accountable to their commitment to the Westminster Confession, then there was hope that the church might return to some doctrinal commonalty around Scripture and the Reformed faith.[42]

Most conservative Presbyterians, however, were not sanguine about the possibilities of such reform. Even Nelson Bell noted that "the differences within the Church are primarily *doctrinal*, not operational, and it is a deep cleavage about *the content of the Christian faith* which lies at the root of our trouble." As Kennedy Smartt later remembered, "In the days of and following World War II the issue was not allegiance

---

42. Williamson, "Be Watchful and Strengthen," 7; Ben Wilkinson, "An Open Letter to the Establishment," *PJ* (4 December 1968): 7; Tom Glasgow, "Mystery of Mysteries," *PJ* (25 December 1968): 9.

to the Reformed faith, but . . . the historicity and deity of Jesus, the inspiration and inerrancy of the Scriptures, and whether men were lost and going to hell apart from faith in Jesus Christ as Savior and Lord." Southern Presbyterian conservatives affirmed biblical authority and the evangelical doctrines of the Westminster Standards, and they stood steadfastly for biblical evangelism and missions. If there were to be a division in the PCUS, it would not be the fault of conservatives, who were simply trying to stand for the faith of the fathers.[43]

43. L. Nelson Bell, "One Moment Please," *PJ* (11 December 1968): 10 (emphasis his); Kennedy Smartt, *I Am Reminded: An Autobiographical, Anecdotal History of the Presbyterian Church in America* (Chestnut Mountain, GA: n.p., 1998), 22.

10

"The Right to Present and Be Represented": Southern Presbyterian Conservatives Organize an Institutional Response

Though conservatives tried and failed to have the church discipline itself and remain true to the Bible and the Reformed faith, they did not give up or consent willingly to a withdrawal. Rather, in the 1960s, they organized an institutional response that sought to reinvigorate the PCUS. The organizations thus formed represented both a negative and positive program for the life of the church. Negatively, conservative organizations were formed to "combat harmful trends" and "to oppose the direction the Church has been going." But positively, these new groups were put together to evangelize both at home and abroad and to train ministers "according to our Church's traditional view of its standards, especially in relation to the Scriptures." The ultimate hope was that these organizations would be used by God to "open the eyes of all of us, that we may all see clearly in this day of confusion."[1]

Needless to say, as Concerned Presbyterians, Reformed Theological Seminary, Presbyterian Churchmen United (PCU), and the

---

1. W. A. McIlwaine, "World Missions in Conflict," *PJ* (16 June 1971): 7–9, 18.

Executive Commission on Overseas Evangelism (ECOE, pronounced "echo") formed, southern Presbyterian progressives were less than thrilled. Not only did these new organizations represent an indictment of their leadership, but these groups siphoned away money from conservative churches that tended to support the denomination's ministry to the greatest degree. While Concerned Presbyterians and PCU represented laymen and ministers, respectively, and sought to alert them to issues and organize them at the presbytery level for concerted action, Reformed Seminary and ECOE represented a new seminary and missionary-sending agency that competed with the denominational program. Thus, they challenged most directly the church's self-identity and connectional purpose.

With these new organizations, progressive leaders charged conservatives with making plans for dividing the church. Initially, conservatives were more focused on reforming the church than on dividing it. Yet as the 1960s progressed and as the direction of the church moved harder leftward, southern Presbyterian conservatives began to wonder whether the time had come to foster a new church structure that would continue the witness and testimony of the PCUS. And perhaps these new organizations, meant to present the conservative perspective and represent conservatives ecclesiastically, would serve as the basis of a continuing church.

CONCERNED PRESBYTERIANS

There had been other conservative Presbyterian laymen's organizations throughout the 1950s and early 1960s. Two of the most important were those based in Selma, Alabama, and Jackson, Mississippi. Somewhat confusingly, both organizations bore the name *Presbyterian Laymen*. The Selma group started in 1959 and produced four newsletters before shutting down. The Selma Laymen focused mainly on the fact that E. T. Thompson's election as General Assembly moderator in 1959 was a signal that the church had been captured by the liberals, who were "taking the church into political, economic, and social issues to which an overwhelming majority of the members of our Church are opposed." The liberals were determined to move the church leftward not only politically and socially, but also theologically:

"They are placing less and less emphasis upon a true Bible centered message and spiritual program of our Church." As evidence of this, the Selma Laymen reproduced material from the Thompson-Glasgow affair as well as from the Chapel Hill case involving Charles M. Jones and University Presbyterian Church. They also cited the Christian Relations Division's reports (a successor of the old Permanent Committee on Social and Moral Welfare) and especially its defense of racial integration in 1954 after the decision in *Brown v. Board of Education*.[2]

Southern Presbyterian conservatives associated with the *Presbyterian Journal* felt that the Selma group had little chance of meaningfully effecting reform. Aiken Taylor offered this assessment about the Selma group to one Nashville ruling elder: "Sometimes you can be agreed with another person about the estimate of a certain situation, but not be agreed with him as to what should be done about it." The Selma group was simply too negative, Taylor held; the *Journal* sought to present a more "positive approach to our needs." Kenneth Keyes held a similar view. He told fellow conservative Roy LeCraw that if the Selma group continued on its trajectory, it would not achieve the ultimate goal, namely, the recapturing of the denomination's boards and agencies. "I feel that the end result of the Selma group will be a split in the Church—that the men active in the Selma group will be hauled before the courts of the church and accused of disturbing the peace of the Church." A further fault with the Selma group was that it presented itself publicly as an anonymous group. Without someone to take responsibility for making the charges, it was difficult to take seriously its claims about liberalism in the church.[3]

A couple of years later, a second Presbyterian laymen's group organized in Jackson, Mississippi. In the letter that was sent to potential supporters, the leaders (all ruling elders from the Jackson area) declared that "the basis of this organization is the firm conviction

2. The newsletters may be found at the PCAHC: *Presbyterian Layman* (Selma, Alabama) 1–4 (c. 1960); "Southern Presbyterian Group Says 'Liberal' Ministers Ruining Church," *Mobile Register* (20 October 1959), clipping in E. T. Thompson Papers, UPS.

3. G. Aiken Taylor to H. M. Doak, 30 June 1960, *Presbyterian Journal* Papers, box 183, folder 3, PCAHC; Kenneth Keyes to Roy LeCraw, 26 September 1960, L. Nelson Bell Papers, box 31, folder 15, BGC.

that Presbyterian laymen love their Lord and have zeal for the spread of the Gospel." They also believed that once laymen in the church clearly understood the issues facing the PCUS, they would stand for the "teaching of the Bible and the standards of our Church." This organization also produced several newsletters before discontinuing. Not only did the newsletters offer "horse sense" about detecting liberals in a local church's pulpit, they offered hard words about liberalism: "To us, 'liberalism' is the work of the Devil. Humanly speaking, if the Devil can get enough of our preachers denying only parts of the Bible, he will soon have the testimony of the Presbyterian Church U.S. so 'watered down' that our church will no longer be 'Christian soldiers marching as to war.'" Their conservatism also had a racial component: they stood against the National Council of Churches, especially because of that organization's involvement in the Delta Ministry and its larger goal of the civil-rights law. This racial traditionalism led Nelson Bell to express concern that the Jackson laymen would turn their work into "a race protest." In order to work effectively in the church, Bell believed, a laymen's group had to emphasize both the positive and negative sides of the issues then facing the church. In addition, he worried that the Mississippi leaders were "willing (some of them anxious) to split the Church."[4]

Both the Selma and Jackson organizations formed in the belief that if PCUS laymen knew what was going on in the denomination, they would rise up and return the church to its biblical foundation and spiritual mission. This same motivation led conservative leaders associated with the *Presbyterian Journal* to meet in Atlanta to discuss the possibility of their own laymen's organization. That possibility became a reality in August 1964, when the *Journal* board of directors voted to form Concerned Presbyterians with $15,000 in seed money and chose Kenneth Keyes to serve as president of the organization.

4. Grady Johnson et al. to "Fellow Presbyterians," 26 June 1964; *Presbyterian U.S., Laymen Inc.* (Jackson, Mississippi) 1–5 (c. 1964–65) (all in *Presbyterian Journal* Papers, box 201, folder 18, PCAHC); "Dissidents Organize in Mississippi," *PO* (7 September 1964): 4; "Lay Group Devises Test for 'Liberals,'" *PO* (7 June 1965): 8–9; L. Nelson Bell to Horace Hull and Kenneth Keyes, 13 May 1961; L. Nelson Bell to Kenneth S. Keyes, 21 August 1964 (both in L. Nelson Bell Papers, box 31, folder 15, BGC).

The thought was that this laymen's group would combat the liberals through organizing elders at the presbytery level and using the courts of the church to bring about reform. In addition, the desire was for the organization to have a more positive agenda than the Selma and Jackson groups, "an association to heal and not divide, to find solutions in love and not regiment by force."[5]

Keyes had come to the notice of southern Presbyterian conservatives during the 1954 debates over reunion with the northern Presbyterian church. A ruling elder from Shenandoah Presbyterian Church, Miami, Florida, Keyes was a remarkably successful commercial real estate developer in south Florida. His financial acumen involved him in the National Association of Evangelicals at its founding, in which he served as the finance chairman and on the board of directors for over twenty years. He had served quietly on the board of directors for the *Presbyterian Journal* for a number of years, lending his expertise to the business side of the magazine. And it was his financial knowledge that was used to show how foolish the proposed 1954 merger was. His articles in the *Journal* used charts and graphs to show that the PCUS was far more successful than the northern Presbyterian church on every front; to merge with a less successful organization made no sense from a business perspective. For some ruling elders, Keyes's argument made sense and helped them to vote against the proposed reunion.[6]

As a result, Keyes appeared to be the right choice for the new organization, a layman whom other ruling elders and church leaders could trust. From the beginning, however, Concerned Presbyterians experienced division. The original vision for the group had been Nelson Bell's, the most recognized layman on the conservative side. He had hoped that Concerned Presbyterians would "build up the Church" and "heal existing breaches," not serve to divide and separate. But as the organization began to send out materials,

5. "'Concerned Presbyterians'!," *PJ* (1 July 1964): 12; Kenneth S. Keyes, *God's Partner* (Brevard, NC: n.p., 1994), 26–27.

6. Keyes, *God's Partner*, 19; Kenneth S. Keyes, *A Layman Looks at the Merger* (Weaverville, NC: Southern Presbyterian Journal, 1954); Kenneth S. Keyes, "More about the Charts," *SPJ* (26 May 1954): 4–7.

including the first newsletter, which contained a slashing attack on the National Council of Churches, Bell decided not to allow his name to be used with Concerned Presbyterians. Both Keyes and Roy LeCraw, the Concerned Presbyterians vice-chairman, felt betrayed. "I can say to you very frankly that I never would have accepted the leadership of this movement if I had any idea you would object to being openly identified with it," Keyes complained to Bell. And yet Bell would continue to refuse identification with Concerned Presbyterians, signaling his discomfort with the direction of the laymen's group as well as his developing differences with others in the conservative leadership.[7]

This internal disagreement did not prevent Keyes and the other leaders from moving forward. The first issue of the association's newsletter came out in March 1965 and immediately caused a stir. In it, the lay leaders set forward a narrative for why Concerned Presbyterians had been formed and what they hoped to accomplish. On one level, they argued that the politicization of the church represented by organizations such as Concerned Presbyterians had been going on for a long time. They claimed that for many years the liberals had had a "secret organization" called "the Fellowship of St. James," which had worked "quietly behind the scenes to gain control of the political machinery of our denomination." This fellowship had recently come out into the open the previous year, when liberal Presbyterians formed the "Fellowship of Concern." These liberal groups were "well organized, highly articulate and zealous in the attainment of their goals." Part of the reason why the liberals were able to gain control of the church's structures was that conservatives "have been largely content to talk about these matters without setting up an effective organization through which to make our voices heard in the Church courts." That was the purpose of Concerned Presbyterians: to serve as an effective organization that would "return control of our Church once more

---

7. "'Concerns' Endorsed by Group," *PJ* (26 August 1964): 4–5; L. Nelson Bell to Robert Strong, 6 January 1965, L. Nelson Bell Papers, box 69, folder 24, BGC; Kenneth Keyes to L. Nelson Bell, 22 December 1964; Kenneth Keyes to L. Nelson Bell, 5 August 1965; L. Nelson Bell to Kenneth Keyes, 7 August 1965 (all in L. Nelson Bell Papers, box 31, folder 15, BGC).

to those who believe that the Bible is the Word of God and the only infallible rule of faith and practice."[8]

On another level, this first newsletter set the trajectory for Concerned Presbyterians in terms of content and tone. While disavowing any desire to "withdraw from our beloved church," they did want to make it clear that their concerns centered on the fact that "the primary mission of the Church—winning people to Jesus Christ and nurturing them in the Faith"—was being set aside "by over-emphasis on social, economic, and political matters." In addition, they were concerned that the authority of the Bible and the truth of the Westminster Standards were being questioned. Finally, there was deep concern about the National Council of Churches and the effects that its leadership was having in the PCUS. And the bulk of the first newsletter focused right there: on the National Council of Churches. Not only did Concerned Presbyterians offer a packet of information on the National Council free of charge, but they dedicated the rest of the first issue of their newsletter to the ecumenical organization. They sought to demonstrate that a large portion of PCUS money was going to fund the National Council; that the National Council had "associated itself with persons who have not been above suspicion as far as Communist influence is concerned"; that the National Council was involved with the 1964 Delta Ministry and worked to supply college students and others for an "invasion" of Mississippi for civil-rights work; and that it was advocating that young people use "subversion" in order to bring them into conflict with law-enforcement officers to further particular social goals.[9]

8. "Why We Are 'Concerned,'" *Concerned Presbyterian* (March 1965): 1. Keyes repeatedly made this claim, and it was picked up by other conservatives throughout the years; see "Somebody Is Seeing Ghosts," *PO* (22 March 1965): 9; Keyes, *God's Partner*, 26; Frank J. Smith, *The History of the Presbyterian Church in America: Silver Anniversary Edition* (Lawrenceville, GA: Presbyterian Scholars Press, 1999), 90–91. The Fellowship of St. James was a dinner club, started by E. T. Thompson and other Richmond ministers in 1929; according to historian Peter Hobbie, they were largely focused on the work of the *Presbyterian of the South*, which later became the *PO*. That they discussed denomination politics there is little doubt. But their work was no secret—it was evident in the editorial policy of the *PO*. See Peter H. Hobbie, "Ernest Trice Thompson: Prophet for a Changing South" (Ph.D. diss., Union Theological Seminary in Virginia, 1987), 228–29.

9. Peter R. Branton, "The Truth about the National Council of Churches," *Concerned Presbyterian* (March 1965): 3–6.

The October 1965 newsletter continued the attack on the National Council of Churches, this time from the financial commitment that the PCUS had demonstrated to it. In particular, Concerned Presbyterians protested the creation of a central treasury for the denomination that had the power to "equalize" the funds given. Regardless of how the benevolence funds came into denominational headquarters—whether designated to particular causes or undesignated—they would be distributed to the agencies and boards based on a predetermined division. This equalization strategy created outrage among conservative churches; some went so far as to cut off funding completely as a way of protesting the denomination's direction and the displeasure with equalization. While Concerned Presbyterians did not like the equalization plan, they also sought to urge all churches to "continue to support the benevolence program of the church while we are making an earnest effort through the proper constitutional channels to change those policies." Yet churches could also try to ensure that no moneys were sent to the National Council of Churches by instructing their local church treasurers to send world missions dollars to specific causes rather than to the central treasury.[10]

Concerned Presbyterians admitted, however, that even when southern Presbyterian dollars were directed to their own causes, they were liable to be misused. For them, one example was the August 1965 conference that brought Martin Luther King Jr. to Montreat. That invitation "has not only compromised the doctrinal position of our Church but it has provoked more friction in our Church than any other single event in recent years." Not only was King suspect theologically—denying the virgin birth of Jesus, professing a lack of interest in sin and salvation, rejecting the deity of Christ—but "his total emphasis was upon his brand of ethics and it centered on race relations." Further, they claimed that he was not even a trustworthy American: "It has been proven that Dr. King has identified himself with more than 60 Communist-front organizations or activities cited as subversive by official government agencies." Surely most conservative

10. "On Handling Benevolence Gifts for General Assembly Causes," *Concerned Presbyterian* (October 1965): 1–2.

laymen would agree that inviting King to the Presbyterian assembly grounds under PCUS auspices was a waste of valuable dollars and an unnecessarily divisive step.[11]

By early 1966, Keyes and the Concerned Presbyterians had made good strides in organizing at the presbytery level. Through the work of George Peters, the Concerned Presbyterians field director, nearly two-thirds of the presbyteries had been visited; groups within those presbyteries had been encouraged "to develop plans to make the conservative voice effective in the various areas." These plans included alerting the elders and deacons of every local church about the issues facing the PCUS, encouraging them to hold chapter meetings either in conjunction with session meetings or separately, and joining in fellowship, prayer, and discussion of denominational issues. In the end, "a primary objective of each local chapter or group . . . will be to try to have their Sessions appoint men of this caliber to serve at presbytery—men with the courage of their convictions, willing if necessary to differ with their own pastors." If conservative elders attended presbytery meetings educated and empowered, the church could be reformed.[12]

Yet even with this organization, it was not enough to arrest the leftward drift of the church. The 1966 General Assembly was dominated by "the 'liberal' machine," which had outworked the Concerned Presbyterians "to insure that the 'right' commissioners were sent from most of the presbyteries." The Assembly's decisions included a stand for the abolition of capital punishment, support for civil disobedience, criticism of the United States' policy in Vietnam, and agreement to participate in the Consultation on Church Union (COCU) talks. In other words, "Concerned Presbyterians need to be aware that the General Assembly voted, in effect, to (1) re-state the Church's faith; (2) join in union conversations with Churches that are neither Reformed nor evangelical, which means that it was willing to (3) abandon the Presbyterian order." While discouraged, laymen were urged not to leave the church, but to work and to fight to see it reformed. And while it

11. "Paul's Gospel and Today's Social Problems," *Concerned Presbyterian* (October 1965): 2–3.

12. "Keyes Group Says Big Gains Are Made in 'First Year,'" *PO* (31 January 1966): 7.

appeared that the 1967 General Assembly turned slightly to the right, rewarding the efforts of Concerned Presbyterians, the following year's national meeting took such a consistent liberal tack that Kenneth Keyes predicted that "a split in the Church is coming within the next two to three years."[13]

And yet even as it was losing the ecclesiastical battle, Concerned Presbyterians were forced to defend themselves in those same church courts. In January 1966, a Texas presbytery heard charges that Concerned Presbyterians were attempting "to divide and destroy the witness and ministry of the Presbyterian Church U.S." The following spring, Nashville Presbytery expressed its "strong disapproval" of the work of Concerned Presbyterians lay leaders. Even while some church courts expressed their disapproval of Concerned Presbyterians, conservative leaders continued to believe that the majority of southern Presbyterians would actually agree with them if they simply understood the issues: "We sincerely believe that a very large majority of the informed members of the Presbyterian Church U.S. are not in favor of what the minority in the denomination is trying to do." It did not appear, however, that the trajectory of events warranted such confidence.[14]

There was one last attempt to conciliate Concerned Presbyterians with the denominational leadership. It occurred in 1967–68 after Marshall Dendy, executive secretary of the Board of Christian Education, was elected moderator of the General Assembly. Dendy attended the executive committee meetings for both Concerned Presbyterians and the Fellowship of Concern. He then hosted a meeting of forty-eight ministers and laymen in Atlanta in early 1968 in an attempt to "resolve some of the troublesome differences within the denomination." Kenneth Keyes, several other elders, and five

13. "The 1966 General Assembly!," *Concerned Presbyterian* (June 1966): 1; "Don't Leave the Church," *Concerned Presbyterian* (November 1967): 8; "Counsel to the 'Concerned,'" *PO* (11 December 1967): 9; "The 108th General Assembly," *Concerned Presbyterian* (September 1968): 2–3; Kenneth Keyes to Donald Patterson, 27 November 1968, *Presbyterian Journal* Papers, box 206, folder 17, PCAHC.

14. Kenneth S. Keyes, "Are We 'Divisive and Destructive'?," *Concerned Presbyterian* (June 1966): 2; "CP Co-Chairmen Draw Rebuke of Presbytery," *PO* (8 May 1967): 4; "Answering Mr. Hartley," *Concerned Presbyterian* (January 1967): 3.

ministers, who were friendly to their cause, represented Concerned Presbyterians. In Keyes's presentation, he reiterated that "the programs and policies sponsored and promoted by the liberal wing during recent years are the principal causes of the decline in the effectiveness of our Church." These liberal programs and policies involved "their substitution of the social gospel for the Gospel of salvation through the shed blood of our Lord and Savior Jesus Christ." And liberals had pursued these programs and policies with a single-minded focus. Concerned Presbyterians existed in order to pursue a different set of goals: namely, to stop the liberal advance and to return the church to its biblical and confessional basis. "We hope our liberal brethren will recognize that we are just as sincere as they are and that we have the same right to pursue our objectives as they have to promote theirs," he pleaded. Not surprisingly, the meeting accomplished little; but after this, both sides knew that it was a matter of time before division would finally come.[15]

REFORMED THEOLOGICAL SEMINARY

Both conservatives and progressives in the southern church recognized that future control of the denomination centered in the theological seminaries. Denominational progressives such as E. T. Thompson believed that they would eventually win the day on reunion with the northern church as a result of "the new batch of ministers coming in from the seminaries." Conservatives, too, recognized that the liberal domination of the four PCUS seminaries that supplied ministers for the denomination—Union Seminary in Richmond; Columbia Seminary in Decatur, Georgia; Louisville Seminary in Kentucky; and Austin Seminary in Texas—meant that progressives would continue to have an upper hand if things did not change.[16]

15. Marshall C. Dendy, "There Is Room for Differences," *PO* (4 September 1967): 5–7; Marshall C. Dendy, "To a Fellowship of Concern," *PO* (2 October 1967): 6–7; "A Moderator's Meeting," *PO* (5 February 1968): 4–6; "The Moderator's Meeting," *Concerned Presbyterian* (May 1968): 1–5.

16. E. T. Thompson, *Presbyterians in the South*, 3 vols. (Richmond, VA: John Knox, 1963–73), 3:574. This section draws heavily from Sean Michael Lucas, *Blessed Zion: First Presbyterian Church, Jackson, Mississippi, 1837–2012* (Jackson, MS: First Presbyterian Church, 2013), chap. 7.

One solution was to encourage men from Westminster Theological Seminary in Philadelphia to come to southern churches. The founder of Westminster Seminary, J. Gresham Machen, was fondly remembered in southern Presbyterian conservative circles for his valiant defense of the faith in the 1920s and 1930s. Likewise, the faculty of that seminary was viewed as the strongest among evangelical theological schools during the period. While some progressives decried the influence of the "fundamentalist," Orthodox Presbyterian–related seminary, conservative churches throughout the South readily found ministers from Machen's school. Central Mississippi Presbytery had several Westminster graduates, which drew the notice of the liberal *Presbyterian Outlook*, which somewhat ironically suggested that there was an "infiltration" of outside influences that was the basis of agitation in the church.[17]

In the long run, securing ministers from Westminster Seminary was not a permanent solution, nor was the seminary able to supply enough ministers to meet the need of the PCUS churches. And so conservative Presbyterians turned their attentions to their own seminaries and the possibility of reform. The one school that had the best possibility of turning in a more conservative direction was Columbia Theological Seminary in Decatur, Georgia. Founded in 1828 in Lexington, Georgia, and relocated two years later to Columbia, South Carolina, Columbia Seminary had a tenuous existence for its first hundred years. Certainly, it had high points with well-known teachers in the nineteenth century: B. M. Palmer, J. H. Thornwell, J. B. Adger, and J. L. Girardeau all served on its faculty. But there was a constant struggle for students and money, especially after the Civil War brought widespread destruction to the South generally and to Columbia specifically. A full-fledged heresy trial of popular professor James Woodrow in the 1880s did not help the school; at the turn of the century, it nearly closed for lack of money and leadership. While Richard T. Gillespie was president in the late 1920s, the

17. "Infiltration—To What End?," *PO* (17 June 1957): 5–7; R. Milton Winter, "Division and Reunion in the Presbyterian Church, U.S.: A Mississippi Retrospective," *Journal of Presbyterian History* 78, 1 (2000): 75–76. See also G. Aiken Taylor to Walter G. Downie, 11 July 1966, *Presbyterian Journal* Papers, box 196, folder 13, PCAHC.

school relocated to Decatur, Georgia, a growing suburb of Atlanta. The school had two influential conservative faculty members in the twentieth century: W. M. McPheeters, who taught Old Testament from 1888 to 1932, and William Childs Robinson, who taught church history, among other subjects, from 1926 until his retirement in 1967. In 1932, J. McDowell Richards became president and served in that position for thirty-nine years, providing strong, moderate leadership. Columbia Seminary had long had the reputation as the "conservative" PCUS theological seminary. Under the oversight of the Synods of Mississippi, Alabama, Georgia, and South Carolina, the seminary was not as theologically progressive as either Louisville Seminary or Union Seminary. As a result, southern Presbyterian conservatives held out the hope that Columbia would remain a safe place to gain a supply of Bible-believing ministers for their churches.[18]

Starting in the mid-1950s, the board of directors of the *Southern Presbyterian Journal* put together a committee that sought to influence the work of Columbia Seminary. Led by Kenneth Keyes, the committee focused on ensuring that conservative men were elected to the seminary board and investigating whether faculty members were teaching progressive theology. Nelson Bell, in particular, was adroit in working both sides of the fence, guiding the work of the committee on the one hand and intervening with seminary president McDowell Richards to shape his potential response on the other. In addition, Bell sought to influence future faculty appointments in a conservative direction and to block others, especially John Leith, then pastor of First Presbyterian Church, Auburn, Alabama, and later professor of theology at Union Seminary.[19]

18. For a history of the school, see David B. Calhoun, *Our Southern Zion: Old Columbia Seminary, 1828–1927* (Carlisle, PA: Banner of Truth, 2012). For a sketch of Robinson's life, see David B. Calhoun, *Pleading for a Reformation Vision: The Life and Selected Writings of William Childs Robinson* (Carlisle, PA: Banner of Truth, 2013).

19. *Minutes, SPJ Board of Directors*, L. Nelson Bell Papers, box 73, folder 4, BGC; L. Nelson Bell to Board of Directors of *SPJ*, 17 September 1955; L. Nelson Bell to Board of Directors of *SPJ*, 15 November 1956 (both in L. Nelson Bell Papers, box 72, folder 7, BGC); L. Nelson Bell to J. McDowell Richards, 30 October 1956; J. McDowell Richards to L. Nelson Bell, 31 October 1956; J. McDowell Richards to L. Nelson Bell, 5 November 1956; L. Nelson Bell to J. McDowell Richards, 19 March 1957 (all in J. McDowell Richards Papers, box 41, PHS). See also Kennedy Smartt, *I Am Reminded: An Autobiographical,*

The *Journal* was not the only organization that was investigating what was happening at Columbia Seminary. The session of First Presbyterian Church, Jackson, Mississippi, also began investigating the school to determine whether it could continue to send men and money there. In November 1953, the session appointed a three-man committee "to study the schools, institutions, and Columbia Seminary, which are supported by this synod and report back to the session any information that they think will be of interest to the session." This committee was chaired by ruling elder Erskine Wells and joined by elders Russ Johnson and M. B. Swayze and slowly went about doing its work. In May 1956, Erskine Wells reported on a trip to Columbia Seminary that he had taken at the request of Keyes and Bell's *Journal* committee, relaying the news that the seminary had hired Ronald Wallace, a "conservative" professor from Scotland.[20]

By 1960, however, the First Presbyterian Church session committee was ready to report. After discussing its method of study, the committee observed that it was "not satisfied with the situation which has been prevailing at Columbia Seminary during recent years, and, without further information, would be unwilling to recommend that our Church cooperate in said fund-raising campaign." Before releasing any money to Columbia Seminary, as part of its campaign to raise $700,000 in Mississippi, the session invited seminary president Richards to meet with the session to discuss the current situation at Columbia and what could be expected in the future. And the session also voted to invite recent Columbia graduates to meet with the session with their observations on the situation at the theological school.[21]

Anecdotal History of the Presbyterian Church in America (Chestnut Mountain, GA: n.p., 1998), 49–50; Smartt was one of the students who raised questions about Richard Gillespie, a homiletics professor who was committed to Barthianism.

20. As it turned out, while Keyes, Bell, and Wells all claimed that Wallace was "conservative," he actually was Barthian. Because he had an eye to historical theology (his first books were on various doctrinal teaching from John Calvin), he was viewed more acceptably or less threateningly. See Iain R. Torrance, "Obituary: Professor Ronald Wallace," *The Scotsman* (1 March 2006), http://www.scotsman.com/news/obituaries/professor-ronald-wallace-1-1107905.

21. Russ M. Johnson to J. McDowell Richards, 29 January 1960, J. McDowell Richards Papers, box 63, PHS.

After meeting with Richards and the students, the First Presbyterian Church session issued a statement to the congregation. While noting that "some of the faculty and staff of this seminary are very faithful to the standards of our church as set forth in the Word of God, the Westminster Confession of Faith and the Catechisms," other faculty and staff have worked to shift the emphasis of the seminary "toward the neo-orthodox view of the inspiration of Scripture [rather] than toward the high view of inspiration of Scripture which is clearly taught in the Westminster Confession of Faith and particularly in the Scriptures themselves." To show good faith toward the seminary and to provide an incentive for the situation to change, however, the session pledged $1,500 a year for five years, which represented a substantial increase in the church's budget for the school. In addition, the session decided to make "a conditional pledge of $10,000 per year for the next five years, commencing in 1961." The condition was simply that Columbia Seminary move back in a more conservative direction, making "substantial improvement in teaching the doctrines of our church, as set forth in the Westminster Confession of Faith." If the school did, it would receive the money; if the school did not, then the money would "be used elsewhere than at Columbia to promote sound theological training for ministerial students."[22]

Not surprisingly, Columbia Seminary's leadership reacted negatively both to the theological charges made against its faculty and to the conditional nature of First Church's pledge. After its May 1960 board meeting, the seminary's board of directors replied to the First Church session. They protested that the way that the session's decision had been publicized "cast aspersions upon the good name of an honored institution of our Church, and upon the reputation of men who have proven themselves to be humble and faithful servants of Christ." In addition, the board "categorically reject[ed] the clear implication of your paper that Columbia Theological Seminary is teaching a lower view of inspiration than that which the Bible asserts for itself." And finally, the directors rejected the conditional gift: "Because the

22. Russ M. Johnson to J. McDowell Richards, 17 February 1960, J. McDowell Richards Papers, box 63, PHS.

acceptance of your gift of $50,000 at the end of that time under the conditions you have imposed inevitably places us in a false position before the Church and seems to imply an acceptance of a judgment which we reject, we wish to advise you that we would be unable to accept the gift if it is offered in the way suggested."[23]

Even though the First Church session's conditional gift was rejected, the session decided to raise the money anyway because plans were developing that would lead to a new seminary. In 1958, the church's pastor, conservative leader John Reed Miller, had discussed the possibility of a new theological seminary with Belhaven professor Morton Smith and area pastor Al Freundt; by October 1959, the discussions had come to the point of a formal plan, as ruling elders Julius Scott and Robert Kennington joined the group. The plan was shelved for a time, however, as the situation with Columbia Seminary played out.[24]

In December 1962, the liberal *Presbyterian Outlook* ran a symposium with faculty members from the four PCUS seminaries on the topic of "do we need an infallible Bible?" All four faculty members answered the question in the negative. The response by conservatives was swift. Churches such as First Presbyterian Church, Hattiesburg, Mississippi, adopted a protest against these statements, as did Central Mississippi Presbytery; individual ministers, such as Sam Patterson, president of French Camp Academy, wrote to the seminary presidents to ascertain whether this was, in fact, the view of each school. Even more significant than the protests, however, was the fact that this symposium set in motion plans to start a new theological seminary. During the June 1963 meeting of the Synod of Mississippi, five key leaders from across the state gathered to discuss and pray about the need for a new seminary. Led by Patterson, the other ministers were William J. Stanway (First Church, Hattiesburg); Erskine Jackson (First Church, Kosciusko); James Spencer (First Church, Crystal Springs); and John Reed Miller (First Church, Jackson). A month later, these

23. Board of Directors to First Presbyterian Church Session, n.d. [May 1960?], J. McDowell Richards Papers, box 63, PHS.

24. Rebecca Barnes Hobbs, *How Big Is Your God? The Spiritual Legacy of Sam Patterson, Evangelist* (French Camp, MS: RTSFCA Publishers, 2010), 188.

ministers gathered at the Robert E. Lee Hotel in Jackson and addressed specific topics that convinced them that they had to start an institute that would develop into a theological seminary, dedicated to the verbal plenary inspiration of Scripture and the Reformed faith and to the provision of ministers to small PCUS churches.[25]

Key to the development of this new institution was the recruitment of ruling elders. One of the earliest supporters was First Church Jackson ruling elder Erskine Wells. He had led the First Church session committee that investigated the theological position of Columbia Seminary; he knew how necessary a new theological school was. When Sam Patterson challenged Wells to consider "how big is your God?" the young ruling elder came on board the developing seminary project. The next ruling elder whom Patterson recruited to the project was another First Church Jackson ruling elder, Robert Cannada. Again, Cannada had spent a number of years leading the First Church Sunday school program and investigating curricula; he, too, had grown concerned about the theological drift of the denomination and recognized the need for solid theological education. Wells and Cannada in turn recruited Frank Horton and Frank Tindall to serve on the planning committee of the developing institute (First Church elder R. G. Kennington would also join the committee in early 1964). Elliot Belcher from Brent, Alabama, and H. S. Williford, another elder from First Church Jackson who would serve as treasurer, would join these men. These founding board members had determined that the school would remain independent of church control and that it would be led by a self-perpetuating board consisting mainly of laymen with a few ministerial advisers. When Reformed Theological Institute was announced in December 1963, it served as the new beginning of theological education for those who affirmed the inerrancy of Scripture.[26]

25. "Do We Need an Infallible Bible?," *PO* (24 December 1962): 5–6; *Session Minutes, First Presbyterian Church, Hattiesburg, Mississippi* (14 January 1963); W. F. Mansell to J. McDowell Richards, 19 July 1963, J. McDowell Richards Papers, box 50, PHS; Hobbs, *How Big Is Your God?*, 188–92, 196–97.

26. John R. Muether, *The First Forty Years, 1966–2006: The History of Reformed Theological Seminary* (Clinton, MS: Reformed Theological Seminary, 2006), 16–17, 21–23; Hobbs, *How Big Is Your God?*, 199, 200, 208.

When the school first opened in the fall of 1964, it used the campus of French Camp Academy to host lay education classes in English Bible, doctrine, and personal evangelism. Patterson, Leonard Van Horn, and Morton Smith were the main teachers in those first classes as they sought to lay a foundation for conservative, Reformed theological education. Yet there was recognition that French Camp, Mississippi, was not the best place to host a theological school. The board determined to establish the school in Jackson, Mississippi, for several reasons. Not only was there proximity to several colleges in the city—Belhaven, Millsaps, and Mississippi Colleges—but many of the key donors and board members were in Jackson. In addition, Central Mississippi Presbytery was one of the very few PCUS presbyteries that demonstrated a willingness to have the school's future graduates in its bounds.[27]

And so the board members went to work preparing for the new school. They were able to secure land in west Jackson, funded mainly by a forgivable loan from Second Church Memphis ruling elder and *Journal* board member Horace Hull. Other start-up costs were covered by an anonymous donation of $100,000 and the $50,000 that First Presbyterian Church, Jackson, had set aside for theological education. In addition, the board developed an initial statement that set forward its founding and guiding principles: the inspiration and inerrancy of the Bible; the Calvinistic theological system represented in the Westminster Standards; and the spiritual nature and mission of the church. The board further declared that these perspectives "have the right to be presented and represented institutionally in the church."[28]

Even before its doors opened, however, Reformed Seminary received opposition from denominational progressives who questioned

27. Muether, *First Forty Years*, 17; "New Seminary Started by Miss.-Memphis Group," *PO* (25 May 1964): 3–4; "Mississippi Institute Projects Its Plan," *PO* (21 September 1964): 3.

28. Muether, *First Forty Years*, 18–20. Nelson Bell repeatedly urged that the seminary move from Mississippi in order to have greater viability in the PCUS and to escape any association with segregation: see L. Nelson Bell to Robert F. Gribble, 27 November 1964; Morton Smith to L. Nelson Bell, 10 December 1964; Morton Smith to L. Nelson Bell, 11 January 1965; L. Nelson Bell to Morton Smith, 25 March 1969 (all in L. Nelson Bell Papers, box 48, folder 6, BGC).

whether an independent seminary supported by PCUS churches and courts was allowable. The liberal *Presbyterian Outlook* urged neighboring synods to "pose a question as to the integrity of the Mississippi commitment" to Reformed Seminary. Further, it urged "quarantine" against potential graduates who came from such a "disloyal" institution. The Synod of Mississippi did remind its churches that Columbia Seminary was the only school "officially supported and controlled by our synod"; lines from this resolution that opposed Reformed Seminary, however, were removed under protest. The 1966 General Assembly heard a resolution that questioned whether PCUS ministers could serve at independent seminaries; it eventually decided that this was up to the individual presbyteries to determine. Likewise, the Assembly would later say that it was within a presbytery's prerogative whether it would accept Reformed Seminary graduates in its bounds; New Orleans Presbytery, for one, rejected Reformed Seminary as a training school for its candidates until the Association of Theological Schools, the main accreditation body for seminaries, approved it.[29]

And yet the school would prosper. By 1969, the seminary had 1,300 individual donors and 140 church donors from thirty-two states. Student enrollment would grow through these first years, with the result that when the PCA formed at the end of 1973, nearly 20 percent of the teaching elders enrolled at the first General Assembly were graduates of Reformed Theological Seminary. While the administration and executive committee of the seminary board sought to maintain neutrality in the divisions that came to the PCUS—as evidenced by the fact that seminary president Sam Patterson and several other faculty members did not leave that church when the division came—there was little doubt that Reformed Seminary was vital to the formation of a new denomination. Indeed, Aiken Taylor went so far as to call it "our new school," the theological seminary of the continuing church.[30]

29. "Mississippi Seminary," *PO* (17 January 1966): 8–9; "Synod Actions: Mississippi," *PO* (27 June 1966): 4; "New Orleans Presbytery Cautions Its Candidates," *PO* (20 November 1967): 8; Muether, *First Forty Years*, 37.

30. Hobbs, *How Big Is Your God?*, 239; Muether, *First Forty Years*, 40; G. Aiken Taylor, "Our Newest Seminary," *PJ* (29 October 1969): 7–11.

PRESBYTERIAN CHURCHMEN UNITED

Three years after Concerned Presbyterians formed as a laymen's organization, a group of about fifty ministers started to meet for prayer and discussion about the state of the church. As Paul Settle remembered it, the room where these ministers met was at the top of the Battery Park Hotel in Asheville, North Carolina: "The men gained access to the penthouse by way of a rickety, decrepit old elevator, whose erratic, wheezing, and lurching ascent assured that its passengers were in an attitude of fervent prayer when they finally scrambled off at the top." These hardy souls who gathered for prayer informally called themselves the Presbyterian Ministers' Prayer Fellowship. Led by Donald Patterson, then pastor of McIlwain Memorial Presbyterian Church, Pensacola, Florida, this group wondered whether they needed to organize more formally in order to pursue reformation in the southern church.[31]

Toward the end of 1968, the prayer fellowship gathered in Atlanta with leaders from Concerned Presbyterians in order to see whether there might be a sense of direction, both for the church as a whole and for the ministerial fellowship. Leading up to that meeting, there was some concern that the time would be spent urging one another to pray and preach without any other specific aims for action. D. James Kennedy, for one, voiced that concern; he urged that the meeting have a specific agenda that included "the specific problems facing our denomination and their time table; possible actions that we might take and their time table; the legal questions involved; [and] if a break with the denomination is necessary, when should it take place, how is it to be effected, how is it to be organized and where do we go." Others wanted the focus to be on alternative strategies toward reforming the denomination. Sam Patterson, head of Reformed Seminary, asked, "Is there an alternative to a 'separation exit' on the one hand and a 'staying-in and defend the faith' on the other? . . . We have done nothing in a united way (we conservatives).

31. "How It Started," *PJ* (7 January 1970): 10; Paul Settle, *To God All Praise and Glory: Under God: Celebrating, the Past, Claiming the Future, the Presbyterian Church in America* (Atlanta: Presbyterian Church in America, 1998), 31.

What we have done has been more in defense of the Truth than in aggressively promoting revival and renewal." Clearly, there was not unanimity, even among the ministers, about the future of the church or even this ministerial fraternalism.[32]

When these ministers and elders met in December 1968, their conversation began to coalesce around the idea that southern Presbyterian conservatives needed to stand for faithfulness to their ordination vows and the constitution of the church. John E. Richards, minister at First Presbyterian Church, Macon, Georgia, urged the men toward "a positive dedication to our commitments." Kenneth Keyes agreed that there should be "a statement that could be signed by session after session, by hundreds, stating that there surely will be a church true to the Word of God regardless" of what happened in the PCUS. They also began to believe that a council or mediating structure was necessary in order to maintain contact with the various interests they represented. Perhaps this mediating structure, Keyes suggested, could include a "strong organization of ministers corresponding to Concerned Presbyterians." As these ideas began to gel, these conservatives agreed to meet again in February 1969 to discuss matters.[33]

In the lead-up to the February meeting, Donald Patterson was tasked with coordinating various leaders with the goal of developing "an association for evangelical and reformed witness." In addition, there was hope that work could be done on "an affirmation to be declared by the group organized." During the February meeting, this affirmation was laid out and a steering committee was appointed to refine it with hopes that it could be adopted by a group of ministers who would gather in Atlanta before the August 1969 Journal Day, and then subsequently by ministers and elders as well as entire sessions in the months to come.[34]

32. D. James Kennedy to Donald B. Patterson, 29 October 1968; Sam C. Patterson to Donald B. Patterson, 12 November 1968 (both in *Presbyterian Journal* Papers, box 206, folder 17, PCAHC).

33. G. Aiken Taylor notes of "Atlanta Invitation Meeting, December 26–27, 1968," *Presbyterian Journal* Papers, box 206, folder 17, PCAHC.

34. Donald Patterson to "Brethren" (G. Aiken Taylor, Donald Graham, John E. Richards, and Bob Pitman), 30 December 1968, *Presbyterian Journal* Papers, box 207, folder 2;

That July, as the ministers met in Atlanta, they agreed to the document called "The Declaration of Commitment." The seven-point statement affirmed the necessity of faith in Jesus Christ for salvation, the infallibility of the Bible, a spirit of "love, concern, and neighborliness toward all races of men without partiality and without prejudice," the need for a confessional church, an opposition to any new creed or confessional statement that would undercut the Westminster Standards, an opposition to the grand strategy of church union represented by COCU, and a warning that the signers would do whatever was necessary "to fulfill the obligations imposed by our ordination vows to maintain our Presbyterian faith." Signing this document was no light matter. Arthur Matthews remembered that these leaders "kind of laid their lives on the line by signing the Declaration. It was a terribly difficult thing for them to do."[35]

After Journal Day 1969, when the Declaration of Commitment was announced, the ministers met and formed themselves into a formal organization, calling themselves Presbyterian Churchmen United (PCU). And yet even as they were forming this new organization, there was division in terms of perspective and strategy. Bob Pitman, pastor of Casa Linda Presbyterian Church in Dallas, Texas, and a member of the PCU Executive Committee, was networking with other moderate voices in the PCUS, including William Elliott Jr., pastor of the influential Highland Park Presbyterian Church in Dallas, and J. Layton Mauze, pastor at Central Presbyterian Church, St. Louis, Missouri. These men were "reluctant to be identified with the traditional conservative people of the church"; as a result, they were more willing to consider a "third force group" outside of Concerned Presbyterians and PCU until some future point when the groups could combine. As signatures were being collected for the Declaration of Commitment, these moderates were willing to sign the document, but were unwilling to be part of the new churchmen's group. The moderates would

---

"How It Started," 11; G. Aiken Taylor to Edward B. Cooper, 16 May 1969, *Presbyterian Journal* Papers, box 207, folder 7, both at PCAHC.

35. "Declaration of Commitment," *PO* (6 October 1969): 16; Settle, *To God All Praise and Glory*, 32–33.

meet in St. Louis in November 1969 before the PCU rally, but held their future in abeyance until the new year.[36]

In the meantime, over a thousand ministers received copies of the Declaration, being asked to sign it or to have their sessions declare their support for it. The PCU Executive Committee had agreed not to publish the document until five hundred signatures were received; as it happened, that publication occurred on 4 October 1969. Plans were also being laid for a major rally to be held in December in Atlanta. In the meantime, conservatives had to answer attacks on the Declaration and sort through what they wanted the December rally to accomplish. Aiken Taylor defended the Declaration against criticisms that prominent churchmen had not signed the statement, by noting that "if any considerable number of General Assembly leaders or appointees had been among those taking this strong evangelical stand, it would have suggested that the *Journal*'s estimate of the seriousness of the crisis in the Church had been in error." But if the crisis actually was serious, then the December rally had to address it as such. Taylor confided to Frank Barker that "it seems to me that if we cannot delineate a specific action program, we will waste the opportunity entirely."[37]

The December 1969 rally was a major gathering for southern Presbyterian conservatives. Over fifteen hundred people attended the meetings and applauded the notion that "there will be a continuing Presbyterian Church, Reformed in doctrine, and representative in government." Such a body might be necessary because "there may be a fork in the road ahead," Frank Barker declared, "but, if so, it will not be we who are departing. We will continue straight ahead, and we will invite men from all over the nation to join us, if and when the time comes." D. James Kennedy noted that even talk about denominational division was evidence that liberalism was destroying the church. "Like a creeping cancer, liberal unbelief is killing the church. It is emptying

36. Bob Pitman to G. Aiken Taylor, 29 July 1969, *Presbyterian Journal* Papers, box 207, folder 7; *Minutes, Executive Committee of PCU* (13–14 November 1969), *Presbyterian Journal* Papers, box 207, folder 4 (both at PCAHC).

37. G. Aiken Taylor to Executive Committee of PCU, 4 October 1969; G. Aiken Taylor to Frank Barker, 5 December 1969 (both in *Presbyterian Journal* Papers, box 206, folder 21, PCAHC); G. Aiken Taylor, "The Reaction Sets In," *PJ* (29 October 1969): 12.

the churches, the seminaries, the mission fields and the benevolent causes of the churches." Robert Strong agreed, observing that "the disturbers are those who would change the denomination of which we are a part. Radical ecumenicists caused the crisis in the Church and they plan the liquidation of confessional Presbyterianism in the Southland." The meeting sent a clear note about the doctrinal deviation of the denominational leadership.[38]

But the meeting also signaled some internal divisions among conservatives. One was over race. Many PCU leaders were younger men who believed that the claims of the gospel outweighed the claims of racial solidarity; in this, they were influenced by Billy Graham's example of holding racially mixed crusades in the South from 1953 on. Kennedy Smartt, then pastor of West End Presbyterian Church, Hopewell, Virginia, remembered D. James Kennedy's address not only for its evaluation of liberal theology. He also recalled that Kennedy "made it plain and simple that the continuing church movement was about faithfulness to the Scriptures, to evangelism, and to world missions and not about preserving a segregated way of life." Paul Settle also was at the meeting and later observed that "Kennedy's remarks may have offended some conferees, but they were quite timely" because the younger conservatives were determined that this movement to purify the church was going to be racially inclusive. That was part of the younger ministers' concern about John Richards's serving as executive director for PCU. Though they agreed that Richards had impeccable credentials, a sharp mind, and commitment to the cause, they also worried about his past pronouncements in favor of segregation. Racial solidarity was not going to be part of the agenda for the rising generation of conservative leadership.[39]

38. "Rally Applauds Pledge of Continuing Church," *PJ* (17 December 1969): 7–8; "Trend of the Church Is Deplored," *PO* (22 December 1969): 4.

39. Smartt, *I Am Reminded*, 54; Settle, *To God All Praise and Glory*, 34; Donald Patterson to G. Aiken Taylor, 22 January 1970; G. Aiken Taylor to Donald Patterson, 26 January 1970 (both in *Presbyterian Journal* Papers, box 206, folder 22, PCAHC); Kennedy Smartt to G. Aiken Taylor, 10 February 1971, *Presbyterian Journal* Papers, box 207, folder 2, PCAHC. John E. Richards gave evidence himself of his racial views in his *The Historical Birth of the Presbyterian Church in America* (Liberty Hill, SC: Liberty Press, 1987), 48, 51, 55–60. Of course, not all the PCU leaders were opposed to segregation; see, e.g., Morton H. Smith,

Another internal division among conservatives was over strategy. Though many of the men associated with Pitman, Elliott, and Mauze attended the rally, they decided to go their own way. In January 1970, this group also met in Atlanta and formed the Covenant Fellowship of Presbyterians. Seeking to represent "the silent majority" in the PCUS, the Covenant Fellowship leaders believed that both the liberals and conservatives were "no longer talking to each other but rather to themselves, following the path to 'the sin of schism.'" They also positioned themselves "to speak to the whole church about reconciliation and the proclamation of the whole Gospel of evangelism *and* social action," unlike some among the *Journal* leadership, who stressed evangelism and left social action to the discretion of individual believers. The Covenant Fellowship wanted to be a "movement" within the church rather than a structure that accomplished particular policy goals. Hence, Fellowship leaders did not take a position on reunion with the northern Presbyterian church or on the possibility of a liberal superchurch through COCU. Indeed, the Covenant Fellowship desired to be a positive force for renewal in the church's life; it "sought to counter the impact and influence of both the *Outlook* and the *Journal*," the liberal and conservative magazines and constituencies.[40]

At the outset of its existence, however, Covenant Fellowship leadership—especially Bob Pitman and Andrew Jumper—was willing to strategize and work together with the leadership of PCU and the rest of the conservative organizations. This "conservative coalition" met in June 1970 with representatives from PCU, the Covenant Fellowship, the *Journal*, and Concerned Presbyterians. They spent most of their meeting discussing contingencies if union presbyteries and

---

How Is the Gold Become Dim: The Decline of the Presbyterian Church, U.S., as Reflected in Its Assembly Actions, 3rd ed. (Greenville, SC: Southern Presbyterian Press, 1999), 153.

40. "'Middlers' Form Newest 'Fellowship,'" *PJ* (28 January 1970): 5–6; "New PCUS Group and Publication Emerge," *PO* (26 January 1970): 3; "FOC, CP, PCU, CFP—It's PCUS Alphabet Soup!," *The Open Letter* (31 March 1970): 1–2; Harry Sharp Hassall, *On Jordan's Stormy Banks I Stand: A Historical Commentary of the Life and Times of the Covenant Fellowship of Presbyterians* (Dallas: privately printed, 1989), 17. Progressive leaders reacted quite negatively to the formation of the Covenant Fellowship: "CFP Puzzle," *PO* (2 February 1970): 8; Don M. Wardlaw, "The Latest Reach for Power," *PO* (9 February 1970): 9–10; "CFOP Leaders in Churchwide Effort," *PO* (13 April 1970): 4.

union synods passed the General Assembly; more significant than the subject matter, though, was the willingness to cooperate on strategy. Most of the conservative coalition felt that the 1971 General Assembly would be the key test.[41]

Even during this time of strategizing, the leaders of PCU and the Covenant Fellowship did not really trust one another fully. John Richards warned Kenneth Keyes that one particular Florida pastor was "deeply involved with the [Covenant Fellowship of Presbyterians], and it would be a major blunder for our strategy to be taken over or indirectly guided by that group. One might even believe that it would be best for them not to be informed on our strategy." Likewise, some Covenant Fellowship leaders wanted to pull out of their coalition with PCU because "there was fear on the part of the Covenant Fellowship that PCU was committed to separatism." At one point, Bob Pitman sent a letter to the Executive Committee of PCU, claiming that those who were advocating withdrawal from the PCUS if they failed at the 1971 General Assembly were espousing a position that was "repugnant" to him. And Andrew Jumper publicly accused conservative leaders of working a deal with liberals for the plan of union that would exchange conservative votes for an "escape clause" that would allow them to depart with their church property. He further claimed that the PCU was an "ultra-conservative remnant that will be relatively small and ineffective." Clearly, this was a "grand coalition" that was struggling to hold together.[42]

In the end, there was an agreement to share information, especially between Kennedy Smartt and Andrew Jumper, who served as strategy chairmen for PCU and Covenant Fellowship, respectively. In addition, there was an agreement that at the 1971 General Assembly the Conservative Coalition would run a winsome and successful

41. *Minutes, Executive Committee of PCU* (24–25 June 1970), *Presbyterian Journal* Papers, box 207, folder 4, PCAHC.

42. John E. Richards to Kenneth Keyes, 16 October 1970, *Presbyterian Journal* Papers, box 206, folder 22; *Minutes, Executive Committee of PCU* (3 February 1971), *Presbyterian Journal* Papers, box 207, folder 4; Donald Graham to Executive Committee of PCU, 2 March 1971, *Presbyterian Journal* Papers, box 207, folder 2 (all at PCAHC); Andrew Jumper, "Is This the End for the PCUS?," *The Open Letter* (January 1971): 1, 4; Kenneth Keyes to Harry S. Hassall, 16 March 1971, Covenant Fellowship of Presbyterians Papers, box 10, PHS.

conservative pastor (D. James Kennedy) and a moderate big-steeple pastor (Harry Fifield); the groups would throw their combined support behind whichever nomination garnered the most votes on the first ballot. In addition, they would challenge the moderator's choices for the Nominating Committee. They would work together as well to defeat the restructuring of the synods and oppose any move toward union with either the northern Presbyterian church or the larger liberal "superchurch" in the offing.[43]

As it turned out, however, all the strategizing on the part of the coalition was for naught. The 1971 General Assembly was a complete victory for the progressive element in the church: they elected their choice for moderator over Kennedy by one hundred votes; they defeated the conservatives' floor nominees for the Permanent Nominating Committee, which included Ruth Bell Graham, former moderator Darby Fulton, and missionary Walter Shepard; and they failed to defeat the restructuring of synods. The plan of union with the northern Presbyterians would not come to a vote until after the restructuring of synods, which would mean 1973 at the earliest. Conservatives also failed to stop the Assembly from sending funds to pay for abortions that were deemed social or economic necessities. At every single point, the conservatives' strategy was defeated. As Kennedy Smartt later remembered, "Our efforts were pitiful. We were playing in a league far above our heads. . . . We were totally outclassed and outgunned. We left that assembly knowing that there was little likelihood of ever turning that well oiled juggernaut around." That was Aiken Taylor's feeling at the time, too, writing about the Assembly in the *Journal*, "In short, to all practical purposes, the show is over. . . . The hopes of many for better days have been taken away." For Presbyterian churchmen, the future would lead to a fracture in the conservative coalition and a parting of the ways.[44]

43. *Minutes, Executive Committee of PCU* (12–13 March 1971), *Presbyterian Journal* Papers, box 207, folder 4, PCAHC; Kennedy Smartt to Andrew Jumper, 18 February 1971; Kennedy Smartt to Andrew Jumper, 29 March 1971 (both in Covenant Fellowship of Presbyterians Papers, box 10, PHS).

44. "Rose Wins Moderatorship, 271–170," *PJ* (23 June 1971): 4; "10 Vote Margin Orders Restructuring," *PJ* (30 June 1971): 4–5; "Tighter Abortion Stand Voted Down by Assembly," *PJ* (30 June 1971): 8; Smartt, *I Am Reminded*, 57; G. Aiken Taylor, "The Assembly Tried to Be Gentle," *PJ* (7 July 1971): 14.

EXECUTIVE COMMITTEE FOR OVERSEAS EVANGELISM

While PEF had formed in 1964, the negative trends in PCUS world missions caused southern Presbyterian conservatives to wonder whether more should be done. This became particularly pressing after Ben Wilkinson and Jimmy Lyons, representing PEF, went to Mexico in early 1969 and found that the mission work there was dying, both spiritually and financially. They returned and prepared a paper for the PEF Executive Committee on "mission evangelism." Part of what they suggested was that PEF take on missionary training, especially in the area of evangelism; but they also proposed something more radical— when evangelical missionaries felt that they could no longer work for the PCUS Board of World Missions, PEF should "be ready to take up support." When Bill Hill sought the advice of missionary statesman C. Darby Fulton on this plan, Fulton noted that it involved serious implications: "This, of course, would bring the P.E.F. into possible conflict with the Board [of World Missions], or even with the General Assembly itself." Plus, financial realities were involved with taking on missionary support: the current cost per missionary supported by the Board of World Missions was around $10,000 a year. Could PEF be responsible for raising that kind of money?[45]

When the PEF board met in January 1970, it authorized the formation of a commission that would investigate the situation on the PCUS mission fields and make a report with recommendations on next steps. The new body, ECOE, would be headed by Jimmy Lyons, pastor of First Presbyterian Church, Swannanoa, North Carolina. At the commission's first meeting, it tackled the major question: would ECOE simply be content to be a training or even funding group? Or would it work toward becoming a missionary-sending agency? The ministers and elders on the commission recognized the momentous nature of the question. While the other possible objectives could bring ECOE in conflict with the world missions board, sending out mission-aries would definitely bring about a major conflict. It could mean the

---

45. Settle, *To God All Praise and Glory*, 31; Otto Whittaker, *Watchman, Tell It True* (Manassas, VA: Reformed Educational Foundation, 1981), 414; C. Darby Fulton to Bill Hill, 12 August 1969, C. Darby Fulton Papers, box 2, PHS.

blacklisting of PEF evangelists or the end of PEF as an organization; it could even lead to deposition from church office in the same way that northern Presbyterians had dealt with J. Gresham Machen in the 1930s. The commission decided that ECOE would work toward becoming a missionary-sending group, but would first attempt to work in a cooperative fashion with the Board of World Missions. At the July 1970 PEF evangelistic meetings at Montreat, ECOE announced its formation and its larger purpose of encouraging evangelistic work overseas and of supporting that work "as the way is clear."[46]

Specifically, ECOE leadership desired to send designated money directly to missionaries in order to avoid the denomination's "equalization" process. They believed that part of the reason that the world missions program was financially struggling was not only the move theologically to the left, but also the decision to equalize all financial gifts that were given to the denomination, whether they were designated dollars or not. That decision caused some conservatives not to give to any denominational cause, hurting world missions especially. The question then became whether ECOE should simply act on its own authority or whether it should attempt to work cooperatively with the Board of World Missions. Darby Fulton, for one, strongly urged the new group to work with the denominational missions board: he worried that any attempt to circumvent the missions board with funds and training would raise significant "ethical implications." And so the ECOE leadership agreed to work through Watson Street, the executive secretary of the Board of World Missions. Street agreed to present the ECOE proposal to fund missionaries in a way that avoided equalization to the PCUS General Council as part of a larger request for a "special (unequalized) offering" for world missions. The General Council, however, not only shot down the request from the Board of World Missions, but also looked negatively on this first mention of ECOE.[47]

46. Whittaker, *Watchman, Tell It True*, 414–15; "Missions Policy Dissent Brings Reaction," *PJ* (7 October 1970): 5–6.

47. C. Darby Fulton to Bill Hill, 5 June 1970; C. Darby Fulton to W. A. McIlwaine, 8 June 1970; W. A. McIlwaine to C. Darby Fulton, 15 June 1970 (all in C. Darby Fulton Papers, box 2, PHS); "Council Considers Church Credibility Gap," *PJ* (30 September 1970): 5–6.

That did not stop ECOE from trying to continue working with the Board of World Missions. At the October 1970 meeting of the PCUS missions board, the board heard and approved a proposal from ECOE "to assist some of the board's evangelistic work if guaranteed that its contributions will not be equalized." While the board noted that it was bound by the General Assembly's rules for equalization of funds, "it suggested that an attempt might be made to get the rules set aside." At the same time, Watson Street presented ECOE leadership with a twelve-point statement on evangelism that could serve as a basis for a partnership, which Bill Hill and others felt compelled to reject. Not only was it "impossible for us to lend our support to some of the things that they called 'evangelism,'" Hill later related, but ECOE's conditions of the potential partnership remained firm: the project had to be evangelistic, separate from the National Council of Churches, and free from equalization. When this request to partner with ECOE and set aside equalization rules was presented to the PCUS General Council, it, too, was summarily rejected.[48]

In response, ECOE announced in January 1971 that it would take the major step of becoming a missionary-sending agency for those missionaries who could no longer work with the PCUS Board of World Missions or for those new missionaries who preferred not to go out from the board. Liberal leaders' reaction was swift. William Benfield Jr., then moderator of the General Assembly, called this development "the most rebellious, tyrannical activity I have heard of in the history of the Presbyterian Church." The PCUS General Council agreed, calling ECOE "a serious threat to the peace and unity of our Church." In addition, the council recommended to the 1971 General Assembly that it "express its disapproval of ECOE." And the Board of World Missions sent a mass letter to its missionaries and supporters, charging ECOE with goals and practices that were "detrimental to the unity and effectiveness of our missionary family and to the whole missionary cause."[49]

48. "Board Approves 380 Missionary Budget," *PJ* (28 October 1970): 6; Bill Hill to C. Darby Fulton, 20 October 1970, C. Darby Fulton Papers, box 2, PHS.

49. Ben Wilkinson to C. Darby Fulton, 20 January 1971; C. Darby Fulton to Ben Wilkinson, 3 February 1971 (both in C. Darby Fulton Papers, box 2, PHS); "A Word from E.C.O.E.," *PJ* (10 February 1971): 2; "Benfield Says Division Most Serious in History,"

Before the 1971 General Assembly, ECOE board member W. A. McIlwaine set out the differences succinctly between ECOE and the Board of World Missions. "At the heart of the problem," he observed, "is an attitude towards the Bible." Those who supported an ecumenical approach to missions "treat the Bible as though [it] were the product of human wisdom" and so "change[s] with every passing theological breeze." As a result, they insisted that "ecumenical cooperation is the indispensable condition for making Christ known," a policy that dispensed with a common theology or even a common approach to the Bible and that eventually developed an approach to missions that emphasized social and economic justice. "Modern ecumenism potentially subverts the Gospel, and actually does so in unpredictable ways," he declared. ECOE was committed to sending out missionaries who were true to the Bible and the Reformed faith, offering to lost internationals "God's salvation in Christ, which alone can make them truly free and able to meet every trouble with the strength that comes from God." Once again, the dividing line between conservatives and progressives was the Bible.[50]

Of course, denominational leaders did not quite see it that way. They saw ECOE as a "grave departure from the orderly processes of the Church." That was the evaluation adopted at the 1971 General Assembly by a large majority. In addition, the Assembly demanded that PCUS missionaries reject any money sent from ECOE, which might help in the short term but offered only "the likelihood of grievous harm to the life and health of the Church" over the long term. Bill Hill's immediate reaction was to refrain from answering any of the charges made about ECOE at General Assembly or before the PCUS General Council. As he told Darby Fulton, "We didn't want to get involved in a public quarrel and argument with Dr. Street and Dr. [David] Stitt and any defense we made of ourselves would necessarily have to reflect upon them. This we were unwilling to do."[51]

PJ (10 February 1971): 8; "Council Labels ECOE 'Serious Threat,'" *PJ* (17 March 1971): 6; David Stitt and T. Watson Street to "Missionary Friends," 10 May 1971, *Presbyterian Journal* Papers, PCAHC.

50. McIlwaine, "World Missions in Conflict," 7–9, 18.

51. "Assembly Tags ECOE 'Grave Departure,'" *PJ* (30 June 1971): 7; Bill Hill to C. Darby Fulton, 8 July 1971, C. Darby Fulton Papers, box 2, PHS. Stitt was chairman of the Board

At the August 1971 PEF evangelistic meeting at Montreat, however, Jimmy Lyons delivered an impassioned response to the charges made by the Assembly and the world missions board. While disagreeing that ECOE had offered "public attacks" against the Board of World Missions, he also denied that ECOE offered funds to missionaries on the condition that they not be reported to the board. "No missionary is asked by ECOE to receive funds and not to report said funds," Lyons clarified. "We do ask the missionary that all funds be disbursed in such a manner as to avoid equalization. And if this is not possible those funds are returned to the donor." He also noted that ECOE had come into existence because conservative missionaries were being forced from the field; "giving missionaries a place to jump to required our becoming a sending agency." In addition, ECOE was not asking churches to divert funds from denominational benevolences; rather, it was going to churches that had already withdrawn money from denominational causes and seeking to route that money to conservative southern Presbyterian missionaries.[52]

After defending ECOE, Lyons turned his focus to the real reason that ECOE and other conservative organizations had come into existence. These conservatives believed that "what constitutes Presbyterianism is set forth in the Scriptures, 'the only holy and infallible rule of faith and practice,' and the Westminster Standards." The denomination's organizations had strayed from conformity to the Bible and the doctrines of the Standards. In place of those truths, the agencies and boards had substituted social witness: "Something's gone terribly wrong somewhere. The social, political, and economic witness of our General Assembly and boards and agencies has not only violated Scripture, it is reaching toward proportions of absurdity and treason." That was why conservatives were abandoning denominational causes for new organizations—such as Concerned Presbyterians, Reformed Seminary, PCU, and ECOE—that would present their issues and represent them institutionally in the eyes of the church's courts and

of World Missions from 1966 to 1975; he was also president of Austin Presbyterian Theological Seminary.

52. James Lyons, *We'll Go With Him . . . With Him . . . All the Way* (Hopewell, VA: Presbyterian Evangelistic Fellowship, 1971), 6, 8, 9.

agencies. And these institutions were making plans to form a new denomination that would continue the witness that the old church had left behind.[53]

53. Ibid., 10–12.

11

A Continuing Church:
The Creation of the
Presbyterian Church in America

After the 1971 General Assembly met at the Synod of Virginia assembly grounds at Massanetta Springs near Harrisonburg, Virginia, conservative Presbyterians did not know quite what to do. Their last-ditch attempt to influence the PCUS had dramatically failed. Even though more conservative ministers were strategically working together than ever before—to elect a moderator, to elect conservatives to the Permanent Nominating Committee, to defeat progressive proposals on redrawing synod lines and union with northern Presbyterians—at each point they were defeated. And so leaders from the main conservative organizations agreed to meet together in Atlanta to determine next steps.

As leaders from Concerned Presbyterians, PCU, PEF, and the *Presbyterian Journal* met (along with five representatives from the Covenant Fellowship of Presbyterians) in mid-July 1971, there were differences of opinion about how to proceed. One perspective was represented by Harry Hassall and the Covenant Fellowship leaders: they wanted to evaluate the previous General Assembly and to chart strategy for the next year. When they discovered that others had formed "hard plans for a coordinated massive pullout as soon as possible," they were dismayed. Kennedy Smartt represented another perspective. "There were men present who were ready to go immediately, men who were deeply concerned but hesitant to actually talk about departure, and men who felt that they were just getting started in trying to reform the church and were not ready to do anything radical," he later remembered. In the end, the Covenant Fellowship leaders left the meeting frustrated, and the rest decided to call a second meeting, two weeks later back in Atlanta, with all the representatives of the "Conservative Coalition" to determine what the decision would be. As Smartt recalled, "We all knew that this next meeting would be for many of us 'the crossing of the Rubicon.' "[1]

These differing perspectives serve as an important reminder that the division of the PCUS and the creation of the PCA was not an obvious move in July 1971. While there was a growing sense of inevitability about the division of the church among many conservative leaders, there were also other strong conservative men who could not go along with those who would separate from the PCUS. Nelson Bell and Robert Strong, who had shaped conservative opinion and led conservative protests for nearly thirty years, remained in the PCUS until their dying days. In addition, several conservative leaders who had initially identified with PCU, such as Bob Pitman and Wayte Fulton, ended up withdrawing from that group once it was clear that the majority of the Conservative Coalition had determined to separate. These men sought to serve as a "third alternative" with the PCUS between the progressive leadership and the withdrawing conservatives.

By the time conservatives met at Briarwood Presbyterian Church in Birmingham, Alabama, on 4 December 1973 for the first General Assembly of what was then called the National Presbyterian Church, they had weathered quite a few storms together. Yet through the entire process of forming a new Presbyterian denomination, the majority of conservative leaders never lost sight of what they meant to do. They sought to forge a Presbyterian church that would be a continuation of what they saw to be the best parts of the PCUS story: a conservative, evangelical, mainline Presbyterian body that would be true to the

---

1. Harry Sharp Hassall, *On Jordan's Stormy Banks I Stand: A Historical Commentary of the Life and Times of the Covenant Fellowship of Presbyterians* (Dallas: privately printed, 1989), 29; Kennedy Smartt, *I Am Reminded: An Autobiographical, Anecdotal History of the Presbyterian Church in America* (Chestnut Mountain, GA: n.p., 1998), 57.

Bible and the Reformed faith and obedient to the Great Commission. That they would also carry a lot more into the new church was to be expected as well.

A GROWING SENSE OF INEVITABILITY

Throughout the 1960s, the official position of southern Presbyterian conservatives was that they were working for the reformation of the church. Any talk about the possibility of division was strongly discouraged and denied. When Concerned Presbyterians formed in 1964, its first newsletter declared that "Concerned Presbyterians, Inc., does NOT recommend that anyone withdraw from our beloved Church. Our goal is to reverse the trends that are causing so many members to consider withdrawal." When two conservative PCUS churches in Savannah, Georgia, left the denomination in 1966, Aiken Taylor deemed it "a tragedy." He observed, "We cannot agree that the answer at this time (or for the foreseeable future) is to pull out of the Presbyterian Church US." The denomination "cannot afford to lose the large numbers of evangelicals who are leaving it individually and collectively." By leaving, these two churches were going to make it harder for remaining conservatives to reform the denomination.[2]

One of the things that began to change conservatives' perception about their future in the denomination was the decision of the 1966 General Assembly to participate in COCU. The consultation had begun in 1962 as the brainchild of Eugene Carson Blake, the stated clerk of the northern United Presbyterian Church in the USA (UPCUSA).[3] Under Blake's leadership, the UPCUSA invited the Protestant Episcopal Church, the Methodist Church (USA), and the United Church of Christ to explore whether these four denominations might unite into a single Protestant "superchurch." By the time the PCUS voted to join in 1966, seven other denominations had become

2. "This Is NOT the Answer . . . ," *Concerned Presbyterian* (March 1965): 1; G. Aiken Taylor, "This Is a Tragedy," *PJ* (4 May 1966): 12.

3. After reunion with the PCUS failed in 1954, the northern Presbyterian church (the PCUSA) was able to effect a union with the smaller United Presbyterian Church of North America. Hence, after 1958, the united body was known as the United Presbyterian Church in the USA.

part of the consultation. The move to enter COCU was viewed as a "massive victory for the 'ecumenical' brethren, and a resounding defeat for those interested in the preservation of the Reformed faith."[4]

Indeed, if there was a General Assembly that was a turning point for conservatives, it was the 1966 General Assembly that met at Montreat. Up to this point, they had seen themselves as generally able to parry liberal advances and hold back the radical party. But at this General Assembly, they used words such as *rout* and *stampede* to describe what happened. "The 'liberals' were in the overwhelming majority and the extreme radicals in greater number than ever before," Aiken Taylor claimed. All the advances that liberals had made in the seminaries over the past forty years, all the questions raised about Scripture and the Westminster Standards, all the work done toward ecumenical relations—it all came together at the 1966 General Assembly.[5]

From this point on, at least among themselves, conservatives began to believe that a denominational split was more likely. In 1966, Paul Settle took a call to Coral Ridge Presbyterian Church because "I believe our Church will be divided within five years" and he wanted to be prepared to lead in the area of Christian education. That same year, Nelson Bell observed that if the denominational leaders continued to pursue their dream of a liberal superchurch that would swallow up the PCUS, "they should be ready to negotiate so that we might have an amicable division of individuals, churches, and assets." Conservatives uniformly blamed the coming split on the progressives who were pursuing union with other denominations through COCU: "As to a plan to split the church: Those who apparently have such a plan are those pushing COCU regardless of whether it will split the church or not," Bell observed. Even while they began to voice privately the

4. G. Aiken Taylor, "The Assembly Acted . . . ," *PJ* (11 May 1966): 6–7; William G. McAtee, *Dreams, Where Have You Gone? Clues for Unity and Hope* (Louisville, KY: Witherspoon Press, 2006), 124–27. For a short summary of COCU, see E. T. Thompson, *Presbyterians in the South*, 3 vols. (Richmond, VA: John Knox, 1963–73), 3:579–82; D. G. Hart and John Muether, *Seeking a Better Country: 300 Years of American Presbyterianism* (Phillipsburg, NJ: P&R Publishing, 2007), 214–16.

5. G. Aiken Taylor, "The 1966 Assembly: An Evaluation," *PJ* (11 May 1966): 12; G. Aiken Taylor, "A Shameful Action," *PJ* (11 May 1966): 12–13; G. Aiken Taylor, "What Happened?," *PJ* (18 May 1966): 12.

idea that division was possible or even likely as a result of the COCU negotiations, conservative leaders continued publicly to say that the way forward was renewed interest in evangelism and spiritual renewal. Both Bill Hill and Nelson Bell suggested that "a spiritual awakening within the Church may sweep away indifference, prejudice, preoccupation with secondary issues, lovelessness and all such things, which are hindering the witness of the Church now."[6]

By 1967, not only had conservatives become concerned with the possibility of a liberal superchurch, but they were also seeing a push within the PCUS for a de facto union with the northern church through the creation of "union synods" and "union presbyteries." For decades, northern and southern Presbyterians had supported overlapping works in border states such as Missouri, Kentucky, and Maryland. In addition, northern Presbyterians had heavily invested in planting churches in Texas and Florida as snowbirds went to these southward places and then remained there permanently. Those in the PCUS who desired to work for a genuine union with the northern church saw an opportunity by forging union presbyteries and synods.

The idea of union presbyteries and synods was first broached and defeated in 1966, but the following year there was growing momentum as a second proposal came to the Assembly. On the one hand, the Assembly approved the principle of creating union presbyteries and synods; on the other hand, the Permanent Judicial Commission ruled that the creation of such union presbyteries and synods would require a three-quarters majority of the presbyteries, since it was in effect a denominational merger, not merely a *Book of Church Order* change, which would require only a simple majority. Conservatives saw all of this as creating a new avenue for division in the church: "It now is between those willing to work for their 'ecumenical' objectives (COCU, denominational union, new forms of 'mission') at any cost,

---

6. Paul Settle to G. Aiken Taylor, 21 June 1966, *Presbyterian Journal* Papers, box 154, folder 2, PCAHC; L. Nelson Bell to John R. Richardson, 9 May 1966, L. Nelson Bell Papers, box 69, folder 13, BGC. Bell appeared to summarize these views in "Negotiations Must Come," *PJ* (25 May 1966): 12; L. Nelson Bell, "The Basic Issue," *PJ* (3 May 1967): 13; William E. Hill Jr., "What Can Be Done?," *PJ* (29 June 1966): 9–11; L. Nelson Bell, "A Dilemma and Some Possible Solutions," *PJ* (3 August 1966): 11, 23.

by any means, fair or unfair, legal or illegal; and those not willing to change the rules in order to win the game." Changing the rules meant organic union with the UPCUSA "by the 'back door' or by 'osmosis,'" through union presbyteries.[7]

The 1968 General Assembly decided to send to the presbyteries an amendment to the *Book of Church Order* that would allow union synods; since it was a church-order change, it would require only a simple majority. Conservatives were frustrated that the progressives were going to be able to accomplish de facto union without sending a plan of union down for three-fourths of the presbyteries to approve. Part of their frustration stemmed from the fact that both conservatives and progressives knew that church union was unlikely to get three-fourths of the presbyteries, but this simple polity change could probably garner approval from half the presbyteries. The Synod of Kentucky, for one, was so confident in its passage that it began moving ahead to merge with its UPCUSA counterpart. Likewise, Kenneth Keyes feared that union synods would be the final straw that led to a division of the church. As he told Donald Patterson in November 1968, "My evaluation of the church situation can be pretty well summed by saying that I believe a split in the Church is coming within the next two or three years." Because this was the case, "I feel that we should be making our plans now so that we will not be caught sleeping when the time for the split arrives."[8]

Others, such as Nelson Bell, continued to argue against leaving the church even if union synods and presbyteries were created: "Pull out of the Church? God forbid! That is the cowardly way and there is little evidence to prove that God blesses such a course." History was replete with small separatist movements that had lost "their witness because of endless bickering within their own bodies." In similar fashion, John C. Neville Jr. told his congregation, "I hope we don't take

7. McAtee, *Dreams, Where Have You Gone?*, 130–35; G. Aiken Taylor, "1967: Year of Realignment," *PJ* (5 July 1967): 12; W. Jack Williamson, "Trends in the 107th," *PJ* (6 September 1967): 7.

8. McAtee, *Dreams, Where Have You Gone?*, 140–52; "Kentucky Goes Ahead with Synods' Merger," *PJ* (10 July 1968): 6; G. Aiken Taylor, "How about Swapping?," *PJ* (26 February 1969): 12; Kenneth Keyes to Donald Patterson, 27 November 1968, *Presbyterian Journal* Papers, box 206, folder 17, PCAHC.

steps to get out until we are faced with the necessity to take drastic steps to maintain our confessional integrity." He, too, worried that for those who would separate from the main body, "they are people who have been fighting so long that they have forgotten how to live in peace. They withdraw and set up a new group, and then fighting breaks out among themselves and another withdrawal takes place." Robert Strong agreed, claiming that "it is too early to talk about a division in our denomination. . . . We have several issues to fight out before we can reach the time when we announce that the situation is hopeless and that division must occur."[9]

By March 1969, it appeared that union synods and presbyteries had been defeated at the presbytery level. The vote for union presbyteries was thirty-nine opposed to thirty-eight in favor; the vote for union synods was forty presbyteries opposed to thirty-seven in favor. Kenneth Keyes and the Concerned Presbyterians rejoiced: "In the opinion of many members of the Presbyterian U.S. constituency, Tuesday, February 17th, will go down in history as one of the most important days in the history of our beloved Church. That was the day when the presbyteries of Nashville and Southwest Georgia cast the deciding votes which defeated the Union Synods and Presbyterians amendments *by a majority vote.*" Aiken Taylor saw the vote against union presbyteries and synods as a vote for integrity; there would be no "back door" union with the northern church. And there was some hope among conservatives that liberals would see that they would "never in the foreseeable future be able to muster the three-fourths vote of the presbyteries which they would need to take the Church into the super-church being planned by the Consultation on Church Union."[10]

9. L. Nelson Bell, "Montreat: Retrospect and Prospect," *PJ* (4 September 1968): 8; L. Nelson Bell, " 'Cowardly?'," *PJ* (2 October 1968): 2; John C. Neville Jr., "This Is How I See It," *PJ* (29 January 1969): 7–8; Robert Strong to L. Nelson Bell, 29 November 1968, L. Nelson Bell Papers, box 69, folder 24; L. Nelson Bell to Board of Directors of *PJ*, 15 November 1968, L. Nelson Bell Papers, box 72, folder 7 (both at BGC).

10. "Union Synods, Presbyteries, Defeated," *PJ* (5 March 1969): 4; "Majority of Presbyteries Vote 'No'—Union Amendments Defeated," *Concerned Presbyterian* (April 1969): 1 (emphasis his); G. Aiken Taylor, "Integrity Back in Style," *PJ* (5 March 1969): 13; McAtee, *Dreams, Where Have You Gone?*, 146–47.

But then something happened that was unprecedented in American Presbyterian history: three presbyteries moved to reconsider their votes on union presbyteries weeks before the Assembly was to meet. Through the work of pro-union forces that had sent letters to key people in twenty-one presbyteries, asking them to move their presbyteries to reconsider, Dallas, Mobile, and North Alabama Presbyteries all gained the two-thirds vote necessary to reconsider the matter, and all three switched from voting against union presbyteries to supporting them. Conservatives howled foul play. Aiken Taylor declared that "no body, not even a Church, can continue forever without a high regard for fundamental integrity," and to him, this maneuvering was evidence of a lack of integrity. When the issues came to the 1969 General Assembly, the progressives had the votes to drive through not only union presbyteries, but more besides: establishing a committee to explore reunion with the UPCUSA as well as reaffirming the denomination's full participation in COCU on the eve of the expected production of its plan of union. It was another watershed moment, the culmination of progressive work that had begun three years before at the Assembly in Montreat.[11]

After the 1969 General Assembly, many conservatives recognized that it was a matter of time before the church divided. The Declaration of Commitment developed by PCU was approved in July 1969, and its signers declared that they would do whatever was necessary "to fulfill the obligations imposed by ordination vows to maintain our Presbyterian faith." At the PCU December 1969 rally, the loudest applause was reserved for the promise "that there will be a continuing Presbyterian [Church], Reformed in doctrine and representative in government"; the same cheers were heard at the 1970 Journal Day, when Kenneth Keyes assured the audience that "regardless of what happens there will be a continuing Presbyterian Church that is loyal to Scripture and the Reformed faith." Some leaders, such as Frank Barker, recognized that keeping this promise would likely require

11. "2 Courts Reverse Union Presbytery Vote," *PJ* (30 April 1969): 5; G. Aiken Taylor, "The Church's Integrity Is on Trial," *PJ* (30 April 1969): 12; "Assembly Ok's COCU, UPUSA Talks, Chapter 32," *PJ* (14 May 1969): 7–8; McAtee, *Dreams, Where Have You Gone?*, 147–52.

division. As Barker noted at the PCU rally, "This parting may come amicably or otherwise. It could come amicably by provision in the merger proposal for local churches to remain out of the merger, thus allow us to continue straight ahead. It may come otherwise." In the end, division seemed sure to come.[12]

For others, such as the moderates who had formed the Covenant Fellowship of Presbyterians, there was an unwillingness to move toward separating from the PCUS. Yet the strongest voice against division remained Nelson Bell's. He had consistently argued against any move toward separating from the PCUS, and over the two years after the 1969 General Assembly, he continued to stand resolutely for remaining in the denomination and working to see revival and renewal. While Bell had initially signed the Declaration of Commitment, he asked that his name be removed once he realized that the signatories' names would be published with the statement—he did not want to be identified with anything that smacked of separation. He also began to experience difficulties with Aiken Taylor's separatist leanings as editor of the *Journal*; as he confided to John Richards, "In my judgment Aiken *wants* a split in our church. I know Bill Hill and others do and I simply cannot follow their approach because I am confident we conservatives are on solid ground. To talk of separation at this time, in my judgment, plays directly into the hands of the liberals—that is exactly what they want us to do." He periodically used his column in the *Journal* to argue against separation: "Now that the Church is so thoroughly infiltrated with and compromised by the world, what should be done? Should we pull out and start a new Church of committed believers? In this writer's judgment this is the very last thing which Christians should do, although we respect the earnest convictions of those who differ with us about it." Increasingly, Bell was out of step with the convictions of those with whom he had

---

12. "Rally Applauds Pledge of Continuing Church," *PJ* (17 December 1969): 7; C. Darby Fulton, "Why I Am For It," *PJ* (31 December 1969): 7; " 'Continuing Church' Pledge Is Cheered," *PJ* (19 August 1970): 4; Frank M. Barker Jr., "The Road Ahead," *PJ* (31 December 1969): 10; "COCU Releases 145 Page Merger Plan," *PJ* (25 February 1970): 4–5; "Details of Restructuring Plan Released," *PJ* (15 April 1970): 6–9; L. Nelson Bell, "This Is Not the Time!," *PJ* (17 June 1970): 13; W. Jack Williamson, "Getting Set for What's Coming," *PJ* (16 September 1970): 8.

labored for thirty years in the conservative cause. It would lead to some painful decisions as the increasingly inevitable came to pass.[13]

"CAN TWO WALK TOGETHER?"

After the failure to gain any traction in moving the church in a conservative direction at the 1971 General Assembly meeting at the Massanetta Springs conference grounds in Virginia, the Conservative Coalition met in Atlanta. At that meeting, separation from the PCUS was set out not simply as an option, but as the plan for moving forward. The Covenant Fellowship of Presbyterians leaders who attended the meeting, along with Charles McGowan, who was there with PCU, and Nelson Bell from the *Journal*, "argued long and hard against any kind of pullout or schism." As Covenant Fellowship leader Harry Hassall later remembered, "We made no progress. After hearing of their pullout plans, we gave them our best advice as to how they might proceed with what we considered to be morally wrong in ways least damaging to the whole church." Yet nothing was decided at that meeting; rather, plans were made for a second meeting, to be held at the end of July 1971, again in Atlanta, to make final determinations about the way forward.[14]

In the two weeks between the mid-July meeting where separation was first set forward as the conservative plan and the end-of-July meeting where it would be ratified, moderates made their feelings known. Wayte Fulton wrote to the Executive Committee of PCU

13. McAtee, *Dreams, Where Have You Gone?*, 86, 178–81; L. Nelson Bell to John E. Richards, 12 November 1969, L. Nelson Bell Papers, box 75, folder 16 (emphasis his); L. Nelson Bell to Board of Directors of *PJ*, 21 October 1970, L. Nelson Bell Papers, box 72, folder 7 (both at BGC); L. Nelson Bell, "Separation Isn't the Answer," *PJ* (29 July 1970): 13.

There were two particularly rough exchanges between Bell and Taylor over events at the Asheville Presbytery meeting and the emerging Covenant Fellowship of Presbyterians: G. Aiken Taylor to L. Nelson Bell, [21 August 1969]; L. Nelson Bell to G. Aiken Taylor, 23 August 1969; L. Nelson Bell to G. Aiken Taylor, 20 October 1969; G. Aiken Taylor to L. Nelson Bell, 22 October 1969 (all in L. Nelson Bell Papers, box 75, folder 16, BGC). After a year of Bell's telling Taylor that he needed to resign as editor of the *Journal*, Taylor did offer his resignation (G. Aiken Taylor to Executive Committee of the *PJ*, 22 July 1970, L. Nelson Bell Papers, box 75, folder 16, BGC); it was rejected. Underlying all the emotional exchange was the deep division between Taylor on the one side and Bell and Henry Dendy on the other about separation from the PCUS.

14. Hassall, *On Jordan's Stormy Banks I Stand*, 29.

to declare "that I am unalterably opposed to the strategy of a phased withdrawal from the denomination. . . . I think such a move at this time is utterly unrealistic, unwise, and unnecessary." Such secession with a definite date and plan "would bring a disastrous and irreparable break in the conservative forces of our church." Andrew Jumper reported the consensus of the Covenant Fellowship that "it is our unanimous opinion that any efforts to withdraw from the Presbyterian Church, U.S., at this time are illegal and unconstitutional and violate our ordination vows, especially in the light that no clear-cut issue of conscience is involved. Thus, any withdrawal plans are unjustifiably schismatic." Matthew McGowan felt that "if we did anything like 'set the date now' for separation, we might be prompted by fear in a very short-range view or even a very narrow view." Most importantly, Nelson Bell stood against the plan for separation: "In my opinion, the proposed 'Plan' for a systematic withdrawal from our church is, if carried out, a disaster. It is a concession of defeat before the battle is joined on issues because of which there could be an honorable separation. It is a cold, calculated plan for a schism without the statement of any doctrinal issue whatsoever." Further, the plan would inevitably "split conservatives at a time when a united witness is vitally important. Good men—men who are desperately needed in the conservative witness of our church—will have no part of it." Finally, the plan for secession was "proof positive to the liberals that some of the leadership in the conservative cause is schismatic instead of constructive."[15]

As the Conservative Coalition met on 30 July 1971, a hot, muggy day in Atlanta, they did so knowing that several men who had fought beside them for at least thirty years stood against their proposed move to separate from the PCUS. The twenty-nine men who gathered debated a three-point plan: first, "create a climate of opinion favorable to the continuation of conservative presbyteries and

15. J. Wayte Fulton to Executive Committee of PCU, 28 July 1971, *Presbyterian Journal* Papers, box 207, folder 2, PCAHC; Andrew Jumper to William E. Hill Jr. et al., 26 July 1971; Matthew McGowan to L. Nelson Bell, 30 July 1971 (both in L. Nelson Bell Papers, box 72, folder 6, BGC); L. Nelson Bell to Executive Committee of *PJ*, 20 July 1971, L. Nelson Bell Papers, box 74, folder 1, BGC.

churches loyal to Scripture and the Reformed faith"; second, "identify presbyteries and congregations willing to take such a stand"; third, "accept the inevitability of division of the PCUS" and "move now toward a continuing body of congregations and presbyteries loyal to the Scriptures and the Westminster Standards." That final point of the plan took the most debate. As Kennedy Smartt observed, "It was agony to adopt it. It took hours." Paul Settle recalled that "before taking the final vote, they dropped to their knees and prayed. Many wept." Another man who was there, Jack Williamson, remembered it similarly: "We spent a great deal of time in prayer. We were humbled. We were reticent. Nobody wanted to do this. But we felt that for the honor of the Lord Jesus Christ we couldn't stay in our Church." When the group finally did adopt the plan to withdraw, it did so over the objections of Nelson Bell, who was at the meeting; while he abstained in the final voting, in principle he was opposed to the direction in which his friends were going.[16]

Along with the plan, the coalition adopted a timetable (which proved to be unrealistic) and agreed to organize a steering committee that would have representatives from the four major conservative organizations—*Presbyterian Journal*, PEF, Concerned Presbyterians, and PCU. The steering committee would have twelve men on it: Donald Patterson, Aiken Taylor, and Kennedy Smartt from PCU; Ken Keyes, Leon Hendrick, and Jack Williamson from Concerned Presbyterians; Bill Hill, Jim Baird, and Ben Wilkinson from PEF; and John Richards, Bob Metcalf, and Steve White from the *Journal* board. When this committee met before the 1971 Journal Day, Patterson was elected chairman, with Baird and Smartt serving as vice-chairman and secretary. The hope was that this steering committee would provide "coordination and leadership" for the entire continuing-church movement.[17]

The thought was to announce the continuing-church plans at the August 1971 Journal Days. Before that could happen, the *Journal*

16. Paul Settle, *To God All Praise and Glory: Under God: Celebrating the Past, Claiming the Future, the Presbyterian Church in America* (Atlanta: Presbyterian Church in America, 1998), 37–38; *Minutes, Executive Committee of PCU* (30–31 July 1971), *Presbyterian Journal* Papers, box 207, folder 4, PCAHC; Smartt, *I Am Reminded*, 59.

17. Settle, *To God All Praise and Glory*, 39; Smartt, *I Am Reminded*, 59.

board received a letter from Nelson Bell: "In view of the fact that this 'Plan' will become a basic policy of the *Presbyterian Journal* board, I feel impelled to dissociate myself from the *Journal*. I therefore with deepest regret, with very strong convictions, hereby tender my resignation as a member of the Board of the *Journal* and from my position as Associate Editor, and request that my name be dropped from the masthead of the magazine." Several *Journal* board members—Robert Strong and Tom Glasgow particularly—asked Bell to reconsider and to withdraw his resignation; but in the end, he could not be party to the division of the PCUS. The irony of Nelson Bell was that the man who was more responsible than any other for the movement of conservative dissent within the PCUS could not leave the church even when he admitted that the situation within the church was "tragic" and that the clear teachings of the gospel were being "muted in favor of Humanism, Universalism, and syncretism."[18]

Others were no longer content to remain in such a church. In a letter written to Bell before the end-of-July 1971 meeting, Bill Hill identified the key difference between the conservatives who were determined to withdraw and those who could not leave the PCUS: "I suppose the fundamental difference between your view and mine is that you are strongly convicted that we do not have a mandate in Scripture for separation from unbelief. I do believe that we have a mandate in Scripture for separation from unbelief." Whereas Bell and other moderates were convinced that history taught that separatist groups remained small and divisive, Hill saw it otherwise: "I am convinced that God had His hand in the separation that took place in the 30s from the USA church. These two little bodies resulting are beginning to show vitality, and hold high the witness of truth. They have sacrificed much for it. They have a witness which will increase greatly in days ahead whereas the evangelical witness of the UPUSA church has diminished to nothing."

18. L. Nelson Bell to Executive Committee of *PJ*, 20 July 1971; L. Nelson Bell to Executive Committee of *PJ*, 3 August 1971; L. Nelson Bell to G. Aiken Taylor, 14 August 1971; L. Nelson Bell to Robert Strong, 16 August 1971; "Statement Given at the Request of Bill Lamkin Regarding Resignation," 20 August 1971 (all in L. Nelson Bell Papers, box 74, folder 1, BGC); Tom Glasgow to L. Nelson Bell, 18 August 1971; Tom Glasgow to L. Nelson Bell, 20 August 1971; L. Nelson Bell to Wilbur Cousar and Tom Glasgow, 24 August 1971 (all in L. Nelson Bell Papers, box 72, folder 6, BGC).

Obviously, no one could predict the future about the group that would come into this continuing church, but "it is high time that some convicted and courageous souls stepped into the breach in our Church and dared to sacrifice all."[19]

That was how the newly minted leaders of the Steering Committee for a Continuing Church felt on 11 August 1971 at the Journal Day meeting in Weaverville, North Carolina. Jack Williamson made the announcement that "we have rounded the bend and are heading toward the continuing of a Presbyterian Church loyal to the Scripture and the Reformed faith." Donald Patterson followed the announcement with an introduction of the steering committee, saying that these leaders had "reached a consensus to accept the apparent inevitability of division" in the PCUS and "to move now toward a continuing body of congregations and presbyteries loyal to the Scriptures and the Westminster Standards." The news was greeted by a standing ovation from the assembled congregation. Conservative leaders stressed that "we must move together"—all the organizations needed to coordinate their efforts so that a significant group would move into the continuing church. Kennedy Smartt later remembered that the steering committee had a big job: "They had to keep the many conservative churches and pastors walking in step, they needed to educate all churches that might possibly be interested in moving with us, and they needed to form a framework that would provide a net, a fellowship, for all those who would be ready to leave when the 'right time' came." Keeping conservatives together over the next months would be a greater challenge than the leadership realized.[20]

PLANS OF UNION AND DISUNION

One of the big challenges for the Steering Committee for a Continuing Church was that there were strong differences of opinion

19. William E. Hill Jr. to L. Nelson Bell, 28 July 1971, L. Nelson Bell Papers, box 72, folder 6, BGC.

20. Smartt, *I Am Reminded*, 60–61, 63; "Plans for Continuing Church Announced," *PJ* (25 August 1971): 4–5; W. Jack Williamson, "Getting Set for What's Coming," *PJ* (1 September 1971): 7. See also G. Aiken Taylor, "Towards a Continuing Church," *PJ* (25 August 1971): 12.

among conservatives about how the timetable for separation should proceed. As Paul Settle noted, there were three major approaches. One group was the "sooners." This group believed that conservatives should leave the PCUS directly after the 1972 General Assembly, regardless of what happened. The "keepers" represented a second approach. They believed that conservatives should remain in the PCUS at least until the 1973 General Assembly, especially as the plan of union with the UPCUSA was unfolding. The expectation in 1971 was that this plan would be presented at the 1973 General Assembly; hence, that would make a good breaking point, especially if the plan had an "escape clause." A final group was the "planners," who insisted that conservatives should not leave until the plan of union was presented or some other definite issue was presented that served as a catalyst for departure. This division in approach made the work of the steering committee incredibly difficult. It wanted to come out with as many churches or even presbyteries as possible, but much of its strategy was dictated not by its own plans and desires, but by the denominational leadership negotiating the plan of union with the UPCUSA.[21]

Not only did conservatives want to bring as many churches as possible with them, but also they wanted to bring those churches with their property. Church property was a major issue back in the 1950s when conservatives defeated reunion with the northern Presbyterians; in the fifteen or so years since, conservatives were nervous that PCUS progressives would attempt to change the *Book of Church Order* so as to make explicit the doctrine of "implied trust," the idea that congregations held property in trust for the denomination. Conservatives were heartened by the 1966 Georgia Supreme Court decision that ultimately awarded church properties to departing Savannah congregations, Hull Memorial Presbyterian Church and Eastern Heights Presbyterian Church. Yet most did not want to have to fight it out in the courts with a "loyal minority" that did not want to secede from the PCUS. As a result, many church leaders hoped that a plan of union with the northern church would have an "escape clause," allowing churches that did not desire to join a new "united" church to stay out

21. Settle, *To God All Praise and Glory*, 40.

with their property. While the draft of the plan of union current in 1971 had such an escape clause in it, several prominent Presbyterians north and south opposed it. There was no guarantee that the final plan of union would have such a provision.[22]

When leaders from eighty congregations gathered in Atlanta in September 1971 for an update from the Continuing Church Steering Committee, the number-one question on their minds was the escape clause. Jack Williamson, who served on the PCUS-UPCUSA Plan of Union Committee, told the group that "there is hope that an acceptable clause will be drafted which will permit a person, in good conscience, to vote for the plan either as a vehicle for union with the UPUSA or as a method of continuing our own Presbyterian Church." Also at this meeting, a "Declaration of Intent" was distributed, a document that was meant to encourage sessions and presbyteries to make their intentions known concerning the continuing-church movement. Importantly, the steering committee reiterated its determination to be more racially inclusive than conservatives had ever been before. Ben Wilkinson stressed, "We are not a racist group seeking to build a racial church." While recognizing differences of opinion, Wilkinson wanted to know of "black pastors and elders who might be interested in the Continuing Church." Finally, the steering committee chose four men from this meeting to work with conservative presbyteries to see whether any of them could "vote themselves out of the PCUS" by way of the proposed escape clause. Having entire presbyteries come into the continuing church would not only bring strength in numbers, but also legitimize conservatives' claim that they represented a continuation of the PCUS, loyal to Scripture and the Westminster Standards.[23]

22. G. Aiken Taylor, "What Do You Mean, 'Escape Clause'?," *PJ* (4 August 1971): 12; "For a Continuing Church," *PJ* (3 November 1971): 7. A summary of the legal battle over the Savannah churches can be found in Frank J. Smith, *The History of the Presbyterian Church in America: Silver Anniversary Edition* (Lawrenceville, GA: Presbyterian Scholars Press, 1999), 184–207; see also Douglas E. Cowan, *The Remnant Spirit: Conservative Reform in Mainline Protestantism* (Westport, CT: Praeger, 2003), 50–54. Jack Williamson rightly pointed out that the Georgia legal decision provided only precedence for withdrawing churches from that state, not a legal guarantee for any PCUS congregation regardless of location. W. Jack Williamson, "A Plan for a Continuing Church," *PJ* (2 August 1972): 10.

23. "Leaders Briefed on Continuing Church," *PJ* (20 October 1971): 5–6; "A Declaration of Intent," c. 1971, Paul Settle Papers, box 257, folder 6, PCAHC; Smartt, *I Am*

As PCUS conservatives continued to work toward a continuing church, Aiken Taylor had larger dreams. As early as 1957, Taylor had written about his dream for conservatives to band together to work for a truly national Presbyterian church. At first, he thought that perhaps the PCUS could be the receptor for disgruntled northern churches and the planter of new congregations outside the former Confederate states. As events unfolded, however, he became an advocate for a "grand realignment" that would allow the conservatives in the northern and southern churches to come together and to allow the liberals to do the same. Twice, he broached the idea in letters to his cousin, J. Randolph Taylor, a leader on the progressive side for the plan of union with the northern church. He felt that the only way to withstand the coming liberal superchurch envisioned by the COCU was to bring all the conservative Presbyterian and Reformed groups together into a similarly large and significant body.[24]

It was with this in mind that Taylor led in forming the National Presbyterian and Reformed Fellowship (NPRF). Its initial meeting was in April 1970 in St. Louis with representatives from the PCUS Conservative Coalition and the Reformed Presbyterian Church, Evangelical Synod (RPCES), the Orthodox Presbyterian Church, and the Christian Reformed Church. As plans developed for the public launch of the new group, there was some thought that papers needed to be prepared to support ecclesiastical separation from apostasy and unbelief, which would nerve conservative groups in denominations that had not yet fractured, such as the Reformed Church in America. In early 1971, the steering committee announced the formation of the NPRF

Reminded, 66. Paul Kooistra also reported that he was encouraged "by the stand the Steering Committee took against racism." "Letters," *The Contact* (December 1971): 3. Also on racial inclusion, see "For a Continuing Church," 9.

24. G. Aiken Taylor, "Why Be the Only Sectional Church?," *SPJ* (7 August 1957): 7–8; G. Aiken Taylor to J. Randolph Taylor, 11 May 1966; J. Randolph Taylor to G. Aiken Taylor, 25 May 1966 (both in *Presbyterian Journal* Papers, box 154, folder 16, PCAHC); G. Aiken Taylor to J. Randolph Taylor, 4 December 1970, *Presbyterian Journal* Papers, box 162, folder 17, PCAHC. See also G. Aiken Taylor, "Be Ye Separate," *PJ* (11 December 1968): 12; G. Aiken Taylor, "Not a Split, Maybe a Realignment," *PJ* (4 December 1968): 12–13. Others agreed with Taylor: R. Wilbur Cousar, "A National Church—Amen," *SPJ* (14 May 1958): 4–5; Loren Watson, "Where Do We Go from Here?," *PJ* (18 June 1969): 8; "Conservative Groups Call for Realignment," *PJ* (21 April 1971): 6.

with its purpose to "join for encouragement and mutual assistance those who seek in our time the unity of a pure witness to the Word of God and the testimony of Jesus Christ." The first national meeting of the group occurred in April 1971 in Atlanta, where it declared its willingness and expectation that it would "function as a 'receiving body' or a 'holding body' both for denominations and congregations" if a grand realignment ever were to occur. The ultimate objective of the group was "a national Church professing the system of doctrine contained in the classic Reformed confessions and functioning under a Presbyterian form of government. Such a Church would not, however, simply be an extension of any existing denomination." In a little over a year, Taylor had advanced his dream toward a national Reformed and Presbyterian church quite a bit.[25]

While Taylor worked toward a national conservative super-church, other conservative leaders continued to plan toward a continuing church out of the PCUS. In March 1972, conservatives had to deal with fears that their movement was beginning to lose energy and direction as the leaders sniped at each other over theological distinctiveness. Early in 1972, Aiken Taylor wrote to Morton Smith to complain about two former Reformed Seminary students who had criticized the *Journal* for not being "thoroughly Reformed." In reply, Smith defended the students, noting that "I personally believe that if you were to be more consistent in this matter, the *Journal* would be more respected by those who are truly Reformed. It would also be a better instrument for the preserving of a truly Presbyterian and Reformed church." Both Taylor and Smith agreed that a meeting of the entire steering committee to discuss theological parameters for the continuing church would be helpful. And so a meeting on 8 March 1972 brought about a long discussion about "the various [theological] shades and hues" of people associated with the movement and how

25. John R. Richardson to Steve White, 26 March 1970, *Presbyterian Journal* Papers, box 189, folder 2; Ed Kellogg to G. Aiken Taylor, 6 October 1970, *Presbyterian Journal* Papers, box 188, folder 9 (both at PCAHC); "New Conservative Fellowship Is Formed," *PJ* (27 January 1971): 4; "Fellowship Anticipates 'Receiver' Role," *PJ* (28 April 1971): 4. The NPRF was the predecessor organization to the present-day North American Presbyterian and Reformed Council.

to unite them. It was agreed that the steering committee would take as its motto that it sought "a national Presbyterian church loyal to Scripture, faithful to the Reformed faith, and obedient to the Great Commission." For the time being, the shades and hues agreed to rally around that statement. But Bill Hill predicted that trouble might arise down the road between the "ultra-Calvinistic group" and the evangelistic group: "Their [i.e., the ultra-Calvinists'] presence may cause some tension in the formation of a church; we pray to God, however, that he may overrule this."[26]

Two weeks later, the members of the steering committee met again in Montgomery, Alabama. They planned toward a large meeting in May when the executive committees of the four conservative organizations would meet with the steering committee to discuss a proposed constitution for a new church. Also at this meeting, the committee approved a document written by John Richards that set out once again the purpose and beliefs of the steering committee and, by extension, of the continuing-church movement. Once again, its members affirmed that the Bible was "verbally inspired by God"; that they accepted the Westminster Standards "as containing the system of doctrine taught in Holy Scripture, and that these standards are the most acceptable expression of the Reformed faith"; and that the mission of the church was "to proclaim, to administer, and to enforce the law of Christ revealed in Scripture." But the document also set forward new issues, such as the belief that "any Christian individual, institution, board, agency or judicatory that rejects the authority of Christ as He speaks in His word is apostate from him and in need of repentance." Likewise, the denial of "the infallibility of Scripture" by individual ministers was a sign of apostasy. By extension, "we believe that many institutions, boards, and agencies of the Church are apostate and we see no significant sign of repentance and revival among them." This apostasy in the agencies of the PCUS set the groundwork for separation in order "to continue a Presbyterian Church faithful to

26. Morton Smith to Aiken Taylor, 4 January 1972; Aiken Taylor to Morton Smith, 10 January 1972 (both in *Presbyterian Journal* Papers, PCAHC); Smartt, *I Am Reminded*, 68–69; William E. Hill Jr. to C. Darby Fulton, 22 March 1972, C. Darby Fulton Papers, box 2, PHS.

the Scripture and the Reformed faith and obedient to [Christ's] Great Commission." This claim reflected conservatives' belief that they were not "schismatic" by leaving a church that was "apostate."[27]

One concern for the May committee meetings and the lead-up to the General Assembly was the status of the plan of union in connection with the rapid growth of union synods and presbyteries along with the progressing restructure of the church's synods. Bill Hill worried that if the progressive leadership set the date for restructuring the synods to 1 January 1973, "this could slam the door permanently for any presbyteries that want to maintain their conservative strength to get out." In addition, the new union synods and presbyteries, which was de facto church union with the northern Presbyterians, could lead some progressives simply to delay the plan-of-union vote until they had enough strength to pass it over conservative objections. In that case, too, there was little need to have an escape clause in the plan of union. Any of these changes or events would indicate the need for conservatives "to move in the very near future if the evangelical conservative testimony to the Scripture and the reformed faith is to continue." Another potential difficulty for conservatives was the announced candidacy of Nelson Bell for moderator of the 1972 General Assembly. On the one hand, the Continuing Church Steering Committee agreed to work with the Covenant Fellowship of Presbyterians to see Bell elected as moderator. On the other hand, if he were elected, it would create a great deal of difficulty: could they withdraw and potentially embarrass someone who had done so much for the conservative cause? How would his election affect conservative churches and leaders who were on the fence? There was no real way of knowing.[28]

When the 1972 General Assembly gathered at Montreat, the seemingly unthinkable did happen: Nelson Bell was elected moderator of the Assembly. And yet that election did not signal the mood of the Assembly. Not only was a complete restructuring of Assembly

27. Smartt, *I Am Reminded*, 69–70; "Faith and Purpose of the Steering Committee for a Continuing Presbyterian Church," *Contact* (May 1972): 4; John E. Richards, *The Historical Birth of the Presbyterian Church in America* (Liberty Hill, SC: Liberty Press, 1987), 190–92.

28. William E. Hill Jr. to C. Darby Fulton, 18 April 1972, C. Darby Fulton Papers, box 2, PHS; W. Jack Williamson to L. Nelson Bell, 11 May 1972, L. Nelson Bell Papers, box 54, folder 25, BGC; Smartt, *I Am Reminded*, 71–74. Smartt apparently forgot that the coalition was working for Bell's election, as the Williamson letter to Bell made clear.

operations approved, with a single General Executive Board replacing sixteen separate agencies and boards, but the thorough restructuring of synods was also approved, abortion for social and economic reasons was again defended, and conservative doctrinal issues were once again denied. Even worse, Bell himself changed his long-standing position on church union with northern Presbyterians, telling a press conference upon his election as moderator that "he will not work for union, but as he sees it now, if union is voted between the Presbyterian Church US and the United Presbyterian Church USA, he will go into the united church." As if that were not bad enough, Bell used his position as moderator to challenge the Steering Committee for a Continuing Church to agree publicly "to cease all activity work toward a 'continuing church' during this coming year." Kennedy Smartt remembered the feeling that the steering committee had when it received this letter: "This hit where it hurt the most. Most of us were involved in this enterprise because of the inspiration and leadership he had given us in the conservative Presbyterian cause. It was like our coach, whose inspiration had brought us to the championship game, calling for us to throw the game." The steering committee left it to Donald Patterson to answer the letter, and he gently told Bell that the steering committee was willing "to pursue this dialogue" but that it could not give up its stewardship of the organizations and structures already in motion for a year. In the end, nothing came of any of it, and the steering committee continued its work.[29]

As the steering committee met at the end of June 1972, not only did it have to deal with Bell's request that it cease its activities, but it needed to plan for the way forward. There were increased indications that the committee working on the plan of union between the southern and northern churches might delay everything until 1975; the supposition was that the newly restructured synods would have reworked

29. "L. Nelson Bell Wins Moderator's Post," *PJ* (21 June 1972): 5–6; "Complete Agency Restructure Approved," *PJ* (21 June 1972): 6; Smartt, *I Am Reminded*, 74; "Won't Promote Union; Will Unite—Dr. Bell," *PJ* (28 June 1973): 8; L. Nelson Bell to Steering Committee for a Continuing Presbyterian Church, 29 June 1972; Donald B. Patterson to L. Nelson Bell, 3 July 1972; L. Nelson Bell to Donald B. Patterson, 6 July 1972 (all in L. Nelson Bell Papers, box 69, folder 22, BGC).

the presbyteries in order to secure the necessary three-fourths vote by then. In addition, some conservative congregations and ministers were agitating for withdrawal; while the steering committee wanted them to wait, the leaders also recognized that "they may feel it necessary to leave at this present time. As such, they might become a test case for others." Also, the possibility of a "provisional presbytery" formed by a few ministers and congregations was discussed; such a presbytery could be a holding place for churches that wanted or needed to leave the PCUS before the continuing church had actually been formed.[30]

Conservatives continued to hold out hope, though, that any talk about the delay of the plan of union was simply talk. Jack Williamson wrote an article in the *Journal* in August 1972 in which he laid out a possible timeline for withdrawal if the plan of union were presented to the 1973 General Assembly as planned with the proposed escape clause. He continued to urge conservatives to wait for the plan of union, if possible, because it would give the continuing church "a broader base with a maximum number of churches," it provided ministers with "full protection" in coming to the continuing church, and "it is the guaranteed constitutional method for a local church to elect not to enter the union and still keep its local church property." With this approach, it was possible that a new continuing church could be formed by the 1974 General Assembly. But some churches simply could not wait that long. On 7 September 1972, sixteen ministers and elders representing ten churches formed a new independent presbytery. Called Vanguard Presbytery, it was the brainchild of Todd Allen, the pastor of Eastern Heights Presbyterian Church, Savannah, Georgia, which had successfully fought for its church property. Vanguard would become a provisional option for some churches and ministers who felt conscience-bound to withdraw and a model for others in the days ahead.[31]

---

30. "Bell Cautions against Force in Union," *PJ* (5 July 1972): 5; *Minutes, Executive Committee of PCU* (30 June 1972), *Presbyterian Journal* Papers, box 207, folder 4, PCAHC.

31. Williamson, "A Plan for a Continuing Church," 10; "Churches Form Vanguard Presbytery," *PJ* (20 September 1972): 6; "Vanguard Presbytery," *Contact* (October 1972): 1–2. For a summary of the formation of Vanguard Presbytery, see Smith, *The History of the Presbyterian Church in America*, 211–24.

Much of the fall of 1972 was spent in developing structures for a new denomination, regardless of what happened with the plan of union. Five subcommittees began working to develop these structures: overseas missions (Donald Patterson and Jim Baird); home missions (Bill Hill and Ben Wilkinson); college and seminary (Morton Smith and Aiken Taylor); retirement programs (Russ Johnson and Leon Hendrick); and Christian education (Paul Settle with others). As these subcommittees did their work, they had to work out some knotty issues: what would be the relationship between the continuing church's missions program, PEF, and ECOE? How would the continuing church relate to Reformed Seminary? Would the new church have its own Christian education and publications program, or would it simply partner with nondenominational, evangelical publishers? These questions needed answers, but could not fully receive them until the joint PCUS-UPCUSA committee writing the plan of union with the northern church reported on 10 February 1973.[32]

FORMING A CONTINUING CHURCH

The Continuing Church Steering Committee had voted to have its next meeting on 16 February 1973, after the Plan of Union Committee was scheduled to have met. When the steering committee met, Jack Williamson brought the news: the Plan of Union Committee had voted to scrap all the work that it had done and produce a new plan for the 1974 General Assembly to send out for study. That Plan of Union Committee meeting itself was a donnybrook: even the stated clerk of the UPCUSA charged the southern church's delegation with being "'dishonest' in their dealing with representatives of conservative groups and 'betrayed brethren who trusted your integrity.'" What was at stake, from the perspective of the PCUS delegation, was the escape clause—whether it was constitutional and how to allow congregations to leave if it was. Even more, the PCUS union supporters believed that restructuring the synods and presbyteries would give them the votes needed to procure a union without an escape clause. Regardless of what they thought, conservatives saw this as the last straw. It proved

---

32. Smartt, *I Am Reminded*, 79; Settle, *To God All Praise and Glory*, 42.

what they had known all along: the liberal leadership of the PCUS was "unworthy of confidence—dishonorable, dishonest, and deceitful."[33]

The steering committee in particular had been primed for the step of separation by the preacher whom its members had heard the night before. Their meeting coincided with a rally of the NPRF, which was meeting in Atlanta; preaching that night was Francis Schaeffer, a leader in the RPCES, and a popular evangelist and apologist. The steering committee heard Schaeffer say, "When it is no longer possible to practice discipline in the church courts, then you must practice discipline in reverse and leave. But your leaving must be with tears, not with flags flying and bands playing." Those words made a huge impact on the leaders of the steering committee, along with the other continuing-church leaders who were there; as they prayed and planned, they were now committed to "practice discipline in reverse and leave" the PCUS. They voted to bring the new church into being that year, 1973. In order to do this, they sent out a call for a "Convocation of Sessions" that would meet at Westminster Presbyterian Church, Atlanta, Georgia, in May. In order to attend the May convocation, the steering committee asked church sessions to affirm the "Reaffirmations of 1973," a document drawn up by John Richards that once again set out the PCUS departures on Scripture, Reformed doctrine, Christ as head of the church, the church's constitution, the church's mission and spirituality, ethics and church discipline, and union presbyteries, synods, restructuring, and centralization of power. Against these departures, the reaffirmation document committed the new church to the historic principles of the PCUS as the continuing expression of that body.[34]

As churches prepared to attend the May 1973 convention in Atlanta, they received yet another blow when Robert Strong, pastor

33. Settle, *To God All Praise and Glory*, 42–43; "Committee Votes to Scrap Plan of Union," *PJ* (21 February 1973): 4–5; "Report on the Committee on Presbyterian Union," *Contact* (March 1973): 5–6; W. Jack Williamson, "Steering Committee Report: Law and Procedure," *PJ* (6 June 1973): 10; G. Aiken Taylor, "They Cannot Be Trusted," *PJ* (28 February 1973): 12.

34. Settle, *To God All Praise and Glory*, 43; Smartt, *I Am Reminded*, 82–83; G. Aiken Taylor, "The Time Has Come for Love," *PJ* (7 March 1973): 12; "Continuing Church Slated for 1973," *PJ* (28 February 1973): 5–6; "Reaffirmations of 1973," *Contact* (March 1973): 1–5.

of Trinity Presbyterian Church, Montgomery, Alabama, and longtime conservative leader, announced that he was not leaving the PCUS. Strong held that his ordination vows "require me to continue to work in the denomination to which I have professed loyalty." There was not currently a doctrinal issue facing the church, nor was church union a live possibility for several years now that the proposed plan of union had been set aside. Though the church was extremely flawed doctrinally, it had not "so degenerated as to become apparently no Church of Christ." In addition, Strong had already been through one church division: he had been part of the group that formed the Orthodox Presbyterian Church in the 1930s; he was unwilling to go through that process again. Strong made this statement in the *Journal*, but he was also working behind the scenes with Nelson Bell to persuade churches and ministers to stay in the PCUS. In the end, however, his influence would wane with those whom he had previously led.[35]

The Convocation of Sessions gathered at Westminster Church in Atlanta on 18–19 May 1973, with 261 churches represented; the total number of communicant members in these churches totaled around seventy thousand. The meeting accomplished several goals. First, because the steering committee believed that it did not have authority to create a new denomination, these sessional representatives voted to start a new denomination (the vote was 349 to 16). Next, the Reaffirmations of 1973 were passed by the convention, with only one dissenting vote, to signal the new church's theological commitments. The meeting also elected a chairman and clerk who would guide the process through the first General Assembly: ruling elder Jack Williamson as chairman and Reformed Seminary professor Morton Smith as clerk. There was also a general agreement to meet again in August for an Advisory Convention, which would hammer out a range of details for recommendation to a constituting assembly for the continuing church.[36]

35. Robert Strong, "Why Some of Us Are Not Leaving," *PJ* (2 May 1973): 11, 18; Robert Strong to L. Nelson Bell, 26 April 1973, L. Nelson Bell Papers, box 69, folder 24; John E. Richards to L. Nelson Bell, 1 May 1973, L. Nelson Bell Papers, box 69, folder 22 (both at BGC). Strong reiterated many of these points in "Why I'm Not Leaving My Church," *Eternity* (September 1973): 44–45, 47–48.

36. "Convocation Calls for Another Church," *PJ* (6 June 1973): 4–6.

There were also a variety of reports about the progress that had been made in putting together new structures for the denomination. In overseas missions, Jim Baird reported for his subcommittee that "the Continuing Presbyterian Church adopt the suggestion of the Steering Committee that the Executive Commission on Overseas Evangelism of the Presbyterian Evangelistic Fellowship (ECOE) assist the new denomination by serving as the overseas sending agency for the first two years of our existence or until such time as the new formed denomination is able to direct its own overseas program." On home missions, Ben Wilkinson, PEF executive director, noted that his group had started a domestic counterpart to ECOE, called Mission to the United States. As a result, Wilkinson called on the continuing church to adopt Mission to the United States as its vehicle for home missions work. Paul Settle reported for the Christian Education Subcommittee and recommended that conservative southern Presbyterians use the Sunday school curriculum produced by Great Commission Publications, the literature arm of the Orthodox Presbyterian Church. Aiken Taylor noted that the new church would not be initially able to support a college or seminary; for theological education, a number of schools would be worth supporting, although Reformed Seminary had not been fully supportive of the continuing-church movement and had known a "level of controversy [that] is regrettably evident in student and graduate attitudes."[37]

Other decisions were made at the Convocation of Sessions. A significant decision concerned which version of the Westminster Standards and the *Book of Church Order* to recommend. After all, a major complaint for conservatives was the way in which the progressive leadership had amended the doctrinal standards through the years; in a similar fashion, the *Book of Church Order* had also been heavily amended over the past decades. It was decided to recommend the version of the Westminster Standards dating to 1881 and the PCUS *Book of Church Order* as it had been in 1933 with the elimination of

37. James M. Baird, "Steering Committee Report: World Missions," *PJ* (6 June 1973): 13; Ben Wilkinson, "Steering Committee Report: Mission to the United States," *PJ* (6 June 1973): 14; G. Aiken Taylor, "Steering Committee Report: Colleges and Seminaries," *PJ* (6 June 1973): 17–18.

synods as a church court. The decision to use the 1881 version of the Standards was an interesting one: in that year, a debate had begun regarding WCF 24.4 over whether someone could marry his deceased wife's sister, which the confession forbade. After five years of debate, the PCUS struck the final clause of that confessional paragraph (hence allowing such marriages to occur). As a result, the continuing-church movement was going back to the version of the Standards that had remained unchanged for the first twenty years of the PCUS's existence. And yet the continuing-church leaders then proceeded to make a change to those Standards, removing language from WCF 25.6 that identified the pope as the antichrist; hence, there was a small irony in using a nonamended version of the Standards, only to amend them at the start of the church's life. The *Book of Church Order* had one significant change to it: a lengthy section that guaranteed local church ownership of property with the proviso that commitment could never be amended or changed.[38]

As important as these plans were, it was more important to ensure that as many large churches came into the new denomination as possible. One of the most important was Coral Ridge Presbyterian Church, Fort Lauderdale, Florida. Its pastor, D. James Kennedy, had long been associated with the Conservative Coalition. He attended the convocation as an observer, but had a number of questions about the new denomination. At one point he told Kennedy Smartt, "I want to be sure that you are not creating a racist or sectional church. If you are, count me out, but if you are not, and if you do not name it 'the Southern Presbyterian Church,' then I will be with you. Not immediately, but you have my word, Coral Ridge will come." Later, Kennedy and Aiken Taylor exchanged letters in which Kennedy questioned the viability of the new denomination, which concerned him in the light of the large mortgage that Coral Ridge was carrying on its property at that

---

38. "Continuing Church Plans Are Announced," *PJ* (13 June 1973): 5; Smartt, *I Am Reminded*, 94–95; *A Digest of the Acts and Proceedings of the General Assembly of the Presbyterian Church in the United States, 1861–1965* (Atlanta: Office of the General Assembly, 1966), 3. For much more on the debate over WCF 24.4, see Barry G. Waugh, "The History of a Confessional Sentence: The Events Leading Up to the Inclusion of the Affinity Sentence" (Ph.D. diss., Westminster Theological Seminary, 2002).

point. Taylor replied by urging Kennedy to "examine the moral and spiritual considerations of the matter and make [a] determination on what [you] think would honor Jesus Christ and his Word most of all, without considering the financial crunch." As it turned out, Kennedy and Coral Ridge would come into the new denomination in 1977.[39]

Other large churches were ready to move forward. From the time the continuing church was announced in 1971, First Presbyterian Church, Jackson, Mississippi, had been one of the major forces in its development. At its 4 June 1973 session meeting, the session formally voted, with only two elders out of thirty-six dissenting, to leave the PCUS. It also adopted a resolution, presented to the congregation later that month, that laid out the reasons for separation: that the people in the congregation "for more than twenty-five years have felt out of step and out of accord with the distinct and progressive trends in the Presbyterian Church, U.S."; that the church was determined to "remain true to the creed and historic attitude toward the Scripture of the Presbyterian Church, U.S."; and that the church desired to focus on "its primary mission—to win others, at home and abroad, to faith in Jesus Christ." In addition, First Church Jackson observed that "we feel that our denomination has been leaving us" and that because this was the case, it was time for the church to "withdraw from Central Mississippi Presbytery and the Presbyterian Church in the United States" and to declare itself to be "an autonomous and independent church." By the end of October, the church would vote to join the continuing-church movement. Briarwood Presbyterian Church in Birmingham, Alabama, and Trinity Presbyterian Church in Montgomery, Alabama, would join it as the three largest churches when the continuing church was formed.[40]

Some churches entered independent status until the new denomination formed, but others formed new presbyteries or joined others already formed. By August 1973, fourteen presbyteries had formed to receive churches that were leaving the PCUS for the continuing church:

---

39. Smartt, *I Am Reminded*, 93; G. Aiken Taylor to D. James Kennedy, 25 June 1973, *Presbyterian Journal* Papers, box 165, folder 11, BGC.

40. Sean Michael Lucas, *Blessed Zion: First Presbyterian Church, Jackson, Mississippi, 1837–2012* (Jackson, MS: First Presbyterian Church, 2013), 143–44.

Vanguard, Warrior, Gulf Coast, Westminster, Central Georgia, North Georgia, Southern Florida, Covenant, Calvary, Grace, Mississippi Valley, Gold Coast, North Texas, and Evangel. Most of these presbyteries represented southeastern states: Alabama, Mississippi, Florida, Georgia, and South Carolina. Some of these presbyteries would be quite large by the time the new denomination formed; Mississippi Valley, for example, would have fifty churches by the end of 1973.[41]

When these churches' representatives finally gathered in Asheville, North Carolina, in August 1973, there was a growing sense of direction, but also a developing ethos that would characterize the new denomination going forward. The direction was clear: the new church would be born and the call was issued for the first General Assembly to meet at Briarwood Presbyterian Church, Birmingham, Alabama, on 4 December 1973. The new denomination would have four program committees: committees on Mission to the World, Mission to the U.S., Christian Education and Publications, and Administration. But the ethos was also coming clear; as the *Journal* reported, "Clearly skittish of top level control of anything, the delegates meeting at Grove Park Inn here allowed 'plans' and 'promotions,'" but not anything more substantive than that. In addition, the advisory convention shot down any thoughts of having a central treasury, a centralized budget, or the equalization of any benevolent funds. Particularly impassioned on this point was Jimmy Lyons, the head of ECOE, who urged the new church to charge "every committee to raise its own funds in competition with the other committees."[42]

Another way to keep control on any church bureaucracy was through "committees of commissioners." Initially, the Assembly required the program committees to submit any new policies to the court through committees of commissioners; these committees would be formed at each General Assembly for the sole purpose of making recommendations on the proposed policy changes. In a way, this structure mirrored what was done in the PCUS through its structure

41. "Vanguard Receives Four Churches, Six Ministers," *PJ* (25 July 1973): 6; "Central Mississippi Loses More than Half," *PJ* (1 August 1973): 6. Information on presbytery order and date is from http://www.pcahistory.org/presbyteries.html.

42. "Convention Clears the Way for Assembly," *PJ* (22 August 1973): 4–5; Smartt, *I Am Reminded*, 95.

of permanent and standing committees; the standing committees were put together each year from commissioners to the Assembly for the purpose of reviewing the work of the agencies and permanent committees. In addition, the advisory convention had little interest in moving forward toward any ecumenical relations or possible church union, refusing to recommend a committee on interchurch relations or to consider working with the NPRF. Aiken Taylor, for one, worried that "we fear that in the long run it may prove costly to that dream which good men are laboring so hard to turn into a reality," namely, a large national conservative Presbyterian and Reformed witness. He blamed Concerned Presbyterians especially for the tone of the rejection, and he feared "that this decision will be interpreted to mean the reborn Church will embody a provincial and defensive regional mentality."[43]

But the leadership of the continuing-church movement did not intend to be provincial or regional. As Donald Patterson told Taylor later, "Not only do I want us to be in NPRF but also the NAE [the National Association of Evangelicals] and the WRC [the World Relief Commission], but it is going to take some selling and a lot of work." In addition, Patterson and the rest of the conservative leadership earnestly desired to be a national church, not simply a southern one. The names batted around for the new denomination all had the word *national* in them; there would be a national focus and aspiration to be a conservative *mainline* body. Yet it was not possible for most conservative leaders to focus on birthing a new denomination and then immediately to lead that new church into negotiations for a conservative "superchurch" that would stand against whatever might come out of COCU. As James Francis Miller told Taylor, "This is no time to talk of union. Our people are in full flight from union—and rightly so—union with the Northern Church. . . . Let's get our own house in order, the new church established and a going concern. Then we can educate our people on this conservative union and lead them to it."[44]

43. Smartt, *I Am Reminded*, 96; G. Aiken Taylor, "One Unfortunate Decision," *PJ* (22 August 1973): 12.

44. Donald B. Patterson to G. Aiken Taylor, 20 August 1973; James Francis Miller to G. Aiken Taylor, 22 August 1973 (both in *Presbyterian Journal* Papers, PCAHC); James Francis Miller, "'Union' a Dirty Word?," *PJ* (10 October 1973): 13, 22.

When the First General Assembly of the Continuing Presbyterian Church finally convened on 4 December 1973 in Birmingham, Alabama—112 years to the day of the founding of the PCUS—there was a sense of hope and relief. Hope that this new denomination being birthed would be free from the acrimonious debates that had characterized life in the PCUS for nearly two generations; hope because the new denomination would be recommending and adopting a first-year budget of over $1.2 million, with over half that amount going to international missions; relief because they had finally created a church that continued all that the founders saw to be good from the PCUS, a church that would be true to the Scriptures and the Reformed faith and obedient to the Great Commission. The church's first actions were electing a moderator and clerk and choosing a name. The moderator and clerk were obvious; they had already been serving in those roles since February: Jack Williamson and Morton Smith. The name would be chosen from three: *Continuing Presbyterian Church*, *National Presbyterian Church*, and *Presbyterian Church in America*. On the third ballot, *National Presbyterian Church* was chosen. Inauspiciously, that name would not last the year; as a result of a court challenge from the National Presbyterian Church, Washington, D.C., the new denomination would select *Presbyterian Church in America* at its second General Assembly in September 1974.[45]

The majority of that first General Assembly was spent hammering out polity details. The changes to the *Book of Church Order* that vested property in the local congregation were easily approved, as was the provision that allowed a church to withdraw from the new denomination with its property "at any time for reasons which seem to it sufficient." The new *Book of Church Order* offered no position "on the controversy of limited service (rotation [of elders]), local congregations are left free to decide for themselves." Another issue involved whether miraculous gifts of the Spirit had in fact ceased; two hours were spent on that issue, and it would return again at future Assemblies. There would be no synods in the new church, "at least until the

45. "Committee Reports to the General Assembly," *PJ* (21 November 1973): 8–9; "National Presbyterian Church Is Born," *PJ* (19 December 1973): 4–5.

denomination is large enough to need them," and the future General Assemblies would have membership determined in the same way as presbyteries, all the ministers and a proportional number of ruling elders, "until size makes it impractical." An additional decision that the Assembly made included taking over all the functions of ECOE into the new Mission to the World and instructing that committee to affiliate with the National Association of Evangelicals for the services it provided through the Chaplains Commission, the World Relief Commission, and the Evangelical Foreign Missions Association. It related the new Women in the Church to the Christian Education Committee and also instructed that committee to partner with the Orthodox Presbyterian Church on curriculum development. Three of the new committees gained coordinators at this first Assembly: Dan Moore to head Administration; Larry Mills for Mission to the U.S.; Paul Settle for Christian Education and Publications. Mission to the World would wait for its new coordinator until the second Assembly. These committees would not be allowed to be in the same city for at least the first five years of the church's existence as another way of holding back any centralizing bureaucracy.[46]

As important as the polity issues were and as significant as the other decisions would prove to be, two documents were vital for the self-understanding of this new denomination. One was "A Message to All Churches of Jesus Christ throughout the World," a document that meant to echo the founding document of the PCUS in many respects. The message sought to justify the church's separation from the PCUS, declaring that "as a whole, and in its leadership, [the PCUS] no longer holds those views regarding the nature and mission of the Church, which we accept as both true and essential." Top of the list for any church's life and well-being was "the Bible [which] is the Word of God written and carries the authority of its divine author." The new church would affirm verbal plenary inspiration and biblical inerrancy: "We declare, therefore, that the Bible is the very Word of God, so inspired in the whole and in all its parts, as in the original

46. "BCO Monopolizes Assembly Attention," *PJ* (19 December 1973): 5–6; "Assembly Made Other Important Decisions," *PJ* (19 December 1973): 7–8; "Assembly Approves Top Staff Nominees," *PJ* (19 December 1973): 8; "National Presbyterian Church Is Born," 5.

autographs to be the inerrant Word of God. It is, therefore, the only infallible and all-sufficient rule of faith and practice." This had been the original position of the PCUS, and it would be the position of this continuing church. Once this position on biblical authority had been jettisoned, everything went wrong in the PCUS: doctrinal aberration, polity abuses, social pronouncements, and failures to discipline. The new church also affirmed "the system of doctrine found in God's Word to be the system known as the Reformed faith." That system was summarized in the Westminster Standards, and that doctrinal statement would serve as the basis of fellowship with all who would unite with the new church. A third affirmation centered on the headship of Christ over his church. Christ ruled over his church by his Word for an express mission: to glorify God by going into the world to fulfill the Great Commission. Hence, the new church would be evangelistic and would seek to plant new Presbyterian churches in the United States and throughout the world.[47]

The other major statement was Jack Williamson's opening sermon at the first General Assembly, which one observer described as "a very statesmanlike pronouncement [that] will be a permanent source of satisfaction and pride to the Church." Williamson stressed that the formation of this new denomination was an effort "to continue a true branch of the Church of our Lord Jesus Christ." As such, the purpose of the church was clear: "The origin of this Church is in God, its form is from God; and from beginning to end, its purpose is and shall be to magnify God's glory." The church was a spiritual institution with a spiritual mission. While the new denomination was forced to separate from the PCUS, it did so to maintain principle—the church was ruled by Christ through his Word for his glory. And the church was bound by this commitment: "We have committed ourselves to be the rebirth and continuation of a Presbyterian Church loyal to the Scripture, the Reformed faith, and committed to the spiritual mission of the Church as Christ commanded in the Great Commission."[48]

47. "A Message," *PJ* (26 December 1973): 7–8.
48. C. Darby Fulton to Paul Settle, 25 December 1973, C. Darby Fulton Papers, box 2, PHS; W. Jack Williamson, "To the Glory of God," *PJ* (26 December 1973): 9–11, 18.

Southern Presbyterian conservatives had centered their message on those three issues from the earliest coalescence of their dissent. They wanted to maintain a church—at first, the PCUS and then this continuing church—that would affirm biblical authority, the Reformed evangelicalism of the Westminster Standards, and the evangelistic passion of the Great Commission. They wanted this new Presbyterian church to pass these truths and values on to the next generation so that those not yet born would love the Bible and the faith of the fathers. They felt that in this way, they would be able to maintain a position within American culture that would bring about social good as men and women came to faith in Christ. The threefold motto perfectly summarized what they desired to accomplish. And at least at the beginning, they were all united around that vision and those goals.

12

Epilogue: Presbyterian Identity and the Presbyterian Church in America, 1973–2013

In 1936, when he preached at the first General Assembly of what would become the Orthodox Presbyterian Church, J. Gresham Machen exulted that "we became members, at last, of a true Presbyterian Church; we recovered, at last, the blessing of true Christian fellowship." Though the little group that followed him out of the northern Presbyterian church was small, only thirty-four ministers representing around five thousand communicant members, Machen believed that its future was bright because it was "the Church of the living God, the temple of the Holy Ghost." He also thought that eventually more conservative Presbyterians would join with this small group. While it is not completely clear that Machen sympathized with those who wanted to make the new denomination a conservative mainline church, Machen's death in 1937 shifted the balance of power to those who believed that a true Presbyterian church meant a more limited, smaller, confessionally particular one. Less than a year after it formed, the Orthodox Presbyterian Church split into two groups, and a small church became even smaller.[1]

1. For more on Machen and the division of the northern church, see Sean Michael Lucas, *J. Gresham Machen* (Darlington, UK: Evangelical Press, 2015), chap. 8.

The lessons represented by their northern cousins loomed large for the southern Presbyterian conservatives who wrestled with the liberal trends in their denomination and who left it to start the PCA. When conservatives raised the specter of the "sin of schism," they did so with an eye cast back in history to the events in the northern church, the Orthodox Presbyterian Church, and its division of 1937. The great fear was that the forces that would bring about a division in the southern Presbyterian church would not be containable; the resultant church would divide into smaller and smaller parts and the dream of a continuing Presbyterian church faithful to Scripture and the Reformed faith and obedient to the Great Commission would die.[2]

Forty years after the formation of the PCA, it is safe to say that the fear of further division was unfounded. Even more, it seems clear that the founders were, in a measure, vindicated and those who counseled remaining in the PCUS were proved to be wrong. In 2013, the PCA reported a total membership of 364,019 in 1,777 churches, a membership number that is undoubtedly low because only half the churches report their statistics annually; more than three hundred mission churches were in process at that time. Meanwhile, the mainline Presbyterian church—formed as the Presbyterian Church (U.S.A.) in 1983 through a finally accomplished reunion of the northern and southern branches—has dwindled from 4.25 million members in 1965 to 1.84 million members in 2012; its trajectory continues downward at a rapid pace. And many of those conservatives associated with the Covenant Fellowship of Presbyterians who urged continuing in the mainline body themselves left the PCUS in 1982 to form the Evangelical Presbyterian Church; that body reported 464 churches and 150,924 total members in 2013. Conservative Presbyterianism

2. On the "sin of schism," see, for example, Andrew Jumper to William E. Hill Jr. et al., 26 July 1971; Charles McGowan to L. Nelson Bell, 5 August 1971 (both in L. Nelson Bell Papers, box 72, folder 6, BGC); L. Nelson Bell to Executive Committee of *PJ*, 3 August 1971, L. Nelson Bell Papers, box 74, folder 1, BGC; L. Nelson Bell to Morton Smith, 25 April 1973; Morton Smith to L. Nelson Bell, 3 May 1973 (both in L. Nelson Bell Papers, box 48, folder 6, BGC).

continues to grow through church-planting and accessions from the PC(USA) while that mainline body is dying.[3]

That apparent success and vindication do not mean that the way forward for conservative Presbyterians has been easy. In fact, from the first months in the new denomination, conservatives struggled to understand truly what they had done in forming the PCA. Aiken Taylor, writing in *Christianity Today* after the second PCA General Assembly met in Macon, Georgia, observed, "Ever since the organizing assembly in December [1973] in Birmingham, where the original lines had been drawn between hardline followers of latter-day Calvinists and those referred to by the hardliners as 'evangelical,' the trenches had been dug and the guns loaded." Taylor's observation was an important indicator of fault lines in the newly formed denomination: what it meant to be Presbyterian, how those in the church would relate to one another and other evangelicals, and how they would move forward around the three parts of their motto without fragmenting.[4]

In other words, the struggle for the PCA was over its identity. The problem of identity was not simply an issue of what the new church would believe, but how it would carry out those beliefs. And these beliefs and practices were connected to particular stories— stories that went back to the 1920s and 1930s when denominational progressives seized control of the PCUS machinery and stories about PCA origins and what the founders intended to accomplish. As these beliefs, practices, and stories combined in the unique way that shaped the PCA, the church would take its place as the largest conservative Presbyterian denomination in the country. And yet that Presbyterian identity continues to be contested to the present day as the founding

3. L. Roy Taylor, "Actions of the 41st General Assembly of the Presbyterian Church in America," http://www.pcaac.org/wp-content/uploads/2013/07/Actions-41st-GA.pdf; Leslie Scanlon, "Joining the Exodus," http://www.pcusa.org/news/2013/9/20/whos-joining -exodus/; Jeff Jeremiah, "Evangelical Presbyterian Church 33rd General Assembly: Report of the Stated Clerk," http://995cf4d644fcb80e0622-5442b5726517b59ac42d093bb8ff9c67 .r51.cf2.rackcdn.com/uploaded/3/0e2210545_33ga-ch-stated-clerk-report-attachment-a -churches-of-record--final.pdf.

4. G. Aiken Taylor, "Presbyterian Church in America: In Quest of Name and Niche," *Christianity Today* (11 October 1974): 48.

generation moves off the scene, as the second generation prepares for retirement, and as the third generation takes its place of leadership in the church.[5]

EVANGELICAL PRESBYTERIANS

Issues of identity often center on original intent: what did the founders intend to do when they set out? That is the case for various forms of national or religious identity, and it is the case for Presbyterian identity as well. For example, when Machen and his followers left the northern Presbyterian church in 1936, they wanted to create a "true" Presbyterian church. And yet even that vision—what constitutes a "true" Presbyterian body?—would morph and change over time, especially in the aftermath of Machen's death and the division of 1937.[6]

It seems incontrovertible that the majority of the PCA founders desired to form a conservative mainline Presbyterian church. That is to say, their orientation was toward continuing the largely evangelical and evangelistic emphases of the southern church while upholding the inerrancy of the Bible and the truth of the WCF. So they did not intend to get bogged down in battles over details in the Reformed system of doctrine, nor did they desire to create litmus tests on doctrinal matters as the determining factor for shared ministries. Their instincts were to be evangelical Presbyterians—but evangelical Presbyterians who had the cultural influence that they had known as part of a mainline Protestant denomination. As Aiken Taylor told Andrew Jumper in 1971, "It has been my dream to help bring about a revitalized Presbyterian and Reformed witness that would be nation-wide." This was not Taylor's dream alone, but the dream of most of the other founders of the PCA.[7]

5. For this use of beliefs, practices, and stories for the formation of Presbyterian identity, see Sean Michael Lucas, *On Being Presbyterian: Our Beliefs, Practices, and Stories* (Phillipsburg, NJ: P&R Publishing, 2006).

6. Charles G. Dennison, *History for a Pilgrim People: The Historical Writing of Charles G. Dennison*, ed. Danny E. Olinger and David K. Thompson (Philadelphia: Orthodox Presbyterian Church, 1999), 91–176.

7. G. Aiken Taylor to Andrew Jumper, 2 August 1971, Covenant Fellowship of Presbyterians Papers, box 10, PHS.

These instincts toward a new conservative mainline Presbyterianism helps to explain why the founders reacted negatively in the early years of the PCA to the younger generation of "TRs" who sought to exert their own influence in the new church. The "TRs" were the "hardline followers of latter-day Calvinists" that Taylor identified for the *Christianity Today* readership; they desired to be "thoroughly Reformed," and their self-chosen moniker distinguished them from evangelical Presbyterians whom they viewed "to be falling short or drawing back in some important particular of Reformed Christianity." Many of these men were graduates of Reformed Theological Seminary and were especially critical of Taylor and other conservative Presbyterian leaders who they felt were not working to form an explicitly Reformed denomination. These younger ministers found support from Morton Smith, professor of systematic theology at Reformed Seminary and the first stated clerk of the PCA, who agreed that the *Presbyterian Journal* was not "thoroughly Reformed" and that the goal of the younger ministers, who were "truly Reformed," was to preserve a "truly Presbyterian and Reformed church." This emphasis on doctrinal particularity could potentially upset the dream of a conservative mainline denomination united for national witness.[8]

And yet as these younger "TR" ministers sought various pathways to be "distinctively Reformed"—whether through the courts of the church or through idiosyncratic theological movements such as theonomy—they never gained critical mass in the life of the PCA. Instead, the founding generation kept the denomination focused on being true to Scripture and the Reformed faith broadly construed, but especially on the evangelistic mandate in domestic and international missions. Churches continued to hold evangelistic meetings, using men from PEF and continuing to support Billy Graham: for example, First Presbyterian Church, Jackson, Mississippi, hosted Bill Hill in 1970 and Bill Bright the following year; and when Billy Graham

8. O. Guy Oliver, "'T-R': The Anatomy of a Slogan (c. 1976)," MS in possession of author. I thank the Rev. Bill Smith for providing me with a copy of this document. Morton Smith to G. Aiken Taylor, 4 January 1972; G. Aiken Taylor to Morton Smith, 10 January 1972; G. Aiken Taylor to Frank M .Barker Jr., 3 May 1974 (all in *Presbyterian Journal* Papers, PCAHC).

came back to Jackson in 1975, the church strongly supported the meetings with personal counselors and financial backing. Likewise, the influence of D. James Kennedy's Evangelism Explosion was significant in the 1970s, with large churches such as McIllwain Presbyterian Church in Pensacola, First Presbyterian Church in Jackson, Mississippi, and Briarwood Presbyterian Church in Birmingham, Alabama, all committed to that evangelistic method. And international missions drove the denominational agenda, even as the PCA had to sort out what "co-operative ministries" were acceptable for its denominational agency, Mission to the World (MTW). As Kennedy Smartt later remembered, "One of our dreams in starting the PCA was to see the opportunity provided for our people to go out under our own mission organization," even while partnering with other "non-Reformed" agencies. Churches such as First Church Jackson and Briarwood, along with Coral Ridge Church in Fort Lauderdale, would be leaders in sending missionaries; notably, by 1983, First Church Jackson had fifty-seven church members serving with MTW around the world.[9]

This evangelistic imperative, both domestically and internationally, has tended to keep the PCA in the middle of the Reformed tradition theologically. Undoubtedly, this centrist instinct has the added benefit of keeping as many people and churches as possible within the "big tent" of the PCA for the purpose of mission and witness. Yet the centrist instinct is itself a reflection of the founders' intention: they envisioned a "Continuing Presbyterian Church," a church that continued the mainline approach to evangelism, missions, and witness that they felt characterized the southern Presbyterian church at its best. In order to do this, the founders emphasized a Reformed evangelicalism that emphasized core truths, starting with inerrancy and flowing outward into the fixed points of orthodoxy and winsome Calvinism. Whenever difficult doctrinal matters came up to the General Assembly—whether theonomy, creation days, or confessional

---

9. Sean Michael Lucas, *Blessed Zion: First Presbyterian Church, Jackson, Mississippi, 1837–2012* (Jackson, MS: First Presbyterian Church, 2013), 149; Kennedy Smartt, *I Am Reminded: An Autobiographical, Anecdotal History of the Presbyterian Church in America* (Chestnut Mountain, GA: n.p., 1998), 115, 117.

subscription—the PCA has tended toward solutions that move toward the center and keep as many people within the church as possible. That evangelical and evangelistic instinct is exactly what the founders intended: that the PCA would be a conservative mainline body representing evangelical Presbyterianism.[10]

PRESBYTERIAN EVANGELICALS

Not only did the founders intend for the PCA to be a *conservative* mainline body, but they also intended for the PCA to be truly *mainline*, both in its national reach and influence and in its ecumenical relationships. That is to say, while the PCA separated from the PCUS, it did not have the history of or the interest in ecclesiastical separation represented by other American fundamentalist groups. While some conservative Presbyterians were content to see themselves as fundamentalists of a certain kind, they were extremely uncomfortable with the fundamentalism represented by Bob Jones Jr. and his Bob Jones University and by Carl McIntire and his Bible Presbyterians. This discomfiture with Jones and McIntire was of long standing, harking back to the 1950s and the disagreements over Billy Graham.[11] These conflicts with hard-line fundamentalists caused leaders such as Nelson Bell and Aiken Taylor to emphasize that southern Presbyterian conservatives were *evangelicals*, not fundamentalists. These conservatives were heavily involved with the National Association of Evangelicals, the Billy Graham Evangelistic Association, and *Christianity Today*;

10. For examples of the centrist approach, see the PCA Position Papers on theonomy (http://www.pcahistory.org/pca/2-555.pdf) and creation days (http://www.pcahistory.org/creation/report.pdf). Likewise, the solution on confessional subscription, called "good faith subscription" and found in the PCA *Book of Church Order* 21–24, is evidence of a "middle of the road solution" between "system subscription" and "strict subscription"; on these issues, see David W. Hall, ed., *The Practice of Confessional Subscription* (Lanham, MD: University Press of America, 1995).

11. L. Nelson Bell, " 'Separation' Can Become Dislocation," *SPJ* (22 May 1957): 5–8. On the transition from fundamentalism to evangelicalism, see Joel A. Carpenter, *Revive Us Again: The Reawakening of American Fundamentalism* (New York: Oxford University Press, 1997); on the discomfiture with Jones and McIntire, see chapter 7 above. For one study that argues that fundamentalism by definition requires ecclesiastical separation, see David O. Beale, *In Pursuit of Purity: American Fundamentalism since 1850* (Greenville, SC: Unusual Publications, 1985).

and when they brought in speakers, they chose men such as Harold Ockenga and Carl Henry, luminaries of the new evangelicalism.[12]

As these evangelical Presbyterians worked together with others to evangelize, they did so with one eye on reviving Christian civilization in America. From its founding in 1942, the *Presbyterian Journal* regularly ran articles that emphasized America's exceptionalism as a Christian nation and urged Presbyterian conservatives to evangelize for the purpose of maintaining that status. "America needs to get back to the pathway of righteousness," Bruce Wideman declared. "America is a great land. America is a wonderful land. . . . But sadly, there is much that is wrong in America. There is a great lack of righteousness in our land." In order to return to that position of greatness, America needed to return to righteousness, which would happen by means of evangelism. Robert Strong agreed and went further: "I regard it as the fundamental stone in that structure which undergirds American life: the tradition of Christian theism." This tradition was in danger and could be reversed only through biblical evangelism. Bill Hill noted that America's difficulties throughout the 1950s and 1960s were a warning that must be heeded. "Only the return of people to that living God in true repentance can save this nation from the fate that all nations have experienced when they departed from God," Hill warned. The kingdom of God in America was always a large part of the conservative Presbyterian focus.[13]

Perhaps as a result, these conservative Presbyterians tended to follow their fellow evangelicals in a rightward political direction as

12. L. Nelson Bell, "The Evangelical Faith vs. Fundamentalism," *SPJ* (27 July 1955): 2–3; L. Nelson Bell, "The New York Campaign—Sifting the Wheat," *SPJ* (3 July 1957): 3–4; L. Nelson Bell, "True Ecumenism," *PJ* (12 December 1962): 11, 23; L. Nelson Bell, "Thoughts about Fundamentalism," *PJ* (31 March 1971): 13; G. Aiken Taylor, "Evangelical Ecumenism Works," *PJ* (21 April 1965): 12; Henry B. Dendy, "Welcome and Congratulations to Christianity Today," *SPJ* (10 October 1956): 6–7. See also the exchange between Taylor and Bob Jones Jr.: Bob Jones Jr. to G. Aiken Taylor, 26 March 1966; G. Aiken Taylor to Bob Jones Jr., 30 March 1966; Bob Jones Jr. to G. Aiken Taylor, 31 March 1966; Bob Jones Jr. to G. Aiken Taylor, 4 April 1966 (all in *Presbyterian Journal* Papers, box 166, folder 30, PCAHC).

13. Bruce Wideman, "Turn Back, America," *PJ* (1 July 1964): 7; Robert Strong, "The American Tradition in Danger," *PJ* (1 July 1964): 9; William E. Hill Jr., "Warning to a Nation," *PJ* (27 September 1961): 7.

well. The narrative in this book has highlighted how conservative Presbyterians emphasized anti-integration, anticommunism, and anti-centralization; in this, of course, they were not alone. Such were the intellectual poles of modern American political conservatism; as evangelicals fueled the rise of political conservatism starting in the 1960s, southern Presbyterian conservatives helped to shift the American South from the Democratic party to the Republican party. It was no accident that when sociologist Corwin Smidt and his colleagues examined PCA leaders in 2000, they discovered that "the clergy of the Presbyterian Church in America are socially homogeneous from almost every possible viewpoint." Politically, this worked out in nearly unanimous support for George W. Bush against Al Gore; 93 percent of PCA leaders voted for Bush, while less than 1 percent voted for Gore. The study concluded that "PCA pastors are politically engaged, conservative evangelicals. They form a solid block in the Republicans' evangelical base." This shift toward the Republican party started in the 1960s as the South moved toward Goldwater and the Republican party shifted toward modern American political conservatism. Along with other groups, the PCA has been a mainspring of the new Religious Right.[14]

Perhaps the most notable change over time on social and political issues for these conservative Presbyterians has been on the issue of race. In this, other southern evangelicals have certainly joined them; conservatives in the Southern Baptist Convention are a notable comparable. Until the 1960s, most conservative Presbyterians in the South supported racial traditionalism and opposed civil rights, often loudly and vociferously. Yet the same evangelistic dynamic that drove them toward theological moderation also served to challenge their views on racial segregation. Prodded on by the example of Billy Graham and Bill Hill, both of whom held integrated evangelistic meetings and who argued the folly of segregation at home while doing international

14. Brent F. Nelsen and Beverly A. Gaddy, "Presbyterian Church in America," in *Pulpit and Politics: Clergy in American Politics at the Advent of the Millennium*, ed. Corwin E. Smidt (Waco, TX: Baylor University Press, 2004), 141–52. See also the sociological data in Earl Black and Merle Black, *The Rise of Southern Republicans* (Cambridge, MA: Harvard University Press, 2002), esp. 227–29.

missions in African countries, younger conservative evangelicals stood against racial segregation when the PCA formed in 1973. As the PCA has continued its ministry over the past forty years, it has worked at local and national levels to correct its past commitments to injustice and racial segregation. As historian Peter Slade demonstrated, one of these then-younger ministers, Jim Baird, would be a vital force in the formation of Mission Mississippi, an interracial organization that pursued a theology of friendship in overcoming racial division. When Baird became pastor of First Presbyterian Church, Jackson, Mississippi, he did what he had done elsewhere: developed relationships with area black pastors and leaders. This relationship-building would bear fruit when Baird along with First Church Jackson ruling elder Lee Paris would work with John Perkins, Dolphus Weary, and Neddie Winters to form Mission Mississippi.[15]

At a denominational level, the PCA took two significant actions that addressed the issues of race. In 2002, the General Assembly adopted a resolution that confessed the PCA's involvement with "the heinous sins attendant with unbiblical forms of servitude—including oppression, racism, exploitation, manstealing, and chattel slavery." The resolution further recognized that the effects of these sins "continue to create barriers between brothers and sisters of different races and/or economic spheres." As a result, the PCA pledged to work "for the encouragement of racial reconciliation." In 2004, the denomination approved a pastoral letter on racism that declared racism to be sinful, a denial of the gospel, and the breaking of several of the commandments. It, too, declared that "it is crucial that we repent of those teachings and actions in our history that are sinful, make a clear break from them and establish a new beginning in obedience by God's grace." While the denomination and its local churches have a long way to go in undoing the difficulties created by their past stand for racial segregation, these represented beginning steps along the way. From a historical perspective, such transitions on race are in line with those

15. Barry Hankins, *Uneasy in Babylon: Southern Baptist Conservatives and American Culture* (Tuscaloosa, AL: University of Alabama Press, 2002); Peter Slade, *Open Friendship in a Closed Society: Mission Mississippi and a Theology of Friendship* (New York: Oxford University Press, 2009); Lucas, *Blessed Zion*, 164–65.

of other conservative evangelical bodies, which now recognize how racial solidarity evidenced a betrayal of the gospel they proclaimed.[16]

The involvement in political and social conservatism in partnership with other evangelicals is a continued reminder that conservative Presbyterians represented in the PCA are not content to withdraw from American society or believe that their faith has little to say to their national or social context. For these Presbyterian evangelicals, there remains a sense of cultural responsibility or custodianship that is a remnant of mainline Protestant ways of viewing one's place in American society. While there remains a continuing dialogue about the relationship of the "spirituality of the church" doctrine with this sense of cultural responsibility, this dialogue is set firmly within the context of the PCA's mainline Protestant heritage and aspiration.[17]

ON BEING PRESBYTERIAN

In many ways, then, because the PCA was formed to be a conservative mainline Presbyterian denomination, the conflict that it has known over the past forty years has replicated—in tone if not in substance—that which belongs to most other mainline Protestant bodies. While there are not any true "liberals" in the PCA—especially compared to the progressive PCUS element described in this narrative—the language of "conservatives" and "progressives," or "right" versus "left," continues to be used in the denominational life. While this language has become increasingly prevalent over the past twenty years—dating back to the initial dialogue over creation days and confessional subscription in the 1990s—it takes its cues not simply from

16. PCA Position Paper on Racial Reconciliation (2002): http://www.pcahistory.org/pca/race.html; PCA Pastoral Letter on Racism (2004): http://pcahistory.org/pca/racism.pdf. See also Michael D. Hammond, "Conscience in Conflict: Neo-Evangelicals and Race in the 1950s" (M.A. thesis, Wheaton Graduate School, 2002); Mark Newman, *Getting Right with God: Southern Baptists and Desegregation, 1945–1995* (Tuscaloosa, AL: University of Alabama Press, 2001).

17. Historian D. G. Hart has argued that conservatives and progressives shared the same activistic approach to religion in American life. In many ways, my accounting here agrees with his argument, albeit without the negative connotation that he attributes to the activist approach. I would argue that this activism is part of the mainline Protestant sense of cultural responsibility and custodianship that moves toward cultural engagement. See his *The Lost Soul of American Protestantism* (Lanham, MD: Rowman and Littlefield, 2002).

the political arena but from the learned habits and fears of mainstream Protestant denominational life. Likewise, large-steeple pastors and seminary faculty members often have a disproportionate influence in denominational affairs, creating or soothing doctrinal or ecclesiastical crises. As these leaders have sought to shape and guide the denomination's ethos and trajectory, they have resorted to a range of conferences, organizations, and manifestos to accomplish their goals—PCA Vision 2000, the Presbyterian Pastoral Leadership Network, Presbyterians and Presbyterians Together, along with informal groups that met for a time and then disbanded.

Undoubtedly, this internal dialogue was complicated by the 1982 joining and receiving of the RPCES. At one level, joining and receiving accomplished the larger goal of making the PCA a truly national denomination. The RPCES was a descendant body from the northern Presbyterians who came out with Machen and then split from the Orthodox Presbyterians in 1937. Their strength was in the midwestern United States, but they also had congregations on the West Coast and in the northeastern states. They also brought into the union a college and seminary—Covenant College in Lookout Mountain, Georgia, and Covenant Theological Seminary in St. Louis, Missouri—that allowed the PCA finally to take up denominational education. In all these ways, joining and receiving helped to advance the PCA's sense of being a mainline church.

At another level, however, joining and receiving brought into the church ministers and elders who held to different beliefs, practices, and stories and who represented a slightly different variant of Presbyterianism that has challenged PCA identity. Most notably, the RPCES affirmed the freedom of individual congregations to call and ordain women deacons, or *deaconesses*. And yet at the same time, they developed standards for ecclesiastical separation that were more rigorous than anything that the PCA had contemplated. More important was the different story that the RPCES had. As a remnant group that developed its own agencies and institutions, and as a separatist body that sought various ecumenical relations and eventually mergers, these Presbyterians did not have the same sense of cultural responsibility that the southern Presbyterians who made up the PCA had. And yet because of the influence of Francis Schaeffer, the evangelical theologian-apologist who was an RPCES minister, there was a richer theological rationale for cultural engagement to be found in the RPCES than in the PCA. Trying to merge together variant identities into a single conservative mainline church has taken a great deal of time, effort, and understanding.[18]

Indeed, probably the most challenging aspect of the past forty years for the PCA has been working through what it means to be Presbyterian and what it means to be a conservative mainline Protestant body in a postdenominational world. Especially coming out of a denomination in which progressive leadership moved the southern Presbyterian church away from historic norms on biblical inerrancy and confessional Calvinism, the conservatives who made up the PCA struggled to figure out how to trust each other and denominational leaders. They struggled to trust one another doctrinally and especially financially: one of the greatest challenges that the PCA has experienced over its history has been the general lack of funding for its ten permanent committees and agencies. While its denominational offices have centralized outside of Atlanta, Georgia, the PCA continues to grapple with what connectional ministry means and requires.

And yet the PCA has hung together for forty years and represents the largest conservative Presbyterian body in North America. For better or for worse, it represents a conservative mainline Presbyterian tradition. In that regard, perhaps, maybe the most difficult years are behind it. When Westminster Seminary president Edmund Clowney spoke at the first commencement of Reformed Theological Seminary

18. "Women Deacons," Documents of Synod: Study Papers of the RPCES (1965 to 1982), http://pcahistory.org/findingaids/rpces/docsynod/156.html; "Apostasy and Ecclesiastical Separation," Documents of Synod, http://pcahistory.org/findingaids/rpces /docsynod/045.html. This document on ecclesiastical separation was adopted by the PCA in 1985. For the history of the RPCES, see George P. Hutchinson, *The History behind the Reformed Presbyterian Church, Evangelical Synod* (Cherry Hill, NJ: Mack, 1974). For an account of Schaeffer's influence in evangelicalism and on conservative Presbyterians, see Barry Hankins, *Francis Schaeffer and the Shaping of Evangelical America* (Grand Rapids: Eerdmans, 2008). This does not even take into account the failure (twice!) to merge with the Orthodox Presbyterian Church; for more on this, see D. G. Hart and John Muether, *Fighting the Good Fight: A Brief History of the Orthodox Presbyterian Church* (Philadelphia: Orthodox Presbyterian Church, 1995).

in spring 1968, he opened by saying, "I am greatly honored to be invited to speak to you on the occasion of your first commencement. Westminster Seminary will be celebrating its fortieth academic year next year, and I want to report to you that the first forty years are the hardest." Perhaps they are. If that is the case, then the next forty years should see the PCA—evangelical Presbyterians and Presbyterian evangelicals—prosper as a witness to the inerrant Bible, the Reformed faith, and the Great Commission.[19]

19. "Our First Commencement," *Reformed Theological Seminary Bulletin* (Fall 1968): 2. I thank John Muether for this reference. The language of evangelical Presbyterians and Presbyterian evangelicals follows R. Albert Mohler Jr., "A Call for Baptist Evangelicals and Evangelical Baptists: Communities of Faith and a Common Quest for Identity," in *Southern Baptists and American Evangelicals*, ed. David S. Dockery (Nashville: Broadman and Holman, 1993), 224–39.

Select Bibliography

PRIMARY SOURCES

Papers

J. Bulow Campbell Library, Columbia Theological Seminary, Decatur, GA
    Melton Clark Papers
    William Childs Robinson Papers
First Presbyterian Church, Hattiesburg, MS
    Session Records, 1934–74
First Presbyterian Church, Jackson, MS
    Historical Files
    Session Records, 1934–74
Presbyterian Church in America Historical Center, St. Louis, MO
    Concerned Presbyterian Papers
    Continuing Presbyterian Church Records
    W. A. McIlwaine Papers
    Presbyterian Churchmen United Records
    Presbyterian Journal Papers
    John E. Richards Papers
    Paul Settle Papers
    Hay Watson Smith Collection
    Morton H. Smith Papers
    G. Aiken Taylor Papers
Presbyterian Historical Society, Philadelphia, PA (Montreat, NC)
    C. Darby Fulton Papers
    Covenant Fellowship of Presbyterians Papers
    J. McDowell Richards Papers
    John M. Wells Papers
William Morton Library, Union Presbyterian Seminary, Richmond, VA
    Robert Lewis Dabney Papers
    Ernest Trice Thompson Papers
Special Collections, University of Kentucky, Lexington, KY
    Samuel M. Wilson Papers

Billy Graham Center, Wheaton College, Wheaton, IL
    L. Nelson Bell Papers

Periodicals and Journals

Central Presbyterian
Christian Observer
The Citizen (1961–73)
The Citizen's Council (1955–61)
The Concerned Presbyterian
The Contact
Mississippi Visitor
The Open Letter
Presbyterian Journal (1959–74)
Presbyterian of the South
Presbyterian Outlook
Presbyterian Quarterly
Presbyterian Standard
Presbyterian Survey
Southern Presbyterian Journal (1942–59)
Union Seminary Review

Church Court Records

Minutes, General Assembly, PCUS
Minutes, Presbytery of Arkansas, PCUS
Minutes, Presbytery of Central Mississippi, PCUS
Minutes, Presbytery of East Hanover, PCUS
Minutes, Synod of Arkansas, PCUS

Books

Chester, Samuel Hall. *Memories of Four-Score Years*. Richmond, VA: Presbyterian
    Committee of Publication, 1934.
Gamble, W. A. *Ten Sermons for Ten Years*. Raymond, MS: Keith Press, 1940.
———. *Trumpets of the Lord: Proclaiming God's Wonderful Words of Life*. New York:
    Vantage, 1971.
Glasgow, Tom. *Did the Southern Assembly Err in the Case of Dr. Ernest Trice Thompson?*
    Charlotte, NC: privately printed, n.d.
———. *Is Union Wise between the Northern and Southern Presbyterian Churches—
    Now?* Charlotte, NC: privately printed, 1939.
———. *A Statement For and Against Dr. Thompson*. Charlotte, NC: privately printed,
    1941.

Hassall, Harry Sharp. *On Jordan's Stormy Banks I Stand: A Historical Commentary of the Life and Times of the Covenant Fellowship of Presbyterians*. Dallas: privately printed, 1989.

Keyes, Kenneth S. *God's Partner*. Brevard, NC: n.p., 1994.

———. *A Layman Looks at the Merger*. Weaverville, NC: Southern Presbyterian Journal, 1954.

Lingle, Walter L. *The Bible and Social Problems*. New York: Revell, 1929.

Lyons, James. *We'll Go With Him . . . With Him . . . All the Way*. Hopewell, VA: Presbyterian Evangelistic Fellowship, 1971.

McAtee, William G. *Transformed: A White Mississippi Pastor's Journey into Civil Rights and Beyond*. Jackson, MS: University Press of Mississippi, 2011.

McPheeters, W. M. *The Facts in the Case of Dr. Hay Watson Smith and Arkansas Presbytery*. Decatur, GA: n.p., 1931.

———. *Facts Revealed by the Records in the So-Called Investigation*. Decatur, GA: n.p., 1934.

———. *A Reply to a Communication of Rev. Dr. Hay Watson Smith*. Decatur, GA: n.p., 1930.

Ogden, Dunbar Hunt. *Reunion of the Presbyterian Churches, U.S.A. and U.S.* N.p.: privately printed, [1939?].

Richards, John E. *The Historical Birth of the Presbyterian Church in America*. Liberty Hill, SC: Liberty Press, 1987.

Smartt, Kennedy. *I Am Reminded: An Autobiographical, Anecdotal History of the Presbyterian Church in America*. Chestnut Mountain, GA: n.p., 1998.

Smith, Hay Watson. *The Charge, The Facts, The Resolution*. Little Rock, AR: n.p., [1927?].

———. *Evolution and Intellectual Freedom: A Compilation of Opinions*. Little Rock, AR: Jordan-Foster-Hamilton, 1927.

———. *Evolutionism and Presbyterianism*. Little Rock, AR: Allsopp and Chapple, 1923.

———. *Prestige and Perquisites*. Little Rock, AR: n.p., 1930.

———. *Some Facts about Evolution*. Little Rock, AR: n.p., 1928.

Smith, Morton H. *How Is the Gold Become Dim: The Decline of the Presbyterian Church, U.S., as Reflected in Its Assembly Actions*. 3rd ed. Greenville, SC: Southern Presbyterian Press, 1999.

Thompson, Ernest Trice. *The Spirituality of the Church: A Distinctive Doctrine of the Presbyterian Church in the United States*. Richmond, VA: John Knox, 1961.

Vance, James I. *Being a Preacher: A Study of the Claims of the Christian Ministry*. New York: Revell, 1923.

———. *The Eternal in Man*. New York: Revell, 1907.

———. *Predestination*. Richmond, VA: Presbyterian Committee of Publication, 1898.

————. *Royal Manhood.* New York: Revell, 1899.

————. *The Young Man Four-Square.* New York: Revell, 1894.

————. *A Young Man's Make-Up.* New York: Revell, 1904.

SECONDARY SOURCES

Books

Alvis, Joel L., Jr. *Religion and Race: Southern Presbyterians, 1946–1983.* Tuscaloosa, AL: University of Alabama Press, 1994.

Arsenault, Raymond. *Freedom Riders: 1961 and the Struggle for Racial Justice.* New York: Oxford University Press, 2006.

Bartley, Numan V. *The New South, 1945–1980.* Baton Rouge, LA: Louisiana State University Press, 1995.

————. *The Rise of Massive Resistance: Race and Politics in the South during the 1950s.* Baton Rouge, LA: Louisiana State University Press, 1969.

Beale, David O. *In Pursuit of Purity: American Fundamentalism since 1850.* Greenville, SC: Unusual Publications, 1985.

Bederman, Gail. *Manliness and Civilization: A Cultural History of Gender and Race in the United States, 1880–1917.* Chicago: University of Chicago Press, 1995.

Billingsly, William. *Communists on Campus: Race, Politics, and the Public University in Sixties North Carolina.* Athens, GA: University of Georgia Press, 1999.

Black, Earl, and Merle Black. *Politics and Society in the South.* Cambridge, MA: Harvard University Press, 1987.

————. *The Rise of Southern Republicans.* Cambridge, MA: Harvard University Press, 2002.

Boyd, Lois A., and R. Douglas Brackenridge. *Presbyterian Women in America: Two Centuries of a Quest for Status.* Westport, CT: Greenwood, 1983.

Calhoun, David B. *The Glory of the Lord Risen Upon It: First Presbyterian Church, Columbia, South Carolina, 1795–1995.* Columbia, SC: R. L. Bryan, 1994.

————. *Our Southern Zion: Old Columbia Seminary, 1828–1927.* Carlisle, PA: Banner of Truth, 2012.

————. *Pleading for a Reformation Vision: The Life and Selected Writings of William Childs Robinson.* Carlisle, PA: Banner of Truth, 2013.

Carpenter, Joel A. *Revive Us Again: The Reawakening of American Fundamentalism.* New York: Oxford University Press, 1997.

Chappell, David L. *A Stone of Hope: Prophetic Religion and the Death of Jim Crow.* Chapel Hill, NC: University of North Carolina Press, 2004.

Cobb, James C. *The Brown Decision, Jim Crow, and Southern Identity.* Athens, GA: University of Georgia Press, 2005.

Conser, Walter H., Jr., and Robert J. Cain. *Presbyterians in North Carolina: Race, Politics, and Religious Identity in Historical Perspective*. Knoxville, TN: University of Tennessee Press, 2012.

Crespino, Joseph. *In Search of Another Country: Mississippi and the Conservative Counterrevolution*. Princeton, NJ: Princeton University Press, 2007.

————. *Strom Thurmond's America*. New York: Hill and Wang, 2012.

Daniel, Pete. *Lost Revolutions: The South in the 1950s*. Chapel Hill, NC: University of North Carolina Press, 2000.

Dennison, Charles G. *History for a Pilgrim People: The Historical Writing of Charles G. Dennison*. Edited by Danny E. Olinger and David K. Thompson. Philadelphia: Orthodox Presbyterian Church, 1999.

Diamond, Sara. *Roads to Dominion: Right-Wing Movements and Political Power in the United States*. New York: Guilford, 1995.

Dowan, Douglas E. *The Remnant Spirit: Conservative Reform in Mainline Protestantism*. Westport, CT: Praeger, 2003.

Dupont, Carolyn Renee. *Mississippi Praying: Southern White Evangelicals and the Civil Rights Movement, 1945–1975*. New York: New York University Press, 2013.

Feldman, Glenn, ed. *Politics and Religion in the White South*. Lexington, KY: University Press of Kentucky, 2005.

Foster, Gaines. *Moral Reconstruction: Christian Lobbyists and the Federal Legislation of Morality, 1865–1920*. Chapel Hill, NC: University of North Carolina Press, 2002.

Friedland, Michael B. *Lift Up Your Voice like a Trumpet: White Clergy and the Civil Rights and Antiwar Movements, 1954–1973*. Chapel Hill, NC: University of North Carolina Press, 1998.

Gatewood, Willard B., Jr. *Preachers, Pedagogues, and Politicians: The Evolution Controversy in North Carolina, 1920–1927*. Chapel Hill, NC: University of North Carolina Press, 1966.

Gill, Jill K. *Embattled Ecumenism: The National Council of Churches, the Vietnam War, and the Trials of the Protestant Left*. DeKalb, IL: Northern Illinois University Press, 2011.

Glass, William R. *Strangers in Zion: Fundamentalists in the South, 1900–1950*. Macon, GA: Mercer University Press, 2001.

Grantham, Dewey W. *Southern Progressivism: The Reconciliation of Progress and Tradition*. Knoxville, TN: University of Tennessee Press, 1983.

Hall, Donald, ed. *Muscular Christianity: Embodying the Victorian Age*. Cambridge: Cambridge University Press, 1994.

Hankins, Barry. *Francis Schaeffer and the Shaping of Evangelical America*. Grand Rapids: Eerdmans, 2008.

————. *Uneasy in Babylon: Southern Baptist Conservatives and American Culture*. Tuscaloosa, AL: University of Alabama Press, 2002.

Hart, D. G. *Deconstructing Evangelicalism: Conservative Protestantism in the Age of Billy Graham*. Grand Rapids: Baker, 2004.

———. *From Billy Graham to Sarah Palin: Evangelicals and the Betrayal of American Conservatism*. Grand Rapids: Eerdmans, 2011.

———. *The Lost Soul of American Protestantism*. Lanham, MD: Rowman and Littlefield, 2002.

———. *That Old-Time Religion in Modern America: Evangelical Protestantism in the Twentieth Century*. Chicago: Ivan R. Dee, 2002.

Hart, D. G., and John Muether. *Fighting the Good Fight: A Brief History of the Orthodox Presbyterian Church*. Philadelphia: Orthodox Presbyterian Church, 1995.

———. *Seeking a Better Country: 300 Years of American Presbyterianism*. Phillipsburg, NJ: P&R Publishing, 2007.

Harvey, Paul. *Freedom's Coming: Religious Culture and the Shaping of the South from the Civil War through the Civil Rights Era*. Chapel Hill, NC: University of North Carolina Press, 2005.

Haynes, Stephen R. *The Last Segregated Hour: The Memphis Kneel-Ins and the Campaign for Southern Church Desegregation*. New York: Oxford University Press, 2012.

———. *Noah's Curse: The Biblical Justification of American Slavery*. New York: Oxford University Press, 2002.

Hillis, Bryan V. *Can Two Walk Together unless They Be Agreed? American Religious Schisms in the 1970s*. Brooklyn, NY: Carlson, 1991.

Hobbs, Rebecca Barnes. *How Big Is Your God? The Spiritual Legacy of Sam Patterson, Evangelist*. French Camp, MS: RTSFCA Publishers, 2010.

Holifield, E. Brooks. *The Gentleman Theologians: American Theology in Southern Culture, 1795–1860*. Durham, NC: Duke University Press, 1978.

Hulsether, Mark. *Muscular Christianity: Manhood and Sports in Protestant America, 1880–1920*. Cambridge, MA: Harvard University Press, 2001.

Hutchinson, George P. *The History behind the Reformed Presbyterian Church, Evangelical Synod*. Cherry Hill, NJ: Mack, 1974.

Kruse, Kevin. *White Flight: Atlanta and the Making of Modern Conservatism*. Princeton, NJ: Princeton University Press, 2005.

Lassiter, Matthew D. *The Silent Majority: Suburban Politics in the Sunbelt South*. Princeton, NJ: Princeton University Press, 2006.

Lewis, George. *The White South and the Red Menace: Segregationists, Anticommunism and Massive Resistance, 1945–1965*. Tallahassee, FL: University Press of Florida, 2004.

Link, William A. *The Paradox of Southern Progressivism, 1880–1930*. Chapel Hill, NC: University of North Carolina Press, 1992.

Longfield, Bradley J. *Presbyterians and American Culture: A History*. Louisville, KY: Westminster John Knox, 2013.

Lowndes, Joseph E. *From the New Deal to the New Right: Race and the Southern Origins of Modern Conservatism.* New Haven, CT: Yale University Press, 2008.

Lucas, Sean Michael. *Blessed Zion: First Presbyterian Church, Jackson, Mississippi, 1837–2012.* Jackson, MS: First Presbyterian Church, 2013.

———. *J. Gresham Machen.* Darlington, UK: Evangelical Press, 2015.

———. *Robert Lewis Dabney: A Southern Presbyterian Life.* Phillipsburg, NJ: P&R Publishing, 2005.

Marsden, George M. *Fundamentalism and American Culture.* 2nd ed. New York: Oxford University Press, 2006.

Martin, William. *Prophet with Honor: The Billy Graham Story.* New York: William Morrow, 1991.

McAllister, J. Gray. *The Life and Letters of Walter W. Moore.* Richmond, VA: Union Theological Seminary, 1939.

McAtee, William G. *Dreams, Where Have You Gone? Clues for Unity and Hope.* Louisville, KY: Witherspoon Press, 2006.

Miller, Steven P. *Billy Graham and the Rise of the Republican South.* Philadelphia: University of Pennsylvania Press, 2009.

Muether, John R. *The First Forty Years, 1966–2006: The History of Reformed Theological Seminary.* Clinton, MS: Reformed Theological Seminary, 2006.

Murray, Peter C. *Methodists and the Crucible of Race, 1930–1975.* Columbia, MO: University of Missouri Press, 2004.

Newman, Mark. *Divine Agitators: The Delta Ministry and Civil Rights in Mississippi.* Athens, GA: University of Georgia Press, 2004.

———. *Getting Right with God: Southern Baptists and Desegregation, 1945–1995.* Tuscaloosa, AL: University of Alabama Press, 2001.

Nutt, Rick L. *Toward Peacemaking: Presbyterians in the South and National Security, 1945–1983.* Tuscaloosa, AL: University of Alabama Press, 1994.

Pascoe, Craig S., Karen Trahan Leathem, and Andy Ambrose, eds. *The American South in the Twentieth Century.* Athens, GA: University of Georgia Press, 2005.

Patterson, James T. *Brown v. Board of Education: A Civil Rights Milestone and Its Troubled Legacy.* New York: Oxford University Press, 2001.

Pryor, Mark. *Faith, Grace, and Heresy: The Biography of Rev. Charles M. Jones.* Lincoln, NE: Writer's Showcase, 2002.

Rutosila, Markku. *The Origins of Christian Anti-Internationalism: Conservative Evangelicals and the League of Nations.* Washington, DC: Georgetown University Press, 2008.

Schoenwald, Jonathan M. *A Time for Choosing: The Rise of Modern American Conservatism.* New York: Oxford University Press, 2001.

Scott, E. C., ed. *Ministerial Directory of the Presbyterian Church, U.S., 1861–1941.* Austin, TX: Von Boeckmann-Jones, 1942.

Settle, Paul. *To God All Praise and Glory: Under God: Celebrating the Past, Claiming the Future, the Presbyterian Church in America*. Atlanta: Presbyterian Church in America, 1998.

Slade, Peter. *Open Friendship in a Closed Society: Mission Mississippi and a Theology of Friendship*. New York: Oxford University Press, 2009.

Smith, Frank J. *The History of the Presbyterian Church in America: Silver Anniversary Edition*. Lawrenceville, GA: Presbyterian Scholars Press, 1999.

Sonsa, Morton. *In Search of the Silent South: Southern Liberals and the Race Issue*. New York: Columbia University Press, 1977.

Stricklin, David. *A Genealogy of Dissent: Southern Baptist Protest in the Twentieth Century*. Lexington, KY: University Press of Kentucky, 2000.

Thompson, E. T. *Presbyterians in the South*. 3 vols. Richmond, VA: John Knox, 1963–73.

Tuveson, Ernest Lee. *Redeemer Nation: The Idea of America's Millennial Role*. Chicago: University of Chicago Press, 1968.

Webb, Clive, ed. *Massive Resistance: Southern Opposition to the Second Reconstruction*. New York: Oxford University Press, 2005.

Whittaker, Otto. *Watchman, Tell It True*. Manassas, VA: Reformation Education Foundation, 1981.

Witherspoon, E. D., Jr., ed. *Ministerial Directory of the Presbyterian Church, U.S., 1861–1967*. Doraville, GA: Foote and Davies, 1967.

Woods, Jeff. *Black Struggle, Red Scare: Segregation and Anti-Communism in the South, 1948–1968*. Baton Rouge, LA: Louisiana State University Press, 2004.

Wuthnow, Robert. *The Restructuring of American Religion*. Princeton, NJ: Princeton University Press, 1988.

Essays and Articles

Brandon, Betty J. "A Wilsonian Progressive—Alexander J. McKelway." *Journal of Presbyterian History* 48 (1970): 2–17.

Clarke, Erskine. "Presbyterian Ecumenical Activity in the United States." In *The Diversity of Discipleship: The Presbyterians and Twentieth Century Witness*, ed. Milton J. Coalter, John M. Mulder, and Louis B. Weeks, 149–69. Louisville, KY: Westminster John Knox, 1991.

Flynt, J. Wayne. " 'Feeding the Hungry and Ministering to the Broken Hearted': The Presbyterian Church in the United States and the Social Gospel, 1900–1920." In *Religion in the South*, edited by Charles Reagan Wilson, 83–137. Jackson, MS: University Press of Mississippi, 1985.

Goodloe, James C., IV. "Kenneth J. Foreman, Sr.—A Candle on the Glacier," *Journal of Presbyterian History* 57 (1979): 467–84.

Hill, Samuel S. "Northern and Southern Varieties of American Evangelicalism in the Nineteenth Century." In *Evangelicalism: Comparative Studies of Popular Protestantism in North America, the British Isles, and Beyond*, edited by Mark A. Noll, 275–89. New York: Oxford University Press, 1994.

Hobbie, Peter H. "Prophet under Fire: Ernest Trice Thompson and the Glasgow Case." *Affirmation* 6, 2 (Fall 1993): 129–45.

———. "Walter L. Lingle, Presbyterians, and the Enigma of the Social Gospel in the South." *American Presbyterians* 69 (1991): 191–202.

Leith, John. "The Westminster Confession in American Presbyterianism." In *The Westminster Confession in the Church Today*, edited by Alasdair I. C. Heron, 95–100. Edinburgh: Saint Andrew, 1982.

Lucas, Sean Michael. "J. Gresham Machen, Ned B. Stonehouse, and the Quandary of Reformed Ecumenicity." *Westminster Theological Journal* 62 (2000): 197–222.

Marshall, Mary-Ruth. "Handling Dynamite: Young People, Race, and Montreat." *American Presbyterians* 74 (1996): 141–54.

Mounger, Dwyn M. "Racial Attitudes in the Presbyterian Church in the United States, 1944–1954." *Journal of Presbyterian History* 48 (1970): 38–68.

Nelsen, Brent F., and Beverly A. Gaddy. "Presbyterian Church in America." In *Pulpit and Politics: Clergy in American Politics at the Advent of the Millennium*, edited by Corwin E. Smidt, 141–52. Waco, TX: Baylor University Press, 2004.

Nutt, Rick L. "The Tie That No Longer Binds: The Origins of the Presbyterian Church in America." In *The Confessional Mosaic: Presbyterians and Twentieth-Century Theology*, edited by Milton J. Coalter, John M. Mulder, and Louis B. Weeks, 236–56. Louisville, KY: Westminster John Knox, 1990.

Putney, Clifford. "Character Building in the YMCA, 1880–1930." *Mid-America* 73, 1 (1991): 49–70.

Smith, Morton H. "The Southern Presbyterian Church and the Presbyterian Church in America." In *Interpreting and Teaching the Word of Hope*, edited by Robert L. Penny, 189–218. Taylors, SC: Presbyterian Press, 2005.

Smylie, James H. "The Bible, Race, and the Changing South." *Journal of Presbyterian History* 59 (1981): 197–216.

Thompson, E. T. "Southern Presbyterians and the Race Problem." *Austin Seminary Theological Bulletin* 83 (1968): 5–28.

Weeks, Louis B., III. "Lewis Sherrill: The Christian Educator and Christian Experience." *Journal of Presbyterian History* 51 (1973): 235–48.

Winter, R. Milton. "Division and Reunion in the Presbyterian Church, U.S.: A Mississippi Retrospective." *Journal of Presbyterian History* 78, 1 (2000): 67–86.

Dissertations

Brandon, Betty Jane. "Alexander Jeffrey McKelway: Statesman of the New Order." Ph.D. diss., University of North Carolina, 1968.

Bridges, Glenda Lynelle. " 'Rescue the Perishing': Alexander Jeffrey McKelway, Social Gospeler and Social Reformer." M.A. thesis, Western Carolina University, 1997.

Hammond, Michael D. "Conscience in Conflict: Neo-Evangelicals and Race in the 1950s." M.A. thesis, Wheaton College Graduate School, 2002.

Harsch, George. " 'Puff Graham': American Media, American Culture, and the Creation of Billy Graham." Ph.D. diss., University of Southern Mississippi, 2005.

Hobbie, Peter H. "Ernest Trice Thompson: Prophet for a Changing South." Ph.D. diss., Union Theological Seminary in Virginia, 1987.

Montgomery, George Robert Martin, Jr. "A Historical Study of the Social and Moral Welfare Committee and Its Successors, with Special Emphasis on Its Role of Involving the Presbyterian Church in the United States in the Social, Economic, and Political Implications of the Gospel, 1934–1969." Th.M. thesis, Austin Presbyterian Theological Seminary, 1970.

Petersen, David. "Southern Presbyterian Conservatives and Ecclesiastical Division: The Formation of the Presbyterian Church in America, 1926–1973." M.A. thesis, University of Kentucky, 2009.

Rayner, Robert Patrick. "On Theological Grounds: Hattiesburg Presbyterians and the Civil Rights Movement." M.A. thesis, University of Southern Mississippi, 2009.

Waldrep, B. Dwain. "Lewis Sperry Chafer and the Development of Interdenominational Fundamentalism in the South, 1900–1950." Ph.D. diss., Auburn University, 2001.

Index of Subjects and Names